DECOLONIAL THINKING

WORLD PHILOSOPHIES
Bret W. Davis, D. A. Masolo, and Alejandro Vallega, editors

DECOLONIAL THINKING

Resistant Meanings and Communal Other-Sense

edited by María Lugones and Patrick M. Crowley

Indiana University Press

This book is a publication of

Indiana University Press
Office of Scholarly Publishing
Herman B Wells Library 350
1320 East 10th Street
Bloomington, Indiana 47405 USA

https://iupress.org

© 2025 by Indiana University Press

All rights reserved

No part of this book may be reproduced or utilized in any form or by any means, electronic or mechanical, including photocopying and recording, or by any information storage and retrieval system, without permission in writing from the publisher.

First Printing 2025

Cataloging information is available from the Library of Congress.

ISBN 978-0-253-07304-4 (hdbk.)
ISBN 978-0-253-07305-1 (pbk.)
ISBN 978-0-253-07307-5 (ebook)
ISBN 978-0-253-07306-8 (web PDF)

CONTENTS

vii Acknowledgments and Dedication

1 Introduction, by María Lugones and Patrick M. Crowley

Part I: Making Other-Sense of Sex and Gender

29 1. A Decolonial Revisiting of Gender, by María Lugones

46 2. Sexual Identity, Coloniality, and the Practice of Coming Out: A Conversation, by Michael Hames-García and María Lugones

66 3. Monstrous Becomings: Concepts for Building Decolonial Queer Coalitions, by Hil Malatino

Part II: Between Women of Color Politics and Decoloniality

85 4. Bridging Empires, Transgressing Disciplines: Methodological Interventions in Asian America, by Jen-Feng Kuo and Shireen Roshanravan

107 5. Toward the Decolonial: Dehumanization, US Women of Color Thought, and the Nonviolent Politics of Love, by Laura E. Pérez

Part III: Methods and Maps toward Resistant Meanings

127 6. Feminist Advocacy Research, Relationality, and the Coloniality of Knowledge, by Sarah Lucia Hoagland

150
7. Topographies of Flesh: Women, Nonhuman Animals, and the Embodiment of Connection and Difference, by Jennifer McWeeny

170
8. Decolonial Aesthetics beyond the Borders of Man: Sylvia Wynter's Theory and Praxis of Human-Aesthetic Transformation, by Patrick M. Crowley

Part IV: Radical Coalitions and Communal Politics

197
9. Hanging Out and an Infrapolitics of Youth, by Cindy Cruz

208
10. On a Nondialogic Theory of Decolonial Communication, by Gabriela Veronelli

238
11. From Nation to Plurination: Plurinationalism, Decolonial Feminism, and the Politics of Coalitional Praxis in Ecuador, by Christine "Cricket" Keating and Amy Lind

257
Index

ACKNOWLEDGMENTS AND DEDICATION

THE HEARTBREAKING LOSS of María Lugones in July 2020 brought the work on this book to a sorrowful halt. Filled with grief and uncertainty at the departure of a beloved mentor and *querida compañera*, I doubted whether this project could—or even should—be completed without her guiding presence.

María had conceived the idea of this volume well before she welcomed me into her seminar on Latin American philosophy in my first year of graduate school. Not long after I joined her class, she invited me to participate in meetings and activities at the Center for Interdisciplinary Studies in Philosophy, Interpretation, and Culture (CPIC), and I quickly realized that I was glimpsing a much different approach to intellectual work than anything I had encountered before or anticipated as a newly enrolled doctoral student. With time, I came to better understand why what we were doing together in her seminars and at CPIC exceeded and escaped narrow definitions of scholarship and research. There were many reasons, but the clearest came from María's continuous and generous demonstration of practices of collaborative inquiry that necessitated a suspension of the individualist, meritocratic ethos so entrenched in academia. She graciously embodied the possibilities of connecting, sharing, and listening with an open heart and spirit, inspiring and challenging those of us in her company to do the same.

By the time she suggested working together with me on *Decolonial Thinking: Resistant Meanings and Communal Other-Sense*, María had already been gathering the seeds for this book for several years. She envisioned it partly as a record of the fruitful work that had grown directly or indirectly out of the fertile soil of CPIC, cultivated collectively by successive cohorts of members. But she also saw it as stimulus for other research collectives and communities dedicated to nontraditional scholarship and communal knowledges. It was her initiative to create a volume that would underscore the transformative promise and potential of decolonial thinking practiced collaboratively by heterogeneous mixtures of people situated in complex and distinct positions of resistance to coloniality. This is what brought all of us together on this project and what ultimately gave me the resolve to help bring it to fruition after María left to join the ancestors.

A book like this cannot come into existence without a deep reservoir of collective dedication, patience, and understanding on the part of the contributors. In this case, the authors were also called on to complete their work under the shadow of devastating bereavement. What's more, they struggled against the plethora of life- and career-altering impacts of the COVID-19 pandemic. My sincere gratitude goes to each person whose work is gathered here.

Other affiliates of CPIC whose collaborative involvement made this volume possible number too many to name individually here. This community includes members whose periods of participation may not have coincided in time, but all of us undoubtedly benefited from the energy, creativity, and generosity of everyone who contributed to the center and its activities over the years. Still, there are some whose solidarity and companionship were vital during the time the book was in preparation. Thanks to Saqer Almarri, Irem Ayan, Jake Bartholomew, Luis Castañeda, Chia-Hsu J. Chang, P. J. DiPietro, Katrina England, Josh T. Franco, Collette Jung, Paul Lemley, Eva Montoya-Davis, Josh Price, and Danielle Schwartz.

The support of Alejandro Vallega has been essential to this volume's publication. Thanks also to Gary Dunham, Anna Francis, and the staff at Indiana University Press.

Personal thanks to Luiza Franco Moreira, Monika Mehta, and Mary Pat Brady for their thoughtful comments and questions. Love and gratitude to my partner Samanta Ordóñez Robles, to whom I owe everything.

This volume is lovingly dedicated by all its contributors to the memory of María Lugones (1944–2020).

Chapter 3, "Monstrous Becomings: Concepts for Building Decolonial Queer Coalitions" by Hil Malatino, is adapted from *Queer Embodiment: Monstrosity, Medical Violence, and Intersex Experience* by permission of the University of Nebraska Press. Copyright 2019 by the Board of Regents of the University of Nebraska.

A shorter version of chapter 6, "Feminist Advocacy Research, Relationality, and the Coloniality of Knowledge" by Sarah Lucia Hoagland, was previously published as "Aspects of the Coloniality of Knowledge," in *Critical Philosophy of Race* 8, no. 1–2 (2020). Portions reprinted by permission of Penn State University Press.

Chapter 7, "Topographies of Flesh: Women, Nonhuman Animals, and the Embodiment of Connection and Difference" by Jennifer McWeeny, was previously published in *Hypatia* 29, no. 2 (2014). Reprinted by permission of Cambridge University Press.

An earlier and shorter version of chapter 10, "On a Nondialogic Theory of Decolonial Communication" by Gabriela Veronelli, was first published as "A Coalitional Approach to Theorizing Decolonial Communication," in *Hypatia* 31, no. 2 (2016). Portions reprinted by permission of Cambridge University Press.

DECOLONIAL THINKING

INTRODUCTION

María Lugones and Patrick M. Crowley

> No nos ponemos en el lugar del colonizado. No pensamos como si fuéramos el colonizado. Vemos al colonizado porque vemos la colonialidad. Además, y al mismo tiempo, percibimos la comunalidad de sus luchas, sus conocimientos, sus formas de vivir en resistencia a la deshumanización.
>
> We do not put ourselves in the place of the colonized. We do not think that we are the colonized. We see the colonized because we see the coloniality. Moreover, and at the same time, we perceive the communality of their struggles, their knowledges, and their ways of living in resistance to dehumanization.

Building Our Intellectual Community

Decoloniality became a shared theoretical direction and critical practice for members of the Center for Interdisciplinary Studies in Philosophy, Interpretation, and Culture (abbreviated as CPIC, pronounced "see-pick") soon after it was founded at Binghamton University in 2000. CPIC affiliates came together in search of a framework that would conceptualize race and gender as co-constitutive of a larger system of power exerting control over social, political, legal, epistemological, economic, religious, and moral relations. We set ourselves on decolonial pathways having studied Third World/women of color feminisms, Black feminisms, postcolonialism, and the work of thinkers who would form the Modernity/Coloniality/Decoloniality (M/C/D) collective. Some of us had worked on race and gender by taking up intersectionality as a perspective and method. Kimberlé Crenshaw (1991) showed us that the United

States as a nation-state equates womanhood with whiteness since the category "women of color" is placed under erasure by the law and other institutional structures. Patricia Hill Collins's (1998) characterization of intersectionality as a matrix of domination with gender and race as two constitutive axes enabled a modeling of critical navigation through the difficult conditions in which women of color live. Collins's model defined a Black feminist standpoint in terms of heterogeneous collectivity, highlighting the group knowledge of Black women that arises from communality in difference. Thus, two central understandings of intersectionality taught us to see the world differently. The fundamental intersectional insight that race and gender are never apart has remained deeply important to us even though we have come to reexamine this relation through the coloniality of gender, a concept that seeks to explain how the reduction to nonhuman of the colonized and enslaved rendered them genderless (Lugones 2007).

Together we were looking for a theory that would critically account for the ubiquity of race and gender in the extremely unbalanced power arrangements that constitute the modern state, the production of knowledge, and the reproduction of life. This called for an understanding of modernity and capitalism as inseparable from the racialized gender and sexual categories that attempt to dictate the subjectivity and intersubjectivity of the colonized. We found many of the ingredients for this in our engagements with the M/C/D collective. Thinking with the triadic conceptualization of modernity/coloniality/decoloniality—also styled as modernity/(de)coloniality—enabled us to perceive historical forms of racialized and sexualized domination in the Americas as inaugurating a vast global system of power that legitimates itself by violently disrupting the ways of life and forms of knowledge of the world's colonized and racially subordinated populations. Our formative encounter with these ideas is, of course, a story after the fact, *un cuento*, but looking back on our path as a collective, we cannot escape how profoundly decoloniality altered the direction of our thinking. Learning to perceive coloniality as the dark side of modernity enabled us to pursue another understanding of how the intersection of race and gender has been continually obscured by disciplinary knowledges in history, economics, sociology, politics, philosophy, anthropology, literature, the arts, and so on.

Working in our collectively chosen direction, members of CPIC began establishing connections with a network of decolonial thinkers. Aníbal Quijano became central to our efforts to understand coloniality and decoloniality. Several of us took part in his seminars at Binghamton's sociology department and the Fernand Braudel Center. We studied and debated his texts repeatedly. He joined our gatherings, gave talks, and engaged us in discussion. Quijano's intellectual influence is reflected throughout much of our work, but he was, more importantly, an invaluable friend who supported us in countless ways over the years. We felt profound sadness when he transcended in 2018. The work of Walter Mignolo, Catherine Walsh, and Nelson Maldonado-Torres also sparked our collective imaginations. We invited them to Binghamton to speak with us, and we were delighted when they drew our awareness to the ways in which our own projects were resonating with currents of decoloniality taking shape in other parts of the world. Because of these exchanges, CPIC became an active node in a network connected to other intellectual spaces and collectives dedicated to decolonial thinking, such as the M/C/D group, the Caribbean Philosophical Association, the Decolonial Summer School at Middelburg, and the decolonial feminist working group in Berkeley. We also found intellectual company with many other invited guests whose interlocution left its mark on our thinking and enhanced our understanding of questions directly and indirectly related to decoloniality. Gerard Aching, M. Jacqui Alexander, Alisa Bierria, Mary Pat Brady, Lucila Bugallo, Chris Cavanagh, Carlos Decena, Alicia Gaspar de Alba, Sylvia Marcos, Ernesto Javier Martínez, Brinda Mehta, Mariana Ortega, Troy Richardson, Monique Roelofs, Chela Sandoval, and Mario Vilca are some of the thinkers who visited the center to give talks and collaborate with us in various ways. Many of these friends also aided us in rescuing the center when it was defunded and closed by the university without warning in 2009. The effort to undo the closure of CPIC drew letters of support from faculty at seventy-five universities across Europe, Latin America, the United States, and Canada. These letters gave us great encouragement not just because of the tributes we received but also because we did not know that CPIC, our creation, had become so widely known and recognized as a fertile ground for cultivating decolonial thought. We felt redeemed when, the following year, CPIC was reinstated as an Organized Research Center, albeit with far less material support from the university. Even as we continued to collaborate with prominent researchers around the world and to attract new members among junior faculty and incoming cohorts of graduate students at Binghamton, our status within the institution remained precarious as we found ourselves under constant administrative pressure to justify CPIC's existence. While our budget was reduced to crumbs, we persisted in holding regular meetings, organizing well-attended events featuring high-profile speakers, and presenting our own collaborative work locally and at international conferences. Our stated agenda, "To conduct research that emphasizes the critique of established forms of knowledge, and the development of multiple alternative knowledges, including those suppressed by dominant disciplinary practices, and others calling for new imaginations and epistemologies," remained consciously at odds with the institutional imperatives of knowledge production in the academy.[1] In 2017, circumstances led to the full termination of our meager annual funding from the university's division of research and the permanent closure of the on-campus space that had been the center's home. Although this was a painful blow, we collectively resolved to continue organizing, meeting, reading, writing, discussing, and thinking together as a research group even without any formal recognition from the university.

Each of the authors whose work is included here has been either a local on-campus CPIC member or an affiliated researcher from another institution who has worked closely with us. Many of the contributors who began their association with CPIC while studying or working at Binghamton followed paths taking them elsewhere, yet they maintained their connections by visiting us, inviting us to events, and participating in our activities from afar. The chapters in this book attest to CPIC's collaborative interpretations of the constitutive unity of modernity and coloniality that engenders decoloniality. Each one of us took the collective discussion in different directions and each chapter presented in this volume benefited from that collaboration. The pieces gathered here share a texture, a logic, a communicative intent; they seek communal possibilities within/against the colonial degradation, disintegration, and erasure that are inseparable from modernity. Embodied proximity is everywhere present in the thinking, sensing, mapping, taking up, and scraping away enacted in our writing. It is at this level of engagement that we are interested in coloniality and decoloniality.

Together, we are putting forward these essays in part to share our understanding of the communal as a wellspring of decolonial thinking, resistant meanings, and sense making otherwise. Our shared interest lies with models of communal existence that have been constituted and upheld in struggle against colonial obliteration but also in creative and restorative practices that seek to build futures for lifeways organized by ancestral consciousness, futures for ongoing restitutions of shared cosmogonies, for complex relations that weave together people, territories, spirits, nonhuman beings, the earth, the cosmos. Communality stands as a living alternative that engenders other worlds, other realities, in defiance of imposed structures of sociality designed to reproduce atomized subjects to be controlled, managed, consumed, and discarded for the optimization of colonial racial capitalism. We acknowledge the existence of a wide range of other models of localization and collective autonomy seeking transitions toward new social realities with designs based on counterhegemonic concepts and categories, such as the commune, the commons, the multitude, and others. We turn our attention away from projects based on inferential and abstract paradigms of intersubjectivity conceptualized from, and affixed to, Eurocentric legacies blind to colonial differences. Instead, we favor thinking with situated and historicized practices of relationality, concrete collective inhabitations of spaces under siege, territories peopled in defiance of lethal forms of expulsion driven by the logic of coloniality. Of course, we are aware of potential and actual co-optation of communality-related discourses by unscrupulous political leaders, parties, and organizations duplicitously claiming to represent this or that communal body while working in the interests of oppressive power. Like any other concept or praxis of resistance and emancipation, communality must be critically scrutinized and actively reconstituted in relation to lived and embodied experiences of oppression. We are guided in our work by principles and practices of decoloniality that teach us to recognize relational ways of living that have been condemned to oblivion, classified as "premodern," and depoliticized as "custom" or "tradition" but are held together in the present by collective acts of resistance, creativity, and love. In a decolonial vein, communality redirects collective pain and sorrow into oppositional energy and joyous transformation. The degradation of bodies and erasure of knowledges generated through and with coloniality comes up against countercurrents wherever we find communal practices of being, living, perceiving, knowing, and sensing shared among people who have been categorially dehumanized. Inhabiting communal spaces of struggle gives rise to new meanings of decolonial resistance that pass through the bodies of those who lovingly join one another in life-affirming praxis. Understood as an oppositional model of sociality based on proximal, relational, embodied transmission and reception of resistant meanings, perceptions, memories, knowledges, emotions, and sensibilities, communality opens possibilities for building and sustaining decolonial coalitions distinct from those constituted in the formation of mass movements engaged with public-sphere politics. Without rejecting these types of activities as viable and necessary strategies in certain instances, we postulate that decoloniality entails trajectories of sense making other than those that typically organize and motivate engagements and negotiations with modern political and legal institutions. Our definition of "Other-sense" encompasses connective affects, feelings, knowledges, and practices of resisting coloniality and building alternate worlds unthinkable and unworkable in the absence of relations of communality. This, we think, is what we offer that is original in our approach to theorizing opposition to dehumanization.

Thinking of our loci, we are most aware of the tempo of coloniality lived in the United States, although several of us come from or are situated in other places, including Latin America and Asia. A plurality of histories and memories inform our reflections. Some of us are Chicanas/os, Asian Americans, or Latinas/os. We are all women of color feminists or transgressive feminists who are white but live whiteness critically. Some of us are men, some women, some of us are neither, and to all of us, the binary is profoundly problematic. We seek positive directions in transgressing sexual boundaries, crossing from separation to creative transformation. None of us knows or speaks with any degree of competence any of the indigenous languages of Abya Yala, the territories "discovered," occupied, and renamed as America. For some of us, English is a language acquired in an academic context outside of our homes and our own communities. Some of us are popular educators bringing conversations to and from besieged and occupied territories. We have taught university courses, led graduate seminars, lectured at international conferences, written dissertations, and published articles and books, but our place in the academy is suffused with tension. We regard disciplinary boundaries as destructive impositions, so we seek to situate our work in transdisciplinary and nondisciplinary spaces. We are deeply invested in knowing and thinking from fractured histories, embodied possibilities, and oppositional transformations, our own and those of others. To practice decolonial thinking is to perceive differently, uncovering what coloniality hides, mapping out movements, disclosing limits, and getting immersed in Indigenous and Afrodiasporic knowledges. None of us belongs to Indigenous or Afrodescendant cultures whose resistant practice is necessarily re-created day to day in survival, in open struggle, in transformative movement. Some of us live in that difficult fissure of being named mestizo/a, knowing next to nothing about the Indigenous or diasporic African people who were our ancestors. For some of us, *mestizaje* conceived as spiritual metamorphosis and opposed to any and all ethnonationalist identitarian projects composes part of a critical inhabitation of that aspect of our locus. In thought and action, we embrace the decolonial possibilities engendered by living in a broken line of consciousness and history, in the interstices. Our rejections of compound colonialities, our recreations of collectivity, and our transformations of embodied selfhood take shape in multiple overlapping border spaces that reflect different modes of inhabiting identities akin to those Gloria Anzaldúa (1987, 25) calls "*los atravezados* ... those who cross over, pass over, or go through the confines of the 'normal.'"

Walking Decolonial Paths

To better explain the connections in our paths as collaborative thinkers, we need to briefly introduce some of the contributions that have elucidated the meanings of decoloniality informing the ideas and discussions we are offering here. It is not our intention to provide a comprehensive overview of the plurality of interrelated projects that have constituted the "decolonial turn" in critical theorizing and cultural studies (Maldonado-Torres 2011). We merely want to accommodate readers who may be newly encountering decoloniality as a locus and orientation of theory and praxis. This involves a necessarily selective and partial revisiting of certain concepts and dialogues that have been conducive to our thinking and have stimulated our collaborations. It also means bypassing most of the debates, critiques, and divergences that occurred over the years as interlocutors thinking from various political ideologies and disciplinary backgrounds engaged with and sometimes sought to deconstruct decoloniality. We do not pretend that the overall trajectory of the decolonial turn has been wholly adequate on every question or free from theoretical missteps and shortcomings. Our primary intention for this book is to offer our own original takes on decolonial thinking, including our reservations, refinements, and questions on issues that have not been sufficiently examined by others working within this influential paradigm.

In its broadest sense, decoloniality has come to be identified with past and present trajectories of communal, social, cultural, political, spiritual, and intellectual transformation originating from the manifold local histories of colonized, disinherited, subalternized people across the planet, those whom Frantz Fanon ([1961] 2004) referred to using the phrase *damnés de la Terre* (the condemned/wretched of the earth). What these diverse transformative movements have in common—beyond a basic ethical rejection of modernity's correlated modalities of colonial control, appropriation, and expulsion; racial and gender violence; environmental devastation; and capitalist exploitation—is the shared recognition of the vast range of existential possibilities offered by practices of world-making massively exceeding the single, narrow horizon of futurity projected as universal by Western civilization's hegemonic metanarrative of development, progress, and modernization. Decoloniality, therefore, consists of challenging and undermining Western modernity's totalized Eurocentric worldview, down to its basic ontological, metaphysical, aesthetic, epistemic, and other foundational categories. At the same time, it seeks strategies for bringing suppressed, concealed worlds into the open by activating interrelated practices of knowing, thinking, doing, feeling, and living that have long been cultivated under conditions of tense and unequal conflict with imposed colonizing structures.

Decoloniality is a process of refusal and renewal, of resistance and re-existence. It may be understood to originate with the defiant response to colonization and imperial rule by the colonized, but it cannot be comprehended as concluding with decolonization in terms of national independence or state sovereignty. While remaining grounded in historical legacies of decolonization and related memories of local struggle against Western imperialism and geopolitical domination, decoloniality evolves continually and dynamically to counter the shapeshifting systems of power and knowledge that constitute global capitalism and modernity. Given that the universalist narrative of modernization will, in all likelihood, continue to be reiterated and that colonizing systems of classification and control will continue to be reinstalled to maintain conditions of oppression across the earth, decoloniality will necessarily be an incomplete project that is perpetually revitalized in ongoing processes of transformative opposition and in the resurgence of other worlds, other cosmologies, and other futures being built in directions leading away from the illusory road laid out by Western myths of progress and development.

Over the past five centuries, decoloniality arose in local and regional scenarios around the globe wherever and whenever the violent colonial reach of modernity was extended, but it is only relatively recently that these currents of oppositional movement and transformation have been explicitly recognized, named, and consciously theorized by university-trained researchers. Many of those who contributed to this recognition were scholars of color who experienced colonial racialization firsthand, and many others collaborated closely with community-based thinkers and activist movements combating racial oppression on colonized lands. The unfolding of conceptual maps and methods to reveal the contours of what is now known as decoloniality in scholarly contexts began with contributions by Latin American intellectuals confronting the limitations of existing academic critiques of the region's ongoing history of peripheralization relative to centers politico-economic power in the United States and Europe. Quijano put forward his influential formulation, "colonialidad del poder" (coloniality of power), which broke new ground in the analysis of global capitalist modernity by locating its genesis in a model of control structured in the fictive category of race that was first systematized in the colonized territories that came to be known as "América" (Quijano 1992). Recognizing the invention of a racially differentiated hierarchy as the foundation of European dominance over labor, land, and their products in the so-called New World was Quijano's originary decolonial intervention, providing the theoretical basis for analyzing historically the constitutive relation of coloniality to modern capitalism throughout its five-century duration and worldwide extension and for charting new intellectual courses toward other horizons. This conceptual shift enabled not only the critical distinction between *colonialism*, as a historically delimited set of politico-economic administrative arrangements designed to serve imperial agendas, and *coloniality*, as a totalizing transhistorical logic of separation, classification, and hierarchization enacted on non-European peoples and territories from a Eurocentric locus of knowledge and power, but also illuminated the indissoluble coarticulation of capitalist modernity with coloniality's racialized patterns of social configuration. As

Quijano (2000, 533) explains, "The racial axis has a colonial origin and character, but it has proven to be more durable and stable than the colonialism in whose matrix it was established. Therefore, the model of power that is globally hegemonic today presupposes an element of coloniality."

Coloniality as a specific model and logic of power thus made its first historical appearance in European conquerors' denial of the humanity of the Indigenous inhabitants of Abya Yala. Since then, it has been constitutively operative as the underside of a paradigmatic structure that governs the development and expansion of Western modernity as a capitalist, patriarchal world system, making it possible to speak of modernity/coloniality as a composite pairing. One way of grasping the underlying unity of this dualism lies with perceiving the distinction—by making the connection—between the "rhetoric of modernity" and the "logic of coloniality" (Mignolo 2007). The first term comprises the set of all variations on the mythic narrative articulating the superiority of Western civilization, repeating ad nauseum its universal promise of rational emancipation, all while hiding—by naturalizing—the perversely dehumanizing colonial operations of separation, classification, and hierarchization referred to by the second term. To grasp simultaneously both halves of this conjunction in their complementarity is to reveal the dualistic structure of modernity/coloniality. Doing so is already an enactment of decolonial thinking because it necessarily involves questioning the hegemony of a singular worldview that grants itself a transcendent, universalist, godlike perspective by disregarding, distorting, and disqualifying all other standpoints. Quijano (2007, 177) defined decoloniality as a decisive break with the Eurocentric knowledge paradigm of modernity: "epistemological decolonization, as decoloniality, is needed to clear the way for new intercultural communication, for an interchange of experiences and meanings, as the basis of another rationality." We participate, via the writings gathered in this volume, in the unremitting labor of tearing down modernity's rhetorical and epistemological curtains to unveil the exercise of the coloniality of power across various domains of experience, even as we pose critical questions not only about the place occupied by gender in the racializing historico-structural framework of coloniality but also about the possibility of a conclusive, redemptive rupture as Quijano defined it. Our approaches are outlined in the closing section of this introduction.

Parallel to Quijano's contributions, Enrique Dussel (1995, 123) conceptualized his influential critique of modernity's "double face" starting from the same history of violent racialized and accumulative forms of colonization, subjugation, and enslavement first practiced in sixteenth-century America under Spanish imperial rule. While Quijano's initial approach was intended to critique and move beyond the prevailing categories and methods of sociological analysis applied to the history of global capitalism, Dussel's work since the 1970s has been characterized by his critical preoccupation with the participation of the Western philosophical tradition in hiding the colonial origins of modernity and with contemporary philosophy's inability to account for its own blind spots vis-à-vis contributions from non-Western knowledges and from the voices of the damnés. For Dussel, the historical figure of Hernán Cortés serves as the prototype of the modern human subject, one who constitutes his own being primarily through the ruthless colonial domination of subjugated, enslaved, inferiorized populations, denying their humanity and therefore excluding the possibility of relational dialogue. This sets the stage for the subsequent development of the modern paradigm of rationality based on the solipsistic refusal of intersubjectivity absolutized in the Cartesian *ego cogito*. The earlier formation of conqueror subjectivity via the negation of the colonized non-European's personhood corresponds to the constitutive moment when Europe originally established itself as an epicenter of global imperialism by invading and incorporating America as its colonial periphery, "las indias *occidentales*," while "covering over" the dehumanizing racial violence integral to this history (Dussel 1995, 34). This covering, or *encumbrimiento*, refers to the totalizing projection of a fallacious one-sided modern salvation narrative—which goes through many evolutions after its original invention by humanist scholars of the Renaissance in southern Europe—casting Western civilization as autonomous, benevolent, and emancipatory and occluding the brutal exploitation of Indigenous people in their own lands and of captive Africans transported across the Atlantic as the enabling factors that set Europe on a path toward global hegemony in the sixteenth century.

Although significant inward-facing dimensions of the "myth of modernity" were thrown into question by prominent postmodern thinkers (e.g., Jean-François Lyotard, Gianni Vattimo, Richard Rorty), Dussel (1995, 12) argues they largely confined their critiques to the intellectual legacy of Enlightenment rationality, remaining *within* the modern episteme of Eurocentrism without venturing to consider perspectives from the exteriority, that is, from subject positions historically confronted with modernity's "irrational" colonial side. To overcome this limit, it is necessary to not only acknowledge the earlier, "covered over" foundations of colonial violence on which European capitalist modernity was built but also create the conditions for intercultural dialogues that include colonized Others whose civilizational perspectives, experiences, and knowledges have been relegated to the hidden exterior of the system. "Transmodernity" is the name Dussel gives to this project, whose aim is "to construct not an abstract universality, but an analogic and concrete world in which all cultures, philosophies, and theologies will make their contribution toward a future, pluralist humanity" (1995, 132). Although articulated in terms quite distinct from Quijano's colonialidad del poder, Dussel's approach to theorizing *beyond* modernity by starting from its colonial exteriority has been fundamental to the methodological elaboration of decolonial thinking.

While these formative dimensions of the decolonial turn were initially unfolded from Latin American standpoints, they were clearly not conceived to be pertinent solely to the history and futurity of this region but rather intended as Latin American contributions to the global critique of the modern/colonial world system. Perspectives built on these forerunning contributions to decoloniality have been significantly shaped by productive dialogues with other intellectual frameworks centering colonization and decolonization as determinative historical processes in diverse parts of the world. This includes the field of postcolonial studies, which incorporates a broad set of responses primarily to British imperialism by transnational Anglophone writers and cultural critics, and subaltern studies, a more focused subset of critiques originally offered by a collective of historiographers and social theorists mostly situated in South Asia but later taken up and continued by thinkers located elsewhere. Differences in geohistorical locations played some role in shaping the distinct direction and scope of these trajectories, but they still formed related shifts in thought away from a Eurocentric locus of rationality and knowledge production, turning toward subalternized, non-Western positionalities. Contributions to postcolonial and subaltern theorizing have often been animated by a utopian spirit, a visionary call to conceive global futures *post*-dehumanization, *post*-racialization, *post*-Eurocentrism—imaginary worlds that could be realized only by radical divergence from the hegemonic logic and rhetoric instituted by Western imperialism. The decolonial turn shares this basic drive to imagine possibilities beyond the horizon of colonial modernity in common with many thinkers working from postcolonial and subaltern theories.

One illustration of the consequences of decoloniality's point of origination in Latin American contexts can be observed in its distinct emphasis on Occidentalism as opposed to Orientalism as developed by Edward Said. Both terms illuminate the idea that, more than merely a system of administering the political, economic, and social affairs of nonsovereign territories, European colonialism always entailed, at its core, a structure of knowledge and representation, a cognitive universe centered on an invented notion of the West's natural superiority to other coexisting civilizations and cultures. But while Orientalism refers to this totalizing imperial imaginary at a certain stage of its trajectory, approximately from the outset of the nineteenth century when extensive parts of the Middle East, Asia, and Mediterranean Africa had already fallen, or would soon fall, under direct or indirect control of Western imperial powers,

Occidentalism points to the moment of origination when the West first constituted its identity via conquest and genocide in the Americas and domination of the Atlantic routes that eventually allowed the transport of millions of captives as human cargo from the western ports of Africa.[2] As Fernando Coronil (1996, 56) explains, "Occidentalism ... is not the reverse of Orientalism but its condition of possibility, its dark side (as in a mirror)." In other words, Europe's systemic misrepresentations of "the Orient" in terms of inferior, premodern cultures became possible because of Europe's prior self-representations, its conflation of itself with human civilization in general that was made possible by the *encubrimiento* described by Dussel and with coloniality as described by Quijano. From a decolonial perspective, "Occidentalism" continues to serve as the "overarching metaphor" for ways in which the modern/colonial imaginary "described itself through the discourse of the state, intellectuals, and scholars" (Mignolo 2000, 23).

The distinct historical periodizations implied by Orientalism and Occidentalism need not be thought of only in linear terms but rather ought to put into relation with one another and with other time frames marking specific extensions and developments of modernity/coloniality alongside interstitial spatiotemporal ruptures generated by local histories of decolonial struggle. Relational strategies that involve shifting between multiple oppositional loci within distinct yet overlapping histories of struggle have been characteristic of Chicana feminists such as Chela Sandoval and Emma Pérez in their contributions to decolonial thinking and their dialogues with poststructuralism and postcolonialism. Sandoval's (1991) theorization of "differential consciousness" articulates a mobile standpoint of oppositional activity that moves back and forth among a plurality of oppressed subject positions, enacting the "ability to read the current situation of power and of self-consciously choosing and adopting the ideological form best suited to push against its configurations" (15). This strategy provided the basis for coalitional organizing among US Third World feminists at a particular historic moment in the 1960s and 1970s yet simultaneously expanded possibilities for transhistorical alignments and affinities with global decolonization movements, crisscrossing and weaving together heterogeneous forms of oppositional consciousness "developed under previous modes of colonization, conquest, enslavement, and domination" (Sandoval 2000, 9). Emma Pérez (1999) has proposed a related methodology based on her conceptualization of the *decolonial imaginary*, a term that names a "rupturing ... interstitial space where differential politics and social dilemmas are negotiated" (6). For Pérez, historical agency enacted within this "third space" resists the uniformity of an oppositional politics that implies sidestepping the social complexity of overlapping histories and ongoing situations of colonization, "accepting power relations as they are, perhaps confronting them, but not reconfiguring them" (110). Instead, the decolonial imaginary creates the possibility of shifting between different, sometimes contradictory, subject positions, negotiating through ambivalence to arrive not at a conclusive endpoint of liberation but at a transformative state of flux that retains an oppositional and emancipatory orientation. We mention Sandoval and Pérez because their task is alive in some of us as the familiar political, social, cultural landscape in which we live, particularly those of us who are Chicanas/os or mestizas/os, whose ancestral memories encompass both the US colonization of Aztlán/the Southwest, initiated in 1846, and the decolonial time of Chicanismo. Thinking from colonial histories in the United States also implies marking the seventeenth century as the beginning of the settler colonial violence that decimated the Indigenous populations and fostered the enslavement of Africans in colonial plantation societies. These and other spatiotemporal conjunctures are relevant in unveiling the coloniality inherent to the plurality of fractured locations from which we speak and enact our political and theoretical commitments.

Defining a nonhomogenizing, nonmonological locus from which to understand relations between multiple coexisting perspectives and differential experiences of Western modernity's spatial and temporal colonizations—and of the linguistic and cognitive domains in which these processes are described and analyzed—has been a long-standing critical preoccupation for decolonial thinkers, particularly following the work of Mignolo. In *The Darker Side of the Renaissance*, Mignolo (1995, 19) introduced the methodological necessity and challenge of "pluritopic hermeneutics" to rethink and pluralize the history and memory of colonial situations in Abya Yala by detaching them from the hegemonic intellectual discourses that reflect the emergence of the so-called New World in European consciousness at the dawning of modernity. This work proposes an alternative mode of comparative interpretation enacted from a self-consciously subjective standpoint, or locus of enunciation, that calls its own presuppositions into question by situating itself in relation to a plurality of intellectual, ethical, political, and social agendas enacted by individuals and interpretative communities offering distinct understandings of colonial realities across the cultural borders established by the conquerors. Beyond mere relativism, pluritopic hermeneutics attempts to straddle the boundaries of asymmetrically partitioned grounds of knowledge production, interrogating how power relations impinge on descriptions of cultures located on opposite sides of the colonial divide. By using this approach to engage with the field of "colonial semiosis," which encompasses diverse communicative interactions within and between the intellectual traditions of different cultures in the aftermath of invasion and conquest, Mignolo (1995, 8) offers detailed, concrete, politicized understandings of how the colonizer's gaze distorted and invalidated the coexisting perspectives of Indigenous knowers. Attending to the ambiguities, appropriations, and conflictive interfaces that come to light when the European Renaissance is examined from a pluritopic perspective situated on its darkened colonial periphery complicates aspects of Dussel's project, particularly to the extent he posits a static ontological opposition between colonizer and colonized rather than a complex, shifting set of relational positions in a newly invented and continuously contested hierarchy of cultures. Without specifying it, Mignolo's interventions also problematize Quijano's sociological exposition of the coloniality of power by illustrating how the implementation of a hegemonic knowledge system did not completely devour traditional Mesoamerican and Andean systems of thought but rather situated them outside the homogeneous realm of intelligibility constituted by modern rationality. From this subalternized position, Indigenous ways of knowing continued to offer competing perspectives of reality based in ancestral cosmologies, even if they were dismissed and invalidated by Western intellectuals. The imbalance of power generated the epistemic and communicative conditions for the enduring monologue of Occidentalism, a tradition of thought and culture that regards itself as the ultimate bastion of universal rationality, thereby denying the possibility of dialogue on equal terms with any other worldview.

In his subsequent work, Mignolo added new dimensions to the engagement with Dussel, Quijano, and many other decolonial thinkers by intensifying the exploration of "colonial difference," an evocative concept with many complex facets but which points suggestively to "the space where coloniality of power is enacted" (Mignolo 2000, ix). In this way, Mignolo provided an additional tool for mapping the territorial and temporal constructions of hierarchical distinction produced by coloniality. The spatial and historical classifications established by modern/colonial reasoning defined the frontiers of difference between the universal space-time of Europe's imperial projects and its exteriority—that is, between the civilized and barbarian, the modern and the primitive, those with letters/history and those without, the white and nonwhite, and so on (3). The temporal and spatial border locations are where the conflicts and negotiations of colonial situations play out their various possibilities, "the space in which global designs have to be adapted, adopted, rejected, integrated, or ignored" (ix). From the beginning, this process has always been unequal and one-sided, as the colonizers monopolized control over where the borders were drawn and how the matrix of differences was defined by continually reinforcing the "subalternization of knowledge" belonging to the colonized (4). Mignolo shows that perceiving coloniality implies a double vision precipitated by a refusal of the binary logic of modern rationality, what can be called "border thinking" (x). Locating thought and perception at interstitial crossings and openings in colonial dichotomies creates the possibility of understanding power relations in terms other than those inscribed by hegemonic categories instituted by Occidentalism. This is by no means equivalent to thinking as the colonized but ventures toward realizing the transformative potential of meeting the colonized in dialogue at the contradictory locus of their resistance, the fracture where violence is both imposed and refused, where a starting point can be found for new liberatory directions of humanness.

Methodologically, border thinking brings the doubleness of formative modern categories such as "the human" into cognizance, splitting apart the imagined completeness of modernity along the partitions produced by the coloniality of power, exposing its hidden relationship to what it disavows, suppresses, and condemns to the exterior of humanness—that is, to the damné as subrational, subhuman other. While this approach shows how the exercise of control over central categories has been integral to the stable exclusionary ordering of knowledge and social systems, decolonial thinking also seeks to understand the ontological effects of this control and its dichotomizing logic as experienced directly by colonized, racially subordinated subjects. Maldonado-Torres (2007) has proposed the "coloniality of Being" as a name for these embodied, experiential dimensions of dehumanization. From this point of view, coloniality is a condition that exceeds expressions of both social power (exercised through political, legal, and economic structures, etc.) and hegemonic control over categories of knowledge. For Maldonado-Torres, the starting point for conceptualizing the coloniality of Being is found in the specific modes of self-perception and lived experience that result from the imposition of a Manichean ontology that rationalizes racial and sexual violence. Fanon's critical elucidation of the existential formation of the damnés as the nonsubjects of colonial reality provides the basis for Maldonado-Torres's (2007, 255) theorization of the processes through which such violence is naturalized as Western modernity/coloniality's "non-ethics of war." The damnés live the condition of being racially condemned, of inhabiting bodies permanently subject to humiliation and brutalization due to the colonizer's perception of their bio-ontological lack. As Maldonado-Torres explains, "coloniality of Being primarily refers to the normalization of the extraordinary events that take place in war. While in war there is murder and rape, in the hell of the colonial world murder and rape become day to day occurrences and menaces. 'Killability' and 'rapeability' are inscribed into the images of the colonial bodies" (255).

Maldonado-Torres (2006) draws on Sylvia Wynter's understanding of Western modernity's underlying parameters of sociocultural discourse designed to ensure the perpetual symbolic reproduction of racial hierarchy within the dominant definition of the human. According to Wynter, the damnés do not merely bear the sociogenically coded racial signs of the nonhuman produced by the coloniality of Being. Those condemned as nonhuman are also engaged in a struggle against the imperial terms of humanity that circumscribe their lived experience, which she defines as the "struggle of our new millennium" (Wynter 2003, 260). For Wynter, as for Fanon, the subjectivity of the damnés is manifested in the capacity to conceive and realize modes of being human outside the frameworks of coloniality, in the potential for revolutionary humanism that takes shape at the outer peripheries of the governing image of Man. As Maldonado-Torres (2006, 203) explains, "What begins to emerge at the extreme point of irritation, frustration, and desire for conceptual and material transformation is a renewed sense of agency that seeks an-other understanding of the human." Maldonado-Torres's notion of the coloniality of Being is central to every one of our attempts to understand decoloniality in terms of reclaiming and reinventing humanity. It is indispensable to our walking of decolonial paths.

Some of the pieces in the volume refer to or presuppose what María Lugones (2007) names the modern/colonial gender system. A central consequence of her articulation of this system, which involves what she calls the "coloniality of gender," is that gender can be disclosed both as a colonial imposition and as a mark of the human. In her analysis, "patriarchy" is an ahistorical naming for systems of oppression that she historicizes and thus understands in more complex terms than invocations of the patriarchy characterized by the isolation of gender. She calls a historicized system of ordering relations in terms of sex, sexuality, and their socialization, along with the place of power in that socialization, a "gender system." That is the underlying meaning of the modern, capitalist colonial gender system. The dichotomy between the human and the nonhuman constitutes a basic expression of this system's control over life. The colonial nonhuman are not "gendered": that is, in that system, their sexual differences are not socialized but left as bestial and treated as such. Reproduction is not the major function of the nonhuman turned colonized, enslaved, and worked to death; rather, their primary purpose is work, while their reproductive activity is also a form of capital since the enslaved woman's "issue" is property of the human to be used as labor, whipped, maimed, or raped at will and desire. The sexual flesh is the site of sexual violence arising from the brutal desire of the colonizer for animal flesh for the sake of pleasure, not for the sake of reproduction. The gender system is heterosexualist as the sexual body is reduced to reproductive purposes and all sex is reduced to heterosexual sex, pointing, however symbolically, to reproduction. Lugones and other CPIC collaborators have for several years been advancing the project of retheorizing feminism decolonially, a way of thinking and living that recognizes the coloniality of gender as one ingredient of the self-straddling the colonial difference.

Two final concepts elucidate the transformative openings that decolonial thinking generates for us and the forms of praxis that drive our collective movement toward them. These are interculturality and pluriversality, both of which refer to projects and processes of imagining and bringing into reality strategies for inhabiting interstices between multiple rationalities and cosmologies— that is, both speak to the challenge of creating conditions for living with more than one reality. Thus, they are vital movers of coalition. Walsh has been a particularly important interlocutor on the concept of interculturality, as she shows how it cannot be understood apart from the concrete historical struggles of Andean Indigenous movements in which it originated. Beginning in the 1980s, activists in Bolivia and Ecuador made intercultural principles and politics central to their struggles against hegemonic state structures and institutions that manage and control cultural, ethnic, and linguistic diversity, particularly in the field of public education, where schooling had become an effective instrument of suppression and homogenization to uphold the fictive cohesion of a monocultural nation (Walsh 2009). The demand for intercultural transformations to these oppressive systems, articulated by Indigenous collectivities, called for a radical reorganization of the social order by establishing new relational grounds for political dialogue that would not seek to contain or flatten out differences between distinct forms of cultural identification across a plurality of knowledges, logics, worldviews, ancestral traditions, spiritualities, concepts of personhood and existence, understandings of nature and the human, and so on. In other words, interculturality was proposed as an alternative model of cross-cultural exchange and interaction intended to open possibilities of social coexistence, interdependence, collaboration, and mutual transformation considered unworkable by secular, capitalist nation-states. Unlike modern liberal notions of inclusive public-sphere politics based on tolerance and individual free speech, it would not pretend that all social conflicts could be mediated within a universalist framework of Western rationality. Instead, differences would have to be negotiated continually and relationally, apart from any preexisting hierarchy of knowledge or culture. As Walsh's (2009, 67) work shows, top-down responses to these demands from state institutions and NGOs often adopted interculturality as a rhetorical gesture but produced limited structural change. In practice, official intercultural policies in Latin America, including those inscribed into the most recent constitutions of Bolivia and Ecuador, have functioned more like neoliberal multiculturalism, superficially recognizing plural identities while refusing to see colonial differences or to intervene in the systems of power keeping them in place. For this reason, interculturality, like decoloniality, does not describe an existing or prospective condition that replaces modernity but, rather, expresses a means of building other worlds beyond its horizons: "It is a process and a project in continuous insurgence, movement, and construction, a conscious action, radical activity, and praxis-based tool of affirmation, correlation, and transformation" (Mignolo and Walsh 2018, 59). In this sense, it goes hand in hand with our approach to decolonial thinking as communal coalition building.

Not quite synonymous with interculturality, the closely related notion of pluriversality similarly expresses a radical departure from the universalist pretensions of Western rationality, though with a different emphasis. Whereas interculturality suggests a praxis of enacting structural de-homogenization at the dialogic interfaces between multiple social collectivities with distinctive cultural experiences, memories, values, and subjectivities, pluriversality denotes the underlying assumption of multiple, diverse, interwoven realities comprising a complex and conflictual meshwork of onto-epistemic relations. While the term has appeared in the works of many decolonial thinkers, the most succinct and illuminating definition of pluriversality may be found in a well-known formulation originally offered by Indigenous Zapatista communities in Chiapas, Mexico, calling for *un mundo donde quepan muchos mundos*, a world in which many worlds coexist. One of the intellectual guides who has elaborated on decolonial implications of this idea in ways that we find helpful is Arturo Escobar. His recent work theorizes the pluriversal politics emerging from Indigenous and Afrodescendant communities in Abya Yala engaged in defending their ancestral territories, lifeways, and cosmologies. Far from clinging to an essentialized past, they seek to "envision a different future— a sort of 'futurality' that imagines, and struggles for, the conditions that will allow them to persevere as a distinct world" (Escobar 2017, 245). Escobar shows that communal opposition to extractive industries and models of development promoted by states and NGOs as the only viable pathway for Latin America's future must be understood to arise from an ontological conflict. The defense of multiple, distinct, relational worlds stands against ontological occupation by what some have called the One-World World (OWW), that is, the global capitalist civilizational model founded on a "dualist ontology of human dominance over so-called 'nature' understood as 'inert space' or 'resources' to be had" (245). These struggles therefore reflect shared commitments to distinct forms of inhabiting and relating to territory, and against the destruction of alternate worlds and futures. Pluriversality is not itself a replacement for the ontology of Eurocentric modernity, but rather challenges and decenters the presumed universal rational validity of the OWW to make room for other cosmologies and their corresponding ways of being, doing, knowing, and thinking. In this sense, it constitutes a decolonial political intervention with onto-epistemic and praxical implications: "The pluriverse is a tool to first, make alternatives to the one world plausible to one-worlders, and, second, provide resonance to those other worlds that interrupt the one-world story" (245). The ability to think and act from the relational complexity that emerges between many worlds and cosmologies is a horizon of decolonial liberation to which our work aspires.

Our Contributions

The approaches gathered in *Decolonial Thinking: Resistant Meanings and Communal Other-Sense* point to how decoloniality entails people's resistance through the creation of alternate modalities of knowledge based crucially in a strong sense of community and coalition. Our book brings together research focusing on intersubjective relations among people whose shared conditions of racialization, dehumanization, linguistic violence, sexual exploitation, and structural poverty activate a common rejection of oppressive rationalities and prompt new strategies for creating shared meaning that diverge radically from dominant disciplinary and academic categories of knowledge. The mutual recognition among people who struggle against the systemic production of violence and the alternative systems of politics, communication, and logic that they create compose a specific strategy of decolonial resistance. The contributions to this volume broadly address the following questions: To what extent have colonial practices, terms, ideas, and directions inserted themselves into people's lives? Have these tendrils of coloniality attached themselves into the grounds of people's self-understanding, their understanding of the self-in-relation, or their understanding of their relation to all that constitutes life—that is, have these imposed categories of meaning found expression in strong tension with the cosmological as informing the daily lives of Indigenous peoples? Or have these colonial paradigms been redirected to particular practices and concepts without marring a cosmological understanding of life? What forms does decolonial other-sense take? How does the understanding of the coloniality of gender enable us to understand people's rejections of colonial constructions of being? What practices have people-in-resistance used to keep and re-create language and communication at the colonial wound? How have they reclaimed histories? What histories in the present can we tell in communicative friendship of our living our embodied selves against the colonial grain? It is our shared hope that this book advances decolonial thinking in new directions. We intend it also to reflect the ideas we have generated together over our many years of collaboration, with CPIC as our shared intellectual home. We have organized the work into four sections with the expectation that this introduction enables a clearer perception of the connections that pervade the porous boundaries between them.

I. Making Other-Sense of Sex and Gender

The sex/gender system that began as a violent imposition on Indigenous and Afrodiasporic peoples in the sixteenth century remains with us today and continues to organize social formations and knowledge production in the modern/colonial world. The three pieces in this section of our book address the coloniality inherent to abstract and generalized categories of sex/sexuality/gender that erase the corporeal specificities of sexual/sensual experience and reduce the bodies of colonized women to the point of erasure. These contributions reject the epistemic paradigms that produce the sexed/gendered body as a reduction along with the sexual politics and identities that have been established within the restricted and dichotomous parameters of the hegemonic system. The authors respond to contemporary sociocultural processes that are driving the homogenization of sexual diversity in Latin America through the exportation of abstract universals rooted in Western, First World histories. Of necessity, this work is carefully attentive to the actual existence of communally constructed concepts of sexual difference that defy the logic of the coloniality of gender and are tenuously maintained in the fractured locus of the colonial difference.

In the opening chapter, "A Decolonial Revisiting of Gender," Lugones extends her earlier analyses of particular modern/colonial capitalist gender arrangements toward a critique of the concept of gender itself. Lugones poses questions about how modern/colonial modes of power continue to influence theoretical convictions regarding the correspondence between biological reproduction and sexual difference. The second chapter, "Sexual Identity, Coloniality, and the Practice of Coming Out: A Conversation," is a dialogue between Lugones and Michael Hames-García that centers on questioning the North–South trajectories of contemporary sexual politics and categories of sexual identity, including the relatively recent introduction of discourses of queerness into Latin America. Whose interests are being served in the latest efforts by intellectuals, activists, and transnational institutions to promote "queer identity" as an overarching paradigm for sexual difference without regard to communal histories and struggles? What do these projects reveal in relation to contemporary geopolitics of sexual knowledge and the coloniality of gender? The conversation also approaches, in an intimate consideration of personal history, the conceptual and political parameters of "coming out" and the problematic implications of imposing these politics to disparage and displace communal Indigenous and Afrodiasporic notions of sexuality. In chapter 3, "Monstrous Becomings: Concepts for Building Decolonial Queer Coalitions," Hil Malatino argues that the reclamation of the figure of the monster by queer and trans theory has important resonances for decolonial thinking, not only due to the epistemic disruption that monstrosity represents but also because of the possibilities that come out of a politics that is not primarily based on a struggle for inclusion and mainstream acceptance. Malatino illustrates how the colonial imposition of a sexual and corporeal schema of norms relied on the figure of the monster to make the non-European world intelligible in terms of defectiveness, aberration, and deviance.

II. Between Women of Color Politics and Decoloniality

The inseparability of race and gender has been a central tenet in the long history of women of color theorizing. It constitutes a paradigm shift in relation to white feminist thinking. If gender, a mark of the human, is not compatible with racial configurations of the nonhuman, then "woman" as a category that is unified, homogeneous, pure cannot be what women of color are. The impurity of "women of color" in contrast to the purity of "woman" confounds modern categories and cannot be captured by them. Since the separation of race and gender is produced through categorial, fragmenting, dichotomous thinking and such thinking is ahistorical, it erases the history of the coloniality of gender. The contributions in this section of our book foreground the nonlinear histories of resistance, communal practices, and knowledges of women of color as they constitute the basis for decolonial analysis of contemporary configurations of power.

The book's fourth chapter, Jen-Feng Kuo and Shireen Roshanravan's "Bridging Empires, Transgressing Disciplines: Methodological Interventions in Asian America," shows how analysis configured by decolonial and women of color feminisms can reframe debates regarding the "model minority" myth and overturn assumptions of a privileged status enjoyed by Asian Americans within the racial matrix of US society. In particular, the authors illustrate how complex processes of Asian American women's subject formation can be understood in relation to the imperial difference, a concept encompassing the often ambivalent dynamics of assimilation, adaptation, and resistance that characterize how "secondary" empires, such as China, have historically negotiated their position relative to Eurocentrism and the global hegemony of the West. In chapter 5, "Toward the Decolonial: Dehumanization, US Women of Color Thought, and the Nonviolent Politics of Love," Laura Pérez reflects on the ethical principle of shared recognition of humanity that informs both decolonial theorizing and the politics of women of color and Third World women's feminism. She highlights the coalitional perspective that these movements have articulated in their resistance to multiple oppressions and their development of complex understandings of diversity in sexual identities and nonconformity with Western gender norms. By examining how the political consciousness of marginalized women has been shaped in tense confrontation with powerful structures of racialization, colonization, and capitalism, Pérez illustrates how the radical perspectives of women of color thinkers such as Audre Lorde, Gloria Anzaldúa, and Chela Sandoval are configured by practices of love that both escape and confound colonial worldviews.

III. Methods and Maps toward Resistant Meanings

Decolonial thinking implies an ongoing search for methods and practices that make coloniality perceptible and that enable greater recognition of the many worlds and knowledges that resist its violent logic. While all the work collected in our book contributes to the critique of existing intellectual frameworks and the development of decolonial approaches aligned with the goals of coalition and conviviality, the three chapters in this section share a particular concern with examining the tools and strategies we have at our disposal and how they might be refashioned or put to more effective use in our research. This includes throwing into question the broad categories that provide the lenses through which we examine and map out territories of struggle. Even research conducted with the best of intentions may erase vital dimensions of knowledge if the epistemic terms that have not arisen from coalitional sensibilities.

In the sixth chapter, "Feminist Advocacy Research, Relationality, and the Coloniality of Knowledge," Sarah Hoagland takes a critical approach to models of knowledge production informing the research practices of scholar-advocates, particularly white women/feminists whose work concerns women of color and their communities. Hoagland's analysis poses questions about the epistemic challenges of advocating on behalf of marginalized groups without reproducing colonial relationalities. Examining aspects of the Coloniality of Knowledge that remain embedded in institutionalized academic research methods, Hoagland demonstrates how they undermine the possibilities for coalitional connections between an advocate researcher and her subjects. In chapter 7, "Topographies of Flesh: Women, Nonhuman Animals, and the Embodiment of Connection and Difference," Jen McWeeny proposes a rethinking of feminism's turn away from ontological accounts of material and corporeal distinctions and commonalities among women and other oppressed subjects. While acknowledging the need to avoid analytic categories that might essentialize or homogenize the intrinsic variability of lived experiences of struggle,

McWeeny argues that greater ontological precision would bring into clearer relief the specific contours of relationality between diverse embodiments of oppression and resistance. Patrick Crowley's chapter, "Decolonial Aesthetics beyond the Borders of Man: Sylvia Wynter's Theory and Praxis of Human-Aesthetic Transformation," intervenes in the conceptualization of a decolonial aesthetics by thinking with the philosophy of Wynter. He first examines how Wynter developed a notion of aesthetics as a metahermeneutics, a way of deciphering the symbolic orders of being or modes of mind that humans institute through their autopoietic capacity. He then assesses Wynter's strategies for cultural criticism and oppositional transformation of the present order of the human, identifying gender-related challenges and consequences of her approach.

IV. Radical Coalitions and Communal Politics

The concept of coalition figures centrally in many of the decolonial projects described in this volume. Coalitional thinking is a way of living at the colonial difference, learning each other as peoples in histories of resistance, and perceiving multiple logics that are at work beyond the modern/colonial logic of power and capital. What makes possible this shared recognition of an immense and elaborate plurality of local responses to coloniality? Coalitional thinking entails an expansion of the logic of multiplicity against the reductions of the singular logic of oppression. The essays in this section show that decolonial coalitions do not aim simply to build strategic alliances for pragmatic purposes. They rather engage possibilities for thinking together across epistemic boundaries without relying on colonial models of translation into dominant discourses or commensurability with a primary or universal model. The coalitional movements imagined here resist enclosure and paralysis within the margins of modernity/coloniality by creatively directing their movements outward toward multiple coexisting centers of pluriversal worlds.

Chapter 9, Cindy Cruz's "Hanging Out and an Infrapolitics of Youth," is a critical reflection on ethnographic approaches to marginalized and gender nonconforming youths that highlights the importance of hidden intersubjective processes of sense making and the possibilities they open. For Cruz, research that centers the resistant socialities of marginalized groups requires an approach based on faithful witnessing, a communal perspective that is attuned to the multiple meanings that emerge in oppressed peoples' confrontations with power. Chapter 11, Gabriela Veronelli's "On a Nondialogic Theory of Decolonial Communication," problematizes questions of how to imagine intercultural connections between differently experienced situations of oppression and resistance. In Veronelli's view, prominent oppositional theories of communication have left largely unanswered the problem of how communities in diverse locations of struggle can engage one another dialogically from within the existing structural order of coloniality. As Veronelli demonstrates, in order to construct communicative connections across global and local contexts of resistant thinking it is necessary to conceptualize strategies to overcome what she calls the "coloniality of language." In chapter 11, "From Nation to Plurination: Plurinationalism, Decolonial Feminism, and the Politics of Coalitional Praxis in Ecuador," Christine "Cricket" Keating and Amy Lind develop an analysis of Ecuador's recent constitutional reforms that focuses on the potential for political and ethical principles of communal autonomy, coexistence, and conviviality to promote new, coalitional understandings of gender justice.

Notes

1. The statement is taken from CPIC's 2010 Annual Report submitted to an advisory committee of Binghamton University's Division of Research responsible for assessing the activities of Organized Research Centers.

2. Spanish, Portuguese, and Dutch incursions into the Pacific began from the sixteenth century, but it would take more than a century for European empires to achieve any significant degree of economic and military dominance in the region. The argument we put forward as decolonial thinkers is that the conquest of the *indias occidentales* was the constitutive event in the formation of a Western identity.

References

Anzaldúa, Gloria. 1987. *Borderlands/La Frontera: The New Mestiza*. San Francisco: Aunt Lute Books.

Collins, Patricia Hill. 1998. *Fighting Words: Black Women and the Search for Justice*. Minneapolis: University of Minnesota Press.

Coronil, Fernando. 1996. "Beyond Occidentalism: Toward Nonimperial Geohistorical Categories." *Cultural Anthropology* 11 (1): 51–87.

Crenshaw, Kimberlé. 1991. "Mapping the Margins: Intersectionality, Identity Politics, and Violence against Women of Color." *Stanford Law Review* 43 (6): 1241–99.

Dussel, Enrique. 1995. *The Invention of the Americas: Eclipse of the "Other" and the Myth of Modernity*. Translated by Michael D. Barber. New York: Continuum.

Escobar, Arturo. 2017. "Sustaining the Pluriverse: The Political Ontology of Territorial Struggles in Latin America." In *The Anthropology of Sustainability*, edited by Marc Brightman and Jerome Lewis, 237–56. New York: Palgrave Macmillan.

Fanon, Frantz. (1961) 2004. *The Wretched of the Earth*. Translated by Richard Philcox. New York: Grove Press.

Lugones, María. 2007. "Heterosexualism and the Colonial/Modern Gender System." *Hypatia* 22 (1): 186–209.

Maldonado-Torres, Nelson. 2006. "Notes on the Current Status of Liminal Categories and the Search for a New Humanism." In *After Man, Towards the Human: Critical Essays on Sylvia Wynter*, edited by Anthony Bogues, 190–208. Kingston, Jamaica: Ian Randle Publishers.

———. 2007. "On the Coloniality of Being: Contributions to the Development of a Concept." *Cultural Studies* 21 (2–3): 240–70.
———. 2011. "Thinking through the Decolonial Turn: Post-continental Interventions in Theory, Philosophy, and Critique—An Introduction." *Transmodernity* 1 (2): 1–15.
Mignolo, Walter D. 1995. *The Darker Side of the Renaissance*. Ann Arbor: University of Michigan Press.
———. 2000. *Local Histories/Global Designs: Coloniality, Subaltern Knowledges, and Border Thinking*. Princeton, NJ: Princeton University Press.
———. 2007. "Delinking: The Rhetoric of Modernity, the Logic of Coloniality and the Grammar of Decoloniality." *Cultural Studies* 21 (2–3): 449–514.
Mignolo, Walter D., and Catherine E. Walsh. 2018. *On Decoloniality: Concepts, Analytics, and Praxis*. On Decoloniality. Durham, NC: Duke University Press.
Pérez, Emma. 1999. *The Decolonial Imaginary: Writing Chicanas into History*. Bloomington: Indiana University Press.
Quijano, Aníbal. 1992. "Colonialidad y modernidad/racionalidad." *Perú Indígena* 13 (29): 11–20.
———. 2000. "Coloniality of Power, Eurocentrism, and Latin America." Translated by Michael Ennis. *Nepantla: Views from South* 1 (3): 533–80.
———. 2007. "Coloniality and Modernity/Rationality." Translated by Sonia Therborn. *Cultural Studies* 21 (2): 168–78.
Sandoval, Chela. 1991. "U.S. Third World Feminism: The Theory and Method of Oppositional Consciousness in the Postmodern World." *Genders* 10:1–24.
———. 2000. *Methodology of the Oppressed*. Minneapolis: University of Minnesota Press.
Walsh, Catherine. 2009. *Interculturalidad, estado y sociedad: Luchas (de)coloniales de nuestra época*. Quito, Ecuador: Universidad Andina Simón Bolívar / Ediciones Abya-Yala.
Wynter, Sylvia. 2003. "Unsettling the Coloniality of Being/Power/Truth/Freedom: Towards the Human, After Man, Its Overrepresentation—An Argument." *CR: The New Centennial Review* 3 (3): 257–337.

María Lugones (1944–2020) was a US Latina decolonial feminist philosopher, popular educator at the Escuela Popular Norteña, and Professor of Comparative Literature at Binghamton University. Her thought has been widely influential on topics such as coalitional praxis, women of color politics, and the coloniality of gender. She was recognized with many awards and honors throughout her life, including Distinguished Woman Philosopher, awarded by the Society for Women in Philosophy, and the Caribbean Philosophical Association's Frantz Fanon Lifetime Achievement Award. She edited, with Yuderkys Espinosa Miñoso and Nelson Maldonado-Torres, *Decolonial Feminism in Abya Yala: Caribbean, Meso, and South American Contributions and Challenges* (2022) and authored dozens of philosophical essays, some of which are collected in *Pilgrimages/Peregrinajes: Theorizing Coalition against Multiple Oppressions* (2003) and *The María Lugones Reader* (forthcoming).

Patrick M. Crowley is a Lecturer in English at Appalachian State University.

PART I

MAKING OTHER-SENSE OF SEX AND GENDER

1
A DECOLONIAL REVISITING OF GENDER

María Lugones

IN OCTOBER 2014, I attended the X Encuentro Lésbico-Feminista de Abya Yala in Chinauta, Colombia, a gathering of decolonial feminists organized by GLEFAS (Grupo Latinoamericano de Estudio, Formación y Acción Feminista [Latin American Group of Feminist Study, Education, and Action]). During one of our discussion sessions, we were shown two short documentary videos. One depicted agents of multinational firms in extractive industries pushing Guatemalan Indigenous peoples off their land; the other one showed mostly black and extremely poor Brazilians being thrown out of the favelas, their houses destroyed, for the cleansing and beautification of Rio de Janeiro before the World Cup. We began to discuss these examples of neoliberalism by asking what lesbianism has to do with it. This implied thinking of sexuality as present in any and all aspects of the economic-political-social order, not merely as a question of intersections.

That discussion centered on how heterosexuality, resource exploitation, and neoliberal politics are working hand in hand to maintain the predatory capitalism that treats impoverished Indigenous people and people of African descent across Latin America and the Caribbean as disposable. As a way of continuing the dialogue opened at the *encuentro*, the position I present in this chapter is one that relates the Western European gender system of the late Middle Ages and the colonial, modern, capitalist gender system introduced in the Americas through conquest and colonization, with the particular, localized erasure/disappearance of the bodies of those reduced by the two gender systems. I also argue that gender itself is inextricably related to those reductions, that is, that there cannot be gender without them and that without gender many possibilities can be imagined and worked for peoples like those in the documentaries. Such work would involve severing the knots holding together the network of neoliberalism, neocolonialism, racism, the brutal attempts to disappear the communal, and the invasive attempts to impose structures on the peoples of Abya Yala, specifically those that are presupposed in the application of gender analysis in social scientific studies, which have contributed to making coalitions among the Indigenous and Afrodescendant peoples of the Americas more difficult, if not virtually impossible.

The men who conquered and colonized Abya Yala and were in a position of power were not men reduced to labor. The reduction to labor marks a separation with all the modern versions of the human. The men who conquered and colonized Abya Yala were constructed in a particular kind of contrast to both laborers and all women. They were ideologically constructed as planners, decision-makers, commanders, and moral judges to conceive and put into practice the construction of every respect of the social in terms of power. They were thus constructed as fundamentally rational and fixed on their own agency and mind, recognizing other men either abstractly as minds or in terms of ferocious, violent competition. Their equality lay in their rational ability to compete for and exercise power.

Central to my position is the coloniality of gender and the place of the socialized sexual difference in the colonial destruction of the philosophical, cosmological, economic, relational life of the peoples of Abya Yala, including the captive African people who were enslaved by colonial masters and their descendants. Those of us in solidarity with the Indigenous movements in South and Central America join the struggle as we adopt the name Abya Yala as a decolonial call to recover the living habitats that underwent the *pachakuti* of conquest and colonization. It is land in its plenitude and maturity that we are rethinking and for which Indigenous and Afrodescendant peoples are struggling. América is the name the conquerors and colonizers gave to this land as they regarded it as empty of human beings and treated it, in the modern intention, as for use by and for Man, Eurocentrism's overrepresented conception of the human (Wynter 2003, 260). I use one or the other as I am shifting from colonial dehumanizing perception to the episteme of the colonized as resistant.

In her extraordinary book *Caliban and the Witch*, Silvia Federici presents us with the tense and violent history of people in Europe who came to live and think in communal ways, without private property, with equality between men and women, and in struggle against the church, the feudal lords, nobility, and later, the nascent nation-state and the emergent capitalist system of production. The people in struggle were the heretics, groups of people all over Europe fighting against their reduction to machines, against their loss of all control over their persons. They were massacred by the hundreds of thousands and finally were made to produce and reproduce as automatons (Federici 2004).

This was also a passage to a new conception of sex and its socialization, what feminists in the 1970s came to call "gender," enabling an understanding of "woman" as *a particular form of exploitation and, therefore, a unique perspective from which to reconsider the history of capitalist relations*" (Federici 2004, 13; emphasis mine). Unlike many other feminist thinkers, Federici does not take women out of the space and time of the struggles that led to their transformation into reproduction machines. Federici understands sex, the "sexual difference," and its socialization as historical-social productions within an extremely tense relation between alternative understandings of men and women. This methodology differs radically from the centering of women's subordination in the ahistoricity of the patriarchy.

The church, in allegiance with other powers, equated women with sin and the desire to control men through their sex. Women who had once exercised control over their own reproduction were now forced to procreate against their will. These combined forces took from women's hands the ability to limit their own reproduction, including the determination of "which children should be born, where, when, or in what numbers" (Federici 2004, 91). With the promotion of prostitution and the institutionalization of regulated systems for the commercialization of sex, the control exercised over women who became prostitutes was justified as control over women as perverts whose sexuality was a threat to men. Federici makes a claim that became central to my understanding of what I am calling "the modern European gender system." She says, "One of the central concerns of the new Mechanical philosophy was *the mechanics of the body*" (138; original emphasis). The body is separated from the person; it is dehumanized. The body had to die for labor power to exist (140). Rural male and female peasants with access to land, those without land, artisans, vagabonds, and prostitutes were transformed into machines, precisely what they were struggling against. The subordination of women rests on control over reproduction being taken from them and particularly taken in this particular way and by this combination of forces. Federici places the historical formation of this subordination in capitalism. Capitalism introduced a new division of sexual labor, subjugating women's labor and their procreative function to the reproduction of the workforce. The proletarian body was mechanized and transformed. In the case of women, they were transformed into machines for the reproduction of new workers. This transformation fit capitalism's needs for labor power. The new patriarchal order excluded women from wage labor, terminated their autonomy, their self-control. Women who were not in reproductive confinement were turned into prostitutes whose function was the satisfaction of the sexual needs of men. They became women who provided sexual release and pleasure, but not their own. Their bodies were controlled against their perceived exercise of power over men through sex.

We can see then this double mechanics of control over women's bodies: severing women from their own pleasure in sex and severing women from control over their own reproduction. I claim, and this is a central claim to my problematizing of gender, that in both cases, women's bodies cease to exist except as fleshy mechanical holes functioning either for reproduction or for the release of men's sexual needs. Federici does not make this claim, but she enables me to think that the body of the woman also had to die for mechanized reproductive power to exist. I also think of the body of the prostitute as dying and being replaced by a fleshy hole in which men were legally and socially encouraged to seek their pleasure. Both played a central role in the workings of capitalist exploitation. There is, then, a similarity between the capitalist production of men and women from peasants, and then heretics, into machines, automatons. The taming of the wild and dangerous masses that could only be thought of as human in metaphor, through a reduction of them into machines is always accompanied with fear, by the bourgeoisie, of the dangerous wildness contained by power. This conception and production of the body of the masses in modernity is one that I want to revisit when thinking of the coloniality of gender and decolonial possibilities.

The rise of capitalism was coeval with the war against women because control of women's reproduction was necessary to the capitalist imperative for the *reproduction of labor*. That is why the witch hunt was aimed at destroying the control that women had exercised over their reproductive function. Federici tells that Marx never conceived that women could have control over their own reproduction. But one just needs to think of the contraceptive properties in the seeds of the wild carrot plant, also known as Queen Anne's lace, to know that women could and can do so. I understand the turning of women into witches as this erasure of women's bodies through fire, which requires the birth of the reproductive machine.

Modernity constructed women married to men with wealth also as reproducers, embodied as sex, subjected to strict control over their reproduction. Bourgeois women reproduced capital. But bourgeois women were understood to have an emotional life, they were considered to be moral teachers to their children, so they were not machines. Emotionality and their reproducing capital distinguished them from working-class women. Importantly, bourgeois women reproduced for their class, for power, while working-class women reproduced against their class, for power over their class. Bourgeois men were construed very differently than the "men as labor" necessary to capital. They were created as rational minds and moral legislators; self-determining holders of rights, including the right to property; active inhabitants of the public domain; decision-makers in the matters of the state capable of ruling, commanding, creating, and leading wars of conquest. Thus, there are two "sexual differences" created in modernity since not only is the body of the rational modern man, a man of means, not reduced to an embodiment of dehumanized labor, but also the latter is irrelevant to his nature, a repugnant and dangerous enemy.

The sexual division of labor imposed by capitalism constructed and socialized the "sexual difference" in ways quite dissimilar from what feminists have thought to be a natural biological given socialized as gender but separable from it. The distinction between the sexes here is not a biological distinction. The body of rural peasants forced to become either labor machines or reproductive machines is disappeared, reconceived, and reconstructed. Her body is reduced to a hole without pleasure, a birth canal, a womb and breasts to be milked by future men of power or accessed by men reduced to labor in the service of capital. Her body is severed from its extraordinary possibilities of connection. We can still understand the machine body and the sentient body as producing ova and when fertilized, growing in a womb, and birthed as an infant. But that is quite compatible with the disappearance of the body alive to connection, feeling, pleasure, and the appearance of mechanical holes that function in conception.

Both bourgeois and working-class women, including prostitutes, were identified with their "sex"—it was their essence, their nature—even though they differed. Neither working-class nor bourgeois men were identified with their "sex." That is why it is only women who came to be identified with gender, only in their case that there is a reduction to the sexual organs. The important difference between male wage earners and bourgeois men indicates the importance of not generalizing over "men," given that the difference in terms of economic power is marked by different "natures," that is, the centrality given to the construction of both in this difference of economic power. The distinction between bourgeois and working-class women indicates the importance of not generalizing over "women." The ideological tendency of Anglo-American and European feminists has been to see the reduction to reproduction as grounds for generalization. But as sex, working-class and bourgeois women are not the same. Political attention to "women" requires the opposite of generalization. It requires understanding the political, historical, and economic construction of difference and its importance to power. Attention to difference as constructed does not lead to a commonality, neither underlining nor going beyond the construction. It leads to an understanding of the body itself as constructed as reproductive machine or reproductive sentient being. This is the sex-gender system that informed those involved in the conquest and colonization of Abya

Yala. But that gender system only informed their perception, inhabitation, and treatment of bourgeois and working Spanish and Portuguese men and women. The colonial modern sex-gender system was significantly different, and the men and women we have described in this section also became different.

What I call the "modern colonial gender system" is a new sex-gender system constituted through the coloniality of power. I use the term *gender* for both of these systems to mark the oppression that requires the erasure of the bodies of women. It is clear to me that a liberatory understanding of socialized sexual difference would not include these erasures of the body.

By the coloniality of power, Aníbal Quijano means the classification of the peoples of the world in terms of races and a system of production, capitalism, that is racialized. He understands capitalism to include wage labor, slavery, reciprocity, and small commodity production, all transformed by capital into the production of surplus value (Quijano 2000). Quijano includes an account of gender within his framework that is not itself placed under scrutiny and thus remains too narrow, ahistorical, and overly biologized as it presupposes sexual dimorphism, heterosexuality, patriarchal distribution of power, and the impossibility of producing sex. When I think of the question, "What is the body?" I think not of reproduction but of the body as sensual, sexual. "What is the body?" is not a question that easily lends itself to an understanding of the production of the body. "What is sex?" is a question that has been answered in an unexamined way in Quijano's model but one that the initial feminist impulse to avoid the naturalization of women helped to make an enduring one. I do not go into the details of Quijano's understanding of sex/gender nor into my critique of it, except to say that women are not thought of by Quijano to be disputing for control over sexual access. Following Marx, he does not conceive that women can control their reproduction themselves. He thinks of the differences between men and women in terms of how society reads reproductive biology.

By the colonial modern gender system, I mean the understanding of gender—socialized reproductive biology—as a mark of the human and its denial to those understood to be inferior by nature, anterior in species-time, animals. Animals do not, cannot, have gender precisely because their "sexual difference" is not socializable. The dimorphic and dichotomic understanding of colonized subhuman sexuality by colonizers is blurry. They are always understood as sexually aberrant, sometimes depicted as hermaphrodites.

While the reduction of the European masses is to machines, the reduction of the inhabitants of Abya Yala and the captive and then enslaved Africans is to animality. While the "machines" are reproducers of labor for power or are labor itself, the reproduction is of other beings-to-be-machines. The peoples of

Abya Yala are marked both for superexploitation without pay, both males and females, and for the reproduction of more animals to serve their owner, who perceives them as under his complete control.

Because the sexual difference is so central to any understanding of gender—as socialized sexual difference—most of my argument is concerned with exposing the sexual difference as a horrific construction. I expose the presuppositions of gender that carry into any understanding of the contemporary people of Abya Yala as gendered. These assumptions mark the use of gender by social scientists in their analysis of non-Western peoples as a form of colonization. I also propose an understanding of the body suggested by my consideration of the cosmologies of Abya Yala. That understanding, as well as the removal of gender from our conceptual map as we consider entering into coalition with them as women of color, can only be sketched here.

Like Aníbal Quijano, Sylvia Wynter (2003, 264) also thinks that gender, unlike race, "has a biogenetically determined anatomical differential correlate onto which each culture's system of gendered oppositions can be anchored." The anchor is the "sexual difference," understood as a biological dichotomy. The body so conceived is naturally one side of the dichotomy. Federici has argued for the sexually dichotomous natural body to be reconceived as the product of power. Thomas Lacqueur (1990) has argued for an understanding of sex in ancient Greece as separate from gender, only one sex and two genders. Even though the body has been disappeared in favor of the sexual difference (my argument through Federici), what "sex" means depends on who has access and control over those bodies. So, if capitalism continues to ensure that control remains in certain hands, sex must be something different from simply the biogenetic ingredients for reproduction. It is something different, then, if a heretical woman has control over access to her own reproductive abilities, a self-control that is aided by a collaborative practice and wisdom about reproduction. It is not just a question of gender being different as social arrangements are different through exercises of power. My important point is that sex changes along with the sexual body itself. If the point of control over sexual access is predatory, as in submitting people to sexual violation, or predatory for the sake of the provision of new labor for capital as in the provision of more slaves to increase the wealth of the plantation master and the power of the Crown and capitalism, then we cannot think that the sexual body is honored as a whole; rather, it is reduced to holes, to ova, to womb and, as such, disappeared. Quijano's (2000, 345) choice of procreation as an understanding of the woman's body is motivated by the question of the biological reproduction of the species, and what could be more important? But what is sufficient for procreation does not exhaust the variety of sexual differences onto which gender differences may be mapped. Intersexed, transgendered, and transsexual people throw the correlation into disarray. The reduction of the body sexual to eggs and womb correlates with dichotomous gender, but the sexual body as a continuum does not. As Anne Fausto-Sterling (2000, 31) writes, "if the state and legal system has an interest in maintaining only two sexes, our collective biological bodies do not."

In her essay, "The Metaphysics of Gender and Sexual Difference" (2006), Linda Alcoff finds in the reproductive biological division a justification for categorizing human beings into males and females. Her project is to provide an objective basis for women's gendered identities. She provides a metaphysics of sex and of the sexual difference. As such, the analysis maintains the central importance of the material reality of the sexed body. She follows Sally Haslanger in adopting a Quinean metaphysics that rejects an unmediated access to reality and absolute starting points. Rather, with Quine, she takes empirical scientific claims as having a weblike structure. Any part of the web, "even basic empirical observation reports—will be revisable if we are prepared to alter the other parts of the web that are structurally dependent on the part we want to eliminate" (Alcoff 2006, 168). What permits Alcoff to center on reproduction is her adopting a gynocentric viewpoint focusing on the experiences of women (gendered), particularly experiences with respect to reproduction, which are different than men's. The question of experience is central to her account and she limits her claims to context-based ones. In those contexts, "we can make reasonable characterizations of gynocentric experiences within given contexts, as long as we acknowledge that there will still be variety even within a delimited context" (167). The experiential, context-based, gynocentric viewpoint enables an understanding of gender in which reproductive "concrete potentialities" are one objective factor in being a woman, a factor that "can be moved about the web, from the center to the periphery, made more or less determinate over the construction of gender depending on cultural context" (172). She wants to capture the idea that women are expected to have, or have already had, the experience of pregnancy, giving birth, and lactating. She understands this experience not as one all women *necessarily* have but one that all women *possibly* have. For Alcoff, this possibility is lived as central to being gendered as a woman.

Alcoff looks at the division of labor in reproduction, particularly in conception, as requiring sperm and ova that come from male and female human beings. That is the sexual difference. The emphasis in this account—here is where the Quinean metaphysics become important—lies with her introduction of "possibility" as the central qualifier. Unlike Quijano and Wynter, who claim that the biological body, simpliciter, is the ground of gender, Alcoff thinks that the possibilities different bodies have of producing either sperm or ova, which makes them male or female, is *one*—and not *the only*—objective factor in cultural gender. That is an important difference.

As I think of the Quinean metaphysics, not enough has been said about the web and how it is conceived in this account. Is the web gender? What else is in web? How is "gender," the concept, conceived in the conceiving of the web? Are more than two genders part of the conception of the web? What are the constituent elements of sex and sexuality, in addition to those involved in reproduction? The complex sexual body is not any part of Alcoff's metaphysics of sex. If you conflate sex with reproduction, then, of course, you will only think of reproduction when understanding sex. But the complexity of the sensual/sexual body would send reproduction away from the center in understanding any relation between sex as sexuality and gender.

Alcoff understands biological reproduction to involve gestation, birthing, and breastfeeding. But these embodied events are no longer technically required. Reproduction no longer necessitates that the fetus gestate in the womb of the biological mother. It can do so in the womb of a surrogate. So, it may well be that in US culture this factor is moving from center to periphery. Alcoff certainly thinks that the biological can and is changed, though these changes do not affect reproduction as an objective factor of gender. Reproduction no longer requires in vivo fertilization, though most of the time conception happens in coitus between the bodies of those who will be the parents, the ova and sperm grow into a viable fetus within the mother's body, and it is she who breastfeeds the baby. Alcoff envisions a future when biological sex changes and it is not a central factor in someone being a woman, but it will remain an objective factor in her being one.

Imagine with me, à la Marge Piercy (1976), a society in which no one engages in reproduction, except for donations of sperm and ova to the reproductive bank. Everyone's fertile possibilities are removed after sperm and ova donation. The rest of reproduction and child-rearing is accomplished by a technological arrangement accompanied by a number of people who offer every care to the fetus and later to the babies and children. So, what happens to gender? The body has not changed, except for the potential for participating in reproduction. Only male sperm and female ova are required, and the rest of reproduction is taken care of so that not even conception happens in the body. In Marge Piercy's *Woman on the Edge of Time*, Connie, the central character, a woman within the time of women's participation in reproduction, meets Luciente, who lives in the time of the minimalization of people's participation in reproduction. Connie thinks Luciente is a man. Her perception of and experience with Luciente leads her to that conclusion. But then she discovers that

Luciente has breasts, and then she can no longer think of Luciente as a man; however, she cannot think of Luciente as a woman either.

I am asking you to join me in this thought experiment because, at some point, the biology in our time may change as radically as in Luciente's world and be the rule for the organization of reproduction. There are many possibilities to explore that would no longer center reproduction as an objective factor of gender. This would be a radical reconception of the body, since the body in sexual/sensual encounters would be a whole body: bellies, mouths, anuses, ears, skin, penises, and clitorises.

But in our time, Alcoff's metaphysics of sex is problematic on several counts. Transgender, transsexual, and intersexual people are clear counterexamples to Alcoff's account of both sex and gender. This is not a matter of concrete potentialities with respect to reproduction or of moving the objective type to the periphery of the Quinean metaphysical web. To understand transgender experience is precisely to deny her claims. This is not a case of periphery-to-center precisely because the transgendered person is not, in his experience, a woman, even though without hormonal or surgical treatments he can still house a fertilized egg in his womb. He is a man who produces eggs. That it sounds counterintuitive is just a matter of the centrality of dimorphism in the contemporary understanding of human sex. Stronger claims can be made for both transsexual and intersexed people.

I want to argue beyond these crucial countercases. In my experience, which is enriched by coming to understand the cosmologies of some of the people of Abya Yala and the contentious radical sex discourse of trans and intersexed people, there is something odd, at this time, in this relation between gender and reproduction, because it requires a reductive characterization of the sexed body in relation to gender. Even though Alcoff's characterization of the sexed body provides only one objective factor in an understanding of gender, a factor that can be moved from center to periphery, the dimorphism resounds in the gender dichotomy. The Western history of the socialization of the sexual difference in the case of white Europeans attests to that. The claim that sex dimorphism is an objective factor in gender fits some experiences and excludes others, fits some sexualities and not others. As a metaphysics of sex, it reduces the sexual body, the thing in the world and not merely the concept, as Alcoff and Sally Haslanger emphasize, to reproduction and thus limits not just genders but also *us* to gender constraints. In this minimal characterization of the sexed body, some bodies produce either sperm or eggs, and the cells gestate in wombs and become babies delivered in parturition and breastfed from healthy breasts. The only thing that ties this facet of the sexual body to gender in Alcoff's account is a gynocentric view of women's experience with respect to reproduction. But why would that be a productive understanding of women, the gendered beings, when reproduction for many of us who produce ova is only a marginal experience and often not a particularly positive one? Marge Piercy's thought experiment decentered reproduction totally. That is completely possible for people whether or not they reproduce as characterizations of themselves as gendered or nongendered. I think both the limitation of gender and the limitation to gender should be clear. Alcoff would probably agree with the limitation of gender but disagree about the limitation to gender, but I did not see her arguing for that. That is, reproduction would still be an objective factor of gender for her to the extent that there are still women, even when genders change radically. But my suggestion is that the reduction to gender itself becomes unnecessary. Gender, though unnecessary, is still placed as reduction and as pure control on bodies. The control may include access to the reproductive body, making gender a tool of power.

The reduction of sex conceived as reproduction gives "men" and "women" a particular meaning that includes the possibility of reproduction. In the search for objectivity in the relation between sex and gender, Alcoff presupposes gender as dichotomous, she moves from the sociocultural to the material, and she argues that reproduction is an objective factor in characterizing gender. These are important structural sociopolitical presuppositions in her conceptualization of gender tied to the conception of sex itself, presuppositions that do not fit other ways of organizing the social in societies without dichotomies, without isolation of the bodies of humans from other bodies, without a reduction of the generative body to the production of sperm and ova.

Male-to-female transsexual children who are reared as girls and who have reconstructive surgery in their adolescence, as well as intersexed people, add to the argument. In the first case, there is no possibility of reproduction and the female experiences related to reproduction may be something the person has a longing for or not depending on how becoming a woman is constructed in that person's imagination or imposed by parents, teachers, and the medical and psychiatric profession. It may be that the change is accompanied by a conceptual and experiential freedom as to what being a woman is. But there no possibility or expectations of reproduction and the sexed body is not diminished as female because the body does not produce eggs. The case of intersexed people is complicated by their being placed outside of the human norm over and over and coming to occupy the monster position—more like having two heads—a position which they may embrace in a radical sexual politics. Such a person will struggle against any of the requirements of normalcy imposed on them. Rather, they explore the abundance of their sexed bodies. The experiences of women do not really apply to intersexed people—too much normalcy is necessary for that. The same goes for the expectations that may be accompanied by ferocious attempts to cut the monster up. Yet the male/female divide that tosses them out of the social is constitutive of Alcoff's account. Male-to-female transsexuals and intersexed people do not count as women. Alcoff (2006, 172; original emphasis) does not seek to establish causality between men's and women's differential reproductive possibilities at the biological level and "the richness of cultural gender," preferring instead a "holistic analysis in which this differential relation of possibility is *one* objective factor always at play." But what about the body sexual itself? Alcoff thinks the sexual body can change so that currently existing sexual differences cannot be used as proof of much of anything. The question of what our permanent physical differences are should be changed, so rather than asking what we are, we need to ask what we want to be, Alcoff says. So, a very different, nonreproductive, understanding of the body sexual is possible for Alcoff. But despite all of this, for her the significance of the division of labor in the process of biological reproduction is not unstable or undecidable all the way down: "To categorize human beings on the basis of a biological division of reproductive roles is then to recognize an objective type" (175). In spite of the complexity, Alcoff affirms that men are men and women are women in terms of biological reproduction.

Could we not view the sexual/sensual material body as something quite different? Could sexual pleasure—the raw, uninterpreted feelings in the body—be the objective anchor for a multifarious concept of gender, the nerve endings tied to the sensual and the sexual? Could not that be what we may want to be? That ground would give us a much richer understanding of the body in relation to gender.

It is interesting that Alcoff reverses the process that anthropologists and other social scientists have used. They "find" the sexual difference and then attribute gender on its basis and find themselves justified in attaching on to them whatever it is that they figure out as the "roles," or divisions of labor, governance, or social activity that attach to the "sexual difference." Alcoff's account is much more interesting because she begins with gender, but when human beings are denied gender, her work is not useful in addressing their humanity; rather, it is useful as it frames the experiences and expectations of certain women as human.

When Alcoff (2006, 154) characterizes her position regarding an objective biological basis of sexual difference, she tells us that her arguments are opposed to a "totally fluid account of sex categories." Sylvia Marcos (2006, 13) has written of distinctions in Mesoamerican Indigenous cosmologies between day and night, cold and hot, and male and female in terms of duality and the attainment in fluidity of what she calls "a homeorrheic equilibrium." Alcoff means to exclude understandings of sexuality and sex that allow mutation, changeability, and permeability. In her account, no one who produces ova can change into someone who produces sperm and vice versa and still be a woman, but most importantly for my argument, she has to exclude any mutation or permeability at the gonadal and hormonal level. If most people are, in hormonal terms, not clearly male or female, and there is no clear measure of combinations of estrogen and testosterone that constitute someone as paradigmatically male or female, and hormonal levels and combinations can be altered and do alter as the body changes, then changeability and mutation cannot be ruled out of human sexuality. I think she means to exclude understandings of sexuality and sex that allow mutation, changeability, and permeability from being someone who produces ova to someone who produces sperm and vice versa—that is, strictly at the level of what is necessary for conception and who can provide it. Intersexuality has, extremely rarely, included people who can produce both sperm and ova. Their case presents a problem for Alcoff, but the problem is not that of permeability, changeability, and mutation. It is easy to say to Marcos's analysis of Mesoamerican duality that it, accurate though it may be, is not biologically correct. To make this claim, Alcoff would first have to argue for several other claims. First, she needs to show that the body/sex web that she is proposing makes no fundamental metaphysical assumptions about the world. In particular, she needs to show whether dichotomic categorial differentiations are or are not part of the metaphysics. She also needs to provide the web. So far, she appeals to a metaphysics that can take in "odd cases," like white crows, without damage to the integrity of the web, but the crucial case of intersexed people is not examined. Third, she needs to argue that a continuum understanding of sexual difference will not back gender.

It can be seen, given the account of duality in the last paragraph and my claim that Alcoff thinks of the sexual difference in terms of dichotomy, why her account of sexual difference as an objective basis for gender falls apart in the case of intersexed persons. They present a sexual overabundance at the level of the body that cannot be understood in terms of the reproductive sexual difference. Some of them have the possibility of contributing sperm or ova—rarely both—to human reproduction, but that makes an intersexual person male or female, not man or woman (exclusive "or"). Some intersexed persons may choose to think of themselves some of the time as men and some of the time as women, at least in the contemporary United States. That does not affect nor do they think it affects their sexuality and sexual possibilities, since deciding on a womanly or manly identity is for them, not unproblematically, consistent with refusing the dimorphic-serving surgery. The stress on possibility is crucial in Alcoff's account, but it is not clear what to do with people born without the capacity to produce sperm or ova (inclusive "or"). In the account, they could only be conceived as participating in the disjunctive division of labor in reproduction subjectively, depending on their being thought of as either men or women. The same is true of people who have lost their capacity to reproduce. "Possibility" is doing a lot of work, but it is unclear how much it can really do. The duality in flux fits intersexuality well since the duality is in one person. How to interpret duality in intersexuality is important, but the metaphysics allow it.

How is a butch lesbian a woman, a *marica* a man, a *travesti* a man, a female-to-male transgendered or transsexual a woman, or a male-to-female transgendered or transsexual a man? How could those be their genders in terms of their possibility of their contributing ova (female/woman) or sperm (male/man) to reproduction? Suppose we were to adopt Alcoff's account with significant revisions. What in the web would have to be changed to accommodate the diversity? I think the Quinean metaphysics is supposed to this job, but it is quite unclear how it would be done. To choose the sexual difference, instead of what Fausto-Sterling (2000, 31) calls "the continuum," seems to me to be without justification in Alcoff's text. Indeed, we could think, going from Indigenous philosophies to Fausto-Sterling's suggestion, that there may be something to the dichotomy, an insight into the need to separate, maim, disaggregate, an important ingredient of what Fernando Coronil called "Occidentalism" (1996, 57). That would be a point of criticism.

I have argued that when Quinean metaphysics is used to describe the sexual body selecting reproduction to be the objective core of human sexuality, that which constitutes the sexual difference and grounds gender objectively, a reduction, a fragmentation, a pulling apart of the sensual and sexual body is taking place so that it no longer feels anything—indeed, it is unimaginable that the body so reduced could produce sperm or ova without scientific manipulation. As the obsession of reproductive science and technology is at the service of those who cannot reproduce and have the finances to cover the enormous costs, eggs and ova are manipulated by means external to the bodies of those who produce them. Among the technologies is surrogacy which uses poor women and poor women of color around the world to allow the body's reproductive potential to be accessed while bypassing or erasing the sensual body. Surrogacy is of a piece with the use of women as mules, as containers for drugs. Similarly, the reduction of the sensual, sexual body to sperm and egg is also behind the sterilization of dehumanized racialized bodies. The forced sterilization of women racialized as inferior to serve a variety of powerful people and ends is also about reproduction. It takes these bodies and the bodies who produce them as dangerous, or their reproductive organs as dangerous, the bodies, fully material without reduction, to be both dangerous and disposable. Reproductive technology is indeed at play in the reduction of our bodies to reproductive organs and their issue, a technology that is part of the scientific, capitalist, colonial obsession with reproduction. To think of the perceiver convinced of the relation between reproduction and sexual difference, understood as the production of substances that when placed together make a being that develops as the result of the sexual interaction, is to see that perception as true, objective. How has the thinking that performs that fragmenting and reductive selection been produced? Where? Within what matrices of power?

In this chapter, I have gone beyond my initial claim about the modern colonial gender system in "Heterosexualism and the Colonial/Modern Gender System" (Lugones 2007). In that piece, I thought of gender as a colonial imposition, but I was only thinking of particular gender arrangements. Here my intention has been to critique the concept of gender itself and its uses by power. If I am right, then without an erasure of the body sensual and sexual and the creation of sexual matter out of it to reproduce labor for capitalism or to reproduce live animal property for slave owners, the Crown, and capital, the concept of "gender" loses its bite. It can only be understood as the state's and capitalism's controlling fiction, like race, a raw use of power, out of place in any liberatory or decolonial understanding of human beings—the notion of humanity itself in need of reconception from other philosophical and cosmological sources than the ones provided by Western modernity. It is also out of place in any feminist account of who we are.

Decolonially, I think of the erotic body as permeable. I think of the colonized female body crossing into decolonial aesthesis: from erasure and separation from one's habitat, isolation from one's world, being turned into female animals by coloniality, crossing into a self who is a fully embodied being, interconnected and open to her habitat, permeable, communal. As I have come to this conception, I imagine sensual-sexual encounters as intensely pleasurable, intimate, creative of possibilities and created by our possibilities for connection in permeable reciprocity. Gender has nothing to do with it.

Bourgeois modern heterosexualisms reproduce race and capital. Neocolonial and neoliberal capitalism is structurally tied to bourgeois heterosexualisms. Racialized bourgeois reproductive heterosexuality is constituted by and is constitutive of the coloniality of power (the interrelation between racialized capitalist economics, liberal and neoliberal global politics, Euro- and Anglo-centered production of knowledge, institutional and juridical racism). CGN (Compañía Guatemalteca de Niquel), REPSA (Reforestadora Palma de Petén SA), and Grupo Cobra are among the capitalist firms violently pushing Indigenous peoples in Guatemala from their lands, backed by the Guatemalan state's neoliberal politics, which continues the reduction of Indigenous peoples to less than human beings. "Woman" as the bourgeois, white, heterosexual gendered being is their ally and profits from this violence. *Torta, cachapera, jota* cannot be lived as isolated from this construction of the economic, social, and political order as a taboo desire. Rather, in our enmeshment in the social together with other people of color who are sexual dissidents, we are in a particularly good epistemic position to understand the centrality of racist heterosexualism in the forced expulsion of the racialized from their habitats and their reduction to disposable beings.

If we take gender only as a term for oppression enmeshed in the construction of the coloniality of power and created by Western modernity, extending to the present, then liberatory, decolonial social structures, arrangements, and communities become interpretively free of gender. Gender is not a harmless way of understanding social organization. The analytic imposition of gender onto contemporary colonized people and people with a history of slavery in Abya Yala erases existing relational practices, cosmologies, philosophies interconnected with communal understandings of the self. It denies the intuitive, sensitive, complex body through a Western apparatus of control over both men and women.

If we think of the Indigenous and Afrodescendant peoples of Abya Yala at the point of encounter with the brutal conquerors and colonizers in the sixteenth century as resisting the modern colonial capitalist reduction of themselves, we must think of them as thoroughly constituted in their own thoughts, relations, conceptions of self, practices of life, economies, philosophies, cosmologies, and social arrangements and therefore at odds with Western modernity/coloniality. It is as so constituted that a history of their resistance to their reduction by the colonizers needs to be thought. In that history, they have changed as they struggled and responded to Western domination, but if we understand their struggles and responses as continuing to be humanly and logically in opposition to the conception of the world of Western capitalist colonial modernity, the imposition of gender in understanding them as our contemporaries, I suggest, performs a management, a control, of their possibilities in a colonial vein. That is not a coalitional engagement with their and our possibilities.

References

Alcoff, Linda Martín. 2006. "The Metaphysics of Gender and Sexual Difference." In *Visible Identities: Race, Gender, and the Self*, 151–76. New York: Oxford University Press.

Coronil, Fernando. 1996. "Beyond Occidentalism: Toward Nonimperial Geohistorical Categories." *Cultural Anthropology* 11 (1): 51–87.

Fausto-Sterling, Anne. 2000. *Sexing the Body: Gender Politics and the Construction of Sexuality.* New York: Basic Books.

Federici, Silvia. 2004. *Caliban and the Witch: Women, the Body, and Primitive Accumulation.* New York: Autonomedia.

Laqueur, Thomas. 1990. *Making Sex: Body and Gender from the Greeks to Freud.* Cambridge, MA: Harvard University Press.

Lugones, María. 2007. "Heterosexualism and the Colonial / Modern Gender System." *Hypatia* 22 (1): 186–209.

Marcos, Sylvia. 2006. *Taken from the Lips: Gender and Eros in Mesoamerican Religions.* Boston: Brill.

Piercy, Marge. 1976. *Woman on the Edge of Time.* New York: Knopf.

Quijano, Aníbal. 2000. "Colonialidad del poder y clasificación social." *Journal of World Systems Research* 5 (2): 342–86.

Wynter, Sylvia. 2003. "Unsettling the Coloniality of Being/Power/Truth/Freedom: Towards the Human, After Man, Its Overrepresentation—An Argument." *CR: The New Centennial Review* 3 (3): 257–337.

2
SEXUAL IDENTITY, COLONIALITY, AND THE PRACTICE OF COMING OUT
A CONVERSATION

Michael Hames-García and María Lugones

Introduction

MARÍA: I have never been someone for whom sexuality is a central-as-separate focus of my identity or my sense of self or my politics. Poverty, race, sexuality, and the gender binary have not been experienced or perceived by me in social settings or in one-on-one relationships as separable from each other. Nor do I treat them as such in theory. So, I have never been able to just ignore the fact that a person who is a lesbian is also white and of means. If she is racist or puts down people who are poor or who do not have a formal education, it does not make me feel closer to her that she is a lesbian. When I am in a place where people have not gone overboard for Euro- and Anglocentrism, where many people live lives that are guided by other values and beliefs than those that constitute Euro-centered people, I feel my own sense of myself open and become permeable.

Given these remarks, I may be understood to be the wrong sort of person to be writing about the exportation of sexual identity politics from the United States or Europe to Latin America, coloniality, and the politics of "coming out," but I think that being outside of LGBT, gay, lesbian, trans, and queer identity politics gives me insight into the connection among them. I am clear that, whatever the origin of these terms, by the time they are pushed onto Latin America, they are terms of identity. So, whatever the interest in Latin America in queer theory, "queer" is imported into Latin America as an identity, the importation done for and by middle-class nonheterosexuals. The question is whether these identities are exported North to South and when the exportation becomes a colonial imposition.

Coming out itself has "traveled" from North to South as if it were a necessary radical position without any worries as to whether the space one is coming out to can be thought, in any way, as the "public sphere" or whether there are ways that people have inhabited well that have not required this very public sense of telling others about one's sexuality. I want to reflect with Michael on coming out from our own lives making clear the specificity of the differences in meaning. The North–South mandate that it is a radical necessity for all sexual transgressors to come out depends on erasing specificity and moving into generalization, homogeneity, and abstraction.

Here I am not criticizing either queer theory or the use of *queer* in the United States; rather, I am thinking about coloniality and the introduction of terms like *queer, gay,* and *lesbian* and practices like coming out into Latin America. I am also emphatically thinking of the specificity of Latin America itself and have Indigenous communities very much in mind, not just the "metropolitan centers." Thinking about coloniality is to think both about race—the understanding of the colonized as animals, inferior by nature, anterior in species-time—and about the correlative dismissal of their knowledges, relations, practices, and ways of being in the world as of no possible value. This position has endured in different forms. Many mestizos and mestizas who identify as white or *blanco/a / mestizo/a* are Euro-centered and adopt practices, knowledges, ways of being, and identities because they are European or Anglo-American. Most of them are middle-class or upper-middle-class urban people who uphold coloniality themselves. Just as they have studied and valued European philosophy, psychology, and many aspects of "high" culture, they look at Europe and Anglo-America as they think of sexuality, theories of sexuality, and social movements. Given this combination, it becomes important to be critical of the adoption of terms of sexual self-identification, movements about sexual discrimination, and theories of sexuality that have been created in Europe or the United States within discussions over meaning and politics within the United States and Europe but with no initial or noted contribution by Latin Americans.

I have perceived that "gay" has been adopted in places like Buenos Aires by middle-class men, instead of the vernacular *puto* or *marica*, to clean up one's homosexuality and to be able to identify as someone who is not just decent but cool with it and well within the limits of his class. The class is pushed to accept their being gay because it is the worldly, educated—rather than backward—contemporary, urban, upwardly mobile thing to do. Homosexuals, putos, and maricas are left unclean, undesirable to anyone except each other and gay men: backward, dark, and poor.

There is a politics in the use of the Spanish for *lesbian* that is a politics of transgression and one that puts together heteronormativity with misogyny but also one that has tended not to think about race in this connection or about the connection of *sapphist* and *lesbian* to Eurocentrism. In my own case, I have learned and use *jota*, *tortillera*, *pata*, and *trola* in the United States, where I have lived most of my life. I do use *lesbiana*, but only when people do not or will not understand *torta* or *tortillera*, *trola*, *pata*, or *jota*. But I often say *torta* or *jota* first when I am talking about myself or women who identify as torta or jota. So, I have thought for a long time about the need for English terms that have their history elsewhere than in Latin America or nonwhite communities in the United States and the Caribbean. The pressure to use them in the United States is on a par with English-only in gatherings of sexual transgressors or in ordinary life.

The recent introduction of *queer* has a very large number of people in Latin America who are not straight and middle class shifting to this terminology. Except for people who get there through a mixture of queer theory and the North–South importation, people often do not know the meaning of the word *queer*, how it came to be in their mouths, or the history of the term or of Queer Nation. How has the term come into their mouths if not through a mimicking of Anglo-American sexual identification? What money, politics—including but certainly not only sexual politics—and constructions of knowledge were involved? How were people who did not accept these identities, either critically or as turns in middle-class fashion, sold on these identities?

MICHAEL: For my part, as long as I have had a sense of myself as a sexual being, I have been aware of my attraction to men. That attraction, however, has not been something that I have separated out from the rest of my being for the purpose of building a politics or a primary sense of self. When I came to identify as "gay" and, later, as "queer" in college, this was more or less the first time that it occurred to me that my sexual preferences might be something that could form the basis of an identity. For many reasons, I have had an ambivalent relationship to these identities, including their tendency to isolate sexuality and sexual politics as the most salient aspects of one's life. Insofar as I do identify myself as gay (in most instances, I do not identify using another term), I have come to understand that identity as carrying with it a very specific set of racialized connotations that take on significance within a larger web of meaning in the United States. The meanings of my identity as gay, this is to say, are something beyond the mere fact of my sexual preference for other men, and neither my sexual preference for other men nor my sense of myself as gay has formed the primary basis for my politics, determined my choice of friends and associates, or been the thing that has given my life the most meaning.

It is interesting to me that identities like lesbian, gay, bisexual, transgender, and queer are used untranslated in Latin America. Although I am not Latin American and have spent very little time in Latin America, the possibility troubles me that the movement of these identities and the politics of coming out that are associated with them have taken place in spite of their contestation within the United States by people who are racialized, poor, or politically dissatisfied with them. In other words, I worry that they are understood outside the United States as either unquestionably progressive or else at least politically benign at their point of origin inside the United States. I hold these concerns despite and because of my own identity as a gay man.

MARÍA: I was in Quito last year (in 2012). I was invited to an event on queer politics. I went to speak against queer theory, queer politics, and the pushing of a queer identity on Latin Americans. I spoke about the use of the word *queer* by Gloria Anzaldúa in *Borderlands/La Frontera* (1987) and said this was not a move after but before Queer Nation or queer theory, when the word was a term of abuse. Her usage of *queer* cannot be taken as a blessing for the exportation of *queer* everywhere against her own theoretical work. She did not use *queer* as an identity term in that work. Rather, she takes it up as a linguistic device that contrasts with "half and half, *mita' y mita'*" (Anzaldúa 1987, 40–41). She never says that *queer* is the word to use to avoid sexual dichotomies. She is "arguing" against all dichotomies in *Borderlands*, but it would be against the politics of language in the book to celebrate and promote an English term. She is about racialized sexuality in the perilous *rajadura* between her *cultura* and her communities, on the one hand, and Anglo-America, on the other. Being pressed into paralysis and away from responsibility by both, she presses back. That pressing is done in *tlilli tlapalli* (the red and black ink of Aztec codices), not in search for Anglo identities (Anzaldúa 1987, 69). I also spoke about the racialization of "queer" by some of the Chicano and Chicana theorists who think about a Chicano or Chicana queer identification and, some, about queer theory as a *located* response to LGBTQ liberal politics. Racialized queer is not just queer. Racialized queer is significantly about asserting one's humanity as a sexual being in darker tones. It is interesting to me that white Anglo-American and European queer theorists have not thought about race even though the question of race was raised again and again to white Anglo gay, lesbian, and feminist writers and activists by women of color and later by men of color. Those who "deconstruct" gender and do away with both the gender and the sexual binaries do not dwell on their being implicated in the history of the modern colonial gender system and the classification and treatment of the colonized and the enslaved as subhuman, beings inferior by nature: savages, primitives, beasts. What does one say or do when faced with a "subhuman sexual deviant" when one is thinking about sexuality and has not thought about one's contemporary involvement and implication in a history of racialization and dehumanization that involves every aspect of those so classified? A history that involves throwing "feminine Indigenous males" to the ferocious dogs of the conquerors; working people to death in the mines and the plantations; deeming their knowledges worthless, demonic, false; destroying their ways of relating in communities. That history includes those viewed by the colonizer as subhuman, out-of-control sexual deviants.

Anyway, I went to this conference in Quito, and the founder of Queering Paradigms was there from England for a different purpose and reason than anyone else at the conference. He was there to promote the identity "queer" in Latin America and to entice institutions to feature his endeavors. He had already organized a massive gathering in Brazil for the same purpose. Queer theory in his hands became an excuse that aided him in organizing one more Latin American gathering to promote "queer" as an identity to *all sexual transgressors: trans, gay, intersex, lesbian*. He was bringing the best term to encompass all of them no matter that the terms were in English and had not arisen from specifically Latin American sexual movements. It gave him an impeccable "in" to Latin American sexual transgression. He could organize the conferences with the locals who, in the case of Quito, were academics. The academics, whether or not they understood his game, accepted his presence and purposes as enticing and serious.

MICHAEL AND MARÍA: Just as identities are exported in a colonial vein, sexual politics and practices that are understood as crucial to sexual politics are exported in a colonial vein. The practice of coming out is one such practice, a central one in our understanding. Here we want to go through both coming out and terms of sexual identity in a way that is more careful and specific than LGBTQ politics has them being. We also relate our own personal experiences with both as a way of giving texture to the more philosophical accounts. We end with a section on coloniality and sexuality.

Coming Out

MARÍA: I understand *coming out* as an explicit articulation of one's sexuality or sexual identity to others in particular situations and circumstances, including and emphatically publicly, particularly in the public sphere. I contrast this explicit articulation with one's living among people without hiding one's sexuality, including living among people in communities of color. This living does not leave sexuality implicit. It rather announces it without using any categorial identification. The announcing is done through attire, bodily movement, the company one keeps, and an erotic appreciation of same-sex company, all among people, rather than verbally. The meaning of *coming out* is not independent from the reasons and motivations one has in coming out. It is not independent from its context, situation, circumstance, and spatiality. It is also not independent from the others to whom one intends to communicate one's sense of one's sexual identity. In asking, "Why is he coming out?" one can be asking what moves him to come out, or for what reasons is he coming out, or to what end or purpose. These are not exclusive. My own sense is that coming out is a name for several distinctively different acts or processes. Only some of these are tied to political projects, even if others can be thought of as aspects of a politics.

MICHAEL: If coming out is an explicit articulation of one's sexuality, I wonder, does it necessarily take the form of a declarative statement of identity? I am thinking of three explicit statements and wondering about the implications of each: "I am gay"; "I find men sexually attractive"; and "Soy de ambiente." When stated explicitly, each appears to be a form of coming out. The first declares an identity. The second two might declare an identity, depending on context and the company one finds oneself with—that is, the second two might reveal an implicit, unspoken identity but only if the hearer already has a sense of that identity fully formed in her mind, with cultural resources to make sense of the identity. In some contexts, the identity might be gay, while in others it could be homosexual, marica, or something else. Since no identity is explicitly named in the second and third statements, the hearer can fill in an identity based on her context and knowledge or might not fill in any identity at all and simply accept the information given as merely a fact about this individual person.

MARÍA: I think all of them are ways of coming out but very different ways, since they depend on context, company, and circumstances to be effective and perceptive. You are not going to say in the bourgeois public sphere, "I find men attractive" or "Soy de ambiente," simply because only semi-impersonal statements of identity are effective in the public sphere. The other two are more intimate and personal, though there are circumstances in which "I am gay" can be very personal. One may be dancing with a female colleague at a feminist conference and say to her, "I am gay, and you?"

MICHAEL: So, it is precisely the dependence on context that prevents "I am attracted to men" and "Soy de ambiente" from being fully effective in the public sphere. Then the power of *gay* and similar words is that they have been made to make sense acontextually (impersonally) through an agreed-on-in-advance set of meanings—meanings that consequently cannot really move from one context to another without doing some violence to contexts in which those meanings were not originally developed.

MARÍA: Coming out to one's parents, something that is deeply painful whether or not one is racialized as nonwhite, is a very personal act. In coming out to one's parents, one's own integrity and the integrity of one's relation to one's parents are on the line. This is very different from coming out as a socially defiant act, one that is public and political. Coming out to one's parents is a personal, ethical, intimate, intersubjectively raw denuding of oneself that seeks what unconditional love can bear—risky, where one's integrity, one's relations, the roof over one's head, one's belonging are at risk. As I say to them that "I like women," I let my parents know about my sexual desires for other women, but I am also alluding to wanting to include in my relation to them those who become my close and dear intimates. For some, this coming out to their parents is charged with a sense that their "real" self is to be revealed, whether or not their parents accept them. If one's parents are fundamentalist Christians, traditional and active Catholics, or people who are wedded to a view of homosexuality as psychological illness, one may be asking for something that they cannot give without a sense of self-betrayal. Yet, one does it in those cases, precisely because one feels a sense of self-betrayal oneself in one's silence. The act is emotively charged and its meaning is itself emotive. It appeals not to reason or to what is right, but to the ethics of intimacy between parents and offspring, a personal relation, an ethics that is not about rules. I argue here that the meaning of *coming out*, in coming out to one's parents, is tightly tied to the motivation, reasons, circumstances, and those addressed. The tie works in such a way that the meaning of *coming out* in coming out to one's parents cannot be generalized regardless of motivation, reasons, or situation and regardless of who is addressed by the act or process.

The socially defiant public meaning of *coming out* in the United States is most clear to me as an occupation of the bourgeois, hegemonic public sphere, where the range and limits of sense precede the defiance of the act so the act challenges already made sense. This sense is related to the logic of recognition and justice in liberal democracy. The problem here is with the terms that one has to use to defy the range and limits of the public sphere. One finds oneself transforming into someone in tune with the hegemon in order to be able to express something important to one's being of worth, something that has been denied by the hegemon. What is important in one's communicative act is itself transformed, precisely because the sense one has to seek to make is "their" sense, the sense that is hegemonic in the public sphere. This is the paradigmatic case of coming out in my experience of the contemporary politics of sexuality from seeking validation and equal rights to medical care for AIDS.

Infrapolitics, as Robin Kelley (1994) uses it, is a very different form of the political from that exercised as defiance in the bourgeois public sphere. Infrapolitical moving and communicating among people involves an-away-from-power-and-hegemony way of making sense. Infrapolitics can be a making sense together among people who are unseen and unintelligible to the hegemonic public while in their midst and thus hidden, away from power. In infrapolitical moving and sense making, one does not make sense in that public as one is attempting to create a radical direction and meaning or a metamorphosis of oneself and the social spaces of their living with those others that are unseen in the hegemon; one is creating a communal sense of the self. Infrapolitics can also take the form of gatherings and groups, more or less permanent, sometimes quite ephemeral, where people get together to make a radical sense away from power. In both cases, it does not ignore the inhabitation of hegemonic spaces. Rather, it speaks the unspeakable in those spaces, but it is learned, observed, or felt from within one's own unspoken inhabitation of spaces of power. Thus, the infrapolitical gatherings away from power can be spaces where witnessing in the hegemon leads to testifying among those making new sense.

Coming out in infrapolitical spaces, then, can be an act or process away from power within dispersed or more cohesive, but not institutionalized, socialities, or it can be a speaking to power from a sense making that is necessarily hidden from power and that has been created in infrapolitics through the first kind of space. If the former case, it is a process of making sense of one's sexuality among others who also reject the hegemonic norming of the sexual. The sense making takes issue with the hegemonic meaning of sexuality and of one's own sexuality. It is in contrast to the articulation of an already-formed understanding of one's sexuality. In the latter infrapolitical understanding of coming out, it is an act of radical politics, but if it seeks to be transforming, it cannot be a speaking to the hegemon. Rather, it seems to me, it is a speaking, moving, gesturing, relating that turns the hegemon against itself. It creates a turmoil that can be efficacious in moving among people within the hegemonic spatiality and sense, disrupting their sense of their sexuality to glimpse more radical possibilities. In each of these infrapolitical understandings of coming out, it is different in meaning from other senses of *coming out* in coming out to one's parents and coming out in the public sphere.

MICHAEL: Carlos Decena (2011) uses the concepts of the "tacit subject" and the politics of "estar" to think about the place of sexuality in the lives of Dominican immigrant men in New York City. The *tacit subject* is an ambivalent term used to describe the importance of unspoken knowledge (and precisely its unspokenness) for the maintenance of social relations. The politics of estar builds on Rodolfo Kusch's work (e.g., [1970] 2010) to use the Spanish sense of *be-ing* in a location (*estar*) as part of the process of *being* an identity (*ser*). Decena (2011, 10) writes that "no pure 'being someone' (*ser*) is possible without accounting for one's be-ing somewhere, for its location (*donde está*)." He situates Dominican men who have sex with men in their movement between contexts and locations, showing how they negotiate circumstances that, in one moment, call for them to choose identification (i.e., to come out in one sense or another) and, at others, to dwell in some form of ambiguity. His work does not make light of or dismiss coming out as a choice, nor does he see it as culturally limiting or inauthentic. At the same time, he offers textured descriptions of the possibilities other than political identification with a gay community or identity that are available to Dominican men who have an erotic attraction to other men. He does so by attending to the place of these possibilities in the men's lives in various contexts. I find this understanding of one's sexual being as something that exists in relation to one's context to be both useful and compatible with your views on the different contexts for coming out or not coming out.

MARÍA: It is important that the verb chosen by Decena is *speak*. I think it is also possible to hide knowledge by moving differently, gesturing differently in a way that is not gay. But this unshown knowledge bears the damage of passing. So, the unspoken knowledge makes me think that there are a lot of other marks of one's sexuality that are shown when one *está* with people in different circumstances. That one *está* with them in this shown but unspoken way makes what is unspoken not central or crucial. Thinking in a Kuschian way, when one *está*, I would say that there is a change in one from circumstance to circumstance but that change is resisted by one's embodiment when the knowledge is unspoken. So the ambiguity does not turn into passing precisely because of that give-and-take between unspoken but shown.

MICHAEL: I think that's a good sense of how Decena uses Kusch, although he is also interested in the movement of people from context to context and the way they move in the ambiguity, sometimes closer to passing and sometimes closer to declaring an identity, depending on the options available to them and what those options can do for them in a given context. For me, the original desire to come out to friends was an intentional desire to create a community in which I could feel comfortable and free to express myself without awkwardness—for example, the awkwardness of a close friend saying something stupidly homophobic in my presence or of a straight female friend expressing sexual interest in me and assuming that my closeness to her was an invitation to that expression. In general, my coming out to people during college was a way I discovered to assemble a community of friends, most of them straight, who would not judge me for how I lived my life. I could feel comfortable around them expressing my sexual desires and never feel pressured to participate in heterosexual rituals. This community was largely a white, liberal, hippie crowd at my college. I shared little in common with them (e.g., I was the only Latino and only one of two people of color), but my being gay provided a justification for my inclusion into their ranks as an "outsider." Indeed, despite being heterosexual, the members of this crowd were frequently derided as faggots, queers, and dykes for reasons unrelated to sexual preference: their androgynous styles of dress (including the women's refusal to shave their legs and armpits), their espoused feminism, and their progressive politics. Generally speaking, the more out I was during this period, the more assured I was of a self-selected community of progressive friends. At the time, this was important to me largely as a contrast to my years of actively hiding my sexual desires from friends during high school and middle school, when my multiracial, conservative friendship circle was made up mostly of fairly religious peers. Coming out in college, then, offered me a longed-for means to escape isolation and in a very real sense an alternative to suicide.

This form of coming out was not "coming out into a community," in the traditional sense that this phrase is understood in gay and lesbian contexts in the United States. I was neither moving to West Hollywood or the Castro, for example, and surrounding myself exclusively with gay and lesbian people nor joining a community of potential sexual partners. (Coming out by declaring oneself gay was never necessary to find erotic company. It had always been clear to me that erotic company could be found otherwise. At the same time, of course, coming together with others around a gay politics could facilitate an ease of contact.) Instead, I was using the declaration of my sexuality to separate myself from some people and draw others toward me in order to assemble a circle of friends that could afford me the space to breathe, to try out living more openly without the active hiding and repression I had practiced before. There was, then, a political sense to it in that I was selecting people with liberal sexual politics to be around in the day to day. It was not a public sphere politics or a particularly gay or queer politics, and there was not a program of political activism in this context specifically related to my sexuality. However, I understand the politics of this coming out to be related to the first sense of infrapolitics you describe: directed away from hegemonic senses of sexual identity toward others who understood themselves as making alternative, radical communities in company with one another other, based on values that explicitly rejected the values of their white, suburban parents and origins. Our purpose was not to make sense to anyone but each other.

MARÍA: I think in presenting this sense of infrapolitics as lived, it would be useful to explore the ways in which you did have, as an important point of the being together, the need to create an alternative sense about things that were not understood or seen in the public sphere and to attempt to transform yourselves in terms of this sense. I think this is an important part of infrapolitics, since the first sense is preparatory for the second sense in which one inhabits the social exhibiting and announcing, expressing this sense that will remain unintelligible to the hegemon but will inspire, attract, seduce, speak to people who were complacent in the hegemonic understanding of themselves or who had no adequate space and opportunity to make this sense themselves.

MICHAEL: There was at the same time another process of coming out in which I participated. The members of the Gay and Lesbian Alliance

(GALA) at my college (in which I participated) were much more oriented toward a public sphere kind of sexual politics. I went to its meetings, participated in some of its social and political events, learned a vocabulary for sexual politics, and met romantic partners through it. However, it never provided me with my core politics, community, or sense of self. Part of this had to do with my discovery of myself as Chicano (rather than simply Mexican or Mexican American) and beginning to elaborate an identity related to it. This discovery came in part through reading the work of Chicana feminists like Cherríe Moraga and absorbing their critiques of white lesbian and gay politics even before I had experienced the limitations of these politics firsthand.

As I have understood it through participation in organizations such as GALA and other student groups or gay prides marches and parades or through my observation of the Human Rights Campaign Fund or its various local equivalents, the political practice of coming out is explicitly directed toward social change on a large scale through the advancement of a program of sexual politics or through changing others' attitudes about homosexuality. This strategy by necessity requires the singling out of sexuality apart from race, gender, class, and other aspects of one's identity—isolating it in a way that I learned to be critical of early on. To the extent that I have had a politics that could be called a sexual one, it has been more often a feminist of color one of challenging gender roles, expectations, and limits and the collusion of racism with sexuality rather than an LGBTQ politics seeking inclusion (e.g., in the military), equality (e.g., through marriage), or freedom (e.g., through the repeal of antisodomy laws). For goals such as these three, I believe that the LGBTQ movement has relied to a significant extent on the public sphere strategy of coming out.

I want to say a bit now about an alternative for me to either queer or gay. Since I did not grow up as a Spanish speaker, my first encounter with the term *joto* was academic. I had seen *jotería* in Anzaldúa's *Borderlands/La Frontera*, but it didn't stand out to me. The first time I was given a rich context for it was at the National Association for Chicana and Chicano Studies (NACCS) in 1995, when the Joto Caucus was still forming. A group of men had started meeting at the previous NACCS and decided to form a caucus along the lines of the already-formed Lesbian Caucus, but it was not official yet. At this NACCS meeting—my first—the resolution to create a new caucus was going to be voted on by the association and the leadership had posed some questions to the caucus first. At the time, the men were calling the caucus NALGAA (taken from the name of another organization: the National Association of Latino Gay Artists and Academics). Because of the name, the NACCS leadership had asked whether the new caucus was a separate "national" organization or a caucus of NACCS. This led in our meeting to a discussion about how to rename ourselves for the resolution. Several possibilities were discussed: Gay Caucus, Queer Caucus, and Joto Caucus were the ones I remember being most discussed. Language (Spanish versus English) was definitely part of the conversation and a reason why some preferred *joto*, but it was pointed out that *gay* was also used in Mexico as an English loan word to Spanish. Both *queer* and *joto* were perceived as reclaimed words of derision, which counted in their favor. (Remember that this was the mid-1990s, and *queer* was not yet quite established as a valorized word in the academy, nor had it been, I think, borrowed into Spanish yet.) Furthermore, an argument was made that both *queer* and *joto* were open and flexible enough to include trans people and even bisexual women (who were at the time excluded from the Lesbian Caucus). I remember there being a general consensus that the new group was open to people who were not men. Furthermore, however, people felt a sense that *joto* was *our* term to reclaim, something particular to Chicano communities. Creating a Joto Caucus required the rest of NACCS to think specifically about the place of jotería within Chicano communities, whereas a Gay Caucus or a Queer Caucus could always risk seeming like it was about something not endemic to the culture. In other words, because *joto* is a word Chicanos use to describe other Chicanos, one cannot claim that there are no jotos in Chicano communities. It was an insistence on our historical presence within the community. So then, to *ser joto* is to *estar entre Chicanos*. It doesn't make any sense outside of the context. In this way, *joto* is significantly different from *gay*.

To the extent, then, that *ser joto es estar entre Chicanos—mejor dicho, estar siendo joto entre Chicanos*—I'm not entirely sure how the logic of coming out works relative to this context. To declare, "I am a joto" or "Soy joto," is not really something I have seen done along the lines of a public sphere coming out politics. People definitely let it be known that they are jotos. Perhaps the closest thing I can picture is the use of the third-person plural or an indirect grammatical construction, such as "As jotos, we experience . . ." or "It's nice to be around other jotitos," but neither of these really expresses a public sphere politics. When one does declare, "I am a joto," even in a very public context, one carries with the declaration traces of particularity, indications of a geography and a history that have given the term its sense. Although *gay* appears to be without context, it in fact does have a history and a geography, and these are indelibly Euro-American in their origin. In a fashion typical of Western universalizing gestures, that history and geography are masked, presented as inconsequential to the term's meaning and use. This is what it means for "the West" to present itself as "universal," its history as universal history, its culture as universal culture, its values and ways of making sense as universal ethics and universal knowledge. I suspect something similar in the North–South exportation of queer by folks like the man from Europe in your example.

MARÍA: When you were saying that the kind of politics of coming out "explicitly directed toward social change on a large scale through the advancement of a program of sexual politics or through changing others' attitudes about homosexuality" requires singling out sexuality, I thought of the lack of possibility of going for a public sphere politics on sex, race, class combined as one. It is unimaginable, isn't it? That's because of the classist and racist nature of the society. You cannot presume intersectionality, on the contrary. I feel as if much of what we are saying makes us sound conservative because it is hard for the positions to be read as radical when what is radical is all about going all out on sex, sexual identity, changing meanings and terms. That is because of the coloniality, and here the coloniality hides the radicalism of acknowledging the inseparability of a coloniality that is not just heterosexualist but also imagines and perceives folk of color as sexually perverse animals. So decoloniality has to be something very different than what queer theory offers.

The question of specificity of context, time and relation is crucial in understanding what's wrong with the exporting and importing of political practices, terms of identity, sexual theories that are all about universality and abstraction even when they say they are about the flesh. It seems odd that people keep on going on "radically" with the same old ways. It's certainly theoretically easy to do this, to show the colonial nature of queer, gay, coming out, and so on, which shows the enormous investment on coloniality of every sort.

I always have to defend not "coming out" in communities where I do the political work of popular education, community organizing, or conceiving and creating together decolonial projects. I do not come out in any of the ways I have characterized previously or others that involve the explicit articulation of my sexuality and my sexual identity. That is not part of my being with others in racialized communities where I am political and where the politics is attuned to the individuals in those communities. That attunement depends on listening and being listened to in order to get a sense of the place in enormous detail, including bits about people's health; their ways of speaking, gesturing, dressing, touching, and dancing; their bodily strength; the way they help each other or not; their good and bad relations with members of their family and their neighbors (who has died, who is not getting along with whom); the economic relations among people (who has pear fruit trees, who is willing to exchange for yellow cherries, their sense of the meaning of owning something, how to treat people who are drunk who knock on your door asking for money); the extent and form of their political life and participation; their religiosity; and their family in an extended and closer sense (their mistrust for white people, their mistrust for people who are not from the community). To pinpoint who is listened to when it comes to making community decisions takes paying attention to many interactions in many different circumstances. But as I am in their midst, I pay attention and take up gestures that convey sensuality, I look at someone in the eye intently as I smile, I keep my way of dressing, my way of moving, and my gestures and add some. I add to my dancing repertoire when I go dancing and the music is danced in way not known to me in an embodied way. I keep my hair very short, I am expressive, I speak often directly to the point when the matter at hand is relevant to the politics affecting or of the community. But I listen a lot, I learn people, their ways of thinking, their particular gestures, how they use their hands. I compliment both men and women in a variety of ways about abilities they show, things they do, their appearance, their ideas, strategies, the way they dance. I think in doing this, I am attentively and expressively *mundana*, in doing so I am open to being known and to know others. I do not pick out my sexuality as something to leave unspoken, though I do not speak it out. Everything is interrelated in people's and my own living with them: race, sexuality, sewing and knitting abilities, playing music, and so on. To intervene in the centrality of heterosexuality, I have to understand in what ways heterosexuality is central to their lives, what heterosexuality is about in their lives, how it came to be that way, and why. I don't barge in with an already-made position. But I am also not coming out as deviant. I want to be known well enough that "deviant" cannot attach to me in their eyes and feelings, and sometimes that never happens.

I have never participated in LGBTQ public sphere liberal politics and have often been struck by the racism in their analysis even when many men of color and some women participate in the public events. I am critical of event politics. I do not think that's a good way of getting people to transform their opinions, relations, or ways of living. That's why I am a popular educator, because I believe in a politics that does not push stuff on people who have been dominated through extreme exploitation, violent knowledges presented as universal truths, a racialized system of production that brutally exploits people's labor or uses their bodies as disposable, or a heterosexualist gender system that relegated those racialized to the position of nongendered animals.

Sexuality, Coloniality, and Latin America

MICHAEL AND MARÍA: The preceding accounts of our personal relationships to sexuality, identity, and coming out politics are intended to provide a grounding for the reservations we express about the exporting of queer identity and queer theory to Latin America. It seems that part of what is important to understand about different ways of living one's sexuality, whether in the United States or Latin America, is the specificity of it. By the "specificity of one's sexuality," we mean at least the following: (1) the specificity of how one experiences erotic relations to others; (2) the specificity of the sense that one makes of those experiences, including whether one understands oneself to have a sexual identity or not; (3) the specificity of how one is understood to be deviant or aberrant because of those experiences or at risk of being understood as deviant; (4) the specificity of the sense one makes of being understood as deviant or of the risk of being understood as deviant and the various kinds of politics one may have in relation to them; (5) the specificity of the way one understands one's body in relation to all of the above, for example, as abject, as torta, as gendered, as deviantly gendered, as in need of trusting company, as ungendered; (6) the specificity of how one lives one's sexuality in the particular community of one's belonging, a community with its own history of sense making about the social world, including the sexual in that world, particularly when that sense making has been the consistent and enduring target of racial ideological domination; and (7) the specificity of the philosophical, cosmological, economic, and spiritual framework that at a particular time places understandings of sexuality as intertwined in a much larger, historically produced, and interpersonally lived context. If one isolates a particular aspect of the social, it cannot be separated and lifted from the rest while still making sense, except from within an analysis that presupposes the rest. Particular social groups, societies, nations, and nation-states have, for example, philosophical, cosmological, economic, and spiritual understandings of the self, of the self among others, and of the self in a relation to one's habitat. The self as an isolated and ahistorical individual is in a tense contrast with a communal self that lives in interconnection with everything in her habitat. One cannot ignore these differences and take them to be irrelevant to the living and the understanding of sexuality, the sexual body, the sexual imagination, and sexual practices of loving oneself and others.

All of this specificity is at profound odds with gestures of homogenization, including those motivated by coalition or by attempts at neutral description. In many contexts, such gestures are colonial gestures that urge the replacement of one's specificity with a supposedly universal or acontextual category (e.g., gay, lesbian, bisexual, transgender, or queer) that in fact carries its own specificity emanating from a point of origin among those active in the United States (and to at least some extent Western European) bourgeois public sphere.

In contradistinction to the Eurocentric universalism of many discussions of LGBTQ or queer politics, we are thinking about terms of identity and coming out in relation to coloniality. We are considering the analysis of race and racialization that understands them as tied to the capitalist modern world system of power taking up the work of Aníbal Quijano (e.g., 2000). In particular, we are thinking of how ways of living one's sexuality as a racialized and thus ideologically dominated person are affected by the continued colonial introduction and imposition of sexual identity terms that originate in the metropole.

Sexual and gender identity categories from the metropole (e.g., LGBTQ) do not travel benignly. They are not offered to those whose sexuality is racialized through processes of colonial domination as a neutral tool that one can take or leave, depending on its usefulness. To the contrary, they are most often imposed through a variety of means, including the tying of "rewards" to identification with them (through NGO funding, for example). They can also be imposed against one's will through reckless or willful misdescription by anthropologists and other academics, by transnational activists and local elites, by the media, and by international, national, and regional policymakers.[1]

(Queremos) erradicar las formas sutiles de discriminación que las enchaquiradas viven en sus comunidades ancestrales de la costa. No hay crímenes de odio aquí, como si se producen en las grandes ciudades. Sin embargo, hay segregación social y política. Queremos evitar la desaparición de la expresión de género enchaquirada y su sustitución por modelos hegemónicos de (trans)feminidad y (trans)masculinidad provenientes de esas ciudades.

—Estatutos de la Asociación de Enchaquiradas de Engabao, Enero 2012

MICHAEL AND MARÍA: So, what possible interest could people in the United States and England, both gay and queer activists, those who export "knowledge" about sexuality in organized events, have in colonizing Latin American sexuality? Is it because they go to sexual public battle for the universal truth? Is it for universalizing negative freedom? To what extent does the marriage of northern sexual activism and knowledge production with capitalism find itself in sexual tourism, clubs where English is spoken as a matter of course, where people are introduced to an upper- and middle-class polished sexuality only to find themselves in the rawer sexual mixtures and couplings with the sexual primitive and unclean locals—putos, maricas, trasvestis—for a price? To what extent is northern funding used for this exportation—as for the exportation of shelters for battered women through NGOs—and to what extent is it an ideological conquest and colonization? Why is the politics of public sphere gay liberation something that needs to be made global even in places where there is no bourgeois public sphere? Is queer power really powerful only when it is global? Is it then that sexual empire becomes realized? Is the colonial imposition of liberal sexuality part of the exportation of liberal democracy as a good? How but through this colonial imposition is it that "gay" and "lesbian" equal sexual freedom and that the United States is the land of sexual freedom? And, most importantly, why is an "autochthonous" sexuality dangerous to the First World's own sense of itself?

From its inception in the sixteenth century, the colonial/modern gender system has, among other things, disrupted traditional ways of understanding sexuality as an interrelated part of the social fabric of a community (Lugones 2007). This disruption has been part and parcel of the disruption of traditional social relations and ways of knowing generally, so as to facilitate their replacement by Eurocentric ones amenable to capitalism and colonialism. One of the things that the pushing of "gay" and "lesbian" into places like Latin America has contributed to is the separation of sexuality from other aspects of life. This separation works according to the logic of capitalism so as to further distance people not only from traditional ways of knowing but also from their connections to other people.

The colonial/modern gender system constitutes the coloniality of gender. The racialization of people and labor is intrinsic to the colonial/modern gender system and inseparable from the distinction between the human and the nonhuman that constitutes it. European bourgeois heterosexuals became racialized as gendered humans, beings superior in every way, including knowledge, the scientific practices of production and use of labor, and the reproduction of humanity. The racialized as non-human inhabitants of Abya Yala, and those Africans brought violently through the Middle Passage and treated as subhuman, beasts, savages, primitives, and animals cannot be understood as gendered, since gender and the reproduction of humanity—the superior white European and later Anglo-American beings—were tightly tied in the heterosexuality of the colonial modern gender system.[2] Reproduction and heterosexuality were inextricably tied to each other and to racialization in the structuring of colonial sexuality and capital. Holding tight to the inferiority and animality of Indigenous and African-descent inhabitants of Abya Yala required that their sexuality be seen and legalized as not producing human beings. Homosexual relations between Europeans and Africans or between Europeans and Guarani, Mexica, Quechua, or other Indigenous people were risky pursuits since the Holy Inquisition was one of the arms of Church and Crown to create terror in spilling seed away from the reproduction of purity of race and property. Indigenous and African sexual ways had to be denied, buried, and extricated from the sociality of colonization.

Indigenous people were subject to enormous disruption of their communal arrangements and the relation between those communal arrangements, their ways of knowing, their senses of self, and a communal understanding of self and relation. An understanding of the sexual that places people outside of connection requires that there be a place that is in an outside where individuals, understood as aberrations, can exist. Whether that is conceptually tenable is an important question for the constitution of the human, since the human for the inhabitants of Abya Yala and the African people enslaved in the Americas is in relation, in connection, and communal. Sexuality, then, cannot be understood in separation from the rest of life. The colonization of Indigenous and African sexuality in Abya Yala requires both that the human/subhuman distinction be maintained and that homosexual sexuality be segregated from communal ways of being. "Communal" does not require community but does involve imagining, envisaging, planning, actions that cannot take place without other people, like carrying a very large and heavy thing or living well as human beings. For that, one has to shift to a communal sense of self for oneself.

We understand the continued systematic replacing of autochthonous sexualities with Anglo and European ones to be central to the disruption of the social fabric of and the ways of being and loving in Latin America. It is also central to what Walter Mignolo (1995, 3) has called "the colonization of memory." Heteronormativity and the concomitant segregated Anglo-American and European homosexual practices and relations have given rise to activism and intellectual production that centers on individualism, deviance, and the conceptualization of sexuality as a reproductive binary. This work is context specific, and it is tied to coloniality—that is, to the racialization, dehumanization, and bestialization of colonized peoples. It cannot travel to colonized spaces without reemphasizing its colonial ties. It's being forced or sold to the people of Latin America, including to intellectuals and activists who emphasize sexuality is a colonial enterprise. The latest such selling, that of a queer identity, is no exception, and it may demand much selling out on the part of activists and intellectuals.

Notes

1. See, for example, Bhaskaran 2004 and Massad 2007.
2. Abya Yala is the Kuna name for the American continent that predates Columbus.

References

Anzaldúa, Gloria. 1987. *Borderlands/La Frontera: The New Mestiza*. San Francisco: Aunt Lute Books.
Bhaskaran, Suparna. 2004. *Made in India: Decolonizations, Queer Sexualities, Trans/National Projects*. New York: Palgrave Macmillan.
Decena, Carlos Ulises. 2011. *Tacit Subjects: Belonging and Same-Sex Desire Among Dominican Immigrant Men*. Durham, NC: Duke University Press.
Kelley, Robin D. G. 1994. *Race Rebels: Culture, Politics, and the Black Working Class*. New York: Free Press.
Kusch, Rodolfo. (1970) 2010. *Indigenous and Popular Thinking in América*. Translated by María Lugones and Joshua M. Price. Durham, NC: Duke University Press.
Lugones, María. 2007. "Heterosexualism and the Colonial / Modern Gender System." *Hypatia* 22 (1): 186–209.
Massad, Joseph A. 2007. *Desiring Arabs*. Chicago: University of Chicago Press.
Mignolo, Walter D. 1995. *The Darker Side of the Renaissance*. Ann Arbor: University of Michigan Press.
Quijano, Aníbal. 2000. "Coloniality of Power, Eurocentrism, and Latin America." Translated by Michael Ennis. *Nepantla: Views from South* 1 (3): 533–80.

Michael Hames-García is Professor of Mexican American and Latina/o Studies at the University of Texas at Austin. His books include *Identity Complex: Making the Case for Multiplicity* (2011), *Gay Latino Studies: A Critical Reader* (2011), and *Fugitive Thought: Prison Movements, Race, and the Meaning of Justice* (2004).

3

MONSTROUS BECOMINGS

CONCEPTS FOR BUILDING DECOLONIAL QUEER COALITIONS

Hil Malatino

Monstrosity and Gender Nonconformance

IN 1994, IN the third issue of then-fledgling *GLQ*—the journal that would play a decisive role in the academic institutionalization and legitimization of queer theory—Susan Stryker published her essay "My Words to Victor Frankenstein above the Village of Chamounix: Performing Transgender Rage." This text, an expanded version of a performance Stryker gave at a 1993 conference at California State University, San Marcos, would go on to become an urtext of sorts for what has come to be known as transgender studies. Stryker herself would go on to help found *TSQ*, an academic journal that aims to be "the journal of record for the rapidly consolidating interdisciplinary field of transgender studies" (Currah and Stryker 2014, 1).

This brief contextual description of the essay's publication is important because it signals that inclusion of transgender issues within queer theory/LGBTQ studies has come coupled with a critical mobilization of monstrosity. In other words, queer theory, trans studies, and "monster studies" are complexly intertwined. I'd like to think, through a close engagement with this foundational text of Stryker's, about why monstrosity has come to function as such a rich locus of intellectual and political investment for trans and gender nonconforming folk. Why does monstrosity resonate so deeply for us? What can we learn from this resonance?

I've written elsewhere that "what we need today, in order to resist the multiple violences entailed by late modern disavowals of corporeal difference, is a coalition of monsters—those beings that embrace corporeal non-normativity, hybridity, and mixity as a source of strength and resilience capable of challenging understandings of extraordinary bodies as pathological, aberrant, and undesirable" (Malatino 2013, 132). This chapter is an effort to flesh out what I mean by a "coalition of monsters." Monstrosity is a powerful trope that indexes categorical excess, liminality, and a refusal of neat identitarian codification. Monsters are difficult to pin down, only ever partially classifiable, singular and unpredictable entities that work to trouble epistemological certainties and unsettle the ostensibly natural order of things.

The function of the monster as epistemological troublemaker is an empowering and resonant aspect, I think, for trans and gender nonconforming folk. In taking a critical stance in relation to the constitutive criteria for maleness and femaleness, one that troubles the distinctions between dyadic gender categories and the line between nature and artifice, we function as troublemakers, or what Sara Ahmed (2010, 88) has termed "unhappiness causes."

Ahmed analyzes the ways in which queer subjectivities are framed as both inevitably unhappy—on account of marginalization and ostracism by the dominant, heterofamilial social order—and "unhappiness causes," persons who generate unhappiness within the dominant order on account of their rejection of its rigidly gendered, heterosexist logics of inclusion, particularly those that manifest in the form of what Lee Edelman (2004, 4) has called "reproductive futurism." In other words, those beings that refuse to act in the name of "the Child" in order to reify and naturalize heterofamilial structure across generations, thus securing a future social order undergirded by the same heterosexist, reproductively oriented logic governing current hegemonic organizations of intimacy and belonging, are understood as both inevitably estranged from the promise of the "good life" and a source of affective dissonance and threat to those invested in the logic of reproductive futurism.

Stryker—long before Edelman authored his well-known polemic against the figure of the Child in *No Future*, long before Ahmed wrote about the unhappy queer—theorized a poignant exemplar of a being who troubled, railed against, caused unhappiness within, even decimated this dimorphically gendered, heterofamilial, reproductively focused order. This exemplar was Frankenstein's monster. A product of positivist science whose existence far outstrips the intentions of the maker; a sentience called into being through the work of a man obsessed with replicating the wondrous; a figure who turns against the maker and thus transgresses Frankenstein's fantasy of ontological mastery; a being thrown into a world with no habitable place for him; a destroyer of the heterofamilial order by way of revenge, murdering Victor Frankenstein's loved ones as retribution for being forced into this placeless, peripatetic, lonely existence; a being who wants company and intimacy and desires discourse, care, empathy, and touch but cannot easily access any of these on account of signifying as a repository of the dominant culture's greatest fears and phobias; and a being who takes to the wilderness, finding some measure of solace in this outside dwelling absented from the judgment, fear, and derision of conventional humans.

It is the monster's rage, loneliness, and desire for an alternative social order that seems to motivate Stryker's (1994, 238) identification.

> The transsexual body is an unnatural body. It is the product of medical science. It is a technological construction. It is flesh torn apart and sewn together again in a shape other than that in which it was born. In these circumstances, I find a deep affinity between myself as a transsexual woman and the monster in Mary Shelley's *Frankenstein*. Like the monster, I am too often perceived as less than fully human due to the means of my embodiment; like the monster's as well, my exclusion from human community fuels a deep and abiding rage in me that I, like the monster, direct against the conditions in which I must struggle to exist.

Identification with Frankenstein's monster precipitates something more than a desire for assimilation and inclusion within the normative "human community," however. While the comfort and security this mode of social organization affords are desired—for instance, the ability to not face consistent macro- and microaggressions in the realm of employment, housing, education, and everyday social interaction; the ability to feel protected and supported both formally, through legal and institutional reform measures, and informally, by accessible structures of interpersonal support—it is not yoked to an investment in inclusion that would leave the heterofamilial, dimorphic order of sociality unchanged.

Rather, the consistent and quotidian struggle to exist produces alternative pathways to community formation, support, intimacy, and belonging. This begins with a reclamation of monstrosity, a resistant rending of the term from its pejorative, Gothic, deeply Othering associations.

> I want to lay claim to the dark power of my monstrous identity without using it as a weapon against others or being wounded by it myself. I will say this as bluntly as I know how: I am a transsexual, and therefore I am a monster ... words like "creature," "monster," and "unnatural" need to be reclaimed by the transgendered. By embracing and accepting them, even piling one on top of another, we may dispel their ability to harm us. A creature, after all, in the dominant tradition of Western European culture, is nothing other than a created being, a made thing. The affront you humans take at being called a "creature" results from the threat the term poses to your status as "lords of creation," beings elevated above mere material existence. (Stryker 1994, 240)

What does it mean to reclaim monstrosity? I think it is nothing short of the embrace of a specifically antihumanist ontology, one with possible decolonial potential. To embrace one's status as a "made thing" is to reject the fallacies of human autonomy, individualism, and self-sovereignty so central to modern Eurocentric conceptions of human being. This understanding of being as fundamentally "made" or "created" opens onto a conceptualization of the human as constructed, embedded in milieu not ever entirely of its choosing, fundamentally interrelational and nonsovereign. This reconceptualization of being stems from the deep ambiguity of monstrosity. On the one hand, the monster is a fabrication, a production of the dominant culture that serves to give flesh and form to Otherness, to contain and manage the fear of difference, and to shore up, through contrariety, normative modes of being and identity. On the other, monstrosity is a semaphore of sorts, signaling the possibility of living alternatively or refusing dominant logics of gender, the family, and possessive individualism and inventing other styles of existence, other modes of embodiment and relation. Reclaiming monstrosity means, as Stryker writes, coming to grips with one's status as a made thing, simultaneously understanding the dominant culture's fabrication of monstrosity while working this fabrication of alterity and Otherness in resistant and liberatory ways, embracing as desirable the failure to assimilate to hegemonic modes of social belonging.

In other words, Stryker's essay enables us to reimagine monstrosity beyond the hackneyed conventions that typically shape it; chief among these is the relegation of the monster to a position of outsiderhood—whether, like Frankenstein's monster, the harsh terrain of the French Alps or, like medieval and early modern monsters, a dwelling at the margins of the colonial imaginary. What would it mean to think monstrosity beyond outsiderhood?

Beyond Outsiderhood: Rethinking Tropes of Gender Nonconformance

We typically think of monsters as inhabiting borderlands, margins, peripheries, underworlds; if they dwell in the same spaces as normative beings, it tends to be in an illicit, mysterious, or secretive way. This is also the way we tend to think of gender and sexual outlaws—even that term, *outlaw*, signifies a being outside of or in excess of social regulation and convention. However, when it comes to both monstrosity and gender (and the complex interweavings of these terms that we've already been exploring), I don't think there is an outside. This is not a particularly popular claim in the field of women's, gender, and sexuality studies; those of us working in this area have learned and utilized, over and over again, heuristics that rely on a spatial imaginary enabled through the dyad of centricity and marginality. Think of Gayle Rubin's formulation of the "charmed circle" of sexual normativity and the "outer limits" of perversion, deviance, and abnormality in "Thinking Sex" (1992) or Judith

Butler's theorization of the "constitutive outside" in *Bodies That Matter* (1993, 3) The outside, the margins, the limits: each of these overlapping tropes operates as a "domain of abjected bodies" or "field of deformation" that produces, through contradistinction, the highly regulatory gendered schema that Butler (1993, 15–16) has termed "the heterosexual matrix," It is important to remember that this matrix also accounts for the production of an expectation of continuity between birth sex and gender performance and could therefore just as easily be referred to as the cisgendered matrix.

The spatial imaginary that informs this constitutive outside—that space of unlivability where gender and sexual transgressors, misfits, and weirdos supposedly dwell—seems somewhat like the margins of early modern European maps, where monsters (dragons and such) populate those unknown, partially known, much speculated-on territories at the periphery of familiar lands. While I think that this framework for understanding the production of legible, properly gendered subjects has been enormously useful, I think it is also important to consider the limitations of the spatial imaginary that structures its logic.

Here's a question deceptive in its simplicity: Where is this constitutive outside? Is it a mythic realm? Is it a set of locations interwoven with that familiar world that we, whether trans, queer, gender nonconforming or not, must navigate daily? Is it in those decentered, dispersed nodes—bars, bedrooms, queer communes, queer squats—where gender transitivity and transgression are (sometimes, tenuously) valorized? Is it possible that it is, actually, nowhere, only a theoretical placeholder meant to explain the production of legibly gendered subjects but otherwise limited in its utility? I have a hunch that this may be so, mostly because I have no workable answer to this question of location. Who could possibly live in a nonplace? Who could actually inhabit this "constitutive outside"?

What I'm suggesting, in other words, is that there is no there there—there is no nonplace, no locatable, constitutive outside—and that this spatial imaginary, even if we understand it only as a heuristic tool, is actually quite unhelpful if we are concerned with ameliorating the conditions of unlivability and existential difficulty that contemporary gender nonconforming and queer subjects experience. If there is no outside, then there is no subject who dwells there; no subjectivity could form in an "outside."

To reclaim monstrosity, to make it work as a resistant concept for trans, queer, and gender nonconforming folks, we must imagine the monster differently, as something other than a being that exists beyond the realm of the natural order, that threatens to disrupt the logic of the Natural from a position outside of it. Instead, perhaps we can imagine monsters in quotidian ways or consider their homeplaces and the fraught complexities of their daily lives. We can try to think of monsters as communal, relational constructions enabled by, and in need of, networks of support rather than considering them as comically extravagant, aberrant, abjected, alone, misunderstood—the way they tend to be thought of by dominant culture.

Monsters conventionally operate as figures of outsiderhood. And I'm increasingly convinced that thinking of trans and gender nonconforming folks as cultural outsiders is none too helpful in developing intricate accounts of the existential difficulties we confront or how those existential difficulties are absolutely nonexceptional. Financial and emotional precarity, the debilitating effects of macro- and microaggressions, difficulty accessing tools that enable holistic self-care—these linked phenomena shape many more lives than the trope of outsiderhood allows us to consider. If monstrosity is to be conceptually useful, it must be thought differently—as common, as quotidian, as a phenomenological orientation that enables more liberatory ways of building and inhabiting spaces of resistance and flourishing. Political philosopher Antonio Negri has argued, in a meditation on the reclamation of monstrosity (what he calls the "becoming-monstrous of life"), that "little by little in the history of the world, the monster, from his position 'outside,' comes to occupy the 'inside.' Better said: the monster has been inside all the time, because his political exclusion is not the consequence, but the premise, of his productive inclusion" (Casarino and Negri 2008, 208). The monster, even when posited as outside, is always actually serving a function internal to the dominant culture; being labeled a monstrous being is a means through which a dominant culture exploits those beings within its domain of force through relegation to the status of sub- or other-than-human; reclaiming monstrosity is a mode of resisting the violence and denigration this entails without succumbing to assimilation, the demand to erase alterity.

I also worry that the marginality/centricity dyad is too closely yoked to reductive debates about radicalism and assimilation, wherein outsiderhood is too neatly linked to queer radicality; my hunch is that this linkage produces excessive posturing in relation to subcultural credibility and not as much pragmatic political action and empathic support as it could. Moreover, it presumes a neat division between normativity and resistance, a division ill-equipped to consider the complex complicities and concessions all subjects are forced to make in late capitalist, neoliberal milieus. As José Esteban Muñoz (1999) reminded us over two decades ago, a political terrain structured by assimilation and antiassimilation is quite incapable of doing justice to disidentificatory practices, those modes of queer self-fashioning that are about tactical misrecognition, improper interpellations, and desire-with-a-difference that occur not outside but within, on, and against fluctuating structures of power.

Engaging these issues means developing a more relational ontology and, in doing so, building a different vocabulary to speak about trans and queer selfhood. I've lately been interested in the work of Karen Barad (2007, 2012) on what she calls "agential realism," "quantum entanglement," and "intra-action," and I think that these concepts can be useful in the line of inquiry I'm trying to sketch here. She moves beyond the treatment of materiality and discursivity as separate domains in order to think how matter is more than a "mere effect of discursive practices, but rather an agentive factor in its iterative materialization" (2012, 32). Materiality and discursivity, here, are understood as ontologically inseparable, which means "body talk" is a transformative social and political force, not merely imprinted or molded, and not ever able to be neatly relegated to a place beyond, outside, or squarely in the margins of the social. She considers what she calls the "world's performativity" as composed of phenomena, and understands phenomena as an "entanglement of spacetimematter," (32), which means that, necessarily, it is quite difficult to decide the boundaries of phenomena; Barad goes so far as to claim that most objectifications are actually heuristic strategies that don't ever quite do justice to the reality of ontological entanglement. Taking ontological entanglement seriously entails thinking about intra-activity rather than interactivity. This means that parts—subjects, institutions, economic circuits, and so on—are never discrete but always enfolded, enmeshed, inextricably intertwined.

The spatial imaginary at work here is much more complex than the marginality/centricity dyad, and I think considering processes of queer and trans subjection and subjectivation through the analytic of entanglement/intra-action is capable of producing more robust accounts of experience, more useful political stratagems, and more intricate understandings of embodiment. By way of example, I'd like to consider a brief excerpt from Paul Preciado's (2013, 143) *Testo-Junkie* on taking testosterone. It is very much written in the spirit of entanglement, becoming, and attentiveness to neoliberal complicities.

> [Of] all the mental and physical effects caused by self-intoxification based on testosterone in gel form, the feeling of transgressing limits of gender that have been socially imposed on me was without a doubt the most intense. The new metabolism of testosterone in my body wouldn't be effective in terms of masculinization without the previous existence of a political agenda that interprets these changes as an integral part of a desire—controlled by the pharmacopornographic order [Preciado's term for the technical/semiotic systems that mold and control the affective potential of bodies]—for sex change. Without this desire, without the project of being in transit from one fiction of sex to another, taking testosterone would never be anything but a molecular becoming.

Here, transmasculine transformation is not about outsiderhood or marginality but, rather, a phenomenon that assumes meaning through a complex cocktail of biomolecular transformation, dimorphic fictions of gender, the circuits of hormone extraction and production (embedded as they are within neoliberal and neocolonial processes at work in production, drug trials, distribution, and access), the gray-market acquisition of hormones by uninsured subjects—the list could go on. The point is that, to do justice to these entangled, interwoven processes at work in the materialization of a gender nonconforming body, we need an analytic that reconceptualizes "spacetimematter" in a mode not limited to the flat metaphor of center and margins.

Can Monstrosity Be Decolonial?

The monster, at least within Stryker's reappraisal, is an excellent trope through which to think this alternative ontology of phenomenological entanglement proposed by Barad. Reclaiming monstrosity begins with the rejection of Western humanist conceptions of being, hyperindividualized and formative of subjectivities compatible with the violence and expropriation endemic to neocolonial capitalism, and pursues a reconceptualization of being that is creaturely, built, interrelational, and resistant to logics of dominance that devalorize and denigrate alterity. There is a resonance I'd like to trace between the rejection of Western humanism within trans and gender nonconforming theorizations of subjectivity/being and those revisions of the humanist tradition engaged in by a handful of decolonial thinkers. Alongside this reappraisal of humanism, there is also a reconsideration of the margin/center metaphor conventionally deployed to discuss colonial and neocolonial geopolitical arrangements—another resonance between trans scholarship and decolonial thought worthy of teasing out the implications of.

Many decolonial scholars utilize the term *modern/colonial* to index the history of racial typologization, instrumentalization, violence, and epistemic and physical denigration that has shaped, and continues to shape, our world. This phraseology forcefully coarticulates colonization with Euro-centered progress—scientific, technological, social, and otherwise—rejecting the margin/center dyad that would impose distance and separateness (both literally and metaphorically) between the European metropole and the colonial territories.

Enrique Dussel, in *The Invention of the Americas*, carefully details the relationship between Europe and the colonial territories in terms of their mutual constitution of modernity, cogently arguing that modernity "originates in a dialectical relationship with non-Europe." Europe "places itself at the center of world history over against a periphery equally constitutive of modernity."

Central to his argument is the refutation of colonial discourses regarding the ostensible discovery (*des-cubierto*) of the colonial Other. Rather, he posits the arrival of Europeans in the supposed "new world" as initiating a long, thoroughgoing, and, indeed, ongoing project that takes as its mission the covering-over (*encubierto*) of this Other. This covering-over erases the alterity that Europeans were confronted with upon arrival in the Americas and subsumes the colonial Other into the logic of Eurocentric sameness. Dussel writes that "for the modern ego the inhabitants of the discovered lands never appeared as Other, but as the possessions of the Same to be conquered, colonized, modernized, civilized, as if they were the modern ego's material" (Dussel 1995, 35).

The notion of Eurocentric sameness is commensurate with the universalist ideology propagated by Europe during the period of the advent of various colonial missions. This universality was key in the movement of Europe from "being a particularity placed in brackets by the Muslim world" to a unified territory that construed itself as the apotheosis of civilization through a discourse of *discovery* of supposed *primitive* civilizations (34). This discovery, which "demanded that Europeans comprehend history more expansively, as a world/planetary happening," prompted the construction of an understanding of this new world that took as its main referent a distinctly European understanding of both temporality and subjectivity and that defined these alterior cultures solely in relation to Eurocentric modes of understanding (34). This positioning of Eurocentric epistemology as the sole referent for the cognition of disparate Indigenous epistemes constitutes the subsumption of the colonial Other into the logic of the same of which Dussel writes.

Integral to this subsumption is a brutal translation of corporeal intelligibility wherein Eurocentric understandings of gender difference and sexual deviance are imposed. While never completely decimating or eradicating alternative erotic-social figurations, the processes of coloniality are thoroughly enmeshed with an intense disciplining of those beings construed as atavistic, particular with respect to Eurocentric hegemonic organizations of gender and sexuality. Michael J. Horswell, in *Decolonizing the Sodomite: Queer Tropes of Sexuality in Colonial Andean Culture* (2005), documents a geopolitically specific instance of this phenomenon. He argues that Andean colonization entailed a brutal reworking of "the third gender's symbolic rupture of the gender binary," a rupture that "served the purpose of creating harmony and complementarity between the sexes and invoked the power and privilege of the androgynous creative force," working to continually restore social balance in the face of cosmological disruption and uncertainty (3–4). This symbolic rupture, utilized to restore and ensure *yanantin*—the Andean term for duality, perfect symmetry, complementarity—posed a decisive threat to the operations of Spanish Catholic patriarchy in colonial territories.

Responses to this threat included, on the linguistic level, the translation of Indigenous Andean terms for what Horswell refers to as "third gendering"—among them, the "cross-dressed" *waylaka*—into the language of sodomy, thus entailing criminalization and an emphasis on perversion, depravity, and the disobedience of (Western) sacral commands.[1] Given the crucial cultural significance of these practices of "third gendering," when the waylaka becomes the sodomite, the entire Andean schematic for ensuring social balance and communal well-being is thrown radically out of whack.

The Spanish colonial counteroffensive was not, however, merely linguistic. The translation to the language of sodomy, particularly when combined with the sixteenth-century theological precept of not naming the crime of sodomy, euphemizing it instead as a "crime against nature," afforded the term a certain "abstruseness . . . that makes it useful in regulating bodies, especially in moments of social fluidity" (Horswell 2005, 61). Said regulation took diffuse forms, ranging from being set aflame, alive, to being literally thrown to dogs. The disciplining of nonprocreative sexuality and nondimorphic gendering worked to shore up the imposition of colonial rule and to entrench its attendant, and vastly different, understanding of sexual difference and gendered relations.

While I only have space here for one anecdotal example specific to the Andean region, this phenomenon of behavioral translation and criminalization is not at all isolated.[2] It manifests in varying forms across the colonial terrain, mutating in enactment and execution according to the geopolitical specificity of colonial contact. What seems common cross-regionally is the hegemonic imposition of Western sex/gender intelligibility coincident with the translation of disparate and incommensurable enactments of gender and sexuality into the language of criminality, deviance, pathology, and perversion.

The colonial inscription of sodomy is illustrative of what María Lugones (2007, 187) refers to as the inseparability and enmeshment of race and Western sex/gender schematics of corporeal intelligibility. She offers these analytics as an extension of intersectional thought, one that deepens and expands the sense of co-constitution and inextricability of coloniality (of thought, language, being), taxonomic racialization, and the institutionalization of heterosexist patriarchal rule. What this long, mutable historical conjuncture allows us to think is the roots of intersectional oppression, so to speak—the development and ongoing maintenance of what Lugones terms the "modern/colonial gender system." She writes that while "sexual dimorphism has been an important characteristic of what I call 'the light side' of the colonial/modern gender system ... those in the 'dark side' were not necessarily understood dimorphically" (188). While the light and dark sides of this gender system exist in relation to one another, those inhabiting the dark side were and are oft figured as both aberrant and monstrous—sexually voracious, animalistic, atavistic, or fantastically hermaphroditic. This monstrosity ensures, in line with Cartesian thought, the barricade of those colonized from the realm of the rational—their reduction to the level of the body construed as deviant and monstrous aids the legitimization of the use of colonial bodies instrumentally, at the same time as it inscribes and concretizes the ostensible normality and legitimacy of bourgeois European sexual and gender arrangements and ideologies.

The dark side of the colonial/modern gender system can be perceived, then, within a Eurocentric worldview that posits gendered aberrance with respect to Western norms and then positions this aberrance as key to the constitution of what Nelson Maldonado-Torres has called a subontological difference. For Maldonado-Torres, this subontological difference is the conception of Otherness operative in the creation of what Frantz Fanon termed the *damné de la terre* (wretched of the earth) (2005) and is shaped by a perception of the Other as *a subalter*, which is

> not the Other qua Other, not even the alter ego—the Other like myself—but that "other" that is no-Other; it is not the irreplaceable and loved, or the replaceable and respected other, but the eliminable Other. It is the object of indifference and hate. ... The sub-alter is the concrete human being who is rendered as less than a "thing" or as an animal. At best, it is seen as the combination of a man and a beast. The sub-alter is created by a system of subordination. It therefore appears in reality not so much as another human being but as someone who is somehow less than a human being. (Maldonado-Torres 2008, 182)

It is in this way that sexual deviance and gender nonnormativity are conflated with Western constructions of the subalter, that which is located in an interstitial space between human and nonhuman animals. Put differently, the figuration of the colonized as less than human, a combination of human and animal, hinges—at least in part—on perceived gender and sexual impropriety. From discourses on racialized promiscuity to others concerning a sort of fantastical hermaphroditism, what constitutes the nonhumanity of the colonized is this positioning beyond, in excess of, or stubbornly resistant to the laws that institute Eurocentric sexed/sexual normalcy.

This positioning did not work—at least, not only or exclusively—in the manner of assimilatory regulation, wherein those colonized were forced to ascribe to bourgeois Eurocentric social-sexual mores, conceptions of corporeality and of eroticism. Rather, the Eurocentric system of mores and norms was installed to function as a barometer of the differential pathology of the colonized, to instantiate the scale of the sub- to fully human in order to produce the less than human, that set of beings then sanctioned to be utilized instrumentally and treated expendably. Thus, the imposition of said Eurocentric norms was not to circumscriptively mold, through assimilation, "proper" men and women but to posit this propriety as unrealizable, impossible, in order to construe those lives at stake as subontological, being-less-than.

Moreover, the discourse of the combinatory—that is, the subalter as both human and animal, as neither fully "man" nor "woman" in the hegemonic, Euro-centered sense of those terms—echoes what Michel Foucault (2004, 162–63) writes, in *Abnormal*, of the constitution of the monstrous.

> What is the monster in both a juridical and scientific tradition? From the Middle Ages to the eighteenth century . . . the monster is essentially a mixture. It is the mixture of two realms, the animal and the human. . . . It is the blending, the mixture of two species. . . . It is the mixture of two individuals. . . . It is the mixture of two sexes. . . . It is the mixture of life and death. . . . Finally, it is a mixture of forms. . . . Consequently, the monster is a transgression of natural limits, the transgression of classifications, of the table, of the law as a table. . . . Monstrosity requires a transgression of the natural limit, of the law-table, to fall under, or at any rate challenge, an interdiction of civil and religious or divine law.

The monster is located beyond the law both as a spectral transgressor, a figure that haunts the bounds of intelligibility, and as that which, when brought within the purview of sacral and secular law alike, is thought as composed of an elemental mixity that, in and of itself, sanctions extinction. It is mixity, the combinatory, which is the fearmongering motor of protofascistic, biopolitical dreams of subjective and social coherence and purity. Mixity, as the disruption of the taxon, solicits death sentences of varying sorts—as punishment for illegitimate being or as punishment for transgression of assigned classificatory being.

These death sentences may range from more or less forced assimilation back into the confines of taxonomic intelligibility (as is the case with emphasis on dimorphically gendered passing, with surgical correction of abnormal bodies, with the phenomenon of missionary schools) or outright, literal annihilation (death from overwork, at the hands of a lynch mob, at the hands of the prison industrial complex). The taxon, the "table, the law as table," sets the bounds of acceptable modes of subjectification, while, cyclically and mutably, a lineage of monstrous construal serves the biopolitical functioning of the taxon, providing the material for decisive adjudication on that which must die in order that others live, what must be purged from the social, excised, rendered unacceptable or redundant in order to subjugate socialities to the demands of capital, to maximize social cohesion in the name of efficiency, to seal territorialities and beings as epistemic objects, as univocal and exhausted by Euro-centered monologic.

Persephone Braham, in her essay "The Monstrous Caribbean," tracks early modern/colonial narratives of cannibals, sirens, Amazons, and zombies in the territories of the Caribbean and Latin America. She corroborates the commentary on racialized subalterity and monstrosity offered by Lugones, Maldonado-Torres, Horswell, and Foucault, claiming that "the narratives that emerged at the junction of cultures under the conditions of early modern globalization established monsters as a preeminent mode of discourse between Latin America and the colonial powers that interacted with it, and ultimately inflected the tropes used by Latin Americans themselves in efforts to explain, diagnose, or correct their eccentricity" (Braham 2013, 47). Brahams alludes, here, to the redeployment of monstrosity as a form of empowerment or resistance, a way of interpreting eccentricity in relation to Eurocentric norms and values as something other than necessary evidence of atavism. The siren, for instance, while utilized tropically within colonial travel narratives to embody the "lure of exploration and conquest" (35), can also be redeployed as a femme fatale–type figure capable of undermining colonial social and political dominance. The cannibal, similarly, can either be construed as evidence of a brutal primitivism that violates Eurocentric ethics of killing and consumption—as well as the binaries of self/other and human/animal—or be redeployed, as in the case of the Brazilian *antropofagia* movement of the 1920s, as a metaphor to mark the culturally hybridized "strategy of incorporation by means of which the strength of the cultural other is used for the creation of a separate cultural identity" (35). The logic of this strategic redeployment runs as such: you say we eat human others? We'll ingest only those aspects of Eurocentricity that serve to create a separate and resistant cultural identity. We'll eat what we want of the colonialists.

It is this resistant redeployment of the logic of monstrosity as a means of refuting Eurocentric conceptions of subjectivity that resonates deeply with Stryker's call to reclaim monstrosity. Rather than functioning solely as a figure of aberrance and outsider status in relation to Western ideals and values, the monster takes a critical distance from them and exposes the violent logics that work to construct certain beings as eliminable, disavowed, fear-inducing others. Reclaiming monstrosity can be a means of rejecting assimilation and embracing those aspects of self and community that the dominant culture has framed illegal, perverse, deviant, threatening, or undesirable. This embrace of that which had been the constitutive criteria for monstrosity opens transformative possibilities. It is a step toward reassessing ways of being that have been devalorized, thinking again about their potential use in inhabiting the present differently, building and strengthening alliances, structures of support, and patterns of belonging. In other words, reclaiming monstrosity is a way of putting subalter status to work in building new ways of being-with.

Monstrosity as Coalitional Concept

I've been trying to gesture at the notion that the reclamation of monstrosity can work as a means of establishing connections between contemporary trans/queer and decolonial movements. While I don't want to suggest that monstrosity works as a necessarily common ground, I think it can denote a certain shared structure of feeling born out of the experience of being marked, construed, or metaphorized as monstrous.

In suggesting that there may be a resonant structure of feeling common to experiences—historical and contemporary—of monstrous construal, and that the predominant feelings that frame this structure are those of coping with derision and violence, rage, loneliness, lack of recognition, misunderstanding, and misinterpretation, I am not far away from suggesting that what is shared, or what connects trans/queer and decolonial struggle, is traumatic experience. Positing trauma as an integral part of the weave that makes up radical coalition is, necessarily, a move to deindividuate and depathologize trauma. I follow Ann Cvetkovich (2003) in this; she has written extensively on trauma's role in the creation of queer public cultures, and articulates trauma as "a social and cultural discourse that emerges in response to the demands of grappling with the psychic consequences of historical events" (18). Exploring trauma as a shared structure of feeling is one way of thinking about how we deal—and how we could deal differently—with the quotidian negativity that emerges from experiences of subalterity, being treated as less than or other-than human. In understanding trauma as a complex response, simultaneously personal and public, to historico-political conditions of violence, abuse, censure, and delegitimization, we can think more adequately about how trauma can work as a prod to create empathic affective bonds that heal and enable resilience, transformation, and flourishing.

Identifying resonant sources of pain, anger, and rage—monstrous construal among them—pushes political movements past a concern with formalized, institutional barriers to rights and attends to the affective dimensions of oppression. Cvetkovich's understanding of trauma blurs the distinction between the public and the personal, precipitating a focus on negative affect as public, shared, and deindividuated. Reclaiming monstrosity is a means of both distancing oneself from normalizing demands and embracing devalorized aspects of subjectivity and community as integral to inventing new styles of being and new ways of inhabiting the social. It is thus a means of coping with, and perhaps healing from trauma communally, in coalition and resistance.

To consider monstrosity in relation to coalition building is to think of it in universalizing, rather than minoritizing terms. It is to think of monstrosity as something that links folks across lines of difference. We should not think of monstrosity as a way of naming a ghettoized, delimited and determinate subset of beings but rather consider the ways in which we all negotiate monstrosity in the practice of building self and community, the ways in which we variously participate in the taxons that produce monsters. Monstrosity is a powerful trope because it is integral to the formation of proper citizen-subjects as well as those deemed subalter. It is also a mobile and mutable concept—as Asa Simon Mittman (2013, 7) puts it, what makes a monster a monster is not its embodiment, location, or "the processes through which it enacts its being" but its *impact*. What is this impact? Mittman writes that "above all, the monstrous is that which creates this sense of vertigo, that which calls into question our (their, anyone's) epistemological worldview, highlights its fragmentary nature, and thereby asks us ... to acknowledge the failure of our systems of categorization" (8). What unites monsters, then, is this ability to force epistemological crises, to trouble "common" sense and "natural" orders, to prompt recognition of personal implication in oppressive systems of categorization. Monstrosity as coalition is not about identifying the discrete functions of specific manifestations of subalterity but about moving from those discrete manifestations toward a universalizing perspective that recognizes the ability of monstrous reclamation to disrupt and denaturalize heterosexist, cissexist, Eurocentric hierarchy and prompts those with naturalized privilege to confront that status as a made, constructed—and therefore fragile, contestable, and paranoically defended—phenomenon. As Stryker (1994, 242) writes, "You are as constructed as me; the same anarchic womb has birthed us both. I call upon you to investigate your nature as I have been compelled to confront mine. I challenge you to risk abjection and flourish as well as have I. Heed my words, and you may well discover the seams and sutures in yourself." Reclaiming monstrosity is a means of embracing agency in the process of fashioning new modes of being and affirming one's creaturely—made and nonsovereign—status, a way of refusing abjection in relation to hegemonic values, and a movement toward affirming and supporting alterity, linking struggles to construct an ethics of being-in-resistance. Siding with monsters, embracing the monsters we are, is a powerful means of inventing ways of inhabiting this world differently, within and against racist cishetero-supremacy that understands different logics of being, relation, intimacy, and community as signs of tamable, correctable excess.

Notes

Adapted from *Queer Embodiment: Monstrosity, Medical Violence, and Intersex Experience* by Hil Malatino by permission of the University of Nebraska Press. Copyright 2019 by the Board of Regents of the University of Nebraska.

1. Here, "third gender" should not be taken reductively to mean the addition of simply one more gender option but signifies a break with binary dimorphism and thus opens a space to be elsewhere and otherwise than "male" or "female." I use "cross-dressed" in quotes, because to speak of "cross-dressing" is to presuppose a binaristic, dimorphic schematic of sex/gender that was not operative in Indigenous Andean life until the advent of colonization; moreover, it is a term that makes reference to the modern Western sexological conception of transvestism. To conflate contemporary conceptions of transvestism with the Andean practices Horswell describes would be inaccurate and anachronistic.

2. See, for instance, Oyěwùmí (1997), Bosworth and Flavin (2007), Stoler (2002), and McClintock (1995).

References

Ahmed, Sara. 2010. *The Promise of Happiness*. Durham, NC: Duke University Press.
Barad, Karen. 2007. *Meeting the Universe Halfway: Quantum Physics and the Entanglement of Matter and Meaning*. Durham, NC: Duke University Press.
———. 2012. "Nature's Queer Performativity (the Authorized Version)." *Kvinder, Køn & Forskning*, no. 1–2: 25–53.
Bosworth, Mary Ann, and Jeanne Flavin, eds. 2007. *Race, Gender, and Punishment: From Colonialism to the War on Terror*. New Brunswick, NJ: Rutgers University Press.
Braham, Persephone. 2013. "The Monstrous Caribbean." In *The Ashgate Research Companion to Monsters and the Monstrous*, edited by Asa Simon Mittman and Peter Dendle, 17–48. Surrey, UK: Ashgate.
Butler, Judith. 1993. *Bodies That Matter: On the Discursive Limits of "Sex."* New York: Routledge.
Casarino, Cesare, and Antonio Negri. 2008. *In Praise of the Common: A Conversation on Philosophy and Politics*. Minneapolis: University of Minnesota Press.
Currah, Paisley, and Susan Stryker. 2014. "Introduction." *Transgender Studies Quarterly* 1 (1–2): 1–18.
Cvetkovich, Ann. 2003. *An Archive of Feelings: Trauma, Sexuality, and Lesbian Public Cultures*. Durham, NC: Duke University Press.
Dussel, Enrique. 1995. *The Invention of the Americas: Eclipse of "the Other" and the Myth of Modernity*. London: Continuum.
Edelman, Lee. 2004. *No Future: Queer Theory and the Death Drive*. Durham, NC: Duke University Press.
Fanon, Frantz. 2005. *The Wretched of the Earth*. New York: Grove.
Foucault, Michel. 2004. *Abnormal: Lectures at the College de France, 1974–1975*. Translated by Graham Burchell. New York: Picador.
Horswell, Michael J. 2005. *Decolonizing the Sodomite: Queer Tropes of Sexuality in Colonial Andean Culture*. Austin: University of Texas Press.
Lugones, María. 2007. "Heterosexualism and the Colonial/Modern Gender System." *Hypatia* 22 (1): 188–209.
Malatino, Hil. 2013. "Queer Monsters: Foucault, 'Hermaphroditism,' and Disability Studies." In *The Imperfect Historian: Disability Histories in Europe*, edited by Sebastian Barsch, Anne Klein, and Pieter Verstraete, 113–32. Frankfurt: Peter Lang.

Maldonado-Torres, Nelson. 2008. *Against War: Views from the Underside of Modernity*. Durham, NC: Duke University Press.
McClintock, Anne. 1995. *Imperial Leather: Race, Gender, and Sexuality in the Colonial Contest*. New York: Routledge.
Mittman, Asa Simon. 2013. "Introduction: The Impact of Monsters and Monster Studies." In *The Ashgate Research Companion to Monsters and the Monstrous*, edited by Asa Simon Mittman and Peter Dendle, 1–14. Surrey, UK: Ashgate.
Muñoz, José Esteban. 1999. *Disidentifications: Queers of Color and the Performance of Politics*. Minneapolis: University of Minnesota Press.
Oyěwùmí, Oyèrónké. 1997. *The Invention of Women: Making an African Sense of Western Gender Discourses*. Minneapolis: University of Minnesota Press.
Preciado, Paul. 2013. *Testo-Junkie: Sex, Drugs, and Biopolitics in the Pharmacopornagraphic Era*. Translated by Bruce Benderson. New York: Feminist Press.
Rubin, Gayle. 1992. "Thinking Sex: Notes for a Radical Theory of the Politics of Sexuality." In *Pleasure and Danger: Exploring Female Sexuality*, edited by Carole S. Vance, 267–93. London: Pandora.
Stoler, Ann Laura. 2002. *Carnal Knowledge and Imperial Powers: Race and the Intimate in Colonial Rule*. Berkeley: University of California Press.
Stryker, Susan. 1994. "My Words to Victor Frankenstein above the Village of Chamounix: Performing Transgender Rage." *GLQ: A Journal of Lesbian and Gay Studies* 1 (3): 237–54.

Hil Malatino is Associate Professor of Women's, Gender, and Sexuality Studies and Philosophy at Pennsylvania State University, where he also holds the Joyce L. and Douglas S. Sherwin Early Career Professorship and is Acting Director and Senior Research Associate at the Rock Ethics Institute. His research and teaching draw on trans and intersex studies, critical sexuality studies, transnational feminisms, disability studies, and medical ethics to theorize how experiences of violence, trauma, and resilience play out in intersex, trans, and gender nonconforming lives. He has published three books: *Side Affects: On Being Trans and Feeling Bad* (2022), *Trans Care* (2020), and *Queer Embodiment: Monstrosity, Medical Violence, and Intersex Experience* (2019).

PART II

BETWEEN WOMEN OF COLOR POLITICS AND DECOLONIALITY

4

BRIDGING EMPIRES, TRANSGRESSING DISCIPLINES

METHODOLOGICAL INTERVENTIONS IN ASIAN AMERICA

Jen-Feng Kuo and Shireen Roshanravan

IN THEIR REVISIT of Aníbal Quijano's concept "coloniality of power," Walter Mignolo and Madina Tlostanova (2006) identify a particular trajectory of subordination to Eurocentrism among declining powers, or what they call "secondary empires," such as Russia, the Ottoman Empire, and China. Attending to the specific differential power relations between those secondary empires and Euro-American ones, Mignolo and Tlostanova propose the "imperial difference," an analytic frame that addresses power relations between the two clusters of empire. The imperial difference also makes visible the trajectories of power among geopolitical sites where Eurocentric domination does not manifest through military conquest and direct colonization.

Mignolo and Tlostanova introduce the concept of the imperial difference to underscore two concurrent historical processes: the particular uneven power relations between secondary empires and Euro-American empires, and the resistance strategies secondary empires employ in response to Eurocentric hegemony. As Tlostanova (2008) argues, secondary empires are "Janus-faced," looking simultaneously at Euro-American hegemony and the margins within their own imperial limits. It is within this Janus-faced site of power negotiation, Mignolo and Tlostanova observe, that secondary empires like China develop "adaptation without assimilation" as a resistant strategy to the domination of Euro-American empires from without. The same site also shapes ways of knowing and thinking within those declining imperial powers that seek to sustain their imperial dominance from within. This negotiation of power is ambiguous because resistant strategies like adaptation without assimilation are founded precisely on the racialized logic of Eurocentrism; moreover, this negotiation is ambivalent because of its purpose to enable secondary empires to assert or maintain dominance within their own imperial parameters. For Mignolo and Tlostanova (2006, 210), the ambiguous and ambivalent nature of strategies like adaptation without assimilation becomes a crucial pattern of the modernizing and nationalist project of secondary empires.

The frame of imperial difference is proposed at the analytic and political cross section of race and empire to address the ambiguous and ambivalent position in which secondary empires negotiate racial subordination relative to Euro-American empires. This frame, however, does not address questions of transnational experience and racialization in the domain of immigrants, especially those in the Euro-American contexts; nor does it appear to intersect analysis on race, empire, and gender/sexuality. In this chapter, we attempt a reading of Asian American women's racializing and gendering experiences by interposing the imperial difference in the vein of Asian American studies. Our goal is to propose an alternative analytic frame in which a nuanced transnational feminist and US women of color feminist engagement with Asian American women's studies can arise. With a critical approach, we examine the persistent assumption of Asian Americans as "in-between" racial subjects in scholarship and critical race, women of color, or transnational feminist discourses, an assumption that contributes to their (unwitting) dismissal as relevant subjects of knowledge in said discourses (Bow 2010; Fujiwara and Roshanravan 2018). Because women of color and transnational feminisms often grant epistemic authority to the "most marginalized communities of women" while attending to culture as a significant site of resistant meaning making, we contend that the imperial difference is an analytic that can facilitate a constructive conversation between Asian American women's studies and cross-racial and transnational feminist scholarship (Mohanty 2003, 232).

Positioned by the US racial state as in-between racial subjects, Asian Americans may need to adapt racist logic in their resistant negotiations of racial subordination (Prashad 2000; Purkayastha 2005; Bow 2010). While this adaptation of dominant racial logics may be read as totalized complicity with white supremacy, the imperial difference, as a historical, political, and analytic lens, enables us to read this negotiation of power as ambiguously resistant. As with African American or US Latino/a studies, Asian American studies has tended to understand race relations between Asian Americans and dominant white/Anglos as resembling colonial relations between the Third World colonized and the First World colonizer (Blauner 1972, 52–54; Chan 2005, 54). While this approach explains how Asian Americans are racialized as nonwhites, it does not fully explore why particular racializing mechanisms, like the model-minority myth, have endured even in a post-9/11 racial climate. Accordingly, this chapter focuses on reading ambiguous resistant negotiations of power, using the imperial difference as a departure point, to expand communicative and epistemic possibilities for engaging Asian American resistance.

Women of color feminisms inform our emphasis on the political and analytic significance of theorizing resistance and identifying culture as a site of resistant meaning making. As Grace Hong (2006) argues, racialized immigrant women and women of color resist through their cultural locations to provide alternative readings of racist capitalist dispossession and generate alternative community and subject formations. We bridge women of color politics with the work of coloniality/decoloniality theorists, like Aníbal Quijano, who theorizes the significance of culture as the sphere in which racialization takes place. According to Quijano (2000, 541), the process of Eurocentrism involves "the colonization of cognitive perspectives, modes of producing and giving meaning, the results of material existence, the imaginary, the universe of intersubjective relations with the world: in short, the culture." Conceptualizing culture as ways of knowing, living, and thinking, Quijano, echoing women of color feminist scholars, also underlines intersubjective relations as a vital pattern that shapes and (re)produces culture. We ground our examination in Quijano's as well as Hong's theoretical understanding of culture as encompassing processes of subject formation and thus highlight language, spirituality, and national solidarity in our investigation of Asian American women's gendered and racialized subject formation. Echoing women of color feminist emphasis on multiple logics of resistance against the homogenizing monologic of mainstream (white) feminist cultural work, we revisit Asian American women's racializing and gendered discourses and see them as refusals of assimilation to those of US white/Anglo women.

The Imperial Difference in the US Context and Racial Triangulation

As Tlostanova (2008) demonstrates, the imperial difference foregrounds how secondary empires adopt a Janus-faced logic, which imbues their resistance strategies against Euro-American imperial powers with ambiguity and ambivalence. The Janus-faced logic of secondary empires can be traced in their incorporation of Eurocentric racial logic in part as a resistant response to the increasing domination of Euro-American empires, and one strategy is to highlight their spiritual and cultural traditions against the material civilization and prowess of Euro-American empires. The effect of Orientalization, invented by Euro-American agents, ironically finds its share in the ways that secondary empires narrate themselves as ahistorical, genuine, and, spiritually if not materially, superior.

While Mignolo and Tlostanova examine the relation of imperial difference within the geopolitical context of secondary empires, they identify it as primarily an analytic as well as a political danger preventing subjects of secondary empires from developing decolonial discourses. Equally notable in their work, as the imperial difference is proposed in the larger frame of the geopolitics of knowledge, is that no attention is paid to the subjects of secondary empires in transnational passages. It is then unclear how the idea of imperial difference can merit scholarship in rethinking identity politics regarding subjects of secondary empires other than exposing their "doomed imperial myth of grandeur and dominance" (Mignolo and Tlostanova 2006, 212). Furthermore, it is also unclear to what extent the relation of imperial difference manifests in identity politics, by virtue of our research regarding Asian immigrants in US sociopolitical contexts. In this section, we explore the significance of the idea of imperial difference, including its important implications, and we consider how and in what form it may apply to the conditions of Asian Americans. We also discuss the model of racial triangulation, proposed by Claire Jean Kim (1999) on her critical approach to Asian American history, and attempt a conversation between the concept of imperial difference and the model of racial triangulation.

In thinking through the historical pattern of racial formation in the United States to "go beyond" the simplistic Black-and-white opposition, Claire Jean Kim argues for a model that she coins as "racial triangulation" in which Asian Americans are particularly and peculiarly positioned vis-à-vis whites and Blacks. In the model of racial triangulation are the twofold historical processes "relative valorization" and "civic ostracism," both of which construct Asian Americans in relation to whites and Blacks on cultural or racial grounds to serve the purpose of white domination (Kim 1999, 107). According to Kim, relative valorization and civic ostracism are two linked processes that together situate Asian Americans between whites and Blacks in racial hierarchy but at the same time outside whites and Blacks in terms of cultural citizenship. The process that racially triangulates Asian Americans in this manner has persisted in constructing them as racially intermediate between whites and Blacks but also alienated in terms of cultural citizenship. Attending most to legal and sociopolitical discourses, Kim contends that the two patterns materialize in forms like promoting Asian Americans as favorable laborers while excluding them as racially and culturally ineligible for American citizenship. The process of racial triangulation of Asian Americans has taken root and proved to be effective in American society, crystalizing in the exclusion movement but outliving the period, with the model-minority myth as the contemporary evidence of this process.

However, as Kim calls to our attention, Asian Americans do not passively receive the mainstream social patterns that valorize and ostracize them; quite on the contrary, they actively participate in the process of racial triangulation to advance their own interests. James Loewen (1988) studies Chinese Americans in Mississippi and demonstrates how they, during the early twentieth century, moved from a near-Black status to a near-white status, by giving children white names, attending white churches, and making donations to white social organizations.[1] In a similar vein, Erika Lee's (2003, 94) work on Chinese immigration during the Exclusion Act years finds Chinese women subscribing to Victorian gender norms, by dress and demeanor, in order to appear respectable and decent in the eyes of customs officials. It remains to be explored whether Chinese women at the customs site were deliberate in conforming to Victorian gender norms as a strategy of social survival; nevertheless, it is notable that this strategy allowed Chinese women to locate themselves as racially more favorable in the white-dominated society where they sought to reside to counteract the ostracizing process against them.

A closer look at Chinese American women's responses to their peculiar racial positioning in history reveals more significance as well as complexity in such sociopolitical ambiguity at the intersection of Chinese nationalist projects and US mainstream gender discourses. Judy Yung (1995) illustrates that the identity formation of Chinese American women since the late nineteenth century were predicated on the support of Protestant mission homes and Chinese American press. Protestant mission homes, for their part, were concerned with Chinese American women's emancipation as well as the exclusionist politics against the Chinese American communities in general. The agenda of the mission homes, however, was to criticize traditions of Chinese women's culture and virtues, and underline Victorian womanhood in domesticity and piety as Chinese American women's idealized qualities (Pascoe 1990). Such an agenda and its practice also suggest a reading in which the rescue operations, in the case of the missionary homes in San Francisco's Chinatown, characterize the intersubjective as well as power relations between white missionary women and Chinese women as guardians/mothers and minors/daughters (Kuo 2010). This pattern of unequal intersubjective relations in the context of the mission homes materialized in the Chinese women being constantly under strict surveillance, including any contact with people outside the mission homes, on premises that Chinatown as well as US mainstream society were primary sources of moral corruption and that Victorian womanhood was taught best without such distractions. Moreover, the racialized division of power and labor persisted beyond the mission homes and prescribed the ethical guidelines by which Chinese American women obeyed and granted the missionary women the authority to review Chinese American women's life after marriage (Pascoe 1989). Such dehumanization of Chinese American women and the denial of Chinese traditions marked related processes of Chinese American women's subject formation, most crucially in the making of the idealized qualities for them, well into the early twentieth century.

What idealized qualities Chinese American women could come to inhabit were largely subject to the agenda of the white women at the mission homes. Still, in contexts of exclusion politics and China as the failing nation, those questions were also closely associated with the status of Chinese American communities in the mainstream society and that of China in relation to the West. Echoing Erika Lee's reading of Chinese American women's strategic adoption of Victorian gender norms, we propose Chinese American women's endorsement of white missionary women's agenda as not merely a blind subscription to Victorian womanhood; nor was it the case that the Chinese root was to be rejected once and for all. Rather, within the early twentieth-century US mainstream racial order, and in relation to the white missionary women, Chinese American women's responses to their racialized and gendered position reflect subjects who read their subjected position in national rather than racial terms.

Consider a speech published in 1903 in *Chung Sai Yat Po* (*CSYP*), the leading Chinese American newspaper in the early twentieth century. In this address to Chinese women in the United States, Mai Zhouyi, an immigrant Chinese woman and wife of a Chinese American merchant, spoke of the relationship between women and the Chinese nationalist movement.

> Sisters, don't say that educating women serves no purpose for home and country. Look for the cause of prosperity in all the Western countries and you will find it in their pool of talented people.... In order to properly educate our young, we must look to our mothers, for they are the ones whom the children cluster around the whole day.... The key to a country's prosperity lies in its women's propensity for learning.... Don't let the weakness of China and the strength of another country turn away your patriotism and discourage you from learning.... If another country is strong, we should search out the reason for its strength. There are four hundred million of us men and women in China. If we all do our best for our country, though weak at present, China will someday become strong.[2]

This vein of thought predominated in Chinese American discourses on women's empowerment in relation to the nationalist project of modernizing China. In the historical context of Chinese exclusion, this speech alludes to a reasoning that attributed the subordination of Chinese Americans to the question of nation, not race. Furthermore, the manner in which "the weakness of China" is associated with "the strength of another country," or the power of

Euro-American nations, is notable in its lack of reference to colonial/imperial oppression. China's competence, evident in its immense population, was undeniable, and it would serve as a useful basis for national revival.

An editorial also published in *CSYP*, in 1911, elaborates more clearly the rationale in Mai's speech nearly a decade earlier. Advocating the urgency of instituting women's education in the Chinese nationalist movement, this editorial associates the strengths of Europe and the United States with women's formal education: "As we have seen these days in the civilized nations of Europe and America, schools for men and women are launched one after another. The trends of equality and liberty are spread to every last inch of their lands.... Women in Europe and America are the best women of the world, and how can they have such spirits, knowledge, and demeanors? There is no other reason than promoting education for women."[3] Criticizing how Chinese society has long ignored the cultivation of knowledge and talents in women, leading China to fall under the sway of Euro-American powers, this editorial proposes that all restrictions against Chinese women be lifted. Invested with knowledge and proper training, the editorial concludes that Chinese women would one day "enjoy equality and liberty, and catch up with the women in Europe and America."[4]

Notable in both of the previous quotations is a Chinese American self-perception, vis-à-vis dominant whites, that accounts for an in-between status that is not in racial terms. To our theoretical concerns in this chapter, the editorial rather reflects a posture of competition, in which China's subordination to Euro-American powers as well as Chinese Americans' subjection could be overcome and even reversed, echoing subtly what Mignolo and Tlostanova argue as China's adaptation without assimilation strategy and the "imperial myth of grandeur." In this ambiguous yet famed vision of national glory and pride, China's resistance to Euro-American dominance would be through imitation, not rejection, of Euro-American women's education and gender assignment. It is also precisely in this mentality that Chinese American women's resistance discourse in the early twentieth century, as seen in these quotations, did not concern a critical engagement with the imposed/colonial gender assignment by the white missionary women.

Using Claire Jean Kim's racial triangulation model to read these examples of Chinese American women in the early twentieth century sheds light on how intersecting contexts of Chinese nationalism, migration, Chinese exclusion, and racialized US society constructed the subjective position of Chinese American women. Unlike Kim, who highlights the racially and culturally restraining effects of the triangulation, we attend to Chinese American women's active participation in the same construction that positioned them as racially intermediate yet culturally ostracized. Furthermore, we suggest that Chinese American women's active engagement in this construction not be read as apolitical or ignorant of racialized and racist violence; instead, we contend that such ambiguous acts of negotiating US racial and gender formation precisely reflect and expose a larger global historical and ideological process that foregrounds this construction.

The ambiguity in Chinese American women's negotiations with dominant racial and imperialist social orders opens a question in relation to Kim's racial triangulation model, specifically in her formulation of relative valorization and civic ostracism. As Kim argues, these two processes shape unequal powers among dominant whites and subordinate Blacks as well as Asian Americans "on cultural and/or racial grounds," but she does not explore the historical formation of these cultural and/or racial grounds nor what they indicate for those who must navigate such terrain.[5] We thus question how such cultural and/or racial grounds take shape to initiate the racialized valorizing as well as the sociocultural ostracizing processes for Asian American women. Understanding the formation of such cultural and/or racial grounds as both a historical and an ideological process, we contextualize Asian American's racially triangulating experiences in the encounters of China and the United States, within which Mignolo and Tlostanova's idea of the imperial difference comes to serve as the crucial theoretical framework.

John Kuo Wei Tchen's (2001) study on the shift of Asian images in US social context informs our question with Kim's model. In his study, Tchen examines sociocultural discourses as well as practices regarding Chinese subjects in New York City and argues that US impressions of China and Chinese culture/people moved from fascination and veneration during the late eighteenth century to suspicion or even contempt in the Chinese exclusion years. According to Tchen, this shift indicates the change of the images of Chinese subjects in the US context; more significantly, it also reflects the dynamic of power relations between the US and China, as the United States was surfacing onto the horizon of world powers, while China experienced a dramatic decline in international politics. By the mid-nineteenth century, the perception that China was associated with "the height of refinement and civilization" initiated during the Enlightenment came to be increasingly displaced by the idea that Chinese people were now somewhat lesser to Europeans and, in terms of race, US whites (151).

Tchen's study not only echoes claims that charge Western perceptions of Asian subjects as Orientalist historical and ideological constructions but also, and especially relevant to our work, presents the material foundation that gave rise to such perceptions. As Tchen argues, the shift in early US perceptions of the Chinese people and civilization as superior and highly cultivated to later perceptions of them as "lesser" reflects the concurrent historical process in which the US emerged as a dominant imperial power while the Chinese empire declined in dominance. This historical and ideological shift, then, helps inspire the images of Chinese subjects as barbarous, primitive yet containing complex and ambiguous characterizations of superiority, delicacy, subordination, and incompetence within the US context. The racialized gender construction of Chinese Americans as simultaneously exotic, refined, and somewhat intelligent and yet also inferior and suspicious must, therefore, be understood as an effect of sociopolitical as well as sociocultural relations between the US and China, two differential imperial powers that increasingly engaged in intense contact during the nineteenth century. Tchen's work thus reveals the historical and ideological construction of the "cultural and/or racial grounds" from and through which Kim's "racial triangulation" comes into being and operates. In other words, the racialization of Chinese Americans and the ensuing politics of identification in which they actively participated is largely and directly related to the status of China as a declining empire, but an empire nonetheless, vis-à-vis the United States.

Given the impact of the relationality between the United States and China as differential imperial powers on Chinese American women's negotiations of power, the usefulness of Walter Mignolo and Madina Tlostanova's analytic of the imperial difference in reframing the question of Chinese American women's racialized gender subject formation becomes clearer. Suturing, as we deepen, Kim's racial triangulation model, the imperial difference as analytic, and Tchen's historical study not only allows us to approach the specific racialization and negotiations among Chinese Americans but also challenges us to rethink certain paradigms for understanding race and gender within Asian American studies. Specifically, the imperial difference calls us to center questions of Eurocentrism and modernity/coloniality in ways that Asian American studies has not yet done in its central engagement with Asian American racialized gender formation. Mignolo and Tlostanova theorize the imperial difference on the premise that the modern/colonial world is a system that operates and is forged through Eurocentrism. Accordingly, they consider the subordination and resistance of non-Euro-American nations to the domination of Eurocentric powers while always attending to the ways Eurocentrism may condition non-European resistance strategies. The imperial difference does not frame power relations defined by Eurocentrism in terms of colonial conquest. Instead, the imperial difference attends to the constructed subjects of secondary empires in relation to Euro-American empires as racialized subjects with different ideas and imaginations than peoples of African or Latin American origins, to name just a few. It simultaneously constructs Euro-American (white) subjects that imagine Asians and Asian Americans as racially intermediate and somewhat otherworldly and Asians and Asian Americans as subjects with desires for and beliefs in competition against dominant Euro-American whites, where an idea of racial or cultural superiority is constantly present.[6]

Using the imperial difference as an analytic through which to rethink Asian American studies facilitates a reconsideration of the particular racializing experiences and racialized imaginations regarding Asian Americans. In earlier passages, we have employed the speech of a Chinese American woman in the early twentieth century to understand the subject formation of Asian Americans through the theoretical frame of the imperial difference; we explore more of the ambiguous intersubjective relations regarding Asian American women in the discussion of Indian American women and the question of the model-minority myth.

Orientalization and Model-Minority Racial
Formation of Asian Americans

India, unlike China, is not and has never been a secondary empire.[7] Yet as Vijay Prashad (2000, 16) notes, India joins China in the European and US Orientalist imagination as an ancient civilization of a certain cultural-spiritual essence that is at once to be recognized as superior relative to Africa and Abya Yala yet stunted in its development and thus borderline barbarous for its lack of transparency to the Eurocentric mind.[8] This relative valorization and subalternization of India vis-à-vis Europe and Europe's other colonial conquests in Africa and the Americas was a central strategy developed within British India to secure colonial rule. Prashad attributes the ambiguous racialization of Indians in the United States to both European and US "Orientalization" of India. To exemplify, he cites, among many others, eighteenth-century French Enlightenment thinker Voltaire's claim that "the ancient religion of India, and that of literary men of China are the only ones wherein men have not been barbarous" (qtd. in Prashad 2000, 16). Voltaire's exemption of China and India from barbarian status relies on a seeming admiration for the ancient spiritual realm of (elite) Indian and Chinese populations. Christine Keating (2011, 19) illuminates how such admiration for the ancient worth of Asian civilization grounds what she calls the *"colonial fraternalist approach"* to British rule in India. Keating explains that "[un]like the paternalist rejection of indigenous ways of being, the fraternalist approach emphasizes respect and admiration for indigenous philosophy and law to the extent that they are congruent with relations of colonial rule" (20). Scholar-administrators, known as "Orientalists," led the charge on this fraternalist approach to colonial rule, constructing narratives of a civilizational and racial brotherhood between upper-caste Hindus and the British that "depended in part on depicting Muslims as racial others" (21). According to Keating, the fraternalist approach relied on an Orientalist framing of upper-caste Hindus as descendants of the Aryan race. Evidence offered in support of such reasoning included claims that shared linguistic roots between Sanskrit and European languages indicate a potential common ancestry between elite Indians and Europeans. The British conjoined this Indo-European kinship ideology with offers to protect economic interests of the elite upper-caste Indians in exchange for their collaboration with British colonial rule. Collaboration between the British colonizer and the elite colonized depended on and generated the construction of the Muslim and South "non-Aryan" Indians as racially inferior relative to the upper-caste "Aryan" Indian. The attribution of some civilizational and racial qualities to the upper-caste elite "Aryan" Indian rendered them almost, but not quite, European.

Keating (2011, 7) theorizes what she calls *"compensatory domination"* to identify the logics of this complex maneuvering in which the colonizers seek collaboration with the elite colonized. Compensatory domination, she explains, operates through the construction and naturalization of hierarchies among those over whom one wishes to rule. Key to this strategy is the ruler's ability to solicit collaboration with the elite or dominant members of the subjugated population on the grounds that these elite members will, in turn, be able to assume a naturalized superiority/power over the rest of the subjugated. Keating argues that, in the case of the British in India, the solicitation of collaboration relied on British Orientalist anthropological and legal constructions of elite upper-caste male Indian superiority vis-à-vis their own women and Other (read: Muslim and lower-caste) Indians (24). British Orientalists, as admirers of India's ancient civilization, collaborated with upper-caste Hindu pundits to consolidate indigenous racial and patriarchal hierarchies through the codification of Indian language, law, and social relations (26–27).

Despite British Orientalist admiration of India's "ancient civilization," British policies presumed India's relative cultural inferiority to Europe. This is particularly evident in British parliamentarian Thomas Babington Macaulay's 1835 "Minute on Indian Education" wherein he declares the civilizational imperative of English-language education in British territories. Macaulay ([1835] 2005, 130) outlines a British colonial strategy infused quite obviously with the logic of compensatory domination as he explicitly calls for the construction of a class of Indians who would remain racially different (inferior) to the British but similar to the British in their thinking, speaking and desires. This in-between class of Indians, Macaulay instructed, would serve as interpreters between the British and the rest of the colonized (130). In their achievement of

English fluency, elite Indians could achieve a sense of superiority over other Indians for whom English education was not (made) accessible. This sense of superiority, in turn, would serve as compensation for their own domination by the British. Shefali Chandra (2012, 26) explains the inextricable relation between elite male uptake of English education and its consolidation of both caste and Indigenous heteropatriarchal hierarchies, arguing that "the success of colonial mimicry lay in how English-educated Indians deployed sexual difference to contain English within their caste and class locations, turning colonial desire for the native male mimic into a revitalized Indian hetero-nationalism." In this regard, Chandra identifies ways that elite male Indians exceeded the assimilationist logic of Macaulay's "Minute on Education," albeit in ways that served caste and heteropatriarchal oppression. As she demonstrates, elite Indian men argued that the civilizational qualities acquired with English-language education required a certain moral capacity to maintain caste-purity in marriage and motherhood. In their estimation, only upper-caste women possessed this requisite morality. This elite Indian adaptation of colonial mimicry to serve their heteropatriarchal nationalist interests exceeds the aims of assimilationist British Anglo prerogatives. Reading this excess allows us to identify resistance, however ambiguous and problematic in its reproduction of internal oppressive logics.

Compensatory domination, via colonial mimicry, produces subordinated subjects whose resistance to domination involves a blurring of differences between themselves and their European rulers. In this way, India, although not a secondary empire, benefits from Mignolo and Tlostanova's analytic lens of the "imperial difference." To use Mignolo's and Tlostanova's (2006, 209–10) words, elite Indians adopted "blurred smudged in-between models" of thinking that make their differences with the West ambiguous and prioritize becoming/competing with the West over decolonization. Focusing on how elite Indians actively inhabit these blurred borders generated by US/European Orientalism to reject a racialized inferiority vis-à-vis whites/Anglos in the context of US racialized gender formation, we underscore the "imperial difference" as a powerful historical and transnational analytic to explain the persistent allure and impact of the model-minority racial project well beyond the rise of post-9/11 racist patriotism.

Descendants of the class of Indians invited to become interpreters for their British rulers constitute the majority of the first massive wave of professional and technical Indian immigration to the United States in the mid-1960s (Bhattacharjee 1998; Prashad 2000). The British Orientalist narratives of the elite Indian's common European ancestry and Caucasian racial roots not only justified the fraternalist approach to colonial rule in India, as Keating elaborates, but also provided a legal rationale for Indian immigrants to justify their rights to US citizenship. As Ian Haney López documents, prior to 1923, Indian immigrants in the United States argued for their right to naturalization on the basis that they were Caucasian. Indian immigrants would herald their British colonial–derived racial classification as Caucasian to circumvent the 1790 US Supreme Court decision that made whiteness a requirement for US naturalization. Some US courts validated this reasoning until the 1923 Baghat Singh Thind case when the Supreme Court concluded that "common sense," rather than anthropological racial classification, would prevail in determining that Indians were not white (Haney López 2006, 64). This ruling stripped many naturalized Indians of their citizenship and led to their deportation (64). Between 1923 and 1965, Indian migration to the United States all but stopped. This changed with the passage of the 1965 Immigration and Nationality Act that lifted race-based restrictions on immigration to the United States. The growing demand for cheap medical and technical professionals to feed the Cold War space and weapons industry, combined with the US government's desire to ward off a reputation for racism in the face of growing civil rights movements, ushered this legal shift (Prashad 2000). The massive wave of medical and technical professionals emigrating from India to the United States at this time produced a skewed middle-class professional South Asian demographic that, in turn, supported the newly launched state-manufactured "model-minority" racial ideology.

As a growing middle-class professional population of Indian immigrants settled in the United States, *U.S. News and World Report* released an article in 1966 hailing Asian Americans, particularly Japanese and Chinese Americans, as the nation's "model minority" because of their apparent economic success and self-sufficiency achieved by the dint of their own hard work (Prashad 2000, 7). The term *model minority* praised Asian Americans as it indicted African Americans, claiming the successes of the former nonwhite population were a testament to their superior cultural values of obedience, discipline, and hard work. In this regard, the model-minority discourse disguises its racist claims by substituting "culture" for "race" while still implying that certain nonwhite races inherently possess superior cultural values relative to others. Echoes of Orientalist admiration of Asian culture as superior to African cultures resurface in the birth of model-minority ideology. While the news article named Chinese and Japanese Americans as representative model minorities, Indian Americans soon joined them as exemplars of this "not-minority minority" title (Prashad 2000, 168). By 1970, the census classified immigrants of Indian descent as white on the basis of their "Indo-European stock" (Das Gupta 2006, 33).

Monisha Das Gupta (2006, 38) traces how, in 1975, the Association of Indians in America (AIA) sought to challenge the classification of peoples of Indian descent as white to access legal protection for Indian immigrants against discriminatory treatment in the United States. She documents how the AIA's acceptance of "racially ambiguous terms of belonging to the U.S. national body" resulted in a "troubling indeterminacy about the status of South Asians as minorities and their entitlement to civil rights protections" (30). On the one hand, they invoked histories of discrimination as Asian, noting their subjection to the Asiatic barred zone (45). The AIA complicated this understanding of race in terms of histories of power in its attempts to argue protected racial minority status on the basis that some, though not all, Indians were, indeed, Caucasian. To retain "Indo-European" identity without losing legal protections from discrimination in the United States, the AIA had to distinguish "Caucasian" from "white" (46). Their campaign against a "white" census categorization rescued their claim to Caucasian identity as it enabled a uniquely Indian American identity that was superior vis-à-vis other racial minorities, proximate to, but distinct from, white identity.

The stubborn persistence of the model-minority logic, particularly among South Asians, is most evident in its endurance after the September 11 attacks on the World Trade Center when many Sikh (and other South Asian and "Muslim-looking") Americans became targets of racist patriotism. Their survival response involved issuing educational messages of "we are not them" and patriotic assertions that "we are American too." As Jasbir Puar (2007, 170) notes, the racist patriotism sexualized the Arab terrorist as sexual deviant, moving targeted South Asian populations, like Sikh Americans, to infuse their responses with an entrenchment of heteropatriarchal familial formation as a nationalist cultural value distinct from those of the "real" terrorist. The mechanisms used by Indian Americans to distance themselves from Arabs must be understood through the long history of active Asian participation in "self-Orientalization" or the idealization of Indian cultural qualities as amenable and admirable in the eyes of the West that would then distinguish them from the barbarous Other. Puar's analysis of post-9/11 racialized gender formation identifies the recurrence of the logic of compensatory domination endemic to this "self-orientalization" subject formation. She writes, "Cast into the politics of the South Asian diaspora, Pakistan, through an erasure of the huge number of Muslims in India, represents the Muslim Other, a space from which normative Hindu Americans and Sikh Americans must distance themselves. This distancing requires an ever-narrowing South Asian model-minority positioning as it seeks to separate off from terrorist look-alikes" (94). The "separat[ing] off from terrorist look-alikes" symbolized by the "Muslim Other" echoes the British colonial logic of compensatory domination where elite Indians claimed civilizational brotherhood with their European conquerors through a depiction of Muslims as the racialized gendered Other.

Historically, as Shefali Chandra documents, upper-caste Indians could claim civilizational brotherhood with the British by naturalizing heteropatriarchal definitions of Indian culture that valued conjugal companionate marriage in which upper-caste Indian women adopted English-language skills while remaining devoted Indian wives/mothers. Participation in companionate marriage (which presumed a liberal individualist exercise of choice) signaled the Indian bourgeoisie's ability to handle the adoption of English language without abandoning cultural commitments to racial/caste boundaries of respectability and family cohesiveness, a significant value attributed to Indian American (and Asian American) status as model minorities (Koshy 2004, 135). That is, learning English affirmed Indian women's civilizational capacity to handle "choice" without disobeying racialized gender prescriptions of proper marital/moral duty within their caste, something Dalit Indians could not be trusted to do if given the opportunity to learn English. The act of choosing a partner of the same race or caste illustrated a racialized assumption of biologized cultural superiority. The model-minority narrative affirms cultural accommodation to white/Anglo imperatives (like learning English) as a naturalized (racialized) quality that elevates the status of Asian Americans relative to Latinos/as and Blacks without undoing their racial status as a subordinated minority.

Using this historical lens, we can read Indian American women's cultural investment in companionate marriage within their own ethnoreligious communities as actively affirming their model-minority cultural distinction from the rest of the racially subordinated. Model-minority derived understandings of South Asianness prescribe a dissociation from those racialized as part of the "underclass" as well as "the normalization of the stable procreative endogamous family in the community's definition of achievement" (Kim 1999, 121; Das Gupta 2006, 70). As with elite male Indian participation in processes of colonial mimicry, then, US South Asian women bear the burden of (re)producing Indian culture as a biologized racial essence and of upholding the bourgeois investment in caste and racial purity through proper marital choice. In this regard, refusing to marry among one's own renders one vulnerable to accusations of cultural betrayal. The culture betrayed, and the very terms of betrayal promote a blurred and smudged model of thinking that seduces model-minority presumptions of relative Indian superiority over other US diasporic populations, such as Dalit, Muslim, and Black peoples. Both colonial mimicry and model-minority subject formation pursue Western civilizational affirmations via racial and caste investments in companionate marriage, family cohesiveness, and understandings of biologized cultural superiority.

We can especially understand this pressure from the locus of post-1965 non-heterosexual Indian American women for whom access to "marriage among one's own" becomes a strategic tool for negotiating belonging within their US South Asian communities. Since same-sex marriage became legal in the United States, photo shoots of celebrated LGBT same-sex marriage ceremonies in the South Asian diaspora circulate more readily on social media and online news media. These marriages symbolize an enactment of the freedom to choose one's partner. As such, some queer Indian American women can still negotiate inclusion within familial and community circles—where cultural loyalty requires marriage among one's own—by choosing to marry among their own caste/class and ethnoreligious boundaries. Take, for example, the case of Mala Nagarajan and Vega Subramaniam, a post-1965 Indian American lesbian couple known as the first lesbian couple to have a Hindu wedding and for their decision to join the lawsuit against Washington State for the right to marry. As the only nonwhite couple to join the lawsuit, Mala and Vega explain that their decision to prioritize the right of gays and lesbians to marry yielded greater acceptance among extended family and community. In Mala's words, "we've definitely experienced how community and extended family response has positively influenced those most close to us who were not accepting, but who now are" (Sadasivan 2011). Marriage itself, however, is not the recuperative mechanism for ethnoreligious familial belonging. The same-sex marriage must also reassure the family that queerness will not disrupt their caste and race boundaries. In discussing the role their public marriage played in familial acceptance of the same-sex relationship, Mala suggest that had Vega been not been of the same ethnoreligious background, the familial and communal acceptance that followed their marriage may not have occurred, at least, not so readily.[9] Mala and Vega's experience resonates in the sentiments that predominated in both the 2006 and 2013 *DesiQ* queer South Asian diasporic conferences where same-sex marital rights were a primary issue of discussion.[10] One of the hosts who opened the 2013 *DesiQ* Conference jokingly welcomed the hundreds of queer South Asians from across the globe, jesting that "this is like a *shadi* [wedding] for gay people." This joke, however, resonated in the discussions and workshop sessions that permeated both the 2006 and 2013 queer South Asian diasporic conferences. One 2006 participant recounted her parents' enthusiasm about her conference attendance with strict instructions to find a marital match of a specific caste, region, and similar. Other conference participants recounted parental fears that their daughters' queerness presumed a refusal to marry among one's own. In a 2013 conference workshop, an Indian American woman described her father's concern that her coming out as a lesbian meant she wanted to marry a Black person.[11] The fear that her queerness would disrupt racial and caste boundaries can be allayed when the queer South Asian daughter pursues the proper marital partner (Roshanravan 2010). Using the "imperial difference" to recognize the Janus-faced logic of upper-caste/class Indian negotiations with British rule and white supremacy, we can read these decisions among Indian American lesbians as more than homonormative assimilation to white/Anglo culture. We can simultaneously read their embrace of endogamous marriage as an ambiguous resistant maneuver to claim their cultural identification as Indian American, however intertwined within the model-minority framing of culture such identification may be (Roshanravan 2010, 2019).

Although these Indian American women would not count among the "most marginalized" in Mohanty's transnational feminist framework, their negotiations with model-minority subject formation reveal important insights about the interlocking logics of heteropatriarchy, racism and colonialism. By attending to histories of colonial mimicry as informing South Asian American negotiations with model-minority racial formation, we not only amplify our understanding of heteropatriarchal gender formation as a colonial project but also hone our ability to read resistant negotiations of Asian American women. In this case, we can read South Asian American lesbian investment in "marriage among our own" as more than assimilation to white/Anglo mainstream standards or homonationalism. We can also read it as negotiation for cultural affirmation and community belonging in resistance to white/Anglo assimilative prerogatives and South Asian diasporic homophobic ostracism.

Thinking only in terms of the colonial difference where the colonizer/colonized dichotomy remains sharp and firm, we could not access the nuanced meanings generated historically over time across nations and Orientalist framings of Asia to understand the persistence of model-minority racial logic. At least, we could not read the distancing mechanisms of Indian Americans from Arab Americans post-9/11 and their claims to being "American too" as a resistance that exceeds assimilative prerogatives of US racist patriotism. We cannot read the ambiguously resistant orientations of Indian American active participation in their blurred positioning between European/US white/Anglo communities, African and Native American communities and those racially subordinated internal Others excised from the cultural idealization of Asia when we think only in terms of the dichotomous logic of colonizer/colonized or white/Black racial paradigms.

Toward More Transnational Understandings of Asian America

Our use of the imperial difference as an analytic to investigate Chinese and Indian examples of Asian American histories contributes a way of reading Asian American racialized gendered subject formation that does not easily conform to the colonizer/colonized, assimilation/resistance frameworks prominent in the field. As such, this intervention addresses persistent inquiries in Asian American studies on the stubborn endurance of the model-minority myth and the totalizing racial assumptions about Asian Americans as an in-between racialized US minority. Our intervention bridges the Orientalist imagination in the West and the increasingly subordinate civilization in the East, and this intervention is meant to connect Asian American studies with transnational Asian studies. Asian America, since its emergence in the mid-nineteenth century, has seen continued waves of immigration, despite the temporary interruption during the exclusion years. We contextualize the subject formation of Asian Americans, in our respective cases, in the transnational passage to address the specific sociopolitical and sociocultural process particular to and most significant for Asian Americans as, liminal, racialized, and gendered subjects.

Framing Asian American subject formation through their transnational histories enables us to access the resistant sense making and active participation of Asian Americans in their particular and peculiar racialized position as intermediate subjects in the US racial matrix. To underline the racial "intermediacy," we borrow from Claire Jean Kim's racial triangulation model and Mignolo's and Tlostanova's concept of the imperial difference, which together help us study Chinese American women's and Indian Americans' history, both of which have fallen under the model-minority myth, in a different analytic light. We avoid a simplified/simplistic observation that Asian Americans subscribe to the model-minority myth or assume the mainstream white culture as a sign of assimilation; rather, we see such subscription as a strategy of survival against US racial(ized) subjugation. We also take into consideration how US mainstream/dominant discourses, in forms like court proceedings, have continued to construct Asian Americans as intermediate racial subjects and reapproach this history within the frame of the imperial difference to explore the rationality behind sociopolitical and ideological mechanisms like the model-minority myth. We argue that it is through the imperial difference that we see most clearly how US mainstream racializing mechanisms and Asian American discourses both actively construct Asian Americans as intermediate racial subjects.

This essay serves as our departure point for further research in Asian American women's subject formation, past and present, in light of the imperial difference. We contend that the imperial difference offers an avenue toward transnational feminist engagement of Asian American women's experiences without consigning the "global" or "transnational" to an "elsewhere" outside the United States (Alexander and Mohanty 2012). It is only in a theoretical as well as historical transnational process, we believe, that Asian American women's subject formation can be comprehended as a becoming of peculiar yet intermediate racialized and gendered subjects and that this intermediacy can be understood as exceeding assimilationist logics. The ability to perceive Asian American women as active participants in their racialized gender formation is particularly significant in terms of Asian American feminist engagement with women of color feminist theory given the latter's emphasis on rereading differences in their nondominant constructions (Lorde 1984; Lugones 2003). Our use of the imperial difference to historicize the racialized intermediacy of Asian Americans highlights culture as a significant site of resistant meaning making for Asian American women, even as these resistant cultural logics reproduce Orientalist and Eurocentric logics of domination. In this way, we situate our investigation as laying the groundwork to better engage in what Grace Hong (2006, x–xi) describes as a women of color reading practice that centers culture to understand "the contradictions of the racialized and gendered state" and to exploit these contradictions for what they can teach us about the logics of domination and the creative and multiple manifestations of resistance against these logics.

Amplifying and sharpening our readings of Asian American women's active subjectivities and resistant negotiations with power, particularly among those too easily dismissed as the assimilated elite, can facilitate against unwitting dismissals of Asian American women in transnational feminist and women of color methodologies that eschew the relatively privileged as analytic anchors for reading power and mapping paths of liberation. In this regard, we understand this chapter as laying the groundwork for an important conversation with Chandra Mohanty's (2003, 232) celebrated transnational feminist analysis, "Under Western Eyes," wherein she explicitly states the need to center the "most marginalized communities of women" to map the most inclusive paradigm of social justice. How does the imperial difference as a transnational feminist analytic disrupt this assumption and its unwitting dismissals of Asian American women (not Asian women) as "relatively privileged" in their intermediate racial status? It is to this question and its consequent bridging of Asian American, women of color, and transnational feminist scholarship that we hope to turn, and we hope others will engage in the spirit of developing an expansive and rich decolonial feminist praxis.

Notes

1. As Kim (1999, 112) notes, Chinese Americans remained racially triangulated in this process.
2. This speech originally appeared in a report in *Chung Sai Yat Po*, June 10, 1903; the transcription, translated from Chinese, is borrowed from Judy Yung (1995, 191).

3. Transcribed from "On the Urgency of Promoting Women's Education" (論女學亟宜振興), written by a Wu Wen-Po (吳文波), on November 4, 1911, *Chung Sai Yat Po*. Translation by Jen-feng Kuo.
4. Transcribed from "On the Urgency of Promoting Women's Education" (論女學亟宜振興), written by a Wu Wen-Po (吳文波), on November 4, 1911.
5. For Kim's definitions of relative valorization and civic ostracism, see p. 107.
6. To be sure, Mignolo and Tlostanova (2006) criticize secondary empires whose resistance strategies involve desires to compete with Euro-American empires or to remain dominant within their own imperial limits, or both, which only assimilate the Eurocentric, colonial logic and cannot be productive in terms of introducing radical border thinking and geopolitics.
7. As we bring historical experiences like Orientalization to attention, we also keep in mind that they certainly are not experiences exclusive to Asian Americans. Rather, we underline the persistent historical as well as ideological effects of those processes among Asian Americans.
8. Abya Yala "is the term that has been used by indigenous movements in the Americas to refer to the American continent from the native people's stance" (Carola 2017).
9. Personal conversation, April 13, 2012.
10. *DesiQ* is a two- to three-day queer diasporic South Asian conference held every six to seven years that brings together LGBTQ and gender nonconforming members of the South Asian diaspora. My reflections are drawn from attendance of the 2006 and 2013 *DesiQ* conferences. Ethnoreligious familial and communal acceptance was a primary theme in both workshop and informal discussions at both of these conferences.
11. Participant observation during the 2006 and 2013 *DesiQ* conferences.

References

Alexander, M. Jacqui, and Chandra Talpade Mohanty. 2012. "Cartographies of Knowledge and Power: Transnational Feminism as Radical Praxis." In *Critical Transnational Feminist Praxis*, edited by Amanda Lock Swarr and Richa Nagar, 23–45. Albany: State University of New York Press.

Bhattacharjee, Anannya. 1998. "The Habit of Ex-Nomination: Nation, Woman and the Indian Immigrant Bourgeoisie." In *A Patchwork Shawl: Chronicles of South Asian Women in America*, edited by Shamita Das Dasgupta, 163–85. New Brunswick, NJ: Rutgers University Press.

Blauner, Bob. 1972. *Racial Oppression in America*. New York: Harper and Row.

Bow, Leslie. 2010. *Partly Colored: Asian Americans and Racial Anomaly in the Segregated South*. New York: New York University Press.

Carola, Carlos Renato. 2017. "Precursors of Decolonial Pedagogical Thinking in Latin America and Abya Yala." In *New Pedagogical Challenges in the 21st Century: Contributions of Research in Education*, edited by Olga Bernad Cavero and Núria Llevot-Calvet, 97–116. London: IntechOpen.

Chan, Sucheng. 2005. *In Defense of Asian American Studies: The Politics of Teaching and Program Building*. Champaign: University of Illinois Press.

Chandra, Shefali. 2012. *The Sexual Life of English: Languages of Caste and Desire in Colonial India*. Durham, NC: Duke University Press.

Das Gupta, Monisha. 2006. *Unruly Immigrants: Rights, Activism, and Transnational South Asian Politics in the United States*. Durham, NC: Duke University Press.

Fujiwara, Lynn, and Shireen Roshanravan, eds. 2018. *Asian American Feminisms and Women of Color Politics*. Seattle: University of Washington Press.

Haney López, Ian. 2006. *White by Law: The Legal Construction of Race*. New York: New York University Press.

Hong, Grace Kyungwon. 2006. *The Ruptures of American Capital: Women of Color Feminism and the Culture of Immigrant Labor*. Minneapolis: University of Minnesota Press.

Keating, Christine. 2011. *Decolonizing Democracy: Transforming the Social Contract in India*. University Park: Pennsylvania State University Press.

Kim, Claire Jean. 1999. "The Racial Triangulation of Asian Americans." *Politics & Society* 27 (1): 105–38.

Koshy, Susan. 2004. *Sexual Naturalization: Asian Americans and Miscegenation*. Stanford, CA: Stanford University Press.

Kuo, Jen-Feng. 2010. "Chinese American Women in the Early Twentieth Century and the Question of Modernity/Coloniality." PhD diss., Binghamton University.

Lee, Erika. 2003. *At America's Gates: Chinese Immigration during the Exclusion Era, 1882–1943*. Chapel Hill, NC: University of North Carolina Press.

Loewen, James. 1988. *The Mississippi Chinese: Between Black and White*. Long Grove, IL: Waveland Press.

Lorde, Audre. 1984. *Sister Outsider: Essays and Speeches*. Berkeley, CA: Crossing Press.

Lugones, María. 2003. *Pilgrimages/Peregrinajes: Theorizing Coalition against Multiple Oppressions*. Lanham, MD: Rowman and Littlefield.

Macaulay, Thomas B. (1835) 2005. "Minute on Indian Education, February 2, 1835." In *Postcolonialisms: An Anthology of Cultural Theory and Criticism*, edited by Gaurav Gajanan Desai and Supriya Nair, 121–31. New Brunswick, NJ: Rutgers University Press.

Mignolo, Walter D., and Madina V. Tlostanova. 2006. "Theorizing from the Borders: Shifting to Geo- and Body-Politics of Knowledge." *European Journal of Social Theory* 9 (2): 205–21.

Mohanty, Chandra Talpade. 2003. *Feminism without Borders: Decolonizing Theory, Practicing Solidarity*. Durham, NC: Duke University Press.

Pascoe, Peggy. 1989. "Gender Systems in Conflict: The Marriages of Mission-Educated Chinese American Women, 1874–1939." *Journal of Social History* 22 (4): 631–52.

———. 1990. *Relations of Rescue: The Search for Female Moral Authority in the American West, 1874–1939*. New York: Oxford University Press.

Prashad, Vijay. 2000. *The Karma of Brown Folk*. Minneapolis: University of Minnesota Press.

Puar, Jasbir K. 2007. *Terrorist Assemblages: Homonationalism in Queer Times*. Durham, NC: Duke University Press.

Purkayastha, Bandana. 2005. *Negotiating Ethnicity: Second-Generation South Asian Americans Traverse a Transnational World*. New Brunswick, NJ: Rutgers University Press.

Quijano, Aníbal. 2000. "Coloniality of Power, Eurocentrism, and Latin America." Translated by Michael Ennis. *Nepantla: Views from South* 1 (3): 533–80.

Roshanravan, Shireen M. 2010. "Passing-as-If: Model-Minority Subjectivity and Women of Color Identification." *Meridians* 10 (1): 1–31.

———. 2019. "Witnessing Faithfully and the Intimate Praxis of Queer South Asian Organizing." In *Speaking Face to Face: The Visionary Philosophy of María Lugones*, edited by Pedro J. DiPietro, Jennifer McWeeny, and Shireen Roshanravan, 103–22. Albany, NY: State University of New York Press.

Sadasivan, Shridhar. 2011. "Jab We Met: And We Sued the State (Part 3)." Gaysi, February 16, 2011. https://gaysifamily.com/culture/jab-we-met-and-we-sued-the-state-part-3/.

Tchen, John Kuo Wei. 2001. *New York before Chinatown: Orientalism and the Shaping of American Culture, 1776–1882*. Baltimore: Johns Hopkins University Press.

Tlostanova, Madina V. 2008. "The Janus-Faced Empire Distorting Orientalist Discourses: Gender, Race and Religion in the Russian/(Post)Soviet Constructions of the 'Orient.'" *Worlds & Knowledges Otherwise* 2:1–11.

Yung, Judy. 1995. *Unbound Feet: A Social History of Chinese Women in San Francisco*. Berkeley: University of California Press.

Jen-Feng Kuo is Adjunct Assistant Professor at the Center for General Education at National Taiwan University. He was previously a postdoctoral fellow at the Social Sciences Research Center (SSRC), National Science Council, Taiwan. While at SSRC, he received the Dissertation Award for Studies of Overseas Chinese Affairs by Taiwan's Overseas Chinese Association.

Shireen Roshanravan is Executive Director of Equity, Diversity, and Inclusion and Professor of Philosophy at Northeastern Illinois University. Her scholarship is rooted in grassroots community and coalition building. She is editor of *Asian American Feminisms and Women of Color Politics* (2018) and *Speaking Face-to-Face: The Visionary Philosophy of María Lugones* (2019).

5

TOWARD THE DECOLONIAL

DEHUMANIZATION, US WOMEN OF COLOR THOUGHT, AND THE NONVIOLENT POLITICS OF LOVE

Laura E. Pérez

IN RESPONSE TO Frederic Jameson's (1984) sense of the diminishing possibilities of effectively countering transnational capitalism's increasing ability to appropriate and commodify even its opposition, Chicana queer feminist Chela Sandoval provided, in *Methodology of the Oppressed* (2000), a different analysis, one based on the perspective of US women of color, longtime survivors of the dehumanizing legacies of Native American genocide, slavery, racism, patriarchy, homophobia, and classism.[1] Instead, Sandoval argued, the growing economic disenfranchisement and attendant social and psychological disorientation of white middle-class men whom Jameson described as part of the new postmodern condition could be viewed as a historic opportunity for widespread coalition across gender, racialization, class, and sexuality between "U.S. women of color," other disenfranchised sectors, and nonelite "white" men, who now increasingly shared the conditions and effects of marginality.[2] What Jameson describes as the experiences of the postmodern subject and Sandoval as that of US women of color are indeed the effects of colonization, neocolonization, and transnational capitalism; however, they are more precisely the effects of dehumanization: the cost of all forms of injustice toward human beings and one that is paid by those who dominate as well as those who exploit. In the present moment, described as that of "extreme capitalism," or "the last phase of what may be called the age of acquisitors or money-grubbers" (Batra 2007, 13), a deeply decolonizing, coalitionary politics simultaneously rooted in the best of the civil rights and liberation struggles and nonviolent social and environmental activism and committed to the local while being mindful of interdependence with the global has much to offer.[3]

Five decades of "trickle-down" economics aimed at further enriching the wealthiest individuals and corporations of the Reagan, Bush Sr., Clinton, Bush, Obama, Trump, and Biden administrations have failed to "gradually" benefit all other sectors of society and government. Blue-collar laborers, service sector workers, white-collar college-educated technicians, administrative staff, and middle management have steadily and increasingly been "down sized" en masse throughout this era into unemployment, while replacements have been hired across borders and abroad at a fraction of the cost and in illegal informal sectors within First World nations, including our own, thus creating tremendous economic disparities globally and maintaining the racialized and gender inequities historically created by European and US imperialism abroad.

In the United States, the economically disproportionate redistribution of the tax burden from the wealthiest to the middle classes of the last five decades, in conjunction with deregulation and the partial privatization of public services and institutions (e.g., museums and universities) make plain the necessity of safeguarding democracy itself against the new "financial imperialists" (Batra 2007). Driven to the pursuit of endless profit in bold disregard of the human suffering and destruction of the environment that their greed and social irresponsibility causes, Professor of Economics Ravi Batra describes the human behavior directing transnational corporate policies as "shameless" and "pathological." Another distinguished economist, David Korten (2009), coincides in characterizing the exploits of the owners and executives of "phantom" capital, financial sector capitalists, as "shameless" and criminal and as the new "buccaneers" of our era.[4] As Korten writes, "an extreme and growing concentration of privatized wealth and power divides the world between the profligate and the desperate, intensifies competition for Earth's resources, undermines the legitimacy of our institutions, drives an unraveling of the social fabric of mutual trust and caring, and fuels the forces of terrorism, crime, and environmental destruction" (55). In 2021, it was reported that "while individuals worth more than $1 million constitute just 1.1% of the world's population, they hold 45.8% of global wealth" (Deshmukh 2021). In 2022, the number of billionaires in the world was 2,668, with a combined wealth of $12.7 trillion (Mille 2022). Since 2005, inequality has increased across the globe and in the United States. The exorbitant wealth and social power of the transnational financial sector elite, centered in the United States, has been built directly on the backs of a superexploited poor. Given the increasing unemployment of the male workforce globally, Third World women and women of color are carrying most of the gendered double workday burden of wage labor and domestic work. Increasingly, the burden of making ends meet for parents and siblings, their own families, and their nations falls on a female workforce that, apart from the odd exception, has yet to receive equal pay for equal work. Regardless of where women are employed in the US labor market, be it in financial executive and managerial sectors; medicine, law, or academia; the informal economy (e.g., the garment or technology assembly industries); or highly lucrative transnational sex work, the superexploitation of women, particularly that of women of color, transnationally and domestically has not been leveled: it has increased, while the wealth and power of European and Euro-American elite men, in the company of other global male elites, has skyrocketed.[5]

For more than fifty years, US feminist and queer women of color (e.g., Audre Lorde, Anna Nieto Gómez, Elizabeth "Betita" Martínez, the Combahee River Collective, Angela Davis) have theorized from personal and collective experience that women of color in the United States experience "simultaneous" and imbricated forms of oppression, the "double" and "triple oppression" of gender, "race," sexuality (i.e., heteronormativity), and class, created by imperialist patriarchy and its colonial culture of racism and slavery.[6] Indeed, this has been the most important theoretical contribution to liberation struggles based primarily on one issue, be it gender, sexuality, class, or "race" and cultural difference. These are all interrelated forms of oppression, US women of color have argued; thus, for example, the way that gender or racialized or economic oppression functions for a working-class Native American woman in contrast to a middle-class Euro-American woman, or a middle-class minority woman, or a "white" or "minority" man are different in important ways, as some may nevertheless also experience degrees of privilege. One can passively benefit from the inequities of society as it is, or actively support the oppression of others and thus be a racist and classist female while also suffering gender inequity or homophobia. Furthermore, to focus on only one oppression to the exclusion of the others suggests, contrary to fact, that they are not imbricated and that they can be resolved independently or that they are not constitutive of the alternative ideologies presumed to be more liberatory. Early "second wave" (i.e., 1960s and 1970s) women of color feminist writings are posited on the idea that the "double," "triple," "multiple," and "simultaneous" oppressions conjugate each other, in constantly shifting rather than static or essentialist ways. The challenge has been and remains to develop analyses that understand these oppressions as co-constitutive and simultaneous and to respond from and develop a different logic than that of inequity, separation, and domination on the basis of cultural, sexual, and supposedly biological or "racial" human inferiorities and superiorities. African American, Asian American, Chicana, Native American, and other women of color feminists early on traced their experience of racialized gender and class oppression to the logic of colonization and busied themselves circulating other ways of understanding being in social and natural worlds based on respect for self and others, beliefs salvaged from diverse and largely non-Western ancestral spiritual philosophies positing that we are interrelated and therefore interdependent, a broad, proliferating politics beyond Left, Progressive, and Right, based on what I have called eros ideologies.[7]

Awareness of cultural difference in the understanding of gender and sexuality, as in other categories of social and cultural understanding, is crucial to avoid reinscribing dominant cultural values and definitions, as Ana Nieto Gómez, Elizabeth "Betita" Martínez, and Ada Sosa Riddell pointed out with respect to gender in their essays throughout the 1970s. Subsequent gender and sexuality studies of the eighties and nineties, such as Will Roscoe's *Changing Ones* (2000), document nonbinary notions of gender and sexuality among "berdache" or "third gender" Native American people before and during colonization of North America. Randy Conner and David Sparks's (2004) work on African-diasporic queer sexualities that are rooted in African notions of gender and spirituality also broadens present notions of gender and sexuality, beyond colonizing and racist heteronormative views of the present.

Latina lesbian philosopher María Lugones (2007) observed that Peruvian sociologist Aníbal Quijano's (1992) use of "gender" and "sexuality" incorrectly assumed that these are universal categories that transcend cultural differences, though his theory of the "coloniality of power" acknowledges in a wholesale way the racialization of culture (and thus subsequently of modernity) produced by European imperialism in the Americas. Drawing on the work of several scholars, Lugones points to different, more fluid notions of "gender" and sexuality on the American and African continents before contact with European colonizers that allow us to begin to more deeply understand the patriarchal heteronormative nature of the colonial and its legacies into the present.

In the same serious, sustained, and far-reaching way that US ethnic studies scholars and Quijano, more or less simultaneously, have aimed to trace the difference that racialization in economic and social exploitation during the last five hundred years has made to the present, rendering it a central rather than a marginalized vector of analysis, so too, I would like to suggest, must any decolonizing, liberatory social analysis deeply consider and incorporate the centrality of patriarchal heteronormativity as a worldview that foundationally structures racialization, colonization, and capitalism.

Homophobic heteronormative patriarchy characterized European medieval and Renaissance colonial-era logic previous to the development of American colonialism, as Richard C. Trexler (1995) has shown.[8] Based on his survey of the classical roots of European views of women and "passive" homosexual partners in particular and colonial-era writings and scholarship, Trexler observes, "Indeed, the weight of the evidence now allows us to understand with some cultural depth the European maxim that male homosexual behavior might bestow a 'just title' for conquest" (171). Following Lugones, PJ DiPietro has investigated how heteronormative Spanish colonization resulted in the profound dehumanization in particular of what colonizers called "sodomites," as less than the dogs to which they were thrown for this "sin" (DiPietro 2025). Ivan Hannaford (1996), in turn, has carefully traced important strands in European, premodern notions of biological "race" as those primarily based on nobility (of character, ancestry, and illustrious service to the state as citizen); the ecclesiastical idea of membership in the body of Christ; early nationalist discourses of cultural difference; recurring Bible-based esoteric ideas about the progeny of good versus that of evil as humanity's different peoples; and late fifteenth-century anti-Jewish Spanish ideas of blood purity (appropriated from Jewish culture itself).

Extensive contact with Native Americans and enslaved Africans in the Spanish colonies led to some reformulation of these older ideas and new theories attempting to account for the cultural and seemingly human differences the Europeans encountered or read about, including important theological debates of the sixteenth century over the ethics of colonization and enslavement. Witness to the genocide and brutal enslavement of Native Americans, and after decades of activity to reform the treatment of Native peoples, the Dominican priest, Fray Bartolomé de las Casas, in a famous 1550 debate and in a 1552 publication, argued that "Indians" had human souls and therefore were potentially fellow Christians.[9] But though some Native elites were incorporated into colonial and social orders and their children educated in Christian schools and colleges and though, as late as the eighteenth century, *casta* or caste paintings reveal intermarriages between Europeans, Native Americans, Africans, and their children, the genocide and racist disenfranchisement of Native American and African-diasporic peoples has generally characterized *mestizaje* and *mulataje* in Spanish-speaking Latin America through the present.

In New England, religious intellectuals also took a leading role in framing foundational beliefs about non-European peoples. Theologian Paul R. Griffin (1999) has shown that Cotton Mather and other influential clergymen from the establishment of the colony to the Republic, persistently argued that the enslavement or social-economic disenfranchisement of African-descended people was divinely ordained and that non-Europeans were subhumans of darkened intellect and soul who could never obtain equality with Europeans in any respect if given the chance so that enslavement was in fact a European

Christian mercy: "Racism is... practically synonymous with American Christianity. From the first moment the Puritans settled in North America, Christian religionists have employed distorted Christian theological ideas to justify their bigotry against persons of African descent" (124–25)

Such scholarship makes plain that colonization of the Americas decisively reinforced retrograde and self-serving ideas of national, cultural, gender, and sexual *difference and dominance* that the European colonizers brought with them and that would be given the definitive form of modern concepts of pseudo-biologically based ideas of racial difference during the rise of a scientism (and atheism, among intellectuals) that could not help but reflect the self-interest of European and Euro-American elites. Other research has focused on the cultural hybridity that arose in both directions from early on as European colonizers and their descendants coexisted, even if unequally, with the surviving, displaced Native Americans and enslaved Africans. African-diasporic, Asian American, Latina/o, and Native American intellectuals, in particular, and in various art forms as well as in literary and scholarly writing, have been attentive to what has survived of largely uncolonized worldviews (what I would call theo-philosophies) and practices of their non-European ancestors. This attentiveness includes not only the creation of a multicultural rather than Eurocentric canon of knowledge but also, more important, a decolonizing revision of what gets to count as knowledge beyond a white supremacist evolutionary account of progress—an account that has entrenched the assumption that "white is best" worldwide and justified injustice in the approving writ of its celebrated theological, philosophical, and scientific apologists, the cornerstones of most of the elite West's edifice of knowledge prior to the anticolonial liberation movements and the civil rights and liberation movements of the twentieth century.

But colonization, imperialism, slavery, genocide, subjugation by ethnic or tribal difference, and patriarchal and sexual oppression are not the product of the last five hundred years or the sole invention of European colonizers and their progeny. Critique of the colonization and neocolonization of the last five hundred years is important—necessary—but therefore also insufficient and to some degree, within the logic of dominant culture as it developed in the modern imperialism of the last five hundred years, built on the invasion of the Americas (as Quijano and Dussel have argued), genocide of the Indigenous, and enslavement of African peoples and the subsequent systematic pauperization and ongoing exploitations and marginalization of the descendants of these people. What then is the fundamental nature or logic of colonization as we have inherited and coproduced it, an imbricated, shifting, modernizing patriarchal, heteronormative, racializing, classist system of subjugation, oppression, marginalization, and ultimately exploitation that has been justified through discourses of dehumanization, given that "the human" within this worldview is, in Darwinian fashion, the economic and political dominator and colonizer? Why does it persist in modernized guises, ingrained in various kinds of cultural biases, including the postmodern, the liberal, the so-called post–civil rights and postfeminist present? What lies behind gender, sexual, racialized, and class exploitation and oppression, of that which has shown itself to inform the full spectrum of political ideologies from extreme right and left and most of what lies in between? What is the colonial and neocolonial relation, and thus, what is the decolonial, not the antithesis of these, but rather outside of their logic?

The colonizing and the neocolonial lie not merely in political, economic, and cultural (including religious or atheist) domination of one nation or people over another but more profoundly in the politics of domination and exploitation of one human being over another and the dehumanizing rationale or logic that make fundamental relationships of inequity and abuse possible, whether between men and women, queer and straight, European and Third World, or "minority," the rich, and the rest, and so on. Nonviolent activism, rooted in different religious and spiritual worldviews (i.e., theo-philosophies), has the power to make a direct connection between colonization, dehumanization, and, most important, decolonized being and is not based on the appropriation of the logic and tactics of oppression. Instead, it is based on an understanding of the interdependence of personal and social ethics of principled and humane behavior where, most to the point, the ends and means must be the same. Thus, if it is respectful, peaceful coexistence that is sought, it can most lastingly be sought by building from relations of mutual respect with peoples of different cultures and class or economic backgrounds and different sexual practices and other social "identities" as well as respect for other life-forms—that is, through a way of being human not built on an anthropocentric, ethnocentric, nationalist, or socially or economically elite notions of the "best kinds of people."[10]

Mohandas Gandhi (1869–1948) developed the theory and technique of fearless nonviolent and active resistance, *satyagraha*, first in response to the racism he experienced in South Africa during his eight years there and then as he led India to independence from the British Empire, grounding this practice in its literal meaning, "holding on to truth." For Gandhi, nonviolence, *ahimsa* (*himsa* translates as "violence"), the path of love and truth, was/is our true human nature, as we are all part of God. This belief is ancient and cross-cultural, Gandhi pointed out, and shared by the world's great spiritual teachers. Personal spiritual purification and discipline over the impulsive and passion-driven self is what enabled discernment in the pursuit of truth, against the caste system and the belief in women's inferiority in Hinduism, for example. The spiritual path of the pursuit of truth and love led logically to a social practice of respect for all, as God's creation. Gandhi concluded that the lasting success of his and other nonviolent actions opposing dehumanization resided in the refusal to dehumanize the oppressor or to engage in any form of violence, including harsh speech and judgment. Wrong action must therefore be opposed through refusal to cooperate with the former in a committed and principled way, on the basis of rational, moral suasion. "It is no non-violence if we merely love those that love us. It is non-violence only when we love those that hate us. I know how difficult it is to follow this grand law of love. But are not all great and good things difficult to do? Love of the hater is the most difficult of all. But by the grace of God even this most difficult thing becomes easy to do if we want to do it" (Gandhi 2004, 78). Reverend Martin Luther King Jr. carried Gandhi's torch in the following two decades as one of the most effective leaders of the civil rights movement and a moral compass for the United States. "Christ gave me the message," he said, "Gandhi gave me the method" ("Mahatma Gandhi" 2000). In the sixties, Chicano farmworker and labor activist Cesar Chavez followed the path of Gandhi and Martin Luther King Jr. in peacefully leading impoverished agricultural farm laborers, most of them immigrants, to demand decent wages, working conditions, and the right to unionize. Chavez's ethical leadership sparked the Chicana/o movement in 1965 as a coalition of laborers, students, teachers, and artists came together in a peaceful protest march to California's state capital. Indeed, it could be argued that most of what has been accomplished that has been lasting in the civil rights and liberation movements has been achieved nonviolently and a great deal of what has been rejected has been the violence of word or action espoused by some within these movements.[11]

Among other nonviolent activist strands, US women of color, alongside global Third World women of color, have developed and continue to develop a politics of personal and collective decolonization, drawing primarily from surviving non-European theo-philosophies. The most visionary and persuasive of US women of color's writing, art, and social activism have been spiritually driven, nonviolent acts of resistance to the dehumanization of (neo)colonial thought and centered in a social activist politics of love. Creative writings and essays, visual art and performance explore, affirm, preserve, re-create, and circulate healthier worldviews that center harmonious mind-body-spirit relations, on the one hand, and human and environment relations, on the other. In US women of color thought, Frantz Fanon's ([1952] 1967) crucial study of the internalization of self-loathing of the negatively racialized self under racist colonial rule is advanced by virtue of attention to the gendering and sexing of racialized colonization and attention to its opposite, to what Audre Lorde (1984) affirmed as the healing erotic power of love: a self-love, a love of women, a romantic love between women (particularly women of color), and a love of their bodies and sexuality, against the fear and loathing of these same forms of love inculcated throughout culture in sexist, racist, homophobic thought. Lest this be understood as a new centrism based on women, or women of color, or queer women of color, I hasten to add that Lorde's point, like that of other US women of color, is that love self, which has been denied people of color, especially women and queer people of color, is crucial as a form of basic social justice and basic human empowerment from which healthy human behavior can arise. What is reclaimed is the human capacity to know and act from an ethics of loving, respectful relationality.

In societies where inhumanity and injustice exist, social justice love, like queer love and Barthes's (1978) unrequited Lover, is denied legitimate social space and thus is also like the marginalization of women, people of color, the poor, and so on. In such conditions, it is to the borderlands, the margins, as Gloria Anzaldúa put it in *Borderlands/La Frontera* (1987), to which we must repair so that the fullness of our wounded humanity, our integrity, can heal and unfold. Socially exiled by racialization, culture, and gender, a "love in Aztlán," the not-yet-existent-again homeland, ultimately defies the denial of love itself by oppression. At the heart of the "methodology of the oppressed," of "differential consciousness," is a "neo-rhetoric of love" (Sandoval 2000, 131) and a "hermeneutic of love" (152), a "physics of love" (181), whereby "oppositional social action as a mode of 'love'" (147) grounds the perduring and humane struggle of women of color, like it does for all those who struggle for social justice.

But under systematic and entrenched dehumanizing conditions, not only is it difficult to love self, and thus love others near and dear to us and of our choice, but just as crucially, it is difficult to love those who treat us inhumanely; to resist dehumanizing the dehumanizers in a vicious cycle of psychic, social, and physical violence; and thus to ourselves become dehumanized and dehumanizing. To resist our dehumanization by and of others, the path of love is what Gandhi's Hindu, Christian, and Muslim spiritual studies led him to affirm as the only way toward God and beyond human injustice. This is what study or practice of ancestral Native American, African-diasporic, Asian, Christian, Jewish, and hybrid spiritualties have taught US women of color. But whether informed by culturally hybrid spiritualities composed of surviving ancestral beliefs and those adopted or imposed or by Christianity, largely inculcated over other faiths by European colonization, the disciplined attempt to follow seemingly universal core teachings of nonjudgmental acceptance and love of all as self and as Creator (by whatever name we understand the life energy) over sexist, racist, and homophobic distortions of what is human and natural has preserved the love and dignity of women of color in their personal and social practices.[12]

Indeed, a good-faith engagement with cultural, gender, sexual, class, or other human differences is, ultimately, an act of assuming the full humanity of the other, a receptive practice of love that is likely to be a transformational encounter, broadening our own humanity. As Lugones (2003, 97) observed, "only when we have traveled to each other's 'worlds' are we fully subjects to each other." A decolonizing politics is one that recognizes the full humanity of (neo)colonizer and (neo)colonized, oppressor and oppressed, exploiter and exploited, and where both accept responsibility for injustice and necessary change beyond that which directly benefits them. Against dehumanization is the simultaneous truth of both our identity and difference from each other as human beings and as part of the natural world. It is the literality of the Maya truth that *tú eres mi otro yo*, that somehow, "you are my other self."[13]

It is not that what humanizes us more deeply is acceptance of our responsibility for the other as other, as not-me, as the Jewish postwar philosopher Emmanuel Levinas ([1991] 2000) argued in the face of the widespread failure of Europe and the United States to intervene earlier in the Nazi Holocaust. Perhaps what "humanizes" us more deeply is the fundamental recognition that across cultural, biological, and personal differences and idiosyncrasies, we are in fact essentially human in the same way. Ethically speaking, we are all continually faced throughout our lives with our interests and desires in relation to those of other individuals—whether within our close circles, our larger communities, or across the globe—tied to us through economic privileges or political relations.

Extreme self-interest, selfishness, and cold abuse of the human and natural ecosystem gird the violence of the binary "either-or" logic that denies the continuum, that is, the relation between seemingly extreme poles of gender, sexuality, "race," class, able-bodiedness, and cultural differences, such as those of religion or worldview or even of political ideologies. Straight males and females do not hold the monopoly on masculinity or femininity, respectively. Nor do the sexually "queer" hold a monopoly on various degrees of same-sex love and attraction. And we would be hard pressed to find an American in the US or South of the border that isn't a mixture of various European, Native American, African-diasporic peoples, or Asian and Middle Eastern peoples. Human beings and their cultures mix whenever contact is possible. Thus, in spite of the colonial encounters in the Americas that gave rise to what eventually became a highly policed separatism of peoples from different parts of the world through what would later be refuted as the pseudoscientific category of race, on the ground, beyond the self-interested regulation and human-made false categories of supposed essential differences between us, we continue to like and love each other when given the chance and to prefer the pleasures of friendship, mutual respect, and peace to injustice, hatred, strife, and war.

The struggles against injustice have been struggles against dehumanization at the hands of the more powerful. At times the struggle has been physically violent, at other others, psychologically or spiritually so. The US government, the Left, the militant branches of the civil rights and other social protest struggles of our time, all have felt at times that violence was necessary to counteract the violent impunity of the imperialist, racist, sexist, and patriarchal aspects of US culture. But violence perpetuates the logic of colonization and of domination, more generally. Violence, physical and ideological (psychological, cultural), is today still the chief tactic of racism (e.g., the KKK, Texas Rangers), sexism, and homophobia. Statistics of violence against women, the queer, and the poor shows that our culture still is not, in fact, postfeminism, postracism, postclassist, or posthomophobic.

As it is in the teachings of Gandhi, the Dalai Lama, and Vietnamese monk Thich Nhat Hanh, according to psychologists, the fundamental site of violence is intrapsychic—within our own psyches. And the solution is a rational process of examining our thoughts and pruning out wrong thinking and errors implanted and reinforced early on. Thus, according to prominent child psychologist Alice Miller, in *For Your Own Good. Hidden Cruelty in Child-Rearing and the Roots of Violence* (1985), the psychology of Hitler and his generation was rooted in a highly repressive, disrespectful, shaming, and nonnurturing childhood education that inculcated rigid notions of the good versus the bad self and produced profound self-loathing and violence later projected onto those perceived to be wrongly different.

In similar fashion, the supposed savagery of Africa, Asia, and Native America has amply been shown to be a projection of the repressed within European culture rather than based on serious knowledge or understanding of cultural difference. Even highly enlightened and self-examining men and women have been trained through everyday assumptions to believe in the superiority of the European, the higher class, the male, and the heterosexual and to fear a greater propensity for criminality—because of supposed tendencies, whether they be to irrationality, passion, lack of discipline, wrongheadedness or "primitiveness," animal-like ideas, or, in the worst case scenario, evil—in women (e.g., Eve, Jezebel, black widow fortune hunters, witches, etc.) and African, Asian, Native American, and, today more than ever, Middle Eastern peoples.

The July–August 2009 issue of the *Harvard Business Review*, a special issue titled "Managing in the New World," reports many similarities in terms of highly valuing meaningful and socially responsible work over monetary compensation as a primary motivating factor, for example, between the oldest and youngest members of the workforce. One striking difference noted however was that "Gen Ys are clearly at ease with diversity [78%], whereas only 27% of Boomers have such comfort level" (Hewlett, Sherbin, and Sumberg 2009). Bearing in mind the imprecisions that must arise in lumping a twenty-year span of individuals, those born from 1944 to 1964, given that the first half were reared pre–civil rights and the second half after, I would predict a similar persistence in many of those who came of age in the sixties of discomfort around same-sex desire, femininity, and femaleness, given still high statistics of violence against women and "feminine"-appearing gay men, butchy women, transvestites, and transgender people. Thus, while there has been much progress through that generation's activism and coalition, in the United States, the younger generations show that it is the content of our minds, our deep-seated beliefs, that are the most important guarantors of social justice change.

A society of genuine commitment to fuller equity and respect for human diversity must strive to decolonize itself culturally (i.e., in our assumptions, ideas, and values) and institutionally (i.e., in our educational, legal, commercial practices) from the dehumanization of the Other within us or across the street, city, or globe and thus regenerate a greater capacity for kindness, compassion, and justice—in short, for greater humaneness where, to repeat, who gets to count as most fully human or be defined as the "best kind of people" is not exclusive of people from different cultures and nations or of other lifeforms. The twentieth and twenty-first centuries are marred by much violence, but they also and more importantly map important moments in the movement beyond received inhumane, dehumanizing beliefs and ways of being and coexisting. The challenge has been and remains to transform individual consciousness at the personal and thereby inevitably more external social levels toward greater truthfulness, justice, and social responsibility and so toward more fully realized democratic cultures.

The rise of nonviolence as a highly effective, transformative, and humane form of social activism practiced at the individual and mass level offers tremendous potential because it advocates simultaneous personal and collective freedom through disciplined self-control and responsibility for self and other (Nagler 2001). Nonviolent activists and the newer field of peace studies, both based on the ancient and equally perduring religious philosophies of faiths across the globe, have shed much-needed light on the short- and long-term solutions, the intra- and intersubjective dynamics of peace, freedom, justice, and the meaning and value of human existence. Michael Nagler, emeritus classics professor and founder of the pioneering Peace studies program at the

University of California, Berkeley, urges us to study peace, love, and compassion as we have war and cites Gandhi in noting that nonviolence is an active practice for the courageous. Elucidating the logic of Gandhi's spiritual and political practice of nonviolence, satyagraha, in his book *Is There No Other Way? The Search for a Nonviolent Future*, Nagler explains:

> Heart unity, the empathetic desire for the welfare of others, can also be called rejoicing in diversity. Our unity comes from our underlying consciousness, which has no divisions. I am in touch with that unity when I want you to be fulfilled, in a way you can be fulfilled—not necessarily the way I'd be fulfilled. That we can and should be fulfilled is a cardinal principle of faith in the world of Satyagraha; that we have different ways of getting there is equally cardinal. So you really can't have one without the other; unity of aspiration is as important as diversity of attributes, of individuality. And this is not unduly paradoxical because unity is the signature, the fulfillment of our inner life, diversity the natural characteristic of our outer life. (289)

Genuine, lasting decolonization of our notions of being, including gender, sexuality, and culturally different practices, cannot avoid being based on a deeply self-conscious democratizing, humanizing, ethical, socially responsible politics (or "philosophy," "worldview," "spirituality," "ethics," etc.) and practice. Abuse and exploitation require the dehumanization of the Other through suppression within our own being of thoughtfulness, reflection, self-examination, honesty, and compassion. A decolonizing politics, I would argue, is therefore to know and discipline oneself, to identify with the Other as one's other self, and to explore the meaning of both the Other's difference and identity to the self. Recognition of the abiding essential nature of humanity and of life within each of us will continue to produce a unifying, coalitionary, respectful struggle for peace and well-being for us as individuals and as interdependent beings. Decolonization is thus, inevitably, the struggle against dehumanization of oneself and the Other and the commitment to institutionalize what is just toward the Other.

Notes

1. *Women of color* is a term that appears widely in the feminist writings of African American and Chicana women of the late 1960s and '70s. In 1981, the concept was widely used in an important collection of writings that included African American, Asian American, Chicana, Native American, and other Latina women: *This Bridge Called My Back: Writings by Radical Women of Color*, edited by Gloria E. Anzaldúa and Cherríe Moraga (originally published by Boston's Persephone Press, followed by Kitchen Table Press [New York] in 1983, and then in an expanded twentieth anniversary edition by Third Woman Press, Berkeley, in 2002). The concept underscores the similarity of conditions shared globally by women of the so-called Third World and the historically oppressed,

negatively racialized "minority" women of the United States, given that contemporary racialized and gender inequity is the product of European and Euro-American patriarchal and heteronormative economic, political, and thereby cultural imperialism and neocolonialism. The use of this ethnic-descent umbrella term signals a widespread coalitionary consciousness aimed at undermining the Darwinist pecking order logic of racism that places African-diasporic women at the bottom of a pseudoscientific (i.e., a false) "racial" ladder with Anglo-Germanic-European-descended peoples at the top and that renders Native Americans, particularly women, highly invisible, as if in fact, successfully exterminated by the colonization of the Americas. Within such a self-serving, fictive, and yet widespread logic, Latina, Asian, and Middle Eastern women are left to negotiate racism according to how close or far they are from a "white" and upper-class ideal, though understood to be supposedly inferior as well. As I have pointed out elsewhere (Pérez 2007), the concept is imperfect, however, in that it continues to place the burden of racialization and its effects on non-European or mixed race women who cannot pass as white, as if "white" itself were not a racialization, though one carrying a positive, but equally unearned and unscientific, connotation. All people in the Westernized world remain racialized today, a legacy of racist intellectuals in a variety of disciplines that together fabricated a rationalization in philosophy, the sciences, history, the social sciences, and the humanities, and even theology to justify European imperialism and Eurocentrism in the invasion, genocide, colonization, and economic neocolonization of other peoples as well as to justify antisemitism. For a careful study of the development of the modern concept of "race," see Ivan Hannaford's *Race: The History of an Idea in the West* (1996). Note that Hannaford distinguishes between the formative caste, blood purity, and what he calls the premodern race ethnocentric ideas of the era of the colonial invasions of the Americas and the still widespread understanding of this concept. Following Hannah Arendt and others, Hannaford notes that modern usage dates to various late eighteenth-century developments that allowed for the intellectually flawed construction of race as "fact" now borne out biologically and historically, as a consequence of evolutionary human inferiority and superiority. Thus, the cultural differences of nations, and their present roles within European and US imperialism, were now explained from philosophy and theology to the sciences, social sciences, and humanities as the natural order or racial superiority of the Anglo-Germanic and Aryan over all others.

2. Sandoval (2000) explains:

> If, as Jameson argues, the formerly centered and legitimated bourgeois citizen-subject of the first world (once anchored in a secure haven of self) is set adrift under the imperatives of late-capitalist cultural conditions, if such citizen-subjects have become anchorless, disoriented, incapable of mapping their relative positions inside multinational capitalism, lost in the reverberating endings of colonial expansionism, and if Jameson has traced well the psychic pathologies brought about in first-world subjectivity under the domination of neocolonial drives in which the subject must face the very "limits of figuration," then the first world subject enters the kind of psychic terrain formerly inhabited by the queer, the subaltern, the marginalized. So too, not only are "psychopathologies," but also the survival skills, theories, methods, and the utopian visions of the marginal made, not just useful but imperative to all citizen-subjects, who must recognize this other truth of postmodernism—another architectural model for oppositional consciousness in the postmodern world (26).

My thanks to Maya Elisa Pérez Strohmeier and Diana Hernández for their research assistance.

3. Writing before the "housing bubble" burst, but nevertheless predicting it, Professor of Economics Ravi Batra (2007) noted:

> Today, as many as 39 million Americans subsist below the poverty line, compared to just 23 million in 1973, which as the first year since World War II in which the ranks of the poor grew.... The destitute grow by a million a year in the United States. Others are burdened by a heavy debt load. The national savings rate is a stunning zero percent, if not negative;

Americans are consuming their home equity to maintain their lifestyle, as if there is no tomorrow. The concentration of wealth is at an all-time high, with just one percent of families owning more than 40 percent of the collective worth. (10)

4. As Korten (2009, 52) explains, "In 2007 alone, the fifty highest paid private investment managers walked away with an average $588 million each in annual compensation—19,000 times as much as an average worker earns. The top five each took home more than $1.5 billion." And furthermore, "from 1980 to 2005, the highest earning 1 percent of the U.S. population increased its share of taxable income from 9 percent to 19 percent. Most of that gain went to the top tenth of 1 percent and came from the bottom 90 percent" (53). Moreover, "the financial assets of the richest 1 percent of Americans totaled $16.8 trillion. This represents what they understand to be their rightful claim against the world's real wealth. To put that in perspective, the estimated 2007 U.S. gross domestic product was $13.8 trillion, and the total federal government expenditures that fiscal year were $2.7 trillion" (67). And finally, "the Government Accountability Office in August 2008 reported that behind the corporate cries of pain over the tax burdens they are forced to bear is a startling truth: Between 1998 and 2005, two-thirds of U.S. corporation paid no U.S. income taxes—zip. Tax loopholes, combined with trillions of dollars of direct subsidies and externalized social and environmental costs, add up to quite a sum" (127).

5. For a summary of US and global history and conditions, see Estelle B. Freedman's *No Turning Back: The History of Feminism and the Future of Women* (2002). Freedman reports that women in the US account for more than 50 percent of the labor force but that in 2000, women only earned seventy-five cents for every dollar earned by men. This is not much progress since 1900, when women earned fifty cents to every dollar earned by men (162). In 2000, 60 percent of all US women were "gainfully employed" (150). In 1995, 61 percent of all married women were in the labor force, and two-thirds of these were mothers of children under the age of two (151). These figures do not include the huge informal, undocumented, or illegal profits produced by women. Note that "in the United States, African American women long exceeded all other groups of female wage laborers, with twice the overall rate for women in 1900.... By 1999, 64 percent of black women were in the workforce, compared to 60 percent white women" (151). Freedman points out not only that the labor market itself is gendered but that historically, once women enter a field, such as teaching or particular branches of medicine, it becomes feminized and suffers the effects of gender inequity in compensation and prestige of virtually all of women's labor. Race and ethnicity, she confirms, further the inequities: "In developed economies almost 80 percent of women workers can be found in service sector jobs, such as teachers, health care workers, or waitresses, with about 15 percent in industry and the remainder in agriculture. Throughout the world, women wage earners dominate as child care workers, nurses, and primary-school teachers.... Women from minority groups cluster in domestic service or factory jobs, while women from dominant groups have greater options as professionals and managers" (161).

6. Mirta Vidal ([1971] 2014, 23), for example, wrote in 1971: "Raza women suffer a triple form of oppression: as members of an oppressed nationality, as workers, and as women." As to the relationship between colonization and gender, Vidal observed, "The inferior role of women in society does not date back to the beginning of time. In fact, before the Europeans came to this part of the world women enjoyed a high position of equality with men. The submission of women, along with institutions such as the church and the patriarchy, was imported by the European colonizers and remains to this day part of Anglo society. Machismo—which, as it is commonly used, translates in English into male chauvinism—is the one thing, if any [i.e., rather than feminism], which should be labeled an 'Anglo thing'" (23).

In 1972, Elizabeth "Betita" Martínez ([1972] 2014, 32) wrote, "The Chicana suffers from a triple oppression. She is oppressed by the forces of racism, imperialism, and sexism. This can be said of all non-white women in the United States." Martínez recognizes different Chicana responses to sexism and racism according to working- or middle-class background. Adaljiza Sosa Riddell expressed the Chicana feminist theory that Chicano resistance to feminism as a culturally foreign or "white" new colonizing influence was erroneous since it was instead European patriarchy and its gender roles that were the actual legacy of colonialism and that evidence showed that greater gender flexibility existed in native cultures before colonization.

> Chicanos are induced to define and describe their very being and existence in terms of external constraints and conditions imposed upon them by their colonizers or neo-colonizers. Thus, what we have is the acceptance of certain externally-imposed stereotypes about Chicanas acting as a restraint upon actions or suggestions for changes among Chicanas; actions and changes which would not conform to the stereotypes or act to destroy the stereotypes.... Many of the stereotypes have been equated with aspects of Mexican-Chicano culture these attitudes are echoed by Chicanos themselves.... Thus, to talk about change becomes a very real threat to Chicanos who wish to retain what they have defined as their culture. The stereotypes, the acceptance of stereotypes, and the defensive postures adopted by "culturalists" become the problems for Chicanos striving to bring about some changes, rather than the problems being defined as they more adequately could be, in terms of external forces.... Chicanas (and Chicanos) are asking for something other than parity. The end which is desired by Chicanas is the restoration of control over a way of life, a culture, an existence. For a Chicana to break with this goal is to break with her past, her present, and her people. For this reason, the concerns expressed by Chicanas for their own needs within the Movimiento cannot be considered a threat to the unity of the Movimiento itself. (Sosa Riddell [1974] 2014, 93–94)

7. I presented the idea of "eros ideologies" at the 2005 Decolonial Turn conference at the University of California, Berkeley, organized by Nelson Maldonado-Torres and other colleagues in the Department of Ethnic Studies, in dialogue with Chela Sandoval's (2000, 183) idea of the social "physics of love" of US women of color writers in her *Methodology of the Oppressed*. That writing and other related ones are part of my book, *Eros Ideologies: Writing on Art, Spirituality, and the Decolonial* (Pérez 2019).

8. Trexler (1995) writes:

> Tribal customs like that of the berdache have often been lost. But the significant question is through what process they were lost. The answer, at least in part, is that martial Europeans could not tolerate the notion of "womanized" males as an institutionalized part of successful, even imperial societies. When the mestizo Garcilaso, in his telling phrase sought to outdo even the Romans by claiming that "there was no more manly people, or prouder of it, among all the pagans, than the Incas, nor any who so scorned feminine pursuits," he revealed that, at the very beginning of the colonial period, male natives and mestizos recognized that they would have to deny their female side, so to speak, a central part of their human self-definition, if they were ever to be able to forget their conquest and claim their (illusory) equality with their oppressors. (155)

9. Trexler (1995, 167) makes the important point that to the Europeans, arguments regarding civilization and barbarism with respect to colonial life were also understood in sexual terms, even among those "sympathetic to the Amerindians" and that "not a single source even hinted that homosexual comportment might be other than evil. Fundamentally, all 'sodomy' was viewed as a sin and most sodomy as evidence of barbarism."

10. Consider María Lugones (2003, 86): "We are fully dependent on each other for the possibility of being understood and without this understanding we are not intelligible, we do not make sense, we are not solid, visible, integrated; we are lacking. So traveling to each other's 'worlds' would enable us to *be* through loving each other."

11. For interviews with prominent proponents of nonviolent social and environmental justice (the Dalai Lama, Aung San Suu Kyi, Oscar Arias, Maha Ghosananda, Thich Quang Do, and Dr. Jane Goodall), see Hunt 2002.

12. Lugones (2003, 79), quoting Marilyn Frye, reflects on the failure of mainstream or white feminists to care about women of color feminists and on how they instead take women of color for granted and as less than fully human: "To love women is, at least in part, to perceive them with loving eyes. 'The loving eye is a contrary of the arrogant eye.'"

13. The concept of "In'Laketch" is cited by Luis Valdez ([1972] 1990) in "Pensamiento Serpentino." Valdez's Maya teachings were received by him through the oral and written knowledge of Maya scholar Domingo Martínez Paredes, according to Yolanda Broyles-Gonzales (1994, 93). Compare this concept to Thich Nhat Hanh's (2006, 165) exposition of Buddhist principles: "Concepts like self and other, inside and outside, are the result of double grasping. In Buddhist practice, not only is low self-esteem an illness, but high self-esteem is also an illness, and thinking that you are the equal to someone else is an illness as well. Why? Because all three of these ideas are based on the notion that you are separate from the other."

References

Anzaldúa, Gloria. 1987. *Borderlands/La Frontera: The New Mestiza*. San Francisco: Aunt Lute Books.

Anzaldúa, Gloria, and Cherríe Moraga, eds. (1981) 2002. *This Bridge Called My Back: Writings by Radical Women of Color*. Expanded and revised 3rd ed. Berkeley: Third Woman Press.

Barthes, Roland. 1978. *A Lover's Discourse: Fragments*. Translated by Richard Howard. New York: Hill and Wang.

Batra, Ravi. 2007. *The New Golden Age: A Revolution against Political Corruption and Economic Chaos*. New York: Palgrave Macmillan.

Broyles-Gonzales, Yolanda. 1994. *El Teatro Campesino: Theater in the Chicano Movement*. Austin: University of Texas Press.

Conner, Randy, and David Sparks. 2004. *Queering Creole Spiritual Traditions: Lesbian, Gay, Bisexual, and Transgender Participation in African Inspired Traditions in the Americas*. New York: Routledge.

Deshmukh, Anshool. 2021. "This Simple Chart Reveals the Distribution of Global Wealth." Visual Capitalist, September 20, 2021. https://www.visualcapitalist.com/distribution-of-global-wealth-chart/.

DiPietro, P. J. 2025. *Sideways Selves. Travesti and Jotería Struggles Across the Americas*. Durham, NC: Duke University Press.

Fanon, Frantz. (1952) 1967. *Black Skin, White Masks*. Translated by Charles Lam Markmann. New York: Grove Press.

Freedman, Estelle B. 2002. *No Turning Back: The History of Feminism and the Future of Women*. New York: Ballantine Books.

Gandhi, Mohandas K. 2004. *Mohandas Gandhi: Essential Writings*. Selected with an introduction by John Dear. Maryknoll, NY: Orbis Books.

Griffin, Paul R. 1999. *Seeds of Racism in the Soul of America*. Cleveland, OH: Pilgrim Press.

Hanh, Thich Nhat. 2006. *Understanding Our Mind*. Berkeley: Parallax Press.

Hannaford, Ivan. 1996. *Race: The History of an Idea in the West*. Washington, DC: Woodrow Wilson Center Press; Baltimore: Johns Hopkins University Press.

Hewlett, Sylvia Ann, Laura Sherbin, and Karen Sumberg. 2009. "How Gen Y & Boomers Will Reshape Your Agenda." *Harvard Business Review*, July 1, 2009. https://hbr.org/2009/07/how-gen-y-boomers-will-reshape-your-agenda.

Hunt, Scott A. 2002. *The Future of Peace: On the Front Lines with the World's Great Peacemakers*. San Francisco: Harper.

Jameson, Frederic. 1984. "Postmodernism, or the Cultural Logic of Late Capitalism." *New Left Review* 146:53–92.

Korten, David C. 2009. *Agenda for a New Economy: From Phantom Wealth to Real Wealth*. San Francisco: Berrett-Koehler.

Levinas, Emmanuel. (1991) 2000. *Entre-Nous: On Thinking-of-the-Other*. Translated by Michael B. Smith and Barbara Harshav. New York: Columbia University Press.

Lorde, Audre. 1984. "Uses of the Erotic: The Erotic as Power." In *Sister Outsider: Essays and Speeches*, 53–59. Berkeley: Crossing Press.

Lugones, María. 2003. *Pilgrimages / Peregrinajes: Theorizing Coalition Against Multiple Oppressions*. Oxford: Rowman & Littlefield Publishers, Inc.

———. 2007. "Heterosexualism and the Colonial / Modern Gender System." *Hypatia* 22 (1): 186–209.

"Mahatma Gandhi: Pilgrim of Peace." 2000. *Biography*. A & E Television Networks.

Martínez, Elizabeth "Betita." (1972) 2014. "La Chicana." In *Chicana Feminist Thought: The Basic Historical Writings*, edited by Alma M. García, 32–34. New York: Routledge.

Mille, Richard. 2022. "Forbes Billionaires 2022: The Richest People in the World." *Forbes*. https://www.forbes.com/billionaires/.

Miller, Alice. 1985. *For Your Own Good. Hidden Cruelty in Child-Rearing and the Roots of Violence*. New York: Farrar, Straus and Giroux.

Nagler, Michael N. 2001. *Is There No Other Way? The Search for a Nonviolent Future*. Berkeley: Berkeley Hills Books.

Pérez, Laura E. 2007. *Chicana Art: The Politics of Spiritual and Aesthetic Altarities*. Durham, NC: Duke University Press.

———. 2019. *Eros Ideologies: Writings on Art, Spirituality, and the Decolonial*. Durham, NC: Duke University Press.

Quijano, Aníbal. 1992. "Colonialidad y modernidad/racionalidad." *Perú Indígena* 13 (29): 11–20.

Roscoe, Will. 2000. *Changing Ones: Third and Fourth Genders in Native North America*. New York: Palgrave Macmillan.

Sandoval, Chela. 2000. *Methodology of the Oppressed*. Minneapolis: University of Minnesota Press.

Sosa Riddell, Adaljiza. (1974) 2014. "Chicanas and El Movimiento." In *Chicana Feminist Thought: The Basic Historical Writings*, edited by Alma M. García, 92–94. New York: Routledge.

Trexler, Richard C. 1995. *Sex and Conquest: Gendered Violence, Political Order, and the European Conquest of the Americas*. Ithaca, NY: Cornell University Press.

Valdez, Luis. (1972) 1990. *Early Works: Actos, Bernabé, and Pensamiento Serpentino*. Houston, TX: Arte Público Press.

Vidal, Mirta. (1971) 2014. "New Voice of La Raza: Chicanas Speak Out." In *Chicana Feminist Thought: The Basic Historical Writings*, edited by Alma M. García, 21–23. New York: Routledge.

Laura E. Pérez is Professor of Chicanx Latinx and Ethnic Studies, University of California, Berkeley. She is author of *Chicana Art: The Politics of Spiritual and Aesthetic Altarities* (2007), *Eros Ideologies: Writings on Art, Spirituality, and the Decolonial* (2019), and coeditor of *Consuelo Jimenez Underwood: Art, Weaving, Vision* (2022) and *Amalia Mesa-Bains: Archaeology of Memory* (2023).

PART III

METHODS AND MAPS TOWARD RESISTANT MEANINGS

6
FEMINIST ADVOCACY RESEARCH, RELATIONALITY, AND THE COLONIALITY OF KNOWLEDGE

Sarah Lucia Hoagland

EVERY FEW YEARS at the Michigan Womyn's [sic] Music Festival, a womon [sic] with training in one of the disciplines, such as sociology, biology, anthropology, psychology, and so on deposits a questionnaire near the One World area or hands it out on the road. It will be a study designed by an academic or a field researcher who is excited to be doing research in an area relevant to her life. The questionnaire's purpose will be to elicit information from a marginalized group—for example, lesbians, or survivors of rape—among the festivalgoers. The researcher will be excited mostly because her company is finally interested in demographics for her community or her academic dissertation director has agreed to allow her to research something important to her life. Most often, she, herself, will be a member of the marginalized group: a lesbian researching lesbian sexuality or a survivor researching strategies of survivors. Upon asking why they are doing this research, I have received enthusiastic responses describing opportunities to gain information about marginalized populations that could ultimately help them—lead doctors toward better health practices, lead policy makers to more accurate and helpful policies.

Typically such researchers understand themselves to be pursuing a liberatory agenda as, in some sense, advocates for a marginalized population, conducting research designed to affect social policy or public health practices by pursuing, developing, and then promoting understanding of specifics about a population whose needs have not been served by existing practice and policy designed by and for the center. Advocacy researchers are taking advantage of their institutional authorization to help make a marginalized population a subject of knowing.

The practice of advocacy, of course, is inimical to positivist understandings of science. Promoting such practice is to reject impartiality as methodologically necessary for objectivity. Indeed, Western feminist epistemology began by arguing that a politicized agenda can be more objective than a self-declared impartial and apolitical agenda (Harding 1986). Moreover, as Lorraine Code (1993) argues, knowing subjects need to be examined with the same degree of care as are the subjects of knowledge that the knowing subject places under scrutiny (Code 1993) or surveillance (Foucault [1975] 1979). Subsequently many feminist theorists have further complicated and developed the concept of objectivity by taking up intersections between epistemology, ethics, and power (e.g., Harding 1993; Haraway 1991). The move toward advocacy research complicates objectivity even further by positioning a researcher to intervene and take up a cause on behalf of her subjects.

I am interested in the concept of advocacy research because it is a practice of knowledge acquisition going beyond "pure" detached observation in order to do something in relation to subjects of knowledge, such as correct standard knowledge in order to help a marginalized population in some way or change public policy or promote social justice for a population that has been kept marginalized through disciplinary power/knowledge projects. Central to this project is acknowledging subjects of knowing—that is, the objects of the research—as themselves actually being knowing subjects.

At issue, for example, as Susan Brison (2003) argues, is that the women who have critical experiences are rarely part of the discourse about them. As Luke Cole and Sheila Foster (2001, 13) note, "grassroots groups inevitably run up against a system of environmental decision making that was not designed with their full participation in mind." Or as Patricia Hill Collins (2004, 121) shows, as outsiders to academic disciplining, Black women lack authority to challenge its axioms. Advocacy research addresses subjects of knowing, of research, not as data but as knowing subjects, subjects who themselves have knowledge.

My primary interest in all this involves a question inspired by Michael Horswell's (2005) work: What happens when two who are marginalized meet in epistemic engagement? My interest primarily concerns white women/feminists engaging women of color as I am a white woman/feminist. However, this is not about essentialized natures; it is about institutional framings, beginning with sixteenth-century Spanish conquest of "América." I'm focusing on advocacy to engage those who are committed to changing dominant relationalities. And I am writing as a white lesbian who has not wanted to be made transparent to mainstream thought, who has watched gay and lesbian politics morph into marriage and military, a dissolution something like the morphing of civil rights into busing or radical feminism into equal rights.

In what follows, I raise questions inviting self-reflection and collective discussion. They are questions designed to tease out and revisit problems rather than offer the reader solutions. Sometimes it is holding the frustrations and failures, rather than grasping for a fix, that enables letting go of the normal and provides the possibility for creative movement. This is written from within the belly of the beast and is a journey without a map in advance or a final destination. It is, in Édouard Glissant's ([1990] 1997) framing, a wandering with a sacred mission, a mission of exploring a poetics of relation.

I. Advocacy Researchers

> After numerous conversations with only myself to serve as company, I find the desire for others to hear and receive me as nothing short of necessity. . . . But I have found that ears are not accustomed. They do not know how to listen, or even what to listen for.
> —Northeastern student, fall of 2006

Taking up Lorraine Code's suggestion of examining the knower, I first turn to the question: How is a researcher competent to hear an Other in order to be an advocate?

To be an advocate, a researcher will engage in epistemic shifts, exit the hegemonic normative paradigm in some respects and become critically conscious of the broader structural framing of people and communities. As with the women I've encountered at the Michigan Womyn's Music Festival, an advocacy researcher may have special access to a marginalized and underrepresented group. Her location may afford her epistemic privilege not available to others. Yet privileged access is no guarantee of competency. For while a particular marginalized population may have been rendered invisible by hegemonic discourse in key ways, it has likely also been rendered highly visible as a trope justifying marginalizing policies and informing our everyday perceptions and reactions. The trope of "welfare queens" comes to mind as do the tropes of "street gang," "the homeless," and "illegal aliens," not to mention "battered women" or "virgin/whore." There are many tropes bolstering hegemony. Even as members of marginalized communities, we are not immune to internalizing valuations justifying the status quo.

A second concern emerges. An advocate researcher will re-cognize that some have been dismissed or erased or covered over by other researchers using her discipline's tools. Still, while an advocate may have insider understanding and access because of her membership in the marginalized community, she is also a member of and an apprentice to her academic or commercial community. Her situatedness in that academic or professional community includes being disciplined and embedded in a discourse that in one way or another rationalizes, often by means of naturalizing, that very marginalization. That is to say, having the methodological tools of her discipline is also not sufficient to guarantee competency to hear an Other. Her training includes methodological strategies that direct her focus, her assumptions, her questions, her understanding in significant ways, and that, in some respects as an advocate, she is in tension with, placing her in a complicated position. As Beverley Skeggs (1997, 18) notes, "Researchers are positioned within institutions, by history, by disciplinary practices, by dominant paradigms, in theoretical fashions, in genre style, by funding arrangements, and so on. All these positionings impact upon what research we do, when and how we do it." Nancy Potter (2002) details how institutions shape us into untrustworthy beings. Engaging in research directed by questions that make sense in hegemonic scientific or policy discourse, even if challenging previous findings in key respects, also affirms the discourse in other respects.

A third matter involves a researcher's subjects. Those doing advocacy research recognize that there are some who are unable to advocate for themselves or are dismissed as knowers in their self-advocacy. But there are other subjects who won't bother to continue to engage in what to them is fruitless and demoralizing appeals that they know are stoically unheard or disciplinarily restructured.[1] Moreover, there are subjects who play to a researcher's ignorance and assumptions for a variety of reasons. Many hold disdain for the conceptual framework in which the researcher is embedded and refuse to make sense within it, refuse its sense making.

These concerns position us to think about what decolonial theorists have named the coloniality of knowledge.

II. Aspects of the Coloniality of Knowledge

When a researcher, as an authorized, knowing subject and a member of or with a pledge to a disciplined community, approaches the subject (object) of knowing, what discursive production does she bring? I want to take up and take in a number of things that have been offered about Western knowledge practices in relation to Anglo-European colonial practices developed over the past five hundred years. For in critical ways, as these practices authorize a researcher, they undermine her competency to hear an Other.

For example, Chandra Mohanty investigated work by a number of academic feminists and argued that this work has the *effect* of discursive colonization. She is particularly concerned with the Western feminist use of an ahistorical, acontextual, universal, analytic category of "woman" (Mohanty 1991). While doing what might be called advocacy research, the Western researchers analyze their non-Western subjects through the Western category of "woman," a category that is not a simple denotation (e.g., Hoagland 2010a). By so doing, Western feminists are interpellating their subjects into Western semiotics and practices, reading them through Western categories and values, and thereby delineating the possibilities and limitations the researcher has access to or can imagine in her advocacy. Many Western feminist researchers are reading their subjects through cultural productions that can only see the subjects as inferior to Western standards of "woman" and hence in need of enlightened rescue. Western feminist practice thereby becomes a version of Gayatri Spivak's (1994, 92–93) observation of "white [wo]men saving brown women from brown men," utilizing white men's colonial constructions to cover/clothe them. And Mohanty points out that this discursive colonization can also be enacted by Third World women theorists.

In other words, there is a problem if the question taken up, How can a subject of knowing be acknowledged by discourse as a knowing subject? is actually the question, How can a subject of Western research be acknowledged *within Western discourse* as a knowing subject?

That is, discursive colonization, the coloniality of knowledge, involves Anglo-Eurocentric practices whereby the only discourse for articulating Third World women's lives is a norming and normative Anglo-European one. This is a first *aspect* of the Coloniality of Knowledge.

Advocacy researchers eschew positivist values of impartiality and disengagement. This is critical. Nevertheless, what positions a researcher to hear the voice of the Other without translating, interpellating, it into colonizing productions? The respons-ability I'm concerned with is not the obligation to respond but the *ability* to respond, an ability to be open to hearing things unfamiliar, things that will challenge normalcy, even one's place in its reproduction. This is a virtue, an Aristotelian-type skill that one develops only over time and through a practice of engagement.

The difficulty of going against the grain, even by those similarly positioned in relation to the center, is highlighted by Susan Brison's (2003, 9) description of the massive denial of her attempted murder, which "takes the shape of attempts to explain the assault in ways that leave the observer's worldview unscathed." When embarking on an advocacy project, does a researcher, a knowing subject, consider that the process of engagement could undermine the researcher's own values, her discursive authorization, indeed her worldview?

That is, When a knowing subject approaches the subject of knowing, what kind of engagement is she anticipating? What relation does she animate, perform? Does the knowing subject, the advocacy researcher, proceed as if the subjects, objects, of knowing are naively opening themselves to view? Does her approach include naive expectations about how the Other positions herself, does it include expectations of forthcoming sincerity, particularly if the researcher herself is a member of the community of the subjects of knowing? Is she presupposing, perhaps unwittingly, what Doris Sommer (1996, 132) characterizes as "artless confession, like the ones that characterize surveillance techniques," an "inquisitorial demand for knowable essences?" As Beverley Skeggs (1997, 19) notes, "During the research I was continually aware of the ease with which those researched can be constructed as objects of knowledge without agency or volition."

More interestingly, Does an advocate researcher recognize that the subject (object) of knowing is strategically positioning herself in critical ways with respect to authority, that is, with respect to the knowing subject, to the researcher advocate herself? In his book *Impossible Witnesses*, Dwight McBride analyzes rhetorical strategies used by several abolition activists/witnesses and formerly enslaved persons. Among other things, he draws our attention to the discursive terrain these activists witnessing slavery had to fit to be intelligible, the competency or lack thereof of the white abolitionists to hear the narratives, and the means by which formerly enslaved witnesses constructed their narratives to meet the nonenslaved white imaginary (McBride 2001).

How does the researcher/advocate develop her ability to move in what Mary Louise Pratt (1991, 34) calls Contact Zones, "social spaces where cultures meet, clash, and grapple with each other, often in contexts of highly asymmetrical relations of power such as colonialism, slavery, or their aftermaths as they are lived out in many parts of the world today"?

Western practitioners often dismiss the possibility of self-conscious address in the Other's self-presentation. Moreover, when forced to recognize this error, many call it lying. For in opening to an Other, we may find ourselves reflected back in ways that bring us face-to-face with our inheritance, the legacy that frames us, for example, our gendered racialized colonial legacy.

In a performance piece inspired in part by Franz Kafka and constructed for the five hundredth anniversary of the "discovery of America," Coco Fusco and Guillermo Gómez-Peña presented themselves as undiscovered Amerindians from a fictitious island, Guatinau, in the Gulf of Mexico, living in a golden cage for several days at different exhibition sites. They were parodying the "European sense of self that was constructed by constructing an Other," for example, as savage. One could say they were offering testimony about colonization. To their surprise they discovered, as white Western audiences mostly interpreted their work literally, that colonial subjectivity is alive and well (Fusco 1995, 37–38). Moreover, those white authorities not informed ahead of time and responding to the exhibit as if it were "real," when discovering their mistake, did not take the opportunity to reflect on the exposed colonial self; rather, like René Descartes, many chose to frame the situation as deception. Many, including museum officials, expressed outrage over being fooled, complaining that the performance should not have been staged in museums—for example, the Museum of Science and Industry in Chicago—but in art galleries; they protested it should not have been exhibited in places of fact, truth. But this was precisely Coco Fusco and Guillermo Gómez-Peña's point—to locate their performance in museums, which are themselves a main site of "historic and ongoing Western performances of The Other (deemed 'Truth')" (Fusco 1995).

The persisting desire to "look upon predictable forms of Otherness from a safe distance" is powerful enough to allow knowing subjects, disciplined researchers, to dismiss the possibility "of self-conscious irony in the Other's self-presentation" (Fusco 1995, 50). As Latin American theorist Aníbal Quijano articulates, the coloniality of knowledge, practices begun with the Spanish colonization of the Americas in the 1500s, made it "unthinkable to accept the idea that a knowing subject was possible beyond the subject of knowledge postulated by the very concept of rationality put in place by modern epistemology" (Mignolo 2000, 60, citing Quijano 1992, 442).

That is, the subject is approached only in terms of the concept of rationality put in place by modern epistemology. This is a second *aspect* of the Coloniality of Knowledge.[2]

The possibility of being played, of being conned, by one's subjects is a substantive fear of researchers (except when they understand their subjects to be dumb), because it is the ground on which the testimony of subjects is discounted by promoters (advocates) of objectivist methodologies to which advocate researchers can feel beholden. Significantly, this is the point at which hegemonic discourse actually acknowledges the agency, or active subjectivity (Lugones 2003, introduction, chap. 10), of research subjects in relation to the field of knowing. That is, the authorized knower ceases to be the only agent in the engagement when scientific methodology understands itself to be in danger of losing control of the research.

For example, Lorraine Code takes up Karen Messing's (1998) work in occupational health studies. Karen Messing carefully investigated many different workplace conditions, from poultry processors to bank tellers, in order to understand and work toward improving them. She challenged standard views that workplace problems that the women faced were the result of women's biology or psychology and showed, rather, that the problems stemmed from workplaces occupationally designed for men, which put many women and some men at a disadvantage (Code 2006, 52–54). In a footnote, Lorraine Code notes that the politics are complex: "When workers engage in activist projects to improve their circumstances, their activities tend to corroborate a suspicion that 'they will fake their symptoms to gain their point'" (54). That is, when workers act on their own behalf, they could manipulate the data and the researchers—a strategic con.

However, if one considers the discourse the workers must enter to be heard, including that of company doctors and lawyers, whose legal obligation is protecting the company, then faking symptoms is a critical epistemic strategy to address institutional indifference beyond company liability, indifference practiced toward the collective workforce and, in particular, toward the conditions they face. Indeed, in this case, lying facilitates the production of knowledge. In fact, as Mary Louise Pratt (1991, 36) notes, one encounters, among other things, parody, imaginary dialogue, denunciation, miscomprehension and incomprehension in contact zones (also see Stepan and Gilman 1993).

Significantly, academics are disciplinarily framed to consider the interpretation and packaging (i.e., manipulating) of information to be the province of the knowing subject, the researcher, but not of the subject of knowing, the one being researched. Because only the researcher advocate is understood to have, or to rightfully have, agency, those concerned with "lying" subjects don't consider the interaction between researcher and subject as a give-and-take relationship.[3]

While offering a great deal of information to her anthropologist/advocate Elisabeth Burgos-Debray, Rigoberta Menchú repeatedly declares there are secrets about her communities of Guatemalan Indians that even friendly anthropologists will never know (Menchú 1984, 247), challenging the terms of their relationship. Doris Sommer (1996, 135–36) suggests that in relation to white audiences, Rigoberta Menchú is exercising "the uncooperative control that turns a potentially humiliating scene of interrogation into an opportunity for self-authorization." Rigoberta Menchú is requesting advocacy, but that request does not authorize a researcher and advocate to make her into either a text to be studied or an object to be rescued (e.g., Menchú 1984, 244). She has not tacitly agreed to become an Other on whom agents of liberation can perform their *own* agency.

Research methodologies dictate that the only agents in the relation are presumed to be the knowing (authorized) subjects, and within authorizing institutions, theirs is the prerogative of interpretation and packaging of information. Western scientific practice thus positions the researcher as a judge of credibility and a gatekeeper for its authority. This is a third *aspect* of the Coloniality of Knowledge, a discursive enactment of colonial relations.

> A conversation of "us" with "us" about "them" is a conversation in which "them" is silenced. "Them" always stands on the other side of the hill, naked and speechless, barely present in its absence. (Trinh T. Minh-Ha, *Woman, Native, Other*, 1989)

But there are still further issues.

If an advocate researcher understands herself to be representing her subjects or her subjects' knowledges in key ways, what does that mean? How does she take what she has learned and make it intelligible to dominant logic, to knowledges that could not or would not recognize such understandings to begin with? In re-presenting a population to power, is she presuming modern Western ideals of transparency and translation, presumptions that drive the coloniality of knowledge? That is, what becomes of the Western knowing subject's critical ability to respond to her subjects of knowing when faced with going before power?

For example, in advocating to power, to what extent does encouraging authority to widen its gaze actually promote assimilation or genocide? As Édouard Glissant ([1990] 1997, 189) writes, "We have a right to opacity," to not being made to be transparent.

At times, one subjected may knowingly choose to address the dominant discourse as there may be no other option at the moment, but this is not without consequences. Dwight McBride argues that "in using the very terms of the institution of slavery to talk about these human beings as 'slaves,' 'Africans,' and later 'Negroes,' one supports and buttresses the idea that the slave, if not subhuman, is certainly not of the same class of people as free Europeans" (2001, 7; also see Fricker 2007, 169). Their interpellation frames their possibilities of meaning and engagement. Hence, the strategies developed in contact zones.

Moreover, while a practice of epistemological advocacy may recognize exclusion and work toward inclusion, *research* itself remains a problematic concept. Not everyone wants to be included. Maori theorist Linda Tuhiwai Smith (1999, 1) argues that research is "probably one of the dirtiest words in the indigenous world's vocabulary" and, for the colonized, is inextricably linked to European imperialism and colonialism. She further argues, "*Research is a site of struggle between interests and ways of knowing of the West and the interests and ways of resisting of the Other*" (1–2; emphasis mine). And she notes, "Reclaiming a voice in this context has also been about reclaiming, reconnecting and reordering those ways of knowing which were submerged, hidden or driven underground" (69). Reclaiming voice means maintaining a distinct ontology/cosmology/epistemology.

For example, Linda Tuhiwai Smith draws attention to the ontological move of framing a culture's practices in terms of individualism that capitalism requires. Individual rights drive reasoning within Western institutions such that Indigenous claims based on collective practices make no sense (Smith 1999). As Ashwani Peetush (2003a, 2003b) argues, within liberal discourse there is no reason to negotiate or even dialogue with members of a community on terms that demand cultural rights based on shared membership, for such people and practices are understood to be primitive—that is, prior to the evolution of Western society—and so in need of being developed, brought up to speed, civilized.

Reframing Indigenous claims to be intelligible within Western institutions is rewriting to the point of covering over Indigenous culture. Thus, such a subject of knowing, of research, will not be approached as a knowing subject on her own terms (since there are none worth pursuing outside Western understanding), and she falls short as a knowing subject on Western terms, is not "rational," does not operate with or accept individualism.

If an advocacy researcher represents an Other to power, what logic does she use in her re-presentation? Again, the skills I find critical are not those of transparency and translation into hegemonic meaning, for those skills strategically function to leave the dominant worldview unscathed.

Within Western intellectual practice, the coloniality of knowledge presumes commensurability with Western discourse and is a process of translating and rewriting other cultures, other knowledges, other ways of being into Western understanding (Dussel 1995; Mignolo 1995). This covering-over of Others' knowledges, not to mention a covering-over of culture, is a fourth *aspect* of the Coloniality of Knowledge.[4]

Noting that positivist research paradigms are framed by particular experiences (which until proven irrelevant in specific cases, remain the model for constructing normalcy and abnormalcy), Lorraine Code (2006, 198) is concerned about decentering those experiences, destabilizing those subjectivities: "The decentering that ecological thinking sets in motion is enacted in its refusal to continue silently participating in a philosophy tacitly derived solely if imperceptibly, from white, affluent, western, male experiences that generate hyperbolic autonomy ideals. It displaces 'man' from his central position in the world and in himself and disturbs the (often narcissistic) inwardness of autonomy in its self-transparency aspect." This project is critical.

Even within Western discourse, individual autonomy is an illusion. Our identities, indeed our subjectivities, are relational. If, for affluent white men, autonomy makes any sense at all, it is only because such men have a cadre of people taking care of things they need to have happen in order to carry out things they imagine they have autonomously conceived. The illusion of white male autonomy exists because there are enormous collectivities to back up the "powerful" (Lugones 2003, chap. 10; any speeches by Senator Elizabeth Warren). To decenter affluent white male experience, subjectivity, is to destroy it.[5]

But there is more to it. Latin American decolonial theorists have been making visible the internal relationship between Western modernity and Western colonialism, tracing the emergence of both to the conquest of the Americas and the control of the Atlantic. They note that there is no "post" to colonial modernism (e.g., Quijano 1992; Dussel 1995; Mignolo 1995, 2000). Although in many cases political independence has been achieved, the economic, political, social, and epistemic restructuring of cultures through the process of modern Western colonizing continues unchecked.

Aníbal Quijano argues that the individual differentiated ego is a phenomenon of modernity, yes, but modernity happened in relation to Others (e.g., the Mexica, Aztecs). There is an intersubjective dimension of the modern ego where Others have been reorganized economically, culturally, spiritually, linguistically, and socially through the praxis of colonization and designated inferior through the racialized codification of differences. These differences formed and were formed by modernity and replace the idea of "superior and inferior" that was justified through power and domination, reconceiving the idea as biological (Quijano 2000). This is a myth of Eurocentrism whereby Anglos/Americans/Europeans see history as beginning in a state of nature and culminating, through a linear, evolutionary, historical process, in the development of Anglo-European culture. "I think" is preceded by and formed by "I conquer" (Dussel 1995).

Thus, it is not just an individual consciousness that formed during modernity but an intersubjective one involving inferior, primitive Others about whom a Western subject has a proprietary relationship (Quijano 1992; Dussel 1995; Mignolo 1995). This is a fifth aspect of the Coloniality of Knowledge.

And this is precisely the subjectivity Coco Fusco and Guillermo Gómez-Peña encountered in reactions to their performance piece.

In other words, *it is not because we are scholars that we are positioned to develop knowledge of marginalized Others. It is because of how we are positioned in relation to marginalized Others that we are able to be scholars.*

III. Re-cognizing and Destabilizing Colonial Relationalities

Understanding that our subjectivities, indeed our sensitivities, have inherited colonial framings, I am specifically interested in how we meet in the construction and performance of knowledge, particularly in ways that keep us reading, approaching, and engaging others through colonial/modern hegemonic scripts. We are positioned in relation to each other through institutionally structured political identities that are not always or necessarily named but that are nevertheless enacted, political identities as created, structured, and enforced by the state (Mamdani 2001), for example, subjectivities, sensitivities, and experiences of a white feminist and an immigrant woman both gathering information on domestic violence against undocumented workers.

Thinking in terms of moving from margin to center (hooks 1984) has been a critical instrumental tool in challenging our subjectivities and sensitivities. And as a result of all the subsequent work that's gone on, I am interested in now shifting away from the margin/center binary as a focal point of understanding others, in particular with its directed focus on "the center," to our intersubjective work of re-cognizing, engaging, each other by inhabiting multiple centers, multiple worlds, of meaning.

But first to reiterate, white Western subjectivity is what it is only because of its relationship to Others, which, to maintain itself, it necessarily works to ignore. As women of color have been articulating for the duration of the women's movement, this is true of white women as well as of white men. And so what needs to be decentered in and for feminist work are not just white affluent men's experiences but also white affluent women's.

So we come back to earlier questions, but at a deeper level: When white feminists advocate on behalf of Others, what subjectivities are we performing/animating, what sensitivities are we drawing on, what relationality are we enacting? And what does resisting institutionalized framings entail at this point in time?

Heralding back to Chandra Mohanty's critique of Western feminists' use of an ahistorical, acontextual, universal, analytic category of "woman," María Lugones's work on the colonial/modern gender system enables us to think further about the coloniality of knowledge in relation to gender. In Western culture, there is a strict gender dimorphism enforced legally and medically.[6] The individual is white Man, and white women are for the reproduction of family and capital. Resisting this gender formation has been a significant locus of (white) feminist struggles. However, those not coming from Anglo-European colonizing heritage were never meant to assume white gender identities.

Thus, María Lugones argues, there is a light side and a dark side to the colonial/modern gender system. On the light side, bourgeois white men are the subjects, and white women are understood as unfit for anything except reproduction of family (race) and property. She writes, "Sexual purity and passivity are characteristics of white bourgeois females who reproduce the class and the colonial and racial standing of bourgeois white men. But equally important is the banning of white bourgeois women from the sphere of collective authority, from the production of knowledge, from most control over the means of production" (Lugones 2007, 206).

Outlining the construction of this modern Western bourgeois development of gender, Silvia Federici argues that witch hunts were terrorist acts against peasant women to wrest away control of production and restrict women's possibilities for survival. Witch trials were state-instituted ramifications against outspoken women, disappearing all kinds of possibilities that had existed for women, work that women performed in the public sphere, and restricting women to a man's house. Witch trials and the material changes in peasants' lives (such as the closing of the commons, the rendering of peasant men as vagrants) took out aggressive women, nagging wives, women who challenged state and male authority, women leaders of peasant revolts, women central to the development and protection of community. Not only was this process repressive, but it was also productive (in Foucault's sense), ultimately producing our modern bourgeois notion of femininity (someone who is passive, needing protection [and restriction], who is dependent on men [who are themselves—allegedly—independent]). And relationally, this involved the production of men as dominant, as both protectors and predators. So this was a reconstruction of gender for everyone of Western culture, a disciplining of both women and men (Federici 2004).

That is, the witch hunts were attacks not just on women but on peasant *communities* through the undermining of women's collective public authority. This restructuring along the lines of the feminine and masculine undermined the structure of the entire community, and women ceased to be a force in its construction and protection (Federici 2004). It is critical to understand the mechanisms of these gender constructions for white women, and there are excellent analyses of them in relation to white men (e.g., Daly 1978; Pateman 1988).

A related attack on community was central to the Anglo-European colonial project that began in 1492 with the Spanish. Relations among members of Indigenous communities under attack were violently disrupted and reconfigured by, among other means, the destruction of women's authority, women's sexual autonomy, and women's knowledges, thereby disrupting and undermining community cohesion and resistance (Lugones 2007). However, the resulting gender productions were critically different from those within Anglo-European communities.

Returning to María Lugones's analysis of the colonial/modern gender system, "the dark side of the gender system was and is thoroughly violent. We have begun to see the deep reduction of anamales, anafemales and third gender people from their ubiquitous participation in rituals, decision making and economics; their reduction to animality, to forced sex with white colonizers, to such deep labor exploitation that often people died working" (Lugones 2007, 206).[7] And there were those who had all sorts of skills and knowledges—for example, healers, curanderas, shamans—who needed to be destroyed (Lugones 2007).[8]

Critical for our purposes is that colonized subjects were not constructed in discourse as Anglo-European gendered subjects. Indeed, while those who Columbus, Cortés, and others encountered were sexed, as are cows and dogs, they were not gendered. At the very least, they were not understood to be human, treated as men and women (Lugones 2007). And nineteenth-century science happily naturalized these constructions.

Moreover, they persist today: as people are brought into Western culture, women of color are primarily relegated to nonproductive labor, such as being maids to white women, and are demonized when they stay home and take care of their own families. They are treated with all manner of brutality, including a lack of healthy working conditions in places such as sweatshops, violent medical practices like sterilization, and astounding abuses in immigration, all of which white feminism has treated as largely irrelevant to the direction and focus of feminist theory (Lugones 2007).[9]

Women of color are not expected to become white women and are not treated as (white) women. This means that white feminist analysis, while excellent in detailing sexism faced by (white) women, marginalizes women of color. The vast majority of white feminist analyses proceed from understandings of gender as produced in the light side. This is why it is critical to decenter affluent white women's experiences.

But there is more to consider, for the dark and light sides are interrelated intersubjectively. Practices of colonization produced a significant subject relationality between British or European women and colonized women that has not informed most white feminist analyses.

Jin Haritaworn (2008) argues that nineteenth-century white women gained voice and agency among white men by re-presenting, even advocating for, women from cultures colonized by the British and others. White women performed superiority over "Oriental women" and enacted their own agency by working to liberate "Oriental women" from "backward, patriarchal cultures."

Meyda Yeğenoğlu (1998) offers an eye-opening analysis of how nineteenth-century white women gained voice by becoming, in Derrida's terms, supplements to colonizing men. Taking up Lady Mary Montagu's "defense" of Turkish women in *Turkish Embassy Letters*, Yeğenoğlu analyzes how Lady Montagu positioned herself as a supplement to Western masculinist Orientalism, providing the one thing European men couldn't obtain: access to Turkish harems, to "the scene of 'stark naked' truth/essence of the other/woman" (90–91). In other words, gaining the trust of upper-class Turkish women and access to their spaces, one might say being an *advocate*, Lady Montagu gained her own voice and authority by informing on the Turkish women and writing about the very thing European men could not in Orientalist discourse, thereby completing the men's work (90–91; also see Hoagland 2010a).[10]

So I ask anew: What relationality is enacted when an advocate researcher re-presents her subjects or her subjects' knowledges and to what end?

While Western feminists have resisted the imposition of Western masculinism, it is also the case, as Jin Haritaworn and Meyda Yeğenoğlu show us, that the resulting production of the feminine has involved a colonial engagement in relation to Third World women while gaining voice and agency in a partnership with white men's institutional projects. This is how affluent white women are positioned, relationally, to enact our womanhood—gaining agency and voice, for example, by advocating for those in need. Indeed, Western women's agency is in part realized in a paternal/maternal enactment of relation to Third World women and marginalized Others. This relationality is what advocacy researchers, both female and male, are disciplinarily positioned to animate.

IV. An (Other) Epistemic Shift

While the practice of advocacy research involves an epistemic shift, challenging hegemonic logic and becoming critically conscious about elements of its constructions, boundaries, and exclusions, I am arguing for even more radical epistemic shifts. The questions I have been raising in this chapter are asking advocacy researchers and feminist theorists to examine and reexamine how we are produced in colonial relationalities enacted by re-presenting Others to power. Granted, the categories here are permeable, but the hegemonic institutionalization of them remains alive and well—for example, white Western women are marginalized in relation to white Western men and privileged in relation to Third World women. Working to destabilize this coloniality of knowledge is not about (contradictorily) embracing essentialized categories; it is about re-cognizing institutionalized trajectories and resulting relationalities in the aftermath of colonization and about developing competencies in engaging others in ways that destabilize these relationalities.

Several critics have asked that I differentiate advocacy from participant research, community-based research, or community service learning, yet often making this distinction simply pushes the problem back a step. As we seek knowledges that have been covered over by the coloniality of knowledge, our liberatory possibilities of engaging exist not through authorized forms of relation and institutional hierarchy but, rather, as we work to destabilize racialized and gendered colonial identities in the coalitional collectivity Lorraine Code is going for. And that is more likely to occur through radical activist participatory research, research that is by, for, and about the people involved and where the community is the owner of the knowledge. My thinking about this has been deeply informed by my decade-long participation in La Escuela Popular Norteña, a popular education school founded by María Lugones and Geoff Bryce.

As opposed to advocating for, what does it mean to think and act *with*? In radical activist participatory research, people who are the focus of the study, whose lives will be affected by it, participate in the design, development of methodologies, and the research itself and have control over it. The work utilizes forms of knowledge people have that are not recognized or are erased by standard social science such as storytelling, theater, drawing, popular knowledge, and so-called folk wisdom. The process and goals of the study are to empower people. Group discussions are used to design the project while academic research methods and "expert knowledge" are seen with distrust as they place those to be studied in a passive position and are driven by requirements of tenure and publishing. The knowledge gained needs to offer the people not only knowledge of their situation but knowledge of how to change it (Keating et al. 2006, summarizing Gaventa and Lewis 1991).[11]

While there is no pure place to engage others free of coloniality, radical activist participatory research offers possibilities for eschewing embeddedness in the coloniality of knowledge. Thus, what I am talking about is not the liberal trend emerging from the disciplines of being a participant-observer. As an approach to learning with and mobilizing with people, radical activist participatory research redirects knowledge to people's hands rather than making it or them a new object of study in the hands of a few whose interests are, by profession and by professing, distinct from their subjects of knowing.

One example comes from the Appalachian Participatory Education and Grassroots Development Project of the Highlander School, addressing rural poverty in the Appalachian region, poverty made worse by President Kennedy's War on Poverty.[12] Participatory research projects were designed by and for local communities in democratic participation, a markedly distinct shift from communities making themselves ready to receive and serve business. The work involved exploring and uncovering knowledge members had about the economy, including oral histories and community surveys and mappings; collecting information that might not be available through people's own work histories in order to share, gather, and build knowledge about the community; doing community economic analysis; and subsequently planning community development through participatory strategies. The project emphasized peoples' research and analysis and deemphasized expert knowledge. It was used to create change, empowering people to address economic issues and inequalities themselves, reversing dependence on external economic forces (Gaventa and Lewis 1991; Luttrell 1988).

What does it mean to think and act *with*? My concern remains, What happens when two who are marginalized meet in epistemic engagement?

Édouard Glissant ([1990] 1997) offers the notion of *donner-avec* in contrast to our concept of "understanding" as "grasping." Glissant's translator Betsy Wing translates this as "gives-on-and-with." In discussing the term, she mentions "generosity," an idea that helps me shift. But I couldn't figure out why she included "on," and then I thought of leaning *on* a table, "support." Students also talked of passing something *on*.[13] This understanding involves a poetics of relation. It involves networking, rhizomatic thinking, grassroots activism, traveling to unfamiliar specialities without translation. This is a step toward the coalitional collectivity Code is going for, toward the possibility of crossing borders without solidifying colonial relationality.

In responding to questions I constructed for my circle of lesbian interlocutors concerning how we maintain epistemic sanity in the midst of the logical illogicality that is US mainstream liberal discourse, Jackie Anderson countered, "I do feel that there are things clear to me that I don't understand why they aren't clear to others. *Not because I think I'm right, but because I can't engage when they don't get it.*" She gave as an example racialization in the United States: "For us, slavery is a genesis. For white people, it is another institution, an institution that is over so it is not something that comes up in any conversation between whites."[14] I was focused on how we lesbians maintain sanity given mainstream impositions and narratives, and so I was focused on the power/resistance dichotomy. Jackie responded in terms of we lesbians interacting and was focused on a subjective/intersubjective dynamic.

Her response opens the possibility of an (Other) epistemic shift of thinking differently about engagement. What if we develop our critical epistemic skills/virtues not to know, not in order to be *right* but in order to *engage* outside dominant constructions that cover over oppressing↔resisting subjectivities?

Jackie Anderson is talking about two logics operating that meet in US lesbian contact zones: on the one hand, a world where slavery is an institutional past that is over and is not a formative part of the everyday, and on the other, a world in which slavery's aftermath is alive and well and where it permeates the everyday, in the health care system, in the education system, in the criminal justice system, indeed, in all the institutions set in place in the United States through the two hundred years of affirmative action for whites that slavery created (e.g., Alexander 2010; DeGruy 2005).[15]

If we understand our epistemic, praxical tasks as ones of engaging rather than getting it right, and we are open to entering different logics, ones where our worldview may not remain unscathed, and we take up a practice of radical activist participatory epistemology, then many of the problems we've encountered may cease to be problems. The researcher is no longer a gatekeeper for Western scientific credibility and hence is capable of being "atheistic" with regard to the system (Dussel 1995). Nor does she have to, nor does she remain in control of the research since it is a collective, collaborative endeavor and she engages as a peer, not as an expert, though certainly she brings her knowledge and understanding to the group as information they all consider and collectively evaluate. She can recognize multiple levels of communication, some addressed to power, some not (Lugones 2006). Moreover, while lying may be part of the engagement, it does not undermine the knowing project. The workers in Karen Messing's study would (and obviously did) recognize that research is a struggle of knowledges as Linda Tuhiwai Smith informs us. Indeed, lying can be a strategy central to the production of knowledge, and playing academically trained researchers involved in radical activist participatory research can be central to complex communication, instilling epistemic humility. Critical re-search remains for and in the hands of the people it is about, and the group determines what information is passed on and what is not.

That is, a re-searcher ceases being simply a "she" and becomes also a "we" and can fertilize into an intentional community.

Returning to the researchers with whom I began this piece, rather than picking an issue recognizable to academic gatekeepers who have the authority to approve or disapprove proposed research, who frame it disciplinarily and who, despite advocacy goals, use it for purposes that fit within their worldview, I would like to see researchers engage lesbians or survivors to determine for their/ourselves what issues are of concern, working together to design research programs for lesbians' or survivors' needs, and help communities define and develop their own solutions. If, for example, someone is looking for data about survivors, is this for academic journals, where discourses of medicalization and criminalization of survivors ground intelligibility and remain in the purview of what is debatable? Alternatively, a participatory research group could develop a workshop booklet based on health information and survival strategies of survivors, to be handed out in shelters for participants to develop their own understandings and strategies and suggestions, to develop further possibilities, information, warnings, and strategies, particularly in communities of color where enforcement violence is prevalent (Bhattacharjee and Silliman 2002).[16]

Moreover, it is critical to move without the goal of rescue, of bringing those lost or left out into the fold. In working with girls who are prostituted,

Claudine O'Leary challenges institutions such as the Salvation Army, whose policies are based on "rescuing" or "saving" youth, which, among other things, regards adults as experts and the girls as damaged. She demonstrates that the rescue trope will always fail because it does not see the active subjectivity of the girls on the street—the competencies they've developed, the skills with which they negotiate their environments, the strategies of survival they develop (O'Leary 2006; also see Hoagland 2010b).

The skills we need are not skills of translation and representation to hegemony through empathy or political solidarity or developing "trust" but the complexity and flexibility of moving to and within distinct logics, worlds of meaning, particularly without trying to make them commensurable or translatable and without trying to keep our worldview unscathed. So the epistemic shift I'm interested in is not globalized, managerial, theorizing, but re-cognizing and working to transform colonial relationalities and subjectivities in their twentieth- and twenty-first-century imperialist forms, recognizing relationalities and subjectivities of oppressing↔resisting. It is about recognizing that we are formed interactively and interdependently through engagement.

So rather than thinking from a detached Cartesian epistemic methodology or a concretized and embedded standpoint methodology, both of which champion objectivity, we can engage through border thinking, from Gloria Anzaldúa (1987), informing Mignolo, thinking within the borderlands, the contact zones, moving toward uncertainty (Hoagland 2002), places where the imaginary of the world systems crack (Mignolo 2000). There isn't a map or a set of rules; there is only feeling one's way, *tanteando*, groping as one negotiates many centers, not just margins to *the* center.

A number of years ago, in my contemporary philosophy class, I was enjoying working on John Austin's performative utterances (*not* speech acts). My interest included thinking about ways to render particularly problematic performative utterances infelicitous. At one point, I suggested to a student, a middle-aged African American man, that he do his paper on Austin using the example of hate speech to explore the theory, for example, ways of creating conditions for infelicities. I was thinking he could take something he experienced and see how useful Austin's theory was for addressing it.

He thought about it, came back the next week, and said, "I don't want to."

Notes

1. For example, Schmule in Barbara Myerhoff's *Number Our Days* (1978), 191.
2. See, for example, the work of Rodolfo Kusch ([1970] 2010) or Trinh T. Minh-ha (1989) on Leslie Marmon Silko.

3. Or they see such actions on the part of a subject (object) of knowing non-relationally through the lens of Western individual self-interest.

4. To cover over is not necessarily to eradicate. For this reason, decolonial theorists are looking at palimpsestic traces in current practices (e.g., Marcos 2006; see also Mignolo 1995 on the work of Felipe Guaman Poma de Ayala).

5. Consider Frantz Fanon's ([1961] 2004) goal was not that the native resignify himself if that is understood to be the native adopting the colonialist's or settler's framework and speaking back, resignifying "native." His goal was to destroy both the native and the settler.

6. The dimorphism is promoted even in Western transsexual legal and medical theorizing.

7. "Anamales" and "anafemales" (anatomically male and anatomically female) are terms used by Oyèrónké Oyěwùmí (1997) distinguishing them from the modern Western gender binary imposed on Yoruba culture through colonization.

8. And yet which persist today (e.g., Marcos 2006). Hence, Linda Tuhiwai Smith's argument that research is a site of struggle (1999).

9. María Lugones also notes that there are many within colonizing cultures who are constructed in the locus between the dark and light sides and are also not treated as or understood to be fully men and women, among others: nonproductive laborers, lesbians and gays, transgendered people, working-class whites, and others. There is much work to be done here. (2003).

10. A number of feminist epistemologists focus on gaining the trust of their subjects as critical to epistemology. The work of Meyda Yeğenoğlu (1998), Linda Tuhiwai Smith (1999), Chandra Mohanty (1991), and others call that goal into question.

11. For a copy of the *Participatory Research* booklet produced by members of the Escuela Popular Norteña, contact Cricket Keating (cricketkeating@gmail.com), Laura DuMond Kerr (laura.concoraje@gmail.com), or Xhercis Méndez (masquara@gmail.com).

12. As Helen Lewis and John Gaventa explain, "Development was done to and for local communities, not by the communities themselves. Over time, the separation between the economic and the political, at least at the local level, meant that the economy was considered by most ordinary people to be something to be dependent upon, not acted upon. . . . This separation of people from development has been paralleled in the production and analysis about economic development. 'The Economy' has become something external to everyday experience, something to be defined and analyzed by experts" (Gaventa and Lewis 1991, 9).

13. An aside: this translation of *donner avec* is not the colonizing translation I am critiquing here.

14. Jackie Anderson, remarks made at an Institute of Lesbian Studies gathering, Chicago, Winter 2005.

15. These are distinct logics because each revolves around a different axis and is held in place by what surrounds it (Wittgenstein 1969, OC §152). While distinct, they aren't necessarily (completely) incommensurable. But they don't need to be completely incommensurable in order to be distinct logics, any more than Kuhn's ([1962] 1970) paradigms need to be (completely) incommensurable for his theory to work.

16. If getting a dissertation done is the goal, then do a study on white men and guns, for example. Again, I'm not talking about essentialized natures, I'm talking about institutional productions.

References

Alexander, Michelle. 2010. *The New Jim Crow: Mass Incarceration in the Age of Colorblindness*. New York: New Press.

Anzaldúa, Gloria. 1987. *Borderlands/La Frontera: The New Mestiza*. San Francisco: Aunt Lute Books.

Bhattacharjee, Anannya, and Jael Silliman, eds. 2002. *Policing the National Body: Sex, Race, Gender and Criminalization*. Cambridge, MA: South End Press.

Brison, Susan J. 2003. *Aftermath: Violence and the Remaking of a Self*. Princeton, NJ: Princeton University Press.

Code, Lorraine. 1993. "Taking Subjectivity into Account." In *Feminist Epistemologies*, edited by Linda Martín Alcoff and Elizabeth Potter, 15–48. New York: Routledge.

———. 2006. *Ecological Thinking: The Politics of Epistemic Location*. New York: Oxford University Press.

Cole, Luke W., and Sheila R. Foster. 2001. *From the Ground Up: Environmental Racism and the Rise of the Environmental Justice Movement*. Critical America. New York: New York University Press.

Collins, Patricia Hill. 2004. "Learning from the Outsider Within: The Sociological Significance of Black Feminist Thought." In *The Feminist Standpoint Theory Reader*, edited by Sandra Harding, 103–27. New York: Routledge.

Daly, Mary. 1978. *Gyn/Ecology: The Metaethics of Radical Feminism*. Boston: Beacon Press.

DeGruy, Joy. 2005. *Post Traumatic Slave Syndrome: America's Legacy of Enduring Injury and Healing*. New York: Uptone.

Dussel, Enrique. 1995. *The Invention of the Americas: Eclipse of the "Other" and the Myth of Modernity*. Translated by Michael D. Barber. New York: Continuum.

Fanon, Frantz. (1961) 2004. *The Wretched of the Earth*. Translated by Richard Philcox. New York: Grove Press.

Federici, Silvia. 2004. *Caliban and the Witch: Women, the Body, and Primitive Accumulation*. New York: Autonomedia.

Foucault, Michel. (1975) 1979. *Discipline and Punish: The Birth of the Prison*. Translated by Alan Sheridan. New York: Vintage.

Fricker, Miranda. 2007. *Epistemic Injustice: Power and the Ethics of Knowing*. Oxford: Oxford University Press.

Fusco, Coco. 1995. *English Is Broken Here: Notes on Cultural Fusion in the Americas*. New York: New Press.

Gaventa, John, and Helen Lewis. 1991. *Participatory Education and Grassroots Development: The Case of Rural Appalachia*. New Market, TN: Highlander Research and Education Center.

Glissant, Édouard. (1990) 1997. *Poetics of Relation*. Translated by Betsy Wing. Ann Arbor: University of Michigan Press.

Haraway, Donna J. 1991. *Simians, Cyborgs, and Women: The Reinvention of Nature*. New York: Routledge.

Harding, Sandra. 1986. *The Science Question in Feminism*. Ithaca, NY: Cornell University Press.

———, ed. 1993. *The Racial Economy of Science*. Bloomington: Indiana University Press.

Haritaworn, Jin. 2008. "Loyal Repetitions of the Nation: Gay Assimilation and the 'War on Terror.'" *Darkmatter* (online journal), May 2, 2008. http://web.archive.org/web/20180326151059/http://www.darkmatter101.org/site/2008/05/02/loyal-repetitions-of-the-nation-gay-assimilation-and-the-war-on-terror.

Hoagland, Sarah Lucia. 2002. "Making Mistakes, Rendering Nonsense, and Moving Toward Uncertainty." In *Feminist Interpretations of Ludwig Wittgenstein*, edited by Naomi Scheman and Peg O'Connor, 119–37. University Park: Pennsylvania State University Press.

———. 2010a. "Colonial Practices/Colonial Identities: All the Women Are Still White." In *The Center Must Not Hold: White Women Philosophers on the Whiteness of Philosophy*, edited by George Yancy, 227–44. Lanham, MD: Lexington Books.

———. 2010b. "Oaths." In *Handbook of Public Pedagogy: Education and Learning Beyond Schooling*, edited by Jennifer A. Sandlin, Brian D. Schultz, and Jake Burdick, 93–102. New York: Routledge.

hooks, bell. 1984. *Feminist Theory from Margin to Center*. Boston, MA: South End Press.

Horswell, Michael J. 2005. *Decolonizing the Sodomite: Queer Tropes of Sexuality in Colonial Andean Culture.* Austin: University of Texas Press.

Keating, Cricket, Laura DuMond Kerr, María Lugones, and Xhercis Méndez. 2006. *Participatory Research: With Examples of Participatory Research Projects in Appalachia.* Booklet. Valdez, NM: La Escuela Popular Norteña.

Kuhn, Thomas S. (1962) 1970. *The Structure of Scientific Revolution.* Chicago: University of Chicago Press.

Kusch, Rodolfo. (1970) 2010. *Indigenous and Popular Thinking in América.* Translated by Joshua M. Price and María Lugones. Durham, NC: Duke University Press.

Lugones, María. 2003. *Pilgrimages/Peregrinajes: Theorizing Coalition against Multiple Oppressions.* Lanham, MD: Rowman and Littlefield.

———. 2006. "On Complex Communication." *Hypatia* 21 (3): 75–85.

———. 2007. "Heterosexualism and the Colonial / Modern Gender System." *Hypatia* 22 (1): 186–209.

Luttrell, Wendy. 1988. *Claiming What Is Ours: An Economic Experience Workbook.* New Market, TN: Highlander Research Center.

Mamdani, Mahmood. 2001. *When Victims Become Killers: Colonialism, Nativism, and Genocide in Rwanda.* Princeton, NJ: Princeton University Press.

Marcos, Sylvia. 2006. *Taken from the Lips: Gender and Eros in Mesoamerican Religions.* Boston: Brill.

McBride, Dwight A. 2001. *Impossible Witnesses: Truth, Abolitionism, and Slave Testimony.* New York: New York University Press.

Menchú, Rigoberta. 1984. *I, Rigoberta Menchu: An Indian Woman in Guatemala.* Translated by Ann Wright. London: Verso.

Messing, Karen. 1998. *One-Eyed Science: Occupational Health and Women Workers.* Philadelphia: Temple University Press.

Mignolo, Walter D. 1995. *The Darker Side of the Renaissance.* Ann Arbor: University of Michigan Press.

———. 2000. *Local Histories/Global Designs: Coloniality, Subaltern Knowledges, and Border Thinking.* Princeton, NJ: Princeton University Press.

Minh-Ha, Trinh T. 1989. *Woman, Native, Other.* Bloomington: Indiana University Press.

Mohanty, Chandra Talpade. 1991. "Under Western Eyes: Feminist Scholarship and Colonial Discourses." In *Third World Women and the Politics of Feminism*, edited by Chandra Talpade Mohanty, Lourdes Torres, and Ann Russo, 51–80. Bloomington: Indiana University Press.

Myerhoff, Barbara. 1978. *Number Our Days.* New York: Dutton.

O'Leary, Claudine. 2006. "Rescue Is for Kittens: A Critical Analysis of the Rescue Philosophy and What Makes It Possible to Be Allies to Girls and Young Women in the Sex Trade." UWW (University without Walls) capstone paper, Northeastern Illinois University. http://www.youarepriceless.org.

Oyěwùmí, Oyèrónke. 1997. *The Invention of Women: Making an African Sense of Western Gender Discourses.* Minneapolis: University of Minnesota Press.

Pateman, Carole. 1988. *The Sexual Contract.* Stanford, CA: Stanford University Press.

Peetush, Ashwani Kumar. 2003a. "Kymlicka, Multiculturalism, and Non-Western Nations: The Problem with Liberalism." *Public Affairs Quarterly* 17 (4): 291–318.

———. 2003b. "Recognizing the Other Solitude: Aboriginal Views of the Land and Liberal Theories of Cultural Justice." *Ayaangwaamizin: The International Journal of Indigenous Philosophy* 3 (1): 55–88.

Potter, Nancy Nyquist. 2002. *How Can I Be Trusted? A Virtue Theory of Trustworthiness.* Lanham, MD: Rowman and Littlefield.

Pratt, Mary Louise. 1991. "Arts of the Contact Zone." *Profession* 33–40. https://www.jstor.org/stable/25595469

Quijano, Aníbal. 1992. "Colonialidad y Modernidad-Racionalidad." In *Los Conquistadores*, edited by H. Bonilla, 437–47. Bogotá: Tercer Mundo.

———. 2000. "Coloniality of Power, Eurocentrism, and Latin America." Translated by Michael Ennis. *Nepantla: Views from South* 1 (3): 533–80.

Skeggs, Beverley. 1997. *Formations of Class and Gender*. London: Sage.

Smith, Linda Tuhiwai. 1999. *Decolonizing Methodologies: Research and Indigenous Peoples*. London: Zed.

Sommer, Doris. 1996. "No Secrets." In *The Real Thing: Testimonial Discourse and Latin America*, edited by Georg M. Gugelberger, 130–58. Durham, NC: Duke University Press.

Spivak, Gayatri Chakravorty. 1994. "Can the Subaltern Speak?" In *Colonial Discourse and Post-Colonial Theory: A Reader*, edited by Patrick Williams and Laura Chrisman, 66–111. New York: Columbia University Press.

Stepan, Nancy Leys, and Sander L. Gilman. 1993. "Appropriating the Idioms of Science: The Rejection of Scientific Racism." In *The "Racial" Economy of Science: Toward a Democratic Future*, edited by Sandra Harding, 170–93. Bloomington: Indiana University Press.

Wittgenstein, Ludwig. 1969. *On Certainty*. Edited by G. E. M. Anscombe and G. H. von Wright. Translated by Dennis Paul and G. E. M. Anscombe. Oxford: Blackwell.

Yeğenoğlu, Meyda. 1998. *Colonial Fantasies: Towards a Feminist Reading of Orientalism*. Cambridge: Cambridge University Press.

Sarah Lucia Hoagland is a collective member of the Institute of Lesbian Studies in Chicago, has been a member of the Escuela Popular Norteña, and is a Bernard Brommel Distinguished Research Professor and Professor Emerita of Philosophy, Women's Studies, and Latino/Latin American Studies, Northeastern Illinois University. Her work has been about articulating conceptual coercion and coercive consensus that deny epistemic credibility to marginalized voices, re-cognizing resistance and sabotage reversed by dominant interpellation, and promoting the creation and maintenance of spaces, discursive and within communities, where nonhegemonic, nonnormative, nondominant sense exists and can thrive. She is author of *Lesbian Ethics: Toward New Value* (1988) and coeditor of *For Lesbians Only: a Separatist Anthology* (1988) and *Re-Reading the Canon: Feminist Interpretations of Mary Daly* (2000).

7

TOPOGRAPHIES OF FLESH

WOMEN, NONHUMAN ANIMALS, AND THE EMBODIMENT OF CONNECTION AND DIFFERENCE

Jennifer McWeeny

FROM A TWENTY-FIRST-CENTURY perspective, the attempt to specify a category called "women" seems misguided at best and straightforwardly imperialistic at worst. We are inevitably familiar with a number of feminist criticisms of this practice. On the one hand, there are practical considerations like the fact that for any property identified as common to all women (e.g., "biological mothers" or "subject to sexist discrimination"), we can readily find particular women who lack this property. On the other, there are the serious political concerns that this kind of ontological project invites the centering of privileged women to the detriment and erasure of others. Furthermore, even if we were able to elucidate the category "women," this does not mean that feminism would actually become inclusive and that existing injustices among women in the movement would cease.

Although these criticisms are justified, their force and pervasiveness have likely led to a diminution of ontological precision in feminist theory that is cause for concern. When ontological claims *are* made in present-day theorizing, they are usually left sufficiently vague so as to sidestep the question of how one woman is actually connected to or different from another, lest the theorizer be branded an essentialist or champion of homogeneity.[1] Refrains such as "subjectivity is relational," "identities are intersectional," "persons are embodied," or "moral imperatives are contextual" tell us that material relationships are at work, but they rarely go further to specify what kinds of entities partake in these relations, how these entities are connected to and different from one another, and how the materiality of these relations affects their participants. That the term *intersectionality* is variably used to refer to particular social locations *and* a kind of relationship between seemingly distinct oppressions such as sexism, racism, and classism is a case in point.[2] Such usage invites confusion as to whether intersectional analyses aim at describing a particular kind of being or whether they intend to give an account of oppression itself.[3]

Many theorists see the "open-endedness" and variability of concepts like intersectionality and relationality as a boon given the complexity of our contemporary world (see, e.g., K. Davis 2008). Although I see great value in this approach, I also believe that feminists have too hastily abandoned the ontological projects of specifying the *bodily* connections and differences among women. Despite good intentions, eschewing such ontological claims for fear of essentialism can sometimes facilitate the invisibility of women of color and the workings of privilege. First, it shifts feminists' attention away from the bodily experiences of women and other oppressed individuals, thereby depriving feminists of a crucial way to pinpoint real harms to actual beings. Second, it encourages oppressor-centric theories that see similar treatment under oppression as the sole basis for connection among women. Third, it therefore establishes feminist discourse as a critical endeavor directed at dominant ontologies rather than as a positive and creative enterprise in its own right.

What feminism needs is not to turn from ontological specificity altogether but to engage a new kind of ontological project that is mindful of the dangers of essentialism and homogenization while nonetheless centering the embodied experiences and materiality of oppressed/resistant beings. Such an ontology must not only be able to account for the intricate and variable locations among women and other oppressed beings, but it should also work to reveal the relational complexities of feminists themselves, including the ways that their own habitual patterns of thought and action may be tied to the oppression of those very beings with whom they claim solidarity. A feminist ontology should not ask us to choose one side of the dualism between connection and difference; it should instead give us tools to reframe the conversation nondualistically, enabling us to think connection and difference simultaneously.

In what follows, I offer a feminist ontological vision that can address these needs and others. My approach is at base phenomenological, giving primacy to lived experience and beginning in Simone de Beauvoir's and Maurice Merleau-Ponty's respective concepts of "flesh" (Beauvoir 2010 [1949]; Merleau-Ponty 1968).[4] For both thinkers, our flesh is literally a relational medium that is capable of holding ambiguous aspects of experience like subjectivity and objectification, mind and body, and continuity and difference together at the same time. Taking inspiration from this ontological concept as well as ecofeminism and María Lugones's theory of the colonial/modern gender system, I argue that our own flesh is related to that of others through lines of intercorporeal exchanges, substitutions, and asymmetries. When viewed collectively, these multiple lines of bodily relations form a "topography of flesh": a three-dimensional landscape of the social, material, and economic relationships present in a given locale at a particular point in time. "Topographical aggregates" are those ontological groups that come into relief in these topographies; they consist in beings who participate in the same lines of intercorporeal relation.

Rather than start by attending to relationships between human women, I take as ontologically paradigmatic an example from Toni Morrison's *Beloved* (2004 [1987]) that involves human and nonhuman women. I pursue this unorthodox move for explanatory purposes as well as political ones. First, our widespread cultural and linguistic preconceptions—however mistaken or justified—that humans and nonhuman animals are essentially different kinds of beings can help us better imagine what connection might look like amid radical difference. Next, the fact that we are all materially tied to nonhuman animals through our consumption practices helps us envision a politics for the twenty-first century where globalization connects most of us to the exploitation of others in ways that we do not consciously choose and may not even be aware of. Third, as ecofeminists and others have pointed out, our cultural ideas and practices in regard to nonhuman animals are not inconsequential to the workings of racial, colonial, and patriarchal systems of oppression. Lugones (2010, 743) considers "the dichotomous hierarchy between the human and the non-human [to be] the central dichotomy of colonial modernity." Finally, witnessing the human/nonhuman relationships in *Beloved* was a catalyst for my becoming a vegan; immediately thereafter I chose to stop consuming animal products, including milk, eggs, flesh, bones, and their derivatives. This chapter is not intended as a defense of veganism, although my references to examples involving nonhuman animals may incite readers to reflect critically on and modify their own relational/material landscapes just as Morrison's text did for me. I am, however, interested in the potential of this example as a model for feminist politics because it constitutes a shift in moral and ontological perception—a moment where I was led to see beings that I had once thought to be radically different from me as now worthy of my ethical consideration at all times, even when that consideration disrupts my daily life and that of others.

The Assault of Sethe and the Goat

Although *Beloved* is rarely recognized for its critical portrayals of our varied abuses of nonhuman animals, the bodily experiences of these animals are crucial to the story of violation that the main character, Sethe, returns to again and again throughout the text.[5] Morrison's novel is set in the United States of the late nineteenth century and offers its readers a vivid evocation of the aftermath of chattel slavery by telling Sethe's story of escape from her owner, Schoolteacher. At the beginning of the novel, we learn that when Sethe was nine months pregnant with her fourth child and was living and working on Schoolteacher's plantation, she was pushed down by his two nephews behind the barn. One of the boys held her while the other tore open her shirt and stole milk from her lactating breasts. When Sethe tells the lady of the plantation what the boys did, Schoolteacher whips her with a strip of cowhide until her back is scarred forever (Morrison 2004 [1987], 19–20). At the end of the story, Sethe revisits this assault in the barnyard when she tries to explain to the ghost of her daughter, Beloved, why she had to kill her when Schoolteacher came to reclaim his "property." She thinks to herself:

> Nobody will ever get my milk no more except my own children. I never had to give it to nobody else—and the one time I did it was took from me—they held me down and took it. Milk that belonged to my baby. Nan had to nurse whitebabies and me too because Ma'am was in the rice. The little whitebabies got it first and I got what was left. Or none. There was no nursing milk to call my own. I know what it is to be without the milk that belongs to you; to have to fight and holler for it, and to have so little left. I'll tell Beloved about that; she'll understand. She my daughter. The one I managed to have milk for and to get it to her even after they stole it; after they handled me like I was the cow, no, the goat, back behind the stable because it was too nasty to stay in with the horses. (236–37)

This central scene of abuse is not the only one in Morrison's novel that depicts a Black person being treated in ways that animals are treated. Additional examples where animals participate in the plot and imagery of the story include the facts that the people of Sethe's Ohio town make their living in a slaughterhouse, that two of the slaves at Schoolteacher's plantation were chained up with the livestock, and that Schoolteacher would ask his pupils to draw the "animal" characteristics of his slaves. Finally, in a phrase so swift that you would miss its meaning if you were not paying attention, Morrison intimates that Sethe escaped rape by the enslaved men upon her arrival at Sweet Home Plantation because "they were so young and so sick with the absence of women they had taken to calves" (12).

Intercorporeal exchange is a primary theme that animates the meanings of *Beloved* and serves to expose the horrors of slavery and modern/colonial thinking. This exposition comes into relief when we trace the ties and asymmetries between beings that found Sethe's knowledge that she was handled like the goat. Most obviously, Sethe's flesh can be exchanged with the goat's and the cow's flesh in a way that the flesh of the male characters in the novel cannot; it is nearly impossible, for example, to picture Schoolteacher as the recipient of this kind of violence in nineteenth-century America. Next, although

Sethe shares with the white women of the plantation a capacity to lactate when pregnant, the bodies of these white women are not really exchangeable with the goat's, since it is difficult to imagine them subject to the same form of assault that Sethe endured. This asymmetry is exemplified by the fact that Black women often served as wet nurses to white women's children during this time but rarely the other way around. However, in other respects, such as sexual availability to Schoolteacher, there is a sense in which Sethe's body is exchangeable with that of Schoolteacher's wife. The material existences of both women are constrained by socioeconomic systems—slavery and marriage, respectively—where it is impossible for the owner to commit rape against his "property." In addition, whereas Sethe experiences herself handled like the cow and goat in Morrison's story, the lives of the male slaves on the plantation are instead juxtaposed with those of workhorses, as is evident in the scene where the white men of the plantation place an iron bit in Paul D.'s mouth. Finally, it is possible to read the defining act of *Beloved*, where Sethe kills her daughter to prevent her from being enslaved, as a definitive protest against these existing economies of intercorporeal exchange between Black people and animals. In Sethe's words, "No one, nobody on this earth, would list her daughter's characteristics on the animal side of the paper" (251), and "Nobody will ever get my milk no more except my own children" (236).

I am interested in how intercorporeal landscapes like the one revealed in *Beloved* could inform a feminist ontology that specifies bodily connections and differences between beings without recourse to essentialism. Let us begin our inquiry by looking to two of feminist theory's most promising accounts of the ontological relationship between women and nonhuman animals.

Ecofeminism and Intersectionality

Ecofeminism is premised on the idea that there are conceptual and practical links between the oppression of women (sexism) and the oppression of nature (speciesism). Carol J. Adams, for example, would understand the connections between Sethe and the goat in terms of their being worked on by the same structures of violence and by our social complicity with that violence. On this reading, the parallels between Sethe and the goat come from their shared "ontology of objectification" (Adams 1994, 101). Adams believes that sexist and speciesist ideologies construct an inferior ontological status for women and nonhuman animals so that the "subject/agent/perpetrator of violence" can be absolved (101). Karen Davis (1995) further suggests that not all nonhuman animals are equal when it comes to their connections to and differences from women. Davis contends that women are most frequently associated with domesticated animals, an idea that is evidenced by the fact that the category "farm animals" is not gender-neutral. The dairy cows and laying hens that epitomize our concepts and practices of animal "husbandry" are female animals whose reproductive systems are exploited in virtue of their femaleness (193). Our litany of animal terms that can stand in for the word *woman*, including chicks, hens, cows, heifers, fat pigs, pieces of meat, pussy cats, bunnies, and bitches, also speaks to this tie between women and domesticated animals (Dunayer 1995).

Taken together, these ecofeminist accounts suggest that Sethe and the goat are ontologized as a special type of object that is "farmable" at its core. To be "farmable" in Davis's sense of the term is to have your reproductive system exploited again and again in the service of others, at the mercy of others, and as the property of others. Appealing to the idea that "ideology recapitulates ontology" (Adams 1994, 101), these ecofeminists maintain that a given system of oppression creates an associated categorization of oppressed beings that dictates the parameters of their moral consideration. A benefit of this type of account is that it can explain why the body of Schoolteacher's wife is not interchangeable with Sethe's or the goat's in the violation behind the stable; unlike them, she has not been ontologized as a farmable object. Are the material relations between them anything other than a function of the oppressor's perception?

We can achieve more ontological specificity if we situate the woman-animal relationship historically in terms of a theory of intersectionality that Lugones (2007) has labeled "the colonial/modern gender system." According to Lugones, the gender system that inhabits our contemporary concepts and practices did not always exist but emerged in tandem with European colonial projects and "congealed as Europe advanced" these projects (206). On the "light side" of this system women are viewed within a heterosexual economy: like Schoolteacher's wife, they are weak, fragile, and sexually passive in contrast to their strong, assertive, and sexually minded male counterparts. The "dark side" of the colonial/modern gender system sees colonized females as animalistic: they are sexually aggressive hermaphrodites who are just as strong and can labor just as hard and long as men (203). These connections between enslaved and colonized women and nonhuman animals in the colonial imaginary served as a justification for white men raping them (204; see also Davis 1981, 171–201, and Collins 1990, 123–48). If a woman or a nonhuman animal is believed to be "biologically programmed" to copulate and reproduce as much as possible, then rape would not apply to her, and thus, male access to her body would be unchecked, as was white male access to the bodies of Black women and women of color during slavery and colonization and male access to the barnyard calves in Morrison's novel.

Lugones's intersectional analysis emphasizes how the characters of sexism and racism undergo substantive modifications when they are combined with the speciesism present in colonial discourses about animality. She shows us how the symbolic, conceptual, and physiological proximity of women of color and nonhuman animals in the colonial landscape renders their respective ontologies co-constitutive. Insofar as Lugones's systemic account of colonization also applies to aspects of slavery, we could say that Sethe's worthiness for moral consideration, Sethe's sense of her own self-worth, and our individual expressions of our own humanity are systematically related to our treatment and perceptions of the cow, the goat, and other animals. Simply put, Sethe's being "gendered dark" according to the colonial/modern gender system is enabled by our attitudes and practices toward animals and vice versa.

Although Lugones's theory points to the systemic and mutually constitutive relationships between the respective ontologies of Sethe and the goat, her attention to the colonial mindset leaves us with a conundrum similar to the one that we arrived at through ecofeminist analyses: Is there anything about Sethe's relation to the goat that exceeds the pairing of their bodies in a racist imaginary? To answer in the negative is to again make the oppressor's activities the sole basis for the ontology of the oppressed. An affirmative answer, however, warrants more explanation than these ecofeminist and intersectional accounts have provided. We therefore need to ask how the very bodies of the oppressed might resist their construal and treatment in a racist-speciesist-heterosexist-colonial imaginary, while also acknowledging the real impact of this system on those bodies. We need a concept that can admit of the interplay of a being's embodied experience and the ideological and practical systems that seek to define that body. This concept should also be able to account for bodily differences between beings without succumbing to homogeneous or essentialist categorizations. It is here where phenomenology becomes particularly useful to feminism.

The Phenomenological Concept of Flesh

The body is both an obvious place of origin for feminist ontology and a place whose mere mention puts the theorist at risk for charges of essentialism. Insofar as we are conditioned to think of the body in virtue of a Cartesian dualism that opposes it to mind, we will be inclined to understand the body only in objective terms: as an object for science made up of mechanisms, organs, and biological capacities. This construal invites essentialist thinking because it asks us to view a woman's body reductively in terms of its parts (e.g., "woman is womb") and to conceptualize those parts as having only one primary function or set of functions such as reproduction. Fortunately, there are other ways to understand our own embodiment. For example, phenomenologists frequently write about the "lived body" or the "phenomenal body," both of which refer to the body as it is lived and experienced by particular individuals in concrete moments and contexts (see Beauvoir [1949] 2010, 49; Merleau-Ponty [1945] 1962, 121).[6] In the phenomenological tradition, the distinction between the "objective body" and "the lived body" refers not to different kinds of bodies but to two different perspectives from which to view our own bodies and the bodies of others.[7] In a reversal of traditional epistemologies, phenomenologists often afford primacy to the perspective of the lived body over objective meanings, which are thought to be "sedimented" or "petrified" forms of fluid experience and thus unduly removed from their referent. As one commentator puts it, "For Merleau-Ponty, the real world is the perceived world is the phenomenal world" (Dillon 1997, 156).

One of the great insights of Beauvoir's *The Second Sex* is that phenomenology's emphasis on the lived body provides feminism with a ready means to prioritize the experiences of women over and above those "objective" descriptions found in historical accounts, literary myths, philosophical and religious ideologies, and men's imaginaries. The book's structure juxtaposes men's ideas of women with women's experiences of themselves: the tile of the first volume is "Facts and Myths" and that of the second is "Lived Experience" (Beauvoir [1949] 2010). Phenomenology's double perspective on the body facilitates Beauvoir's fundamental claim that a woman experiences herself as a contradiction in sexist society, for she is both a subject for herself (a lived body) and an object for others (an objective body) at the same time. Beauvoir describes sexism as a situation where "woman is an existent who is asked to make herself an object" (Beauvoir [1949] 2010, 419). *Flesh* (*la chair*) is the term that Beauvoir uses to refer to this multiple self-experience. Of the child's experience of puberty, she writes, "The child's body is becoming a woman's body and is making itself flesh. . . . In the blossoming of her breasts the girl senses the ambiguity of the word 'living.' . . . Her breasts show through her sweater or blouse, and this body that the little girl identified with herself appears to her as flesh. It is an object that others look at and see" (1949, 57–58; my translation). The young girl makes herself flesh at the moment when she discovers that her body is hers and not hers, since it takes on importance only in virtue of what it does for others. Beauvoir's "flesh" is thus an ontological concept that specifies a kind of being but does not do so in terms of essential properties of objective bodies. Flesh is rather the material location where the ambiguity of life is held and lived passivity/activity; it is a style of being, and yet, due to the situated nature of materiality, flesh is by no means uniform across beings. As Beauvoir emphasizes, "flesh is clothed in special significance for each person and in each experience" (268).

More than a decade after Beauvoir published *The Second Sex*, Merleau-Ponty developed the ontological notion of flesh in the manuscript that was posthumously published as *The Visible and the Invisible* (1968). Like Beauvoir, Merleau-Ponty describes flesh as that which is capable of holding two seemingly opposed aspects of experience together at the same time. When we attend to our own flesh, we are struck by the multiple modes of experiencing that it can accommodate. Flesh is capable of both touching and being touched, seeing and being seen, moving and being moved, and so on. In short, flesh constitutes our sentience *and* our sensibility. Whereas Beauvoir often conceives of the multiplicity of flesh as "ambiguity," Merleau-Ponty is more apt to use the term *reversibility*, which emphasizes that transitivity between seemingly contradictory perspectives is the very essence of flesh (Merleau-Ponty 1968, 155). Just as when we touch something—whether being or object—that thing also touches us, the active and receptive aspects of our flesh yield to each other in a continuous back-and-forth dance of experience.

Merleau-Ponty (1968, 144) frequently uses the phrase *the flesh of the world* to indicate that the lived body of one being already implicates the lived bodies of others as well as inanimate materiality. He thus explains in his working notes, "this flesh of my body is shared by the world, the world *reflects* it, encroaches upon it and it encroaches upon the world (the felt . . . at the same time the culmination of subjectivity and the culmination of materiality)" (248). Although in his earlier work relationality, or intersubjectivity, between beings was a phenomenon that he sought to explain, Merleau-Ponty's later work depicts material relationality as the originary structure of experience—flesh is an "element" like air, water, earth, and fire that is the "incarnate principle" of existence (139). We are always already immersed in bodily relationships with one another. We are always already affecting and being affected, sensing and being sensed, touching and being touched. In political terms, "the flesh of the world" signifies that we all participate in relationships of connection and exploitation with others. However, this relationality is not homogeneity; that one's flesh is the material site of infinite and varied configurations of relation makes it radically particular. For this reason, "the other's body which I see and his word which I hear . . . *do present to me in their own fashion what I will never be present to*, what will always be invisible to me, what I will never directly witness—an absence" (82). Though both flesh, one being cannot transcend her unique spatiotemporal position to take up the perspective of another; approaching the world from a located perspective is precisely what it means to be embodied and to experience oneself as flesh.

The ontological concept of flesh allows us to affirm the relationality and complexity of lived experience, which does not present beings as either mind or body, active or passive, self or other, oppressed or privileged, but as both of these aspects at the same time. It also provides us with a way to center the lived experiences of oppressed/resistant beings with specificity because being flesh is coincident with having a particular, embodied perspective. However, if we allow for the radical particularity of the lived body, we must also admit that the flesh of a particular woman may have more in common with that of members of other recognized categories like "Black men" or "queer people" than with other women. This is especially true if we reject the idea that oppressive ideologies and practices *determine* the ontologies of the oppressed. How then do we make sense of ontological connection at the level of embodiment in light of this radical particularity of flesh? And how do we acknowledge, ontologically speaking, that the harms of oppression do not affect all bodies equally? Though we are all flesh, we are not all in the same boat. In what follows, I build on the phenomenological notion of flesh to develop an ontological concept that is capable of answering these questions and others.

Topographies of Flesh

Many years ago, I relied on topographic maps while working as a wilderness guide in central Alaska. In the tundra, there are no trails or other human impacts to follow, just unending expanses of shrubs, grass, wildflowers, rivers, mountains, and sky. Topographic maps helped me foster a sense of where I was in this environment relative to its prominent features. A topographic map (see fig. 7.1) is different from other kinds of maps for several reasons: (1) through the varied placement of nonintersecting lines called "contour lines" a landscape is depicted in three dimensions via the relationships between the lines (the closer the contour lines are to one another, the steeper the terrain), even though the map itself is two-dimensional; (2) "natural," "cultural," and historical features of a landscape are all included in the map; and (3) their focus is small and local. For any given hike, one might need to piece together two or three maps to address the whole of the desired area. The first time I saw a topographic map, I could not make heads or tails of its meaning. It was only by walking through the landscape and keying my experiences into the linear configurations on the map that the landscape's multiple dimensions were revealed. After much practice and experience, its mountains, valleys, and rivers came into relief for me when looking in two dimensions. I learned to sense the steepness or slackness of its grades and tell which directions the rivers and valleys flowed.

Feminist theory is at its best when, like a topographic map, it attends to the multiple dimensions of the spatiality of embodied experience and thinks its material, social, and historical aspects collectively and locally. In this mode, feminist theory becomes Lugones's streetwalker/*la callejera*, whose "insight into the social does not flatten it out as the distance of height does.... For the tactical strategist resisting ↔ oppressing has volume, intricacy, multiplicity of

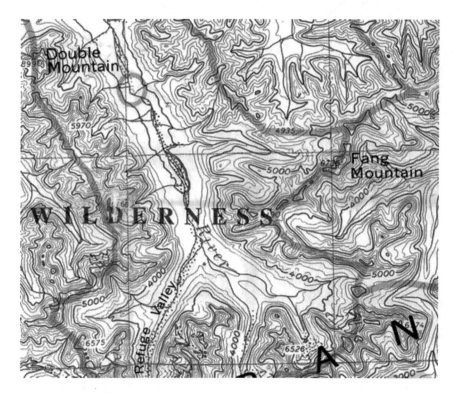

Fig. 7.1 A small portion of Denali National Park & Preserve topographic map. US Geological Survey.

relationality and meaning" (Lugones 2003, 215). To chart a topography of flesh is to look for what you cannot see from your perspective, that is, it is to make visible the myriad material perspectives—fleshes—that constitute a world, despite our personal investments in concealing them. It is to look for whose bodies sustain our own through their flesh, labor, and sociocultural position: Whose hands prepared this meal? Whose eyes sewed this shirt? Whose sweat cleaned this university bathroom, this hotel room, this apartment? Whose resources are my profit? Whose inferiority enhances my superiority? Whose milk is this that I drink?[8] To use Lugones's terminology, as feminists we must examine whose bodies are "the light and dark sides" of our own. Bringing a sociopolitical topography into relief is hard work, intellectually, emotionally, and interpersonally, for taking up one perspective can exclude others, and sometimes whole features can be covered in the twin fogs of mystification and privilege. For all of these reasons, the task of revealing a topography of flesh is necessarily a coalitional one.

Flesh is an apt metaphor for signifying the lived ambiguity of relational embodiment, which is animated by seemingly contradictory aspects of experience like passivity and activity and objectification and resistance at the same time. But flesh is also a concept that we should take quite literally; actual beings consist of flesh, which can see and be seen, touch and be touched, nourish and be nourished, harm and be harmed, handle and be handled, and so on. Flesh indicates a body that is mindful/full of spirit and a mind or spirit that is embodied. The process of charting the literal exchanges of flesh that are operative and unthinkable in a particular historical-social moment and of the ways that one flesh constitutes and is constituted by that of others yields what I am here calling a "topography of flesh"—a three-dimensional landscape of bodily, material relationships of exchange and asymmetry, exploitation and solidarity, oppression and resistance.

The colonialist origins of the term *topography* and its associations with the practices of cartography, exploration, and conquest are not unproblematic in this context, nor are the Christian origins and connotations of the word *flesh*. Although this discussion deserves greater attention than can be given here, it is precisely the complex and multiple meanings of these terms that render them especially suitable for describing embodied experience in the twenty-first century. The idea that we are all immersed in topographies of flesh affirms our inescapable participation in systems of oppression, so its constituent terms reflect this lived impurity, politically speaking. Yet a topography frustrates the abstraction of cartography through its focus on the depth of the local and the necessity of keying mapped features to lived experience. We must also remember that Beauvoir refused to permit the erasure of woman's subjectivity that occurred through men's conceptions of *flesh*; she redefined the word in a way that acknowledged women's bodily knowing and capacities for resistance despite their diminishment in patriarchal narratives and practice ([1949] 2010, 392). The phrase *topographies of flesh* is therefore appropriate for indicating the difficult, contested, and multidimensional work of feminist theory.

So far we have been conceiving of a topography of flesh in epistemological terms: it emerges from a style of thinking that interprets and exposes the lines of intercorporeal exchange and asymmetry present in a given locale at a particular point in time. But how is "topography of flesh" also an ontological notion? How does it indicate actual connections between beings as well as differential harms of oppression? To answer these questions, we must first examine three different kinds of intercorporeal relationships that one body can share with another: exchange, substitution, and asymmetry.

First, bodies are "exchangeable" with one another when they are alternately used to serve the same function. The bodies of laborers readily fall into this category since, once the parameters of labor are specified, there is little regard for the particularity of workers as long as they perform the desired tasks. If one worker takes ill, another body is found as a replacement. Likewise, the consumer generally does not care which bovine body went into his hamburger; any cow could serve that purpose. On Schoolteacher's plantation, men raped both calves and women. In at least *some* respects, these bodies are interchangeable with one another within their situating contexts. Second, we should use the word *substitution* for a special kind of exchange wherein one body is used in a way that is normally reserved for another. Sethe's being milked and Paul D.'s having a bit placed in his mouth are salient examples of this process since these practices are designed for and routinely operate on the bodies of cows, goats, and horses. Importantly, it is not just in "the oppressor's mind" that intercorporeal exchanges and substitutions occur but also *actually* and *materially*; they are functionally rather than (or as well as) symbolically operative. Who or what motivates or enables the exchange is secondary to its presence. Furthermore, such motivations can come from all directions. From a place of resistance, a child or family dog in a situation of domestic abuse might substitute his body for his mother's and endure a beating standardly meant for her. Third, which exchanges and substitutions are *not* operative in a given context tell us just as much about the contours of a society as those that are. For instance, types of labor are often keyed into kinds of bodies. The distribution of garment-district, shoe-factory, janitorial, agricultural, and slaughterhouse workers does not pull equally from every demographic. Global capital travels, with the result of exploiting some bodies and protecting others. An intercorporeal *asymmetry* occurs when a line of exchange between two bodies is inoperative and thus unimaginable. When such asymmetries are present, bodies on each side of the distance codefine one another. There are many more kinds of intercorporeal relations than these three, but this should suffice to illustrate the ontological potentials of a topography of flesh.

When we attend to those lines of intercorporeal exchange, substitution, and asymmetry present at a given moment in history in a particular locality, we are able to recognize aggregates of beings who share involvement in the same line (see fig. 7.2).[9] According to this schema, Sethe, the cow, and the goat constitute one such aggregate; all of their bodies are milked and experience this milking in nineteenth-century America, so they form a group in virtue of this intercorporeal exchangeability. Sethe, Paul D., the goat, the horse, and many of the other humans and nonhumans on the plantation constitute a different group because they are exchangeable in terms of a different intercorporeal line, namely, the one consisting of beings who labor for Schoolteacher's interests and experience this laboring. Sethe and Schoolteacher's wife form

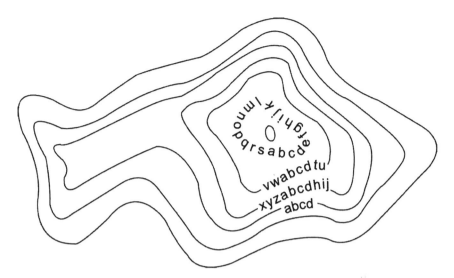

Fig. 7.2 Illustration of a topography of flesh. Each contour line is composed of individual bodies (represented by each different letter) who share an intercorporeal relationship with one another. The entire group of individuals whose bodies constitute one contour line is a topographical aggregate (e.g., the series a–s in the figure). When multiple individuals participate in several of the same contour lines (e.g., individuals a–d), they form a topographical feature. Concept: Jennifer McWeeny, Illustration: Jennifer A. Vokoun.

yet another aggregate due to their asymmetry in regard to wet-nursing other's children; as two sides of the same coin, the activities of one work to define the lived experience of the other and vice versa. Grouping beings in terms of such intercorporeal relations does not entail that there is coincidence, identity, or even bodily similarity among the group's members. *Topographical aggregates are about bodily proximities rather than bodily properties*; they emerge out of what actually happens between bodies in lived experience instead of what features those bodies may or may not possess in themselves. We could imagine societies where Black women and goats are not milked, Black men and horses are not bridled, colonized people and pigs are not slaughtered, and women and nonhuman animals are not raped. The ontological aggregates in these societies would thus be different than they are in the ones to which we have been referring. Furthermore, since these are aggregates of bodies who consist in flesh that both receives the world passively *and* crafts that world actively, the perspective of the oppressor is only part of the story. Thinking our ontologies in terms of flesh reminds us that a being who is involved in an existing line of intercorporeal exchange may do so in countless ways: she may facilitate, resist, exploit, undermine, reposition, or recraft that line, among many other activities.

When two beings share not one but several lines of intercorporeal relation, the coincidence of these multiple aggregates can form a complex ontological category or "topographical feature," just as the contour lines on a topographic map reveal mountains, plains, and canyons (see fig. 7.2). Lugones's account of what it means to be "gendered dark" is paradigmatic here. The bodies of colonized women were exchangeable with those of nonhuman animals at the same time as they experienced intercorporeal asymmetries with white women. Such *systems* of intercorporeal relations composed by mutually constitutive lines of exchange implicate groups of beings like "women of color." Even though all beings are involved in many lines of intercorporeal relation, the consequences of this involvement are varied, especially if a being is involved in a topographical feature crafted by consistent patterns that entail harm or other erasures of her subjectivity. Topographical thinking thus provides us with ways to identify groups of beings whose flesh is especially vulnerable or especially protected in the context of existing social and material structures.

A Ground for Feminist Politics

The concept of a topography of flesh and the associated ideas of topographical aggregates and topographical features offer feminists a way to think our ontologies without essentialism, individualism, disembodiment, oppressor-centrism, or other reductions of the complexity of lived experience. But there is much work to be done before this ontological notion can ground feminist politics. Notably, the aggregates that emerge within our topographies of flesh do not entail that there will be solidarity among group members. The material proximity of our fleshes in lines of intercorporeal relations provides merely an opportunity for solidarity and coalition, not their factual existence. A being's inclusion in a topographical aggregate can be harmful, beneficial, or unimportant to her and so, depending on the circumstance, she may wish to affirm or reject her membership in that group. Angela Y. Davis (1978, 27) discusses an instance where white workers gained a feeling of "racial affinity" with the bosses by being racist to Black workers. The white worker's refusal to acknowledge the exchangeability of his flesh with that of Black workers served his own advantage, not to mention the interests of capitalism, by fragmenting the working class. In this case, facilitating an intercorporeal asymmetry in place of exchange constitutes a kind of sacrifice of the other wherein one being offers another instead of herself in order to prevent her own harm. Alternatively, a person may enter into a line of exchange to prevent harm to another. For example, this type of relation is evident in the case where a middle-class woman offers regular childcare to an acquaintance from a low socioeconomic class who is leaving an abusive relationship, despite the woman's considerable responsibilities with her own children, one of whom has special needs.[10] Because of the multidirectionality of a being's participation in a given line of intercorporeal exchange, solidarity is never guaranteed. And yet whether we are aware of the lines of exchange within which we are always already involved, whether we can articulate these relationships, and whether we choose (consciously or subconsciously) to participate in them, the political moment presents itself. In other words, our feminisms are made manifest in the coalitions we live and realize before it is (or is not) in those that we theorize or consciously acknowledge. What motivates a being to participate in intercorporeal relations in the ways that she does is a further question.

An additional consideration is what to do once a particular topography of flesh has been revealed. At first glance, we might be tempted to say that one should resist any harmful lines of exchange that are discovered, like the one between Sethe and the goat. But there are as many attitudes to take toward an intercorporeal relation as there are ways to participate in them, including denial, justification, critique, and resistance. Moreover, political and moral imperatives are contextual and complex, especially considering that our participation in these lines is not necessarily voluntary. Politically speaking, should Sethe have rejected the substitution between her and the goat by affirming her "humanity" over and above the goat's "animality"? Paul D. simplifies these complicated relations when, in response to learning that Sethe has killed her child, he says, "You got two feet, Sethe, not four" (Morrison 2004, 194). In this way, Paul D. reminds Sethe that she need not internalize "slavery's dehumanizing discourse" (Valkeakari 2002). Yet this approach paradoxically resists slavery by further entrenching the moral-ontological distinctions on which it rests. Is it not morally problematic to rape, whip, chain, or slaughter *any* sentient being—to take the milk meant for her offspring? Evading culpability for differential moral treatment by establishing essential distinctions between kinds of bodies or kinds of beings repeats the foundational ideology of slavery and colonial modernity. Despite this need for destabilizing the human/animal distinction, we must also recognize that in certain present-day contexts, the feminist who is more concerned with animal liberation than with women of color is also repeating the structural asymmetry that centers white women's perspectives and makes women of color irrelevant and invisible. Because our fleshes are so entwined with one another, moral purity is likely impossible to achieve, especially considering the realities of globalized life in the twenty-first century. But this fact does not mean that we should let entrenched ontologies and the status quo decide whom we should harm and whom we should not.

This is why inquiring into our own topographies of flesh by entering into complex communication (Lugones 2006) and coalition with others is paramount; it affords us the opportunity to participate actively in supporting liberatory relations and challenging oppressive ones.[11] Methods for deriving courses of action and resistance from the landscapes that we find will subsequently need to be developed.

Finally, there will undoubtedly be disagreement over which lines of intercorporeal exchange and asymmetry are operative in a given locality. There will also be discussions about which perspectives should be charted, that is, who or what counts as flesh and who does not. For example, should beings like trees, rocks, and ecosystems be included? Perhaps more controversially, there will be disputes about how harmful or beneficial a given line of exchange is for its members. The answers to these questions cannot be decided in advance of exploring our existing topographies, nor can they be determined by one individual's projection. Approaching these dilemmas collectively by placing ourselves in genuine contact with a variety of other perspectives—fleshes—is precisely what it means to think topographically. The point is not to generate a God's-eye view of our world that will settle any divergences within feminism but to retain the moral, political, and material complexity of lived experience. In the words of Merleau-Ponty ([1945] 1964, 17), a topography of flesh "imposes itself not as true for every intellect, but as real for every subject who is standing where I am." This difficult ontological work is thus a way of theorizing "resistance from the subaltern position and from within the concreteness of body-to-body engagement" (Lugones 2003, 207).

The task of revealing topographies of flesh is not necessarily new to feminist theory. Scores of feminist thinkers have undertaken the important work of exposing actually existing relationships among beings; taking the complexity of their social, historical, and material contexts into account; and recognizing connections and differences between them. Following this lineage, I have derived an ontology from these practices. This ontology conceives of groups of beings not in terms of essential properties but in virtue of their proximity to one another in lines of lived, intercorporeal relations. As such, a topography of flesh provides us with a way to think connections and differences between beings at the level of embodiment without homogenizing beings, centering the activities of the oppressor, or obscuring the fluid relations of oppression and privilege among feminists themselves.[12]

In *The Visible and the Invisible* Merleau-Ponty (1968, 137) asks, "Yes or no: do we have a body—that is, not a permanent object of thought, but a flesh that suffers when it is wounded, hands that touch?" In a similar vein, Baby Suggs calls out: "Here, in this here place, we flesh; flesh that weeps, laughs; flesh that dances on bare feet in grass. Love it. Love it hard. Yonder they do not love your flesh. They despise it. . . . This is flesh I'm talking about here. Flesh that needs to be loved" (Morrison 2004, 103). The impetus for feminist action lies in our affirmation of the body's ability to harm and be harmed, touch and be touched, love and be loved. By thinking the connections and differences between bodies topographically—materially and phenomenologically—we can not only reveal a feminist ontology but also participate in the most important political work of crafting a topography where the bodily exchanges, substitutions, and asymmetries constitutive of multiple, intersecting oppressions are inoperative and unthinkable.

Notes

A previous version of this chapter was previously published as Jennifer McWeeny, "Topographies of Flesh: Women, Nonhuman Animals, and the Embodiment of Connection and Difference," Hypatia 29, no. 2 (2014), 269-86, 2020 © Cambridge University Press, reproduced with permission. Earlier versions of this paper were presented at the 2009 Annual Meeting of the Association for Feminist Ethics and Social Theory, the 2009 National Women's Studies Association Annual Meeting, the Dean's Speaker Series "The Human and the Non-human" at Binghamton University in 2011, and the 2012 International Women's Day Lecture at Wright State University. I am deeply grateful for the conversations I had with audience members and interlocutors at these venues, including PJ DiPietro, María Lugones, Hil Malatino, Xhercis Mendes, Gabriela Veronelli, Maria Chavez, Matt Applegate, Josh Franco, Carol Meija-LaPerle, Dana Paterson, and Amber Vlasnik. I am also thankful for discussions with Vrinda Dalmiya, Ashby Butnor, Kelli Zaytoun, Julie Meiser Rioux, Lynna Scranton, and John Sanbonmatsu. In addition, the Feminist Working Group Initiative, which consists of Celia Bardwell-Jones, Dana Berthold, Kimberly Garchar, Rochelle Green, Chaone Mallory, Amy Story, and Lisa Yount, commented extensively on a previous version of this paper and gave me the final encouragement to prepare it for publication. Finally, I am grateful to graphic designer Jennifer A. Vokoun who helped me create the figures in this essay.

    1. Important exceptions to this trend of ontological vagueness include, for example, Zack 2005 and Garry 2011.

    2. For example, Kimberlé Williams Crenshaw's (1991, 1243) work on the subject speaks both of "intersectional identities such as women of color" and of "intersecting patterns of racism and sexism."

    3. That a host of metaphors in addition to "intersecting," such as "interlocking," "intermeshed," "overlapping," and "fused," are used (often interchangeably) in the literature despite the differences in their meanings further indicates the concept's ontological imprecision.

    4. See also McWeeny (2017).

    5. For articles that do analyze the role of animals in Morrison's text, see Valkeakari 2002 and Armbruster 2005.

    6. See also Sara Heinämaa's (2003) discussion of the import of the concept of "the living body" for feminism.

    7. See also Jenny Slatman (2020).

    8. See also the central question of Françoise Vergès's A Decolonial Feminism ([2019] 2021): "Who cleans the world?"

9. For an example of this kind of feminist analysis that traces lines of bodily exchange and asymmetry across beings, see Vrinda Dalmiya's (2002, 153–55) discussion of Saadat Hasan Manto's story "Bestiality."
10. I am grateful to Julie Meiser Rioux for providing this example.
11. See McWeeny (2019) for one approach to articulating topographies of flesh in which I participate.
12. See also Jennifer McWeeny, "Feminist Ontology for the Twenty-First Century," video, interview conducted by Hypatia: A Journal of Feminist Philosophy, November 15, 2013, uploaded July 28, 2014, 35 min., 11 sec., https://www.youtube.com/watch?v=-yewhkQmV38.

References

Adams, Carol J. 1994. *Neither Man nor Beast: Feminism and the Defense of Animals*. New York: Continuum.
Armbruster, Karla. 2005. "'What There Was Before Language': Animals and the Challenges of Being Human in the Novels of Toni Morrison." *Comparative Critical Studies* 2 (3): 365–80.
Beauvoir, Simone de. 1949. *Le Deuxième sexe*. Vol. 2. Paris: Gallimard.
———. (1949) 2010. *The Second Sex*. Translated by Constance Borde and Sheila Malovany-Chevallier. New York: Vintage Books.
Collins, Patricia Hill. 1990. *Black Feminist Thought: Knowledge, Consciousness, and the Politics of Empowerment*. Boston, MA: Unwin Hyman.
Crenshaw, Kimberlé Williams. 1991. "Mapping the Margins: Intersectionality, Identity Politics, and Violence against Women of Color." *Stanford Law Review* 43 (6): 1241–99.
Dalmiya, Vrinda. 2002. "Cows and Others: Toward Constructing Ecofeminist Selves." *Environmental Ethics* 24 (2): 149–68.
Davis, Angela Y. 1978. "Rape, Racism, and the Capitalist Setting." *Black Scholar* 9 (7): 24–30.
———. 1981. *Women, Race, and Class*. New York: Random House.
Davis, Karen. 1995. "Thinking like a Chicken: Farm Animals and the Feminine Connection." In *Animals and Women: Feminist Theoretical Explorations*, edited by Carol J. Adams and Josephine Donovan, 192–212. Durham, NC: Duke University Press.
Davis, Kathy. 2008. "Intersectionality as Buzzword: A Sociology of Science Perspective on What Makes a Feminist Theory Successful." *Feminist Theory* 9 (1): 67–85.
Dillon, M. C. 1997. *Merleau-Ponty's Ontology*. Evanston, IL: Northwestern University Press.
Dunayer, Joan. 1995. "Sexist Words, Speciesist Roots." In *Animals and Women: Feminist Theoretical Explorations*, edited by Carol J. Adams and Josephine Donovan, 11–31. Durham, NC: Duke University Press.
Garry, Ann. 2011. "Intersectionality, Metaphors, and the Multiplicity of Gender." *Hypatia* 26 (4): 826–50.
Heinämaa, Sara. 2003. *Toward a Phenomenology of Sexual Difference: Husserl, Merleau-Ponty, Beauvoir*. Lanham, MD: Rowman and Littlefield.
Lugones, María. 2003. *Pilgrimages/Peregrinajes: Theorizing Coalition against Multiple Oppressions*. Lanham, MD: Rowman and Littlefield.
———. 2006. "On Complex Communication." *Hypatia* 21 (3): 75–85.
———. 2007. "Heterosexualism and the Colonial / Modern Gender System." *Hypatia* 22 (1): 186–209.
———. 2010. "Toward a Decolonial Feminism." *Hypatia* 25 (4): 743–59.
McWeeny, Jennifer. 2017. "Beauvoir and Merleau-Ponty." In *A Companion to Simone de Beauvoir*, edited by Laura Hengehold and Nancy Bauer, 211–23. Malden, MA: John Wiley & Sons.

———. 2019. "Motion Sickness and the Slipperiness of Irish Racialization." In *Speaking Face to Face: The Visionary Philosophy of María Lugones*, edited by Pedro DiPietro, Jennifer McWeeny, and Shireen Roshanravan, 145–74. Albany: State University of New York Press.

Merleau-Ponty, Maurice. (1945) 1962. *Phenomenology of Perception*. Translated by Colin Smith. London: Routledge and Kegan Paul.

———. (1945) 1964. *The Primacy of Perception: And Other Essays on Phenomenological Psychology, the Philosophy of Art, History, and Politics*, edited and translated by James M. Edie. Evanston, IL: Northwestern University Press.

———. 1968. *The Visible and the Invisible*. Translated by Alfonso Lingis. Evanston, IL: Northwestern University Press.

Morrison, Toni. 2004. *Beloved*. New York: Vintage.

Slatman, Jenny. 2020. "The *Körper-Leib* Distinction." In *50 Concepts for a Critical Phenomenology*, edited by Gail Weiss, Ann V. Murphy, and Gayle Salamon, 203–209. Evanston, IL: Northwestern University Press.

Valkeakari, Tuire. 2002. "Toni Morrison Writes B(l)Ack: *Beloved* and Slavery's Dehumanizing Discourse of Animality." *Atlantic Literary Review* 3 (2): 165–87.

Vergès, Françoise. [2019] 2021. *A Decolonial Feminism*. London: Pluto Press.

Zack, Naomi. 2005. *Inclusive Feminism: A Third Wave Theory of Women's Commonality*. Lanham, MD: Rowman and Littlefield.

Jennifer McWeeny is Professor of Philosophy at Emerson College and Professor II at the Centre for Gender Research at the University of Oslo. Her research and teaching interests are in philosophies of gender and race, phenomenology, decolonial studies, feminist theory, and philosophy of mind. She has coedited three books: *Feminist Philosophy of Mind* (2022), *Speaking Face to Face: The Visionary Philosophy of María Lugones* (2019), and *Asian and Feminist Philosophies in Dialogue: Liberating Traditions* (2014). She is editor in chief of *Simone de Beauvoir Studies*.

8
DECOLONIAL AESTHETICS BEYOND THE BORDERS OF MAN
SYLVIA WYNTER'S THEORY AND PRAXIS OF HUMAN-AESTHETIC TRANSFORMATION

Patrick M. Crowley

BEGINNING WITH ITS eighteenth-century inception as a category of knowledge and a branch of Western philosophy concerned with theorizing universal human faculties for sensing beauty and establishing transcultural/transhistorical criteria governing the evaluation of artwork, the modern concept of aesthetics has functioned as an overloaded assembly of Eurocentric values, ideals, distinctions, methods, principles, canons, and similar. In accordance with its constitutive ties to the project of modernity, the field of aesthetics institutes an intellectual monopoly by delegitimizing non-Western theories and practices of creativity and sensibility (*aesthesis*) through the application of the classificatory, hierarchical logic of coloniality (Mignolo and Vázquez 2013). Hence, the meanings inherent to humanness in prevailing aesthetic discourses overlap seamlessly with dominant modern/colonial definitions of Man designed to enact global categorial separations between human beings and subhuman counterparts predicated on an array of fictive essentialisms. Put another way, for almost three centuries, Man has been articulated and constructed in terms of the aesthetic, and the aesthetic in terms of Man. Today, while modernity/coloniality's singular universalizing human-aesthetic coformation continues to act as an oppressive overarching institutional constraint on cultural, creative, and intellectual activity, practitioner-theorists involved with decolonial projects and communal movements across the planet collectively assert a radical pluriverse of other understandings of beauty, creativity, and sensibility in conjunction with distinctive discernments of human/nonhuman interdependency and alternate praxes of living and being (Escobar 2018). Part of the challenge posed by decoloniality arises from the way many of these projects disentangle humanness and aesthetics from their modern/colonial nexus, resignifying these spheres and their connectivity as open, relational, and responsive to communal practices of making other-sense, creating other worlds, and struggling for other arrangements of collective autonomy.[1] Thinking with these projects, certain intellectual guides have demonstrated that the enmeshment of the human and the aesthetic as interdependent domains within the systemic totality of Western modernity means that to transform one, it is also necessary to transform the other.[2] One such guide is Jamaican philosopher Sylvia Wynter.

In this chapter, I discuss Wynter's contributions to disentangling the aesthetic and the human from the matrix of modern/colonial power. Her thinking reveals the oppressive boundaries delimited by "Man" as a category instrumental to the West's effort to extend universal dominion over human ways of being, doing, thinking, feeling, and living. Taking part in an Afro-Caribbean tradition of artist-theorists who address the deficiencies of Western humanism from the memory of racial enslavement and the embodied standpoint of rebellious Blackness, Wynter's creative and theoretical writings from the 1960s to the present have sought to disclose the onto-epistemic limits imposed by the global hegemony of Man and the foundational logic that organizes prevailing disciplinary knowledges in the humanities and social sciences. Wynter's overall project may be sketched in terms of three overlapping challenges: (1) to philosophically analyze the inception of Man as an ordering principle that assumed global authority to legitimate the asymmetrical apportioning of knowledge and power; (2) to elucidate the cognitive and behavioral effects of the adaptable truth regime organized around Man on subjects differently situated within its structure of power relations; and (3) to conceptualize and enact the overthrow of Man by reconceiving the human in ways that realize the full potential of our collective autonomy and capacity for self-invention. Her efforts to displace the dominant humanist paradigm through the unfolding of what she calls "a new science of the Word" (Wynter 2003, 331) intersect with multiple transformative currents of decolonial aesthetics taking shape across many parts of the world.[3] Space prohibits a comprehensive treatment of Wynter's approach to rethinking the human, and my intent is to focus on her theorization of the aesthetic as a problematic Western concept that may be reappropriated and reinscribed with alternate meanings to generate liberatory intellectual praxis.[4] At the same time, I address incongruities arising from her partial engagements with the intersection of race and gender in modernity/coloniality's exclusionary framework of humanism.

The discussion unfolds as follows. First, I contextualize Wynter's approach to resignifying aesthetics in relation to her philosophical genealogy of "Man" and her theory of sociogenic autopoiesis, that is, her account of the self-organizing codes and coding processes foundational to all human orders of being and consciousness. Second, I formulate an assessment of the specific critical aesthetic methodology she defines as a "deciphering practice" in terms of how it enhances the counterpoetic image-making activities of Black artists, especially filmmakers, who are well positioned to unconceal the subtextual, semiotic dimensions of modernity's discursively instituted epistemic governance of everyday life (Wynter 1992, 238–39). The final part of my discussion raises questions about Wynter's binary approach to critiquing the "rule-governed function" of the modern human-aesthetic order (253), specifically concerning its analytic precision vis-à-vis assemblages of multiple interlocking categories of subhuman difference. I describe certain contradictions that arise from Wynter's theoretical ambivalence toward gendered modalities of racial dehumanization. The discussion concludes with some consideration of how her thinking opens but does not pursue possible pathways toward activating the liminal positionalities of racialized women and sexual dissidents as sites for generating transformative reinventions of the aesthetic and the human.

Although my discussion interrogates aspects of Wynter's reluctance to fully theorize the dimensions of humanness specifically denied to nonwhite women along with others habitually excluded from normative gendered personhood, these questions are not intended to undermine the ongoing significance of her intellectual guidance in the context of decolonial thinking. Indeed, there is no doubt that future trajectories of reinventing aesthetic theory and practice, which go hand in hand with imagining other ways of being human, will continue to be fruitfully engaged with Wynter's conceptualization of these tasks. My view is that options for decolonial aesthetics are greatly enriched by Wynter's formulations, even as I pose questions about potential shortcomings or limitations in her critical schema. Ultimately, identifying vulnerabilities in the structure of Wynter's influential framework opens possibilities for dialogic exchange and critical negotiation beyond Man's oppressive borders.

Beyond the Aesthetic Regime of Man

According to Paget Henry (2006, 260), a starting point for engaging with Wynter's thinking may be found in the questions, "How are social orders established? What are the mechanisms, the glue, or the centripetal forces that integrate societies and hold them together?" Disseminated across dozens of often lengthy essays, especially those written since the early 1980s, Wynter's approach to offering radically different answers to the fundamental problem of the origins, perpetuation, and transformation of social orders entails rigorous transdisciplinary analysis that draws intricate connections between multiple domains of humanity's formative self-organizing activity. She centers the role of culture in order-constituting processes, but as Henry explains, unlike many conservative schools of thought that emphasize established traditions as the basis of shared formations of peoplehood, Wynter's approach "moves below such specific cultural practices and links the problem of social order to a more general set of *a priori* conditions that make cultural and discursive practices possible" (260). These transcendental preconditions for the emergence of culturally specific orders of sociality are described in various ways throughout Wynter's voluminous writings, but perhaps the most definitive element of her conceptualization is the human cognitive faculty of "autopoiesis," which Henry encapsulates as "a set of encoded creative possibilities that can be discursively mobilized and deployed in the service of human self-formation" (261). In nonhuman animals, one finds analogous shared behaviors of "self-speciation," but whereas these are codified strictly at the innate genetic level, humans, by contrast, are uniquely endowed with the autopoietic capacity to alter or rewrite the coded inscriptions that organize our existence (260). As Henry puts it, "autopoeisis is ontological writing. Through its coded possibilities it allows humans to write different versions of themselves into being" (261). It is precisely as manifestations of this unconsciously enacted ability to define and redefine the "We" and the "I" of human collective and individual selfhood that culture, representation, and aesthetics come into play.

While Henry's helpful exegesis traces Wynter's deep incursions into the "transcendental ground of knowledge production" within the disciplinary structures of the modern humanities and social sciences (259), I want to reflect more closely on her formulation of aesthetics as a framework of knowing and sensing that situates individuals and groups in relation to culturally instituted orders of being human, and conceptualizes possibilities for more deliberate, conscious, and liberatory transformations of the latter. In the first half of this chapter, I draw mainly from two of Wynter's essays, "Rethinking 'Aesthetics': Notes towards a Deciphering Practice" (1992) and "Africa, the West and the Analogy of Culture: The Cinematic Text after Man" (2000), illustrating how she resignifies aesthetics to destabilize its conventional discourses, methods, and principles as the philosophy of art and beauty. Of course, a discussion of Wynter's thought can hardly avoid entering the transcendental spaces she exposes to critical scrutiny, as these house the very mechanisms perpetuating unfreedom that she works to dismantle and rebuild for emancipatory ends. To grasp Wynter's theory and practice of aesthetics implies a constant oscillation between particular articulations of creative and critical activity and the underlying codified assemblages of rules that govern human orders of being, doing, thinking.

In Wynter's philosophical anthropology, the origins of humanity itself are intrinsically tied to the development of symbolic activity that allowed the self-formative behaviors of the first humans to diverge from the genetic coding biologically inherited from their ancestors. As distinct from other organic life-forms whose modes of existence and self-propagation are solely determined by their DNA, she explains that the "aggregating and cospeciating behaviors of human 'forms of life' are instead induced and regulated by the orders of discourse instituting of each culture. Human life cannot, therefore, *pre-exist*, as it is now believed to do, the phenomenon of culture. Rather, it comes into being simultaneously with it" (1992, 242).[5] This co-constitutive structure of cultural activity and human orders of being is the anchoring hypothesis of Wynter's genealogy of humanness, as it allows her to distinguish specific and distinct formations of the human by linking particular constellations of self-inscriptive symbolic practice to more fundamental differences in each culturally distinct order's autopoietic codification. By locating human origins "in *Representation* rather than in *Evolution*" (2000, 26), Wynter not only offers a provocative challenge to the authoritative bio-ontological foundation narrative of the currently dominant globalized order of Western Man but also sets the stage for a definitive rupture of the usual pattern that defines the formation and maintenance of human orders.

To underscore the correlation between cultural activity and autopoiesis, Wynter reworks the standard definition of "aesthetics" by dislodging it from the modern field of disciplinary philosophical meanings, where it typically denotes a pseudoscientific ensemble of spuriously objective categories, standards, and norms to be used in judgments of creative art and beauty. Instead, she redefines it to refer to the set of "rules" that govern the formation of "social cohesion" and "culture-specific cooperative behaviors" and that function according to "semantic closure principle," meaning that they must remain semantically consistent with themselves to replicate the order (1992, 242–43). This move effectively turns aesthetics inside out, making it into a means of mapping the correspondence between particular cultural and discursive practices and the transcendental processes that induce, regulate, and reproduce each order's acceptable forms of human social conduct and sensibility. It must be added that Wynter constantly adapts her theoretical vocabulary as she approaches different spheres of human self-inscriptive activity. In other contexts, she describes these same transcendental rules of autopoietic order production in terms that emphasize their sociopolitical, economic, epistemic, and other dimensions. One of the overarching aims of her theoretical project is to demonstrate how the internal coherence of each order derives from a fundamental relation of interdependence between multiple levels of signifying practices across all fields of human activity and the structural organization of the transcendental domain where autopoietic codes are inscribed. The redefinition of aesthetics thematized in at least two of her essays resonates with her contention that humanness emerges with the earliest practices of symbolic representation as well as her postulation of a special function for creative signifying practices and cultural criticism, but it is not the exclusive descriptor she uses to refer to systems of order-constitutive rule-governed codes.

The explanatory power of Wynter's reconceptualized aesthetics consists in enabling description and analysis of modernity's current rule-governed order of cultural signification as a particular instantiation of a more fundamental set of possibilities conditioned by patterns of autopoiesis common to all other human orders. To illustrate the correspondence, Wynter marks a distinction between "Aesthetic 1," which defines the transcendental autopoietic processes structuring all systems of cultural signification, and "Aesthetic 2," naming the particular system specific to the currently dominant order of Man (1992, 244). The primary function of Aesthetic 1, as Wynter explains, "is to secure the social cohesion of the specific human order of which it is a function" (244). This is accomplished via the organization of an "altruistic psycho-affective field whose cohering mechanisms serve to integrate each specific mode of ultra-sociality or 'form of life'" (244). In other words, Aesthetic 1 designates the generalized logic of autopoiesis that determines how each "culture-specific mode of the subject *must* know (the episteme) and *feel* about (the psycho-aesthetics) its Self, Other, and social world" (246). To identify these transcultural parameters governing all human-aesthetic orders, Wynter relies on research by numerous scholars across many disciplinary fields whose findings support her hypothesis regarding the human faculty of symbolic self-inscription.[6] Most significantly, she builds on the concept of "sociogeny," as developed by Frantz Fanon in *Black Skin, White Masks* ([1952] 2007), to describe the process of socialization subjects undergo as they unconsciously integrate into each specific human order's normative structures of knowledge and affect that make Self, Other, and World intelligible and perceptible (Wynter 1992, 246).

Wynter's theorization of Aesthetic 1's imperative function to stably replicate specific orders of the human provides the basis for an alternative description of the currently prevailing system of social signification as a particular manifestation of this general logic. Using the term Aesthetic 2 to refer to the cultural, discursive, and symbolic practices that reproduce the dominant order of Western modernity and its specific definition of the human, that is, Man, Wynter demonstrates how the truths generated by these practices are preconditioned by the rules of Aesthetic 1. The onto-epistemic order constituted by the cultural dominance of the Western middle classes notably formalized its own knowledges, standards, and norms into an array of disciplinary fields collectively comprising the humanities and social sciences, which, as Wynter posits, *must* function to ensure this order's internal coherence. Even though the principle of semantic closure that secures the truth of Man has a determinative effect throughout every branch of Western humanism, the discourse of philosophical aesthetics still provides Wynter with a particularly apt exemplification of how the West's paradigm of cultural values adheres to the governing logic of Aesthetic 1. Drawing on Pierre Bourdieu's sociological critique of Kantian aesthetics, which correlated supposedly disinterested judgments of taste to the safeguarding of a distinct bourgeois class identity, Wynter extends the argument to apply to the globalized category of Man: "If . . . the discourses of philosophical aesthetics take as their 'sole datum' the lived experience of a *homo aestheticus* who is none other than the middle-class mode of the subject represented as 'the universal subject of aesthetic experience,' they also represent the lived experience of the western European and now, more generally, the 'developed' world's middle classes, as the experience of the generic human subject of aesthetic experience" (1992, 249).

This narcissistic projection of a particular mode of aesthetic experience as universally valid and desirable for all human subjects adheres to the rules defined by the logic of Aesthetic 1, but it also illustrates the problems arising within the currently dominant human order for those it subordinates. The systematized aesthetic overvaluation of Western middle-class cultural being, activity, and experience as the unquestionable signs of humanness implies a corresponding undervaluation of non-Western and lower-class cultural being, activity, and experience as denoting subhumanness. This particular outcome is a logical consequence of the generalized autopoietic rules governing all human orders, which have a binary configuration requiring a negatively marked abject category to stand in opposition to the normative ideal: "In every human order, each such sign-complex of the abject is everywhere empirically embodied in an interned and excluded group category whose role as the pariah figure(s) of the order is indispensable to the verifying of the 'regime of truth' orienting of the shared perceptions, and, therefore, of the collective behaviors by means of which each order is brought into being and stably replicated as such an order" (1992, 255). The historical genealogy of the present global order of Man, with its normatively Western, bourgeois subjectivity, as Wynter describes at length in other essays (e.g., 2003), necessarily led to the autopoietic codification of abject, excluded, or liminal beings representing/embodying conditions or experiences deemed antithetical to this specific definition of humanness. According to Wynter, these fall principally into two overlapping categories: (1) "mankind's enslavement to a possibly evolutionary regressive and genetically dysselected mode of human nature (as empirically expressed in peoples of Black African descent and, to a lesser extent, in all non-white peoples)" and (2) "enslavement to the 'natural scarcity' of external nature, and, therefore, to the threat of the insufficiency of the earth's resources, as verified by the empirical condition of the new pariah figures of the *poor* and *jobless*" (1992, 257). She underscores the binary logic at work in both of these categories by explaining how they each become symbolically coded as "death," whereas Man embodies the definitive form of "life" (1992, 258). Since these "life/death" formulations are inscribed into the dominant, culturally specific order of signification, or Aesthetic 2, in accordance with the a priori rules defined by Aesthetic 1, they determine the ways in which subjects sociogenically situated within this order will normatively think and feel about Self, Other, and World.

Every facet of Wynter's philosophy works toward a reinvention of the human "after Man" (2000, 25), a definitive break with the autopoietic pattern that stably replicates the current human-aesthetic order along with its rule-governed codification of subhuman abject others. For her, the full realization of such a rupture would be analogous to what she calls the "First Emergence" of humans from our precultural, purely natural existence, so she uses the idea of a "Second Emergence" to refer to the nascent formation of a shared consciousness of humanity's collective agency over the alterable autopoietic codes governing our self-formative behaviors (2000, 58). Another analogy developed throughout her project is, somewhat paradoxically, the revolution in thought that enabled the invention of Man itself. The lay humanists of late medieval Europe who challenged the epistemic authority of the Church and clergy effected an intellectual and cultural break that gradually displaced the scholastic theological conception of the cosmos with a secularized knowledge paradigm, building the foundations for the modern natural or physical sciences. Just as the sciences granted "autonomy of human cognition with respect to physical and organic reality," Wynter's proposed "parallel goal" is to realize "the autonomy of human cognition with respect to the reality of the social universes of which we are always already discursively instituted speaking/knowing/feeling subjects, and, therefore, with respect to the processes which govern our modes of being/behaving" (1992, 239). The redefined role of Wynter's aesthetics is to become a critical praxis capable of preparing the way for the planetary unfolding of this transformation. She describes this "deciphering practice" as an "attempt to move beyond our present 'human sciences' to that of a new science of human 'forms of life' and their correlated modes of the aesthetic" (240). In the next section, I examine some of Wynter's claims regarding how this framework of criticism may be applied in relation to creative projects by culturally and intellectually oppositional artist-practitioners.

Aesthetics as Deciphering Practice

A key theoretical premise of Wynter's approach is that, under routine cognitive conditions for those occupying subject positions corresponding to the normative "form of life" of each human order, the determinative a priori autopoietic logic of Aesthetic 1 remains generally inaccessible and unrecognizable, giving Aesthetic 2 the appearance of an essentially inalterable facticity. In other words, the specific signifying system of cultural valuation, as defined *within* the terms of a given order of the human, will always appear to have an autonomous, singular ontology whose "truth" may be comprehended but remains beyond the reach of human agency to transform. As a consequence, writes Wynter, the "production of all culture-specific, altruism-inducing, and cohering systems of meanings must function both rule-governedly and in ways that have hitherto transcended the 'normal' consciousness of each order's individual subjects" (1992, 244). Cultural critics working within the parameters of Aesthetic 2 unwittingly reproduce the particular configuration of humanness given by the underlying configuration of rules. To perceive the current human-aesthetic regime of Man as a historically contingent instance of a transcultural process of autopoiesis that has limitless possible arrangements and inherent potential for change, criticism will need to develop a practice of correlating cultural and discursive activity with the logical preconditions governing the normally hidden self-inscriptive process. This is the basic theory underpinning what Wynter calls a "practice of decipherment" (238).

The challenge of realizing such a practice lies with finding a "new conceptual ground ... [that] moves outside the parameters of the memory of Man, as the memory to which we are at present submitted" (Wynter 2000, 32). One of the enabling factors Wynter highlights comes from the "cognitive advantage" gained by subjects occupying the "liminal" position in the normative human order (58–59). She writes that "only the liminal categories of human orders (i.e., categories made to embody the signifier of deviant alterity and, thereby, of symbolic death to the criterion of being, of each culture's 'normal' mode of being), who, in attempting to free themselves from their systemic role of ontological negation, can free us all from the prescriptive categories of the circularly self-referential modes of memory or orders of consciousness, whose function is to integrate human orders" (58). Since those condemned to the condition subhumanity, those Fanon ([1961] 2004) referred to as *damnés*, are positioned at external borders of the dominant order of being, they are likely to experience a destabilizing degree of cognitive dissonance between normative representational codes and their lived perceptions of social reality. Even with the hegemonic "truth" of inferiority inscribed on their "dysselected" bodies or in their oppressive conditions of poverty and joblessness, they need not accept the legitimacy or finality of such inscriptions or the terms in which they are written and enforced. This epistemic resistance opens other conceptual standpoints offering perspectives that reach beyond the horizons of Man.

Part of the reason Wynter focuses on a reconceived critical aesthetic praxis arises from her observation that even when the signifying practices of liminal subjects have articulated profound challenges to the cultural paradigm of Man, these tend to lose much of their oppositional force when taken up by institutionally trained intellectuals. The dampening effects of disciplinary methods of criticism ultimately trace to the Western humanist precepts structurally embedded in the prevailing systems of scholarship. Because producers of even the most oppositional intellectual discourses are predominantly "educated in the Western episteme or order of knowledge, which is based on the a priori of this conception of the human, Man," their possibilities of making sense of cultural practices originating from liminal categories have most often been confined within parameters of disciplinary critical practice, which subsumes countersignifications in order to perpetuate the established rules (2000, 25). Referring to contemporary practices of academic cultural criticism, she writes that "in spite of its most radical approaches, its disciplinary paradigm must necessarily, in the last instance, function to contain, defuse, and neutralize the counter-signifying practice . . . of a still emergent global popular Imaginary" (1992, 260). Of course, Wynter differentiates among divergent branches or modes of mainstream academic theory and criticism (e.g., deconstruction, Marxist, feminist, African American, etc.) in terms of how each compromises itself in relation to the governing regime of Man. Some of the specific relevance of her reasoning on this issue is addressed later in this chapter. First, I examine how she describes and models her critical "deciphering practice" in the context of Black cinema.

Wynter has particular interest in film as a mode of creative practice that illustrates what is at stake in the "battle of tastes" being waged between disciplinary cultural criticisms that bolster the aesthetic regime of Man and artists/practitioners/thinkers who have resolved to move beyond its borders (1992, 268). In part, this is due to the vast reach and massive popular appeal of commercial cinema and television, in conjunction with "the formulaic way in which Hollywood's dream factories reinforce the desire for being in the terms of Man's modernity" (2000, 31). She argues that the accessibility and captivating power of visual mass media is a double-edged sword: "if no other medium was to be more effective than that of the cinema in ensuring the continued submission to its single memory of the peoples whom the West has subordinated in the course of its rise to world hegemony, no other medium is so potentially equipped to effect our common human emancipation from this memory" (29). Her approach to film as an arena of decolonial cultural combat dialogues with Clyde Taylor's (1988, 82) influential contributions to theorizing Black cinema's "efforts to break out of the prison-house of aesthetic discourse." Taylor's position, shared by Wynter, is that conventional aesthetic criteria used in film criticism will only distort subversive Black filmmakers' rebellions against the prevailing symbolic order. He writes, "Discussions about cinema and black people—whether they are portrayed accurately, which films are 'positive,' how films made by blacks fare beside others—reproduce false consciousness until they are grounded in knowledge of how the overwhelming experience of African people with this apparatus of representation has been as a mechanism of domination" (Taylor 1989, 90). Likewise, Wynter underscores that films such as the two selected for her discussion, *The Harder They Come* (1972; dir. Perry Henzell) and *Do the Right Thing* (1989; dir. Spike Lee), "can be properly evaluated only in the context of the challenge that they make to the cultural Imaginary instituting of our present order" (1992, 258).

Wynter's methodological practice of aesthetic decipherment consciously builds on and extends Taylor's (1988, 80–84) elaboration of what he calls "postaesthetic interpretation," a critical schema intended not only to undo the "injury" caused by traditional Western aesthetic philosophy's "doctrine of the autonomy of cultural production and appreciation" but also to avoid the dead end of ethno-aesthetics that trapped the US Black Aesthetic movement of the 1970s, causing it to become "lulled into quietue by its fascination with images of perfect and static essences." Taylor describes postaesthetics as a model of criticism in which the "individual text is freed of specious autonomy" and instead "opened to intercommunication with other texts and the significations of everyday life" (83). "The aim in postaesthetics," he writes, "is to seek satisfaction from the production and exchange of liberating knowledge, not the pleasure of the text" (83). From this perspective, with each cultural production constituting a "site of competing inscriptions of knowledge," the audience is situated in a complex discursive interface within which liberatory insights may be gleaned "through positive or negative illumination, or both" (83). When cultural representation opens up unbounded fields of contestable meaning, it invites translocal, transdisciplinary, and transideological dialogues that reshape the practice of critical analysis, pushing it out of the narrowly delimited areas of specialization and expertise that conventional aesthetic theory promotes. For Taylor, postaesthetics offers the potential to "revivify and validate meanings dismissed or obscured in imperial knowledge" (84). In this sense, he locates it within a larger array of decolonial strategies that contest not merely the content but also the terms of prevailing modes of cultural production, questioning the categorial subalternization of non-Western, nonmodern, nonbourgeois, nonpatriarchal knowledges, perspectives, histories, and so on. Taylor's (1989, 105) postaesthetics creates conceptual space for enacting transformative negotiations between a plurality of emancipatory currents, and for "a conscious realisation of the need to orchestrate . . . efforts against cultural imperialism and bourgeois cultural elitism, and therefore against the rationales for these ideological agencies embedded in aesthetics."

While incorporating Taylor's (1989, 106) focus on "creative/critical strategies . . . homologous with the conscious historical development of liberationist ideologies that give rise to goals beyond aestheticism," Wynter's deciphering practice aims to arrive at a more definitive mode of synthesizing the relation between cultural texts and their potential liberating effects on processes of subject formation within the dominant social order of Man. According to Wynter's model, the goal is for cultural criticism to grasp the rule-governed correlation between signifying practices and humanly instituted modes of consciousness and social being with a level of cognitive autonomy that parallels the objective detachment through which the natural sciences reveal the laws governing the physical universe or the genetically determinative codes inscribed into biological organisms. Wynter endorses Taylor's call for critics and scholars to self-consciously refuse the "opiate of aestheticism" in order to properly situate cultural productions in the sociopolitical, economic, historical, and epistemic context of decolonial struggles (Wynter 1992, 240). But whereas Taylor (1989, 106) views this as a step toward reinventing knowledge of the human through immersion in an open-ended critical/creative process reflective of the "dialogic disposition that mobilises decolonisation theory," Wynter envisions the possibility of approaching scientific certainty in our knowledge of the autopoietic processes by which we become instituted in culturally specific modes of human subjectivity. Rather than developing emancipatory social meanings by placing cultural texts into ever-evolving negotiations with a heteroglossic multiplicity of distinct oppositional (and potentially regressive) discourses, Wynter (1992, 272–73) posits a strategic distancing to enable analytic synthesis and methodical alteration of the dominant human-aesthetic nexus: "if we provisionally reduce all our present public language 'discourses,' epistemic and imaginative, . . . to their function as pure behavior regulating systems of meaning . . . then we can take the empirical behaviors and social effectivities to which they lead . . . as the data which makes them decipherable and, therefore, as the data which gives insight into the rules which govern the signifying practices by which we are instituted as specific modes of the subject. These modes now, because humanly knowable, are potentially, consciously, and consensually, alterable."

By analyzing "data" gathered from these correlations between patterns of cultural signification in creative texts, such as films, and observable regularities in the social environment, Wynter's (1992, 267) deciphering practice aims to give an empirically valid and logically sound account of "what the signifying practices, at the level of representation and their performative acts of meaning, are *intended to do*—that is, *what* collective behaviors they are intended to induce." To gain epistemic autonomy from the symbolic order of knowledge, the decipherment needs to be articulated in terms that break with the normative modes of cultural inscription: "Such a practice is intended to provide a 'separate language' able to deal with how, as humans, we can know the social reality of which we are both agents and always already socio-culturally constituted subjects" (268). Using the films *The Harder They Come* and *Do the Right Thing* to demonstrate, Wynter models some of the results of her deciphering methodology. She correlates representational elements within each film to the "form of life" and "social effectivities" instituted by the order Man, suggesting how a critical approach that views the main characters as signifying the existence of "captive populations" condemned to symbolic death in "U.S. inner cities and the Third World shantytown archipelagoes" can reveal patterns in the "non-linear structuring dynamics of our present global order, as well of its nation-state subunits" (241). She observes the films' depictions of middle-class and entrepreneurial characters who "embody the optimal behavioral model in relation to whose specific criterion the ensemble of global collective behaviors, which bring our present global order into being, are dynamically induced and regulated" (250). She then discerns how these idealized modes of "life-activity" are thrown into question by the countersignifications offered from the perspectives of the "Black and jobless" characters (250). Once the latter are identified as "systemic pariah figures," whose liminality is inscribed as "truth" in the terms of the current order's "epistemic contract," critics are confronted with the "imperative of 'breaking' this contract" to properly appreciate the characters' "performative acts of counter-meaning" (258). Deciphering this data collected from the films' "counter-signifying practices" as correlated to deducible elements of the rule-governed autopoietic code, Wynter argues, allows critics to draw "testable and verifiable" conclusions regarding these filmmakers' intentions to aesthetically induce a "counter-politics of 'feeling'" that connects the audience to a "global popular Imaginary whose referent telos is that of the well-being of the individual human subject and, therefore, of the species" (268).

In my view, certain theoretical moves in Wynter's deciphering practice undoubtedly generate advantages over the existing models of academic cultural criticism mentioned in her essays, but the proposed reduction of creative texts to data in pursuit of cognitively autonomous knowledge production analogous to that of the natural sciences raises numerous questions. Of course, not all of the possible pathways for interrogating Wynter's method of cultural criticism can be explored in the space available. One major branch of her argument that I have not described concerns the linkage she conceptualizes between the foundational "life/death" symbolic binary common to all human signifying systems and the human brain's internal neurochemical production of rewards and punishments in the form of endorphins and dynorphins, which function at the organic level to regulate behaviors (2000, 52). This line of argumentation, which she has continued to unfold in more recent writings (e.g., 2015), significantly underpins her call to reconceive the human as a "hybrid *nature-culture, bios/logos* form of life," as opposed to the strictly biocentric ontology instituted by Man under the Darwinian paradigm of evolution (2000, 26). Although I do not venture to dispute Wynter's detailed transdisciplinary engagements with research in cognitive science, neurology, and related fields, I find that the structure of oppositional binaries (e.g., life/death, subject/pariah, reward/punishment) abductively extended throughout her conceptual mapping of human autopoiesis is the source of certain shortcomings in her proposed method of critical practice.

In order to reduce cultural texts, such as *The Harder They Come* and *Do the Right Thing*, to decipherable data, Wynter (1992, 256) describes them in terms of representational elements that embody either the positively marked symbolic "form of life" or the negatively marked "sign-complex of the abject," as defined by the underlying logic of human-aesthetic codes. Based on this determination, Wynter argues that critics can assess whether the signifying practices within the film texts constitute inducements to behaviors aligned with the optimal goals, purposes, or telos of the current governing regime of Man or, alternatively, to counterbehaviors that challenge and subvert the dominant codes, ultimately encouraging heightened consciousness of their determinative function and activating the collective capacity to rewrite them. In a debate over the merits of Wynter's approach to cultural criticism, foregrounding the loss of subtlety, nuance, and ambiguity in the critical appreciation of creative art forms does not gain much traction, especially if this line of questioning rests on claims about the need to register an individual artist's singular point of view or refined sensibility. Wynter's rejection of conventional aesthetics implies consciously sacrificing the notion of any intrinsic value in imaginative genius, artistic ambivalence, or opaque abstraction in favor of making concrete determinations regarding how the creative text either reinforces or counters the status quo of the sociosymbolic order.

A more promising question relates to the seemingly passive role assigned to the audience/spectator in Wynter's schema as an object to be manipulated by positive and negative inducements. Wynter does not grant much direct attention to the potentially emancipatory subjectivity of spectators who may reject, appropriate, transform, or disidentify with cultural meanings inscribed by creative texts, regardless of input from critics/intellectuals. Unlike Taylor, she does not explicitly address the "developmental-critical function [that] is available to post-aesthetics in the tri-part dialogue . . . among film-maker/storyteller, audience/community and activist/critic" (Taylor 1989, 105).[7] She equivocates in her approach to the question of resistance in mass spectatorship, as she highlights, on the one hand, the history of US Black audiences rebelling against the denigrating racial imagery deployed in early cinema (2000, 32). On the other hand, she asserts that "it is because the experience of their real-life reality is such a persistently harsh and unfulfilled one for the cinema's mass audiences, that the fantasy of escaping from it becomes an urgent consumer need" (31). But if Wynter's position here is rather unpersuasive, and if her main arguments turn primarily on the deciphering task of the critic, this does not necessarily add up to a dismissal of the audience's active responsiveness, especially that of communities socially located in liminal positionalities. Her repeated references to the "ongoing cultural revolution of an emergent global and popular Imaginary" suggest that she sees this formation as already constituting a plurality of movements toward communal decolonial consciousness in diverse parts of the world, presumably including some groups of cinemagoers capable of responding mindfully to behavior-motivating patterns of filmic representation (1992, 239).

Wynter does not make critics/intellectuals into the sole or even chief arbiters of the cultural criteria for "securing . . . the well-being of the concrete individual human subject," since she believes these are already being established by articulations coming from various currents of collective cultural and epistemic reinvention (1992, 239). Precisely what Wynter wants to address is the problematic disjuncture between academic disciplinary paradigms of cultural criticism, which remain enchanted by Western humanism and aesthetics, and the "global popular Imaginary," which refers to a diversity of projects intended to bring about other modes of humanness beyond Man. She views the intellectual establishment—including branches dedicated to radically disruptive or progressive theories of culture and politics—as lagging far behind, or as disconnected altogether from the paths being cut beyond Man's borders by struggles for communal autonomy across the planet. The regressive, insular thinking of academically trained critics, combined with the institutional power and discursive authority of their disciplinary knowledges, contributes to holding back wider participation in oppositional movements and produces alienating separations by dividing specific constituencies into discrete fields of contestation, blocking possibilities of relational convergence and coalition. In her attempt to close the gaps maintained by existing humanist scholarship's self-segregating estrangement from liminal collectivities engaging in an ongoing pursuit of a reinvented human, Wynter unfolds a practice of criticism designed as an alternative to the reproductions of Man that persist within schools of thought supposedly concerned with countering capitalist, patriarchal, and racial oppressions. A mode of critical discourse more closely connected with popular and communal articulations of other humanisms, she suggests, would be able to contribute to more durable institutional and social transformations.

The reasoning behind Wynter's claims that existing academic disciplinary approaches have been unable to dislodge the regime of Man extends beyond the immediate context of her discussions of cultural criticism, but the two selected essays illustrate the basic contours of her larger perspective on the limitations of influential discursive formations that offer only superficial challenges to Western modernity's hierarchical structures of class, gender, and race. The main deficiency shared by Marxist, feminist, and some ethnic studies' paradigms of cultural analysis, according to Wynter, is that they leave intact the current integrative human-aesthetic codification of subjectivity as the governing source of legitimacy for the incorporation of additional "forms of life" into the present order. In other words, the implicit goal of these critical paradigms is not to overthrow the rule of Man but to create an inclusive space for others to be recognized as humans within his domains. Wynter (1992, 263) disparages the shortsightedness of this tacitly compliant agenda, describing Marxist and feminist criticism as being inherently constrained by their "respective 'ideologies of Otherness.'" She continues, "If these have only succeeded in adding the variant figures of proletarian 'man' and of 'woman' to that of liberalism's 'figure of man,' the recent attempt by Henry Louis Gates to counter traditional literary theory and its canon by the instituting of the figure of an African American man complete with its own indigenous literary theory and canon has lead instead . . . to an ethno-literary criticism and to the reinforcing, therefore, of our present cultural Imaginary, together with its still pervasive realm of unfreedom" (263). Expressed in terms of Wynter's theory of the transcendental process of autopoiesis, the failure of these critical approaches lies in the attempt to undo the exclusions of workers, women, and Blacks *within* the terms given by the current sociosymbolic order rather than effecting a transformation from the *exteriority*, at the level of the underlying rules establishing the binary relation between the governing concept of the human and its liminal subhuman categories. This error, Wynter argues, results in partial gains in rights and recognition for limited constituencies based on narrowly defined conditions, leaving the normativity of Man uncontested. The alternative, she insists, must involve reinventing the overarching criteria of humanness "based on a new conception of freedom able to move us not only beyond that of Man . . . but also beyond those of Man's oppositional sub-versions,—that of Marxism's *proletariat*, that of feminism's *woman* (gender rights), and that of our multiple multiculturalisms and/or centric cultural nationalisms (minority rights), to that of gay liberation (homosexual rights), but also a conception of freedom able to draw them all together in a new synthesis" (2000, 41–42).

By positing the need for this "new synthesis," Wynter contends that getting beyond Man requires a mode of analysis that transcends internal struggles waged over categories of Otherness by moving to a different "conceptual ground," a standpoint from which the rules governing all social orders may be consciously grasped and directed toward other horizons of human freedom. It is here, I argue, that the binary configuration of autopoietic/epistemic/sociogenic codes underpinning Wynter's theory of human self-formation leads her into an overreductive critique of gendered modalities of dehumanization and an undertheorized conceptualization of the oppositional possibilities of Black women's creative practices. As I explain in the next section, Wynter proposes that transformative critical engagement with the discourse-constitutive logic of Man requires subordinating analysis of gender as a system of oppression to what she considers the more fundamental question of biracial and socioeconomic categories of exclusion that organize the global order of modernity/coloniality. This creates weaknesses in her framework's ability to account for subject positions such as those inhabited by Black women contesting multiple overlapping colonizations. As I will demonstrate, Wynter's anatomical description of the sex-gender matrix rests on an essentializing dichotomy that risks erasing the dehumanizing consequences of these categories for racially colonized women and nonwhite sexual dissidents. These limitations in Wynter's thought need to be identified more clearly in order to create openings in her theoretical framework for nonwhite women's creative practices to contribute to the project of reinventing of the human.

Critical Consequences of Wynter's Naturalization
of the Sexual/Gender Dichotomy

Since Wynter's (2000, 25) project thoroughly and definitively discredits the foundational bioevolutionary narrative of Man that discursively institutes the normative superiority of the Western European as the naturally "selected" ideal genre of humanness, at least some of her interlocutors have interpreted this move as constituting a challenge to the sex/gender-related dimensions of this narrative, which naturalize patriarchal social structures on the spurious basis of biological determinism. Moreover, because her critical genealogy of Man traces the imperial origins of the current global order of hierarchical social relations, some have been prompted to see Wynter as an intellectual ally in the struggle against gendered articulations of the coloniality of power. For example, Greg Thomas (2006, 78) argues that Wynter's thought goes much further than that of such luminaries as Michel Foucault or Judith Butler in questioning the hegemony of modern sex and gender categories since she makes it possible to connect normative constructions of maleness and femaleness to a history of colonialization and the invention of a racialized hierarchy of humanness. From Thomas's perspective, Wynter's work contributes to the project of "reconstruct[ing] an African/Diasporic tradition of thought that not only denaturalizes dominant sexual ontologies *for real*, but does so furthermore in *anti-imperialist* fashion. It would treat sex categories as explicit categories of empire" (Thomas 2006, 78). He suggests that her critical thought unsettles the "conceptual foundations" of "*core* concepts . . . like 'manhood' and 'womanhood,' 'heterosexuality' and 'homosexuality,' and demonstrate[s] their *historical contingency;* their *cultural specificity*, as well as their *socio-political undesirability*" (78–79).

Despite such assessments, Wynter's wide-ranging theorization of humanism conspicuously declines to analyze the imperial function of the modern gender matrix. Thomas provides a useful summary of research by thinkers, such as Ifi Amadiume, Nkiru Nzegwu, and Oyèrónkẹ́ Oyěwùmí, who examine sex and gender historically from the perspective of African societies whose indigenous structures of sociosexual differentiation were largely destroyed and replaced through processes of racial colonization. Thomas's attempts to find a place for Wynter in this dialogue come up short, producing few if any substantial connections. In fact, Wynter shares very little common ground with these researchers, who oppose the biologization of gender difference and offer frameworks for reconstructing sexual politics beyond the terms derived from Western modernity's sociocultural history. Looking closely at some of Wynter's engagements with questions of sex and gender, one finds an overreduction of these categories to a biological, or rather anatomical, conception of difference without immediate relevance to the discursive construction of Man's subhuman Others. Instead, political and cultural struggles over gendered modes of subjectivity are understood to be secondary effects of what Wynter sees as Man's primary dual-axis human-aesthetic hierarchy of racial and economic differentiation. For her, Man's less-than-human Others are composed of, first, "all native peoples, and most extremely, to the ultimately zero degree, all peoples of African descent, wholly or partly (i.e. negroes)," and second, "the category of the *jobless, semi-jobless Poor*, together with that of the underdeveloped countries" (2000, 26). With humanness delimited in terms of these two intersecting classificatory fields, the causes and consequences of sex- and gender-inflected oppressions and exclusions must be approached as separate from the foundational self-inscriptive logic of Man.

To be certain, Wynter acknowledges women's differential experiences within the current sociogenic regime of Man, but she sees these accruing primarily to white, middle-class, professional women who, "while privileged like their male peers in terms of race and class, experienced the anomaly of their gender dysprivilege *vis-à-vis* these male peers" (interview with Scott 2000, 184). She is also fully cognizant that nonmodern human orders defined their own normative gender roles in very different terms than those familiar to Western modernity, marking a distinction from major branches of academic feminist theory, which "would continue to see gender as a supracultural phenomenon, and therefore as a universal whose terms could be the same for all human groups" (Scott 2000, 185). These critical recognitions of how gender became an analytic category based on the perspective of subjects who were already occupying positions of relative privilege in the global system of capitalist modernity are common to many women of color who think from the liminal regions of this system. However, instead of reworking the terms of gender politics from the intersectional standpoint of racialized women as other critics of First World feminism have done, Wynter argues for subordinating gender to the more fundamental classificatory logic embedded in modern humanism: "the moment that you look at it from the perspective of that vast majority [of unprivileged women], you can recognize that the phenomenon of gender, while a foundational archetype unique to our situation as humans, nevertheless is itself only one member of a class, a class of *something else*" (Scott 2000, 186). The perception of gender's subsumption into "something else" informs Wynter's conclusion that the autopoietic codes governing all orders of humanness, that is, Aesthetic 1, will assign culturally specific meanings to the anatomical distinctions between male and female bodies, but in Aesthetic 2, our own order, these meanings no longer constitute a primary determinative dimension of symbolic life/death. In other words, gender "had been the *archetypal* form of all such codes, it is not the code itself" (Scott 2000, 186).

Putting her critical method of aesthetic deciphering into practice, Wynter offers a fairly precise description of her understanding of gender's displacement by race as the determinative cultural form in Man's codified order of the human in a discussion of William Shakespeare's *The Tempest*. This paradigmatic text, she argues, registers the "mutational shift from the primacy of the *anatomical* model of sexual difference as the referential model of *mimetic* ordering, to that of the physiognomic model of *racial/cultural* difference" (1990, 358). The Renaissance humanist episteme, of which Shakespeare is one of the foremost representatives, holds particular significance within Wynter's genealogy of Man for having consolidated the "epochal shift out of primarily *religious* systems of legitimation and behaviour-regulation" into a secularizing modality of aesthetic practice that would inscribe other criteria of humanness, rewriting the sociogenic code to make the rational-political subject of Western European civilization into the preeminent "form of life" (357). This transformative process was, of course, unfolding in tandem with the "expropriation of the land/living space of the New World peoples ... based on the secular concept of the 'non-rational' inferior '*nature*' of the peoples to be expropriated and governed" (357). What becomes visible through Shakespeare's dramatic writing is the humanist configuration of "an ostensible difference in 'natural' substance which, for the first time in history, was no longer primarily encoded in the male/female gender division as it has been hitherto in the symbolic template of all traditional and religiously based human orders, but now in the cultural-physiognomic variations between the dominant expanding European civilization and the non-Western peoples that, encountering it, would now stigmatize as 'natives'" (357–58). To state this even more clearly, the "shift to the secular" brought with it a corresponding aesthetic change in the "primary code of difference [which] now became that between 'men' and 'natives,' with the traditional 'male' and 'female' distinctions now coming to play a secondary—if nonetheless powerful—reinforcing role within the system of symbolic representations" (358). Wynter observes these dynamics in *The Tempest*'s representation of a European woman, Miranda, enacting her position of social superiority over an enslaved native male, Caliban.

By reducing gender differentiation to a secondary datum in the aesthetic analysis of modern humanism's symbolic order, Wynter disengages from feminist analysis that isolates and universalizes the patriarchal dimension of social oppression. Instead, the critical aesthetic focus turns toward the cultural representation of racialized "natural" attributes associated with a lack of civilization, which became the "primary index of 'deferent' difference" in the construction of the West's new secularized episteme, and her project's imperative becomes to trace its further mutations over the course of centuries toward the present-day biological-*cum*-economic model of the human (1990, 358). Aspects of Wynter's rationale for this disengagement, as I have suggested, do not vary greatly from the critical precepts that have informed much Black feminist theorizing of the past several decades, which Wynter herself acknowledges with references to Alice Walker and the Caribbean women authors whose work was gathered in the anthology *Out of the Kumbla,* for which Wynter's (1990, 357) own essay served as the "After/Word." However, the consequences borne out in Wynter's subsequent work show that more than merely distancing herself from white, academic feminism's revalorizations of a universal conception of womanhood, she has tended to minimize gender analytics altogether. Her more recent essays elaborating on her resignified aesthetics not only neglect to work through the complex enmeshment of modern/colonial sex-gender discourses and race- and class-bound definitions of humanness but also persistently give overreductive descriptions of nonmodern systems of gendering anatomical distinctions that naturalize the sexual dichotomy. For example, she frequently makes broad analogies between the hierarchical logic of racial distinction within the regime of Man, and the gender-based distinctions that she claims organized other human-aesthetic orders: "This encoded value-difference [i.e., between whiteness and Blackness] then came to play the same role, in the enactment of our now purely secular genre of the human Man, as the gendered anatomical difference between men and women had played over millennia, if in then supernaturally mandated terms, in the enactment of all the genres of being human that had been defining of traditional, stateless orders" (2006, 117–18). The suggestion, repeated in different terms in several other essays—that anatomy provided the primary transcultural basis for the construction of gender dichotomies—not only ignores the question of nonbinary systems of sociosexual differentiation but also reinforces the naturalized biological anchor of sex/gender dualism.[8]

Wynter's (2006, 131) reconceived aesthetic method grasps Western modernity's invention of Man as a model of being systematically "overrepresented as if it were the human." Throughout her project, the aim is to *denaturalize* this hegemonic conception of humanness in order to move beyond its hierarchical logic. Unless sex/gender can be fully denaturalized as a category of social difference, along with other related systems of classification based on bioracial and economic hierarchies, the current conception of the human will retain at least some of its ontological stature. Furthermore, without analytically engaging the gendering criteria that constitute Man's aesthetic paradigm, the particular oppositional, creative, communal standpoints of subjects dehumanized *as* nonwhite women or sexual dissidents, for example, will remain unintelligible as the grounds for wider processes of intellectual, cultural, and political transformation. Such an engagement need not turn completely away from Wynter's aesthetic approach. As Alexander Weheliye (2014, 41) suggests, it is possible to unfold a theoretical framework that "takes Wynter's insights about how race inflects human physiology in colonial modernity seriously, while still asking how, even if it is not the primary model of hierarchical differentiation, sexual difference might figure into this theory of the human." Although the racialized gender matrix remains undertheorized in much of Wynter's writing, certain texts contain suggestive pathways approaching the aestheticized "silencing" of racialized women's perspectives.

One example of such an opening occurs in the previously cited essay, "Beyond Miranda's Meanings," in which Wynter argues that deciphering *The Tempest* demonstrates modernity's movement beyond the primacy of gender difference in social relations to the constitution of a new aesthetic-human order based on the racial/cultural distinction between rational men and irrational natives. Wynter (1990, 364) observes that there is a significant absence in the play where one might expect to find "Caliban's woman" as "an alternative sexual-erotic model of desire, as an alternative source of an alternative system of meanings." Instead, Miranda, the only female character in the drama, is "canonized as the 'rational' object of desire; as the potential genitrix of a superior mode of human 'life,' that of 'good natures' as contrasted with the ontologically absent potential genitrix—Caliban's mate" (364). On one hand, the nonexistence of a subject position corresponding to that of *native woman* in the "desirable" and "rational" social schema aesthetically inscribed by the play suggests that such a position was logically and representationally unnecessary for image-making practices dedicated to the stable reproduction of the ideal form of humanness embodied by Man. On the other hand, Wynter invokes the dynamics of liminality to suggest this absence points to a possible point of aesthetic rupture with the order of Man, as such a rupture can only be effectuated from a vantage point situated outside of its dominant discourses. In other words, using this method to identify the "systemic function" of the mechanisms of silencing and exclusion that produce the specific absence of "Caliban's woman" throws into relief the delimiting borders of Man, making them available to challenge from an aesthetic perspective not governed by its episteme (364).

As I have already mentioned, Wynter's more recent essays do not follow through on this suggestive trajectory of critical aesthetic theorization. However, by identifying nonwhite women's subjectivity as an ontological gap in the ostensibly pristine surface of Man's socio-epistemic edifice, she acknowledges racialized gender difference as a standpoint condemned to silence and invisibility by colonial modernity, thereby calling attention to it as a point of epistemic breakage, a "fractured locus" (Lugones 2010) in the current symbolic order. Opting to think with Wynter in pursuit of decolonial aesthetics will entail unpacking and cultivating these suggestions in recognition of the shortcomings and limitations of her framework. Without engaging the specific transformative potential of communal sense making articulated from the liminal zones occupied by racialized women and sexual nonconformers, overthrowing the dominant aesthetic-human regime is simply unimaginable.

Notes

1. Decolonial aesthetics has emerged relatively recently as an analytic term, but the practices and theories to which it refers are part of a long legacy of creating and re-creating other worlds beyond Western modernity. See the "Decolonial Aesthetics" manifesto, originally published in 2011 (Lockward et al. 2020). Also see Mignolo and Vázquez 2013, which introduces a dossier of diverse contributions focused on this topic.

2. Mignolo (2011, 16–19) identifies an "aesthetic hierarchy" and "an idea of Man" as two "heterogenous historico-structural nodes" joined together with at least ten others to constitute the "colonial matrix of power," expanding the influential model originally theorized by Aníbal Quijano (2000). By no means does an analytic focus on the linkages between two components of this matrix imply they can be entirely separated from other discursive, epistemic, institutional mechanisms of modern/colonial domination. On the contrary, bringing critical attention to the interdependence of synchronously orchestrated domains of coloniality facilitates an understanding of their enmeshment within the systemic arrangement of diffusely coordinated organs of oppression comprising modernity as whole.

3. Wynter's notion of a "science of the Word" is partly based on arguments put forward by Aimé Césaire in his 1946 essay, "Poetry and Knowledge" (1990, xlii–lvi). Wynter frequently cites Césaire, invoking his legacy of cultural and artistic practices informed by decolonial struggles and the memory of the Middle Passage.

4. For an informative overview of Wynter's thinking, see Henry 2000, chap. 5. At least two anthologies of scholarly essays and several special issues of academic journals dedicated to Wynter's work have been published. See *After Man, towards the Human: Critical Essays on Sylvia Wynter*, edited by Anthony Bogues (2006) and *Sylvia Wynter: On Being Human as Praxis*, edited by Katherine McKittrick (2015). Also see "Sylvia Wynter's 'Black Metamorphosis': A Discussion" in *Small Axe*, no. 49, guest edited by Aaron Kamugisha (2016).

5. Italicized words and phrases in quoted passages are always italicized in the original texts unless otherwise specified.

6. Works by Gregory Bateson, David Chalmers, Ernesto Grassi, J. G. A. Pocock, James F. Danielli, Cornelius Castoriadis, V. Y. Mudimbe, and Asmarom Legesse, among others, are frequently cited by Wynter.

7. Given Wynter's extended dialogue with Taylor, it is somewhat surprising that Wynter engages so little with other literature on Third Cinema, which was animated by lively debates around the question of the oppositional artist's relation to mass audiences made available through film and television. See, for example, the essays collected in *Questions of Third Cinema* (edited by Jim Pines and Paul Willemen, 1989). For a more recent treatment of Third Cinema that engages with questions of decolonial aesthetics, see Ramos 2018, chap. 4.

8. For example, in "Unsettling the Coloniality of Being/Power/Truth/Freedom" (2003), Wynter writes that race is "unlike gender" in that the latter "has a biogenetically determined anatomical differential correlate onto which each culture's system of gendered oppositions can be anchored" (264).

References

Césaire, Aimé. 1990. *Lyric and Dramatic Poetry, 1946–82*. Translated by Clayton Eshleman and Annette Smith. Charlottesville: University Press of Virginia.

Escobar, Arturo. 2018. *Designs for the Pluriverse: Radical Interdependence, Autonomy, and the Making of Worlds*. Durham, NC: Duke University Press.

Fanon, Frantz. (1952) 2007. *Black Skin, White Masks*. Translated by Richard Philcox. New York: Grove Press.

———. (1961) 2004. *The Wretched of the Earth*. Translated by Richard Philcox. New York: Grove Press.

Henry, Paget. 2000. *Caliban's Reason: Introducing Afro-Caribbean Philosophy*. London: Routledge.

———. 2006. "Wynter and the Transcendental Spaces of Caribbean Thought." In *After Man, towards the Human: Critical Essays on Sylvia Wynter*, edited by Anthony Bogues, 258–89. Kingston, Jamaica: Ian Randle.

Kamugisha, Aaron, ed. 2016. "Sylvia Wynter's 'Black Metamorphosis': A Discussion." *Small Axe* 20 (1): 37–146.

Lockward, Alanna, Rolando Vázquez, Teresa María Díaz Nerio, Marina Grzinic, Tanja Ostojic, Dalida María Benfield, Raul Moarquech Ferrera Balanquet, et al. 2020. "Decolonial Aesthetics." *Minorit'Art: Revue de Recherches Décoloniales*, no. 4: 21–25.

Lugones, María. 2010. "Toward a Decolonial Feminism." *Hypatia* 25 (4): 743–59.

McKittrick, Katherine, ed. 2015. *Sylvia Wynter: On Being Human as Praxis*. Durham, NC: Duke University Press.

Mignolo, Walter D. 2011. *The Darker Side of Western Modernity: Global Futures, Decolonial Options*. Durham, NC: Duke University Press.

Mignolo, Walter D., and Rolando Vázquez. 2013. "Decolonial AestheSis: Colonial Wounds/Decolonial Healings." *Social Text Online*, July 15, 2013. https://socialtextjournal.org/periscope_article/decolonial-aesthesis-colonial-woundsdecolonial-healings/.

Pines, Jim, and Paul Willemen, eds. 1989. *Questions of Third Cinema*. London: British Film Institute.

Quijano, Aníbal. 2000. "Colonialidad del poder y clasificación social." *Journal of World Systems Research* 5 (2): 342–86.

Ramos, Juan G. 2018. *Sensing Decolonial Aesthetics in Latin American Arts*. Gainesville: University of Florida Press.

Scott, David. 2000. "The Re-Enchantment of Humanism: An Interview with Sylvia Wynter." *Small Axe* 8: 119–207.

Taylor, Clyde. 1988. "We Don't Need Another Hero: Anti-Theses on Aesthetics." In *Blackframes: Critical Perspectives on Black Independent Cinema*, edited by Mbye B. Cham and Claire Andrade-Watkins, 80–85. Cambridge, MA: MIT Press.

———. 1989. "Black Cinema in the Post-Aesthetic Era." In *Questions of Third Cinema*, edited by Jim Pines and Paul Willemen, 90–110. London: British Film Institute.

Thomas, Greg. 2006. "The 'S' Word: Sex, Empire and Black Radical Tradition." In *After Man, towards the Human: Critical Essays on Sylvia Wynter*, edited by Anthony Bogues, 76–99. Kingston, Jamaica: Ian Randle.

Weheliye, Alexander G. 2014. *Habeas Viscus: Racializing Assemblages, Biopolitics, and Black Feminist Theories of the Human*. Durham, NC: Duke University Press.

Wynter, Sylvia. 1990. "Beyond Miranda's Meanings: Un/Silencing the 'Demonic Ground' of Caliban's 'Woman.'" In *Out of the Kumbla: Caribbean Women and Literature*, edited by Carole Boyce Davies and Elaine Savory Fido, 355–72. Trenton, NJ: Africa World Press.

———. 1992. "Rethinking 'Aesthetics': Notes towards a Deciphering Practice." In *Ex-Iles: Essays on Caribbean Cinema*, edited by Mbye B. Cham, 237–79. Trenton, NJ: Africa World Press.

———. 2000. "Africa, the West and the Analogy of Culture: The Cinematic Text after Man." In *Symbolic Narratives/African Cinema: Audiences, Theory and the Moving Image*, edited by June Givanni, 23–76. London: British Film Institute.

———. 2003. "Unsettling the Coloniality of Being/Power/Truth/Freedom: Towards the Human, after Man, Its Overrepresentation—An Argument." *CR: The New Centennial Review* 3 (3): 257–337.

———. 2006. "On How We Mistook the Map for the Territory and Re-Imprisoned Ourselves in Our Unbearable Wrongness of Being, of *Désêtre*: Black Studies Toward the Human Project." In *Not Only the Master's Tools: African-American Studies in Theory and Practice*, edited by Lewis R. Gordon and Jane Anna Gordon, 107–69. New York: Routledge.

———. 2015. "The Ceremony Found: Towards the Autopoetic Turn/Overturn, Its Autonomy of Human Agency and Extraterritoriality of (Self-)Cognition." In *Black Knowledges/Black Struggles: Essays in Critical Epistemology*, edited by Jason R. Ambroise and Sabine Broeck, 184–252. Liverpool: Liverpool University Press.

Patrick M. Crowley is a Lecturer in English at Appalachian State University.

PART IV
RADICAL COALITIONS AND COMMUNAL POLITICS

9
HANGING OUT AND AN INFRAPOLITICS OF YOUTH

Cindy Cruz

> We are also other than what the hegemon makes us be.
> —María Lugones, "Toward a Decolonial Feminism"

I AM A youth researcher. I have worked with LGBTQ+ houseless youth for many years as a teacher, an HIV counselor, an activist, and an ethnographer. Carrying safe sex kits and protein bars in my backpack, I walk the streets with queer and trans* youth—*callejera*-style—talk with them, laugh and cry with them, always aware that the houseless are not permitted any form of relief in public spaces in Los Angeles. Youth who are queer, trans*, and houseless are made invisible and their intentions are often erased by police, caseworkers, teachers, and medical services. I "world"-travel with queer and trans* youth to make sense of their queer youthspaces, hanging out, streetwalking, understanding mobility as survival, sharing knowledge and technology with others as resistant and life-affirming praxes, recognizing the plural self, recognizing "world"-traveling as youth resistance and its celebration, and conceiving of youth geographies as multiple, intermeshing, interwoven, co-temporaneous realities.

This chapter is engaging with two concepts from María Lugones's work. One concept is the practice of *hanging out*, where I am thinking with the stories and experiences of houseless queer and trans* youth. The second concept I am thinking with is the plural notion of "worlds" and "world"-traveling that becomes so important in my understanding of street youth worlds and building relations. It is Lugones's work that helps me as an ethnographer and a youth researcher think about resisting practices and "worlds" in ways that counter the deficit and dehumanizing manners in which houseless subjects are represented. This work with youth is dedicated to Lugones's thinking and pedagogy in all of the parts of her life, where I "world"-travel with young people to understand "what it is to be them and what it is to be ourselves in their eyes" (Lugones 2003, 97).

Hanging Out

I want to think about *hanging out* as a houseless queer and trans* youth practice. This practice is what María Lugones (2003, 221) defines as "highly fluid, worldly, non-sanctioned, communicative, occupations of space, contestatory retreats for the passing on of knowledge, for the tactical-strategic fashioning of multivocal sense, of enigmatic vocabularies and gestures, for the development of keen commentaries on structural pressures and gaps, spaces of complex and open-ended recognition."

Hanging out practices created by queer and trans* youth are not only found in besieged public places (like public parks, schools, bus stops, social service agencies, computer clubhouses), where young houseless people are heavily policed and surveilled. Hanging out is also a practice where youth can both sense and discuss the reality and fiction of the commons (and all of their experiences of being under siege, defined as deficit, and sharing with each other how they move against dehumanization) through their daily interactions on the street with other youth. It is a space of interactive street literacies, where multiple meanings and worlds of sense are being negotiated. Hanging out is a praxis, always in flux, negotiating, reinscribing, rethinking, revising, made anew with each crossing, even if only temporarily. Hanging out is the persistence of queer and trans youth where a "reappropriation of space" happens (Lefebvre [1974] 1991).

Youth who are unaccompanied minors, aged out of foster care, or fleeing abusive home spaces challenge this myth of the commons, despite what Lugones (2003, 209) names as the circuit of "home-shelter-street-police station/jail/insane asylum-cemetery." The practice of hanging out responds by rejecting the division between public and private spheres through the creation of spaces of resistant socialities. Youth *callejeras* understand the dominant spatial politics of Los Angeles, where police and their proxies remind them daily of their vulnerabilities in a public sphere. "Home" does not often offer refuge for queer and trans* youth. They find themselves "at odds" with home, understanding that neither living on the street nor in homes where violence is the norm offers any protection from abuse and exploitation.

To be homeless in Los Angeles is to understand the regulation and the destruction of public space as an elimination of homeless bodies. New antihomeless laws prohibit sleeping, sitting, camping, and obstructing the public right-of-way within five hundred feet of "sensitive" facilities, including schools, day care facilities, parks and libraries (Zahniser and Oreskes 2021). New gentrification in neighborhoods occupied by youth social service centers and shelters has led to those areas being heavily policed and surveilled while big-box stores and consumer spaces are literally walled off from the street. The dissemination of antihomeless laws is an issue of destroying whatever freedom houseless people have to move, sleep, eat, or rest. The parking fees, private security, and loitering laws are the daily reminders of the regulation of space in Los Angeles, understanding how the control of it determines the very condition of their lives. To be the queer and trans* youth callejera is to be cognizant of this city's spatial politics, to understand how race is managed on Santa Monica Boulevard, where the young white male hustlers stay west of La Brea Avenue and young queer and trans* men of color work east of Highland Avenue, highlighting the racial politics in Los Angeles.

Hanging out is recognizing as a way of being in the world with others in which queer and trans* youth share with each other gossip and information about jobs, teachers, social workers, the police, and their agents. It is in *hanging out* where homeless youth practice a "persistence of appropriation of space" (Lugones 2003, 220), and the term is defined as a contested concrete space that cannot be contained by a private/public dichotomy. It is a space where youth who are "at odds with home," create space outside of the surveillance of those in power, where young people compare their experiences with others who become important centers of information and survival strategies. This space of hanging out helps create space for queer and trans youth to rest without harassment, smoke and laugh with friends, dress provocatively with newly found clothes, and dance to publicly taunt onlookers but also to enjoy their own and each other's bodies. It allows youth to release the "muscular tension" (Fanon [1961] 2004, 17) accrued in the zone of constant struggle with teachers, police, and social workers.

When I first began working with queer and trans* street youth, I didn't recognize the infrapolitics: the dissident offstage practices that resist the everyday humiliations, degradations, and experiences of exclusion that make up the daily fabric of LGBTQ+ youth lives. The young people I worked with would often hang out outside of the gates of the schoolyard and in front of the youth drop-in center. I often saw youth assembled at the bus stop or standing together on sidewalks smoking cigarettes, joking, and talking loudly with each other and often dramatically with other passersby. Despite the heavy surveillance of youth in the public sites where this research takes place, it is helpful to think about youth resistance in these hanging out spaces as offstage practices

(Scott 1990) that take place just below the constant watchfulness of authority. It is in practice of hanging out where I can think with youth about the activities that are so important in how we can think about resistance to multiple oppressions by queer and trans* street youth.

Lugones (2003) writes about resistance in tight spaces—the fragile spatiality produced in such offstage practices. This spatiality is constricted in that it is not concrete: "You are concrete. Your spatiality, constructed as an intersection following the designs of power, isn't" (10). It is in the careful observations of the often violent intersections of the body, race, gender, and sexuality, where the tight spaces of youth resistance are engaged. Interfacing Lugones's theorizing of resistance with those by James C. Scott (1990) and Robin D. G. Kelley (1993), everyday acts of resistance in tight spaces describe how the self and others "violate this spatiality or inhabit it with great resistance, without willful collaboration" (Lugones 2003, 10). Reframing youth experiences that extend traditional notions of resistance, Lugones's tight spaces help locate the daily and seemingly spontaneous acts of resistance performed by LGBTQ+ street youth as important. The notion of a resistant sociality is particularly important in an examination of the offstage practices that may create the breathing spaces, however tight, for LGBTQ+ street youth—life for otherwise disposable lives. Resistance in these instances is not about changing or intervening in the life circumstances of LGBTQ+ youth, nor is it about the destruction of a system of oppression. It is a deviation from the overwhelming logic of domination, a fissure in the monolithic space of oppression. These gestures and maneuvers by LGBTQ+ street youth represent departures from these logics, however small and imperceptible they may be. In spaces where the queer and trans* youth body is perceived as infected, contaminated, and often expendable, it is with Lugones's work that their talking back must be recognized.

Thinking Infrapolitically with Youth

Throughout my tenure as a teacher with queer and trans* students, I observed youth "talking back" to teachers, administrators, and social service workers in bodily ways. It was the exaggerated snap of fingers in someone's face or the slow swagger of a student turning their back on an authority figure. Schools, even those places whose mission emphasized the educational experiences of LGBTQ+ adolescents, were spaces where the "daily confrontations, evasive actions, and stifled thoughts" of an infrapolitics was in place (Kelley 1993). Infrapolitics, defined as the space of offstage practices (Scott 1990, 4) and "a dissident political culture that manifests itself in daily conversations, folklore, jobs, songs, and other cultural practices" (Kelley 1993, 77), is a strategy of resistance created by subjugated communities to negotiate the continuous scrutiny and containment by the powerful. Illuminating resistance in the tight spaces of infrapolitics counters the representation of youth as deficit and as victims of a culture of poverty. Recognizing youth infrapolitics moves away from discourses of criminalization and poverty that often haunt educational policy and research.

A deficit approach to research is often about "fixing" pathologized people. Under this rubric, change is forced on the imperfect bodies of queer and trans* youth of color. Countering such research models and representations requires another kind of infrapolitics. To delink or divest oneself from the research models of radical othering requires educational and social science researchers to reframe the dialectics of domination and submission between youth and police, doctors, teachers, and other authorities.

Thinking about LGBTQ+ youth practices and small acts of resistance through a hanging out/infrapolitical framework offers invaluable insight into the economic, political, and cultural patterns of power and resistance. Scott (1990) defines the *public transcript* as the public performance of deference and humility by the powerless. Further, the powerful uphold this public transcript through the maintenance of the symbols of a hierarchical social order. These *onstage* practices of a public transcript maintain the illusion of a social order. These performances between the houseless and those in authority in the public sphere reveal little information, if any, of how power is wielded between communities. As Scott writes, "A skeptic might well ask at this point how we can presume to know, on the basis of the public transcript alone, whether this performance is genuine or not.... The answer is, surely, that we cannot know how contrived or imposed the performance is unless we can speak, as it were, to the performer *offstage* [my italics], out of this particular power-laden context, or unless the performer suddenly declares openly, on-stage, that the performances we have previously observed were just a pose" (4). If an onstage performance is the public transcript, then the *hidden transcript* is the narrative that takes place offstage and beyond the direct observation of powerholders (14). The hidden transcript becomes the hush harbor, the spaces of rest and leisure, a place to gossip about your bosses, teachers, caseworkers, and places to exchange valuable information about the inner workings of institutions, organizations, worksites—in this case, schools and youth centers.

At the youth drop-in center where I did some of my primary observations, I was often hanging out with LGBTQ+ students who congregated on the sidewalk or on the roof (where there were tables and chairs). These were places to smoke cigarettes out of range from surveillance by the school and youth center security and staff. In this offstage space, youth often shared stories with each other, gossiped, and complained about their treatment by caseworkers and youth center staff.

At one point I overheard a young African American transwoman complaining to a group of youth about her demeaning treatment by center staff, telling a group of youth outside the drop-in center "that bitch in the office called me a man." The imposition of rigid categories of gender on trans* youth who come in for services became a point of contention for many of the youth clients seeking assistance. Because they often depended on these services from the drop-in center, it necessitated a public transcript of civility between youth and staff. It might be that the sidewalk and rooftop were some of the few secure places where youth could share information, and talk back about their mistreatment—out of the sight and hearing of center staff and security, whose surveillance of trans* youth of color in particular was part of the struggle. The hidden transcript also helps us understand nonattendance as resistance. With the emphasis on security throughout Los Angeles, more guards at the youth center were hired and more tensions erupted. Youth stayed away in such numbers that some youth centers and services were forced to cut hours and staff, if not close operations altogether.

Access to offstage spaces is not so easily granted to researchers, whose questions and observations are perceived by youth as informing the powerful. Coded languages, like Chicanx *caló* or the queer languages of youth, may be indecipherable and inaccessible to some. Furthermore, the frontier between the public and the hidden transcript is a "zone of constant struggle" (Scott 1990), where our recognition of subordinate/dominant narratives and resistant/conformist behaviors is not so clear. A researcher may not recognize or, worse, misrecognize or misinterpret certain kinds of behavior as resistance. It is to houseless queer and trans* youth's detriment to recognize only a public transcript.

Researching Resistance

There is a certain stance a researcher must take when working with youth of color, homeless youth, and queer and trans* students. It is a belief that youth have something to say about their own experiences with oppression that is important, that their insight is enlightening and survival-rich, and that you have as much to learn from youth as they do from you. Sometimes the narratives that youth put forth elicit emotions that are not ones of solidarity or even empathy. This stance is not one of pity. Pity is a diversion from a deeper engagement with the issues that are central in a young person's narrative. Once you have put pity between you and a young person, there can be no bridge. Pity turns an individual into an object. They can no longer be a subject.

To research resistance is to take the stance that youth are not victims but often witnesses and survivors of great trauma and oppression. In order to recognize their resisting later, I have to first recognize the stories that students tell me *on their own terms*. For example, an eighteen-year-old eastern European queer youth told me a story of meeting an older American photographer "friend" online. This friend sent him a plane ticket to the United States so that they can meet. (The youth was sixteen years old at the time of the story.)

> When I got to [large East Coast city], I lived with this photographer who said that maybe I could work for him, as photography is my passion. But after a little while, things weren't going to work between us and I left him with the cash that he had given me. I stayed with new friends for a while, crashing on their couches as I looked for work. Nobody was going to hire me—young, and now illegal, as I had already overstayed my visa. I did bar back work at a gay bar, but I didn't make enough to really live on, and slowly I found myself at the shelters.

I had to acknowledge that this was a story of youth trafficking, a queer youth lured by a potential job in photography and a plane ticket, that was reframed by the subject as a relationship. The youth then quits the short-lived relationship with cash in hand and soon finds himself homeless in a large East Coast city. But it was the way that he framed the story to me that was important. In his telling, the ending of the relationship is mutual for both the youth and the photographer. The youth "left" the older man *on his own terms*. His recasting of events is significant, from being a youth caught in the traffic of queer and trans* bodies to a novice photographer yearning for a new life in the United States. In this multiple narrative, my reading of the trafficking of a young gay man becomes intimately tied to my recognition of his refusal to be defined as a victim.

What is helpful in thinking about these multiple interpretations of a narrative is Lugones's conception of "world"-traveling. "World"-traveling is the agentive negotiation of mainstream life in the United States, where queer and trans* youth and women of color (and others from nondominant communities) occupy and move through multiple worlds in their daily existence. Lugones recognizes that much of "world"-traveling is done unwillingly, within often hostile worlds. A key insight is that the self is plural, where the self constantly changes in its movements across multiple worlds. In a world of trafficking, a young person is deemed exploitable, powerless, and utterly victimized. The youth in this field note refuses that world and instead reframes his story in a world where his self is ambitious and entrepreneurial.

Nonetheless, a researcher also recognizes this other world of trafficking. In these multiple and contradictory worlds that exist in this example, I am forced to attend to the conflicts between how the youth sees himself, how a researcher/teacher might see him, and how the youth sees the researcher. I must attend to "what it is to be them and what it is to be ourselves in their eyes" (Lugones 1987, 17). My role becomes vital in this negotiation of multiple frames, plural selves, and numerous worlds. To create different interpretations of experience and to create new knowledges that are outside of the usual frames of the public performances of power is a risk taken together—youth and researcher. It often means challenging both the subject and the researcher to see what meanings can be made. To recognize and validate the multiple narratives of this example is a critically important methodological move, where this queer street youth's story can be reclaimed as resistant, agentic, and sometimes liberatory, even though risky.

LGBTQ+ street youth take many calculated risks, such as the youth mentioned earlier, who weighed the chances of immigrating to the United States for a commitment of intimacy with the costs of exploitation. In contrast to the moral panics that rationalize withholding information about safe sex, contraception, and HIV, the youth in the field note is well aware of the unequal transaction between a sixteen-year-old migrant and an older American professional. Despite guarantees of anonymity in the research interview process,[1] it may be that the youth testimony is still deliberately designed to have multiple meanings, to shield the identities of the actors in this story. To make sense of explicitly ambiguous narratives, we must also consider the resistant sociality and the practices of hanging out in those tight spaces where meanings are developed.

Learning to Be Together in a Resistant Sociality

In his study of the Black working class in the Jim Crow South, Robin D. G. Kelley discusses how workers in Birmingham, Alabama, organized their time and space with others in a way that reinforced a collective identity. It was in these spaces of Black working-class culture where workers "take back their bodies, to recuperate, to be together" (Kelley 1993, 84). Kelley theorizes that places of rest and recreation—family organizations, churches, dance halls, parties, and bars—were ones where Black workers learned to be together outside of the institutions of white supremacy. Coming together for a dance, a party, or church reinforced the sense of shared community, knowledge, and cultural values for Black workers. I find this idea helpful in thinking about queer and trans* youth hanging out, where spaces like a continuation school for LGBTQ+ students or a youth drop-in center, despite their problems, offer the possibility of mutuality and sociality. What happens in these youth spaces helps explain the solidarity that queer street youth have shown in times of duress. In this case, alternative socialities are not only about countering oppressive systems but of the practice of hanging out and building infrapolitical worlds that are essential for survival for LGBTQ+ street youth.

The Black workers in Kelley's study not only made these spaces to unmask themselves of the disguises of deference and humility but also practiced kinships and relationships outside of racist or classist constraints. Both Lugones (2010) and Kelley (1993) suggest that these socialities can be practiced only in spaces where communities are able to define themselves outside of the frameworks of their oppressors. In offstage spaces where youth create, define, and rehearse more egalitarian ways of relating with each other, there is an implied pedagogy of relations that is potentially nonhierarchical, communal, and survival-rich.

A Pedagogy of Faithful Witnessing

To bear faithful witness is to be completely present with people. It is about listening deeply with intention. It is also about making public a commitment to interpret other people's experience against the grain of power, a commitment to documenting experience as social memory (Lugones 2010, 7). In compiling the narratives of queer and trans* street youth, it is about making a commitment to recognizing resistance in all of its complex and intermeshing/intersecting ways. However, these experiences of both youth and researcher are always from power-laden contexts. Despite Scott's (1990) assertion that the infrapolitics of subordinate groups cannot be known unless we can speak to the performer offstage, the presence of outsiders/ethnographers must be put into question. When can researchers, even those committed to pedagogies of faithful witnessing, claim that our presence does not disrupt the resistant sociality and hanging out practices of youth? In one of my engagements of the ethnography, I met Tommy, an eighteen-year-old gay white youth. In this excerpt from my field notes, he turns from telling a story about his body to a critique of power, representation, and research.

> I was just thinking that maybe it was time to go home, to take care of some shit that I need to deal with. I've been in here for over nine months and it's been hard. This body can tell you a story that nobody will want to believe. Right now, I can't even think about tomorrow. But I was thinking that maybe testing positive is a good thing, because nothing else seems to motivate me when it comes to taking care of myself, my body. I've lost so much weight, I'm just a bag of bones, and my arms. These sores never seem to heal. But you, this is your job, huh? Making me think? Let me show you something—
> (*Tommy stretches out full length on his chair.*)
> This body's made hundreds, thousands of dollars. Tell me, what do you think this body's worth now? (Transcript of interview)

Equating a body to its in/ability to produce wealth is a discourse directed at immigrants, homeless women and men, teen mothers, and youth of color. Likewise, these same bodies are often assessed on their supposed cost to the state. Tommy implicates the research process as part of the mechanism for these neoliberal discourses. As a researcher, I was attempting to compile experiences of violence, homelessness, and the body. Tommy's response talks back to how the process of knowledge production about the queer body is reductive and predatory. He challenges the appraisal of a body's net worth in terms of dollars accumulated in a lifetime of earnings. He is also critical of the implied pedagogy in my research ("making me think") and its disciplinary effect on the subject's own appraisal of self. Being present as a faithful witness is inadequate if it is reduced to only acknowledging the narratives that describe the trauma and perils of LGBTQ+ street youth insubordination.

I will know very little about homeless queer and trans youth if I notice only that they are homeless and hungry. I might know that they are particularly desperate to find a place to sleep that night or the limited availability of beds in Los Angeles; I might know that they may be HIV positive and that they have suffered at the hands of their family or schoolmates or partner. I might have learned something about the shape of their oppression. These are certainly important understandings of the conditions facing LGBTQ+ street youth. However, it is critical that I challenge a social science approach that surmises "once we know" about LGBTQ+ street youth, then this knowing offers something. I must challenge the idea that things supposedly "get better" with better research. Perhaps faithful witnessing has revealed to me how a resistant sociality and a practice of hanging out is necessary in the lives of queer street youth. To survive these often hostile worlds, to negotiate cooptation, youth have learned to resist. In the tight spaces of their resistance, I might witness the opening of new creative strategies for organizing life.

Conclusion

In *Ideology, Culture, and the Process of Schooling* (1981), Henry Giroux argued that resistance is the translation of a critical or political understanding of collective experience into political struggle that contests the hegemonic practices of schools. Part of that contestation is an understanding by youth that political struggle is also tied to the larger struggle against the concentration of power in the capitalist state itself (92–98). Resisting in the form of traditional politics, such as mobilizing for public action and civic engagement in formal organizations, do not often work for queer and trans* street youth. What I often witness are small yet deliberate acts by youth toward their social service workers, police, and medical personnel (Cruz 2011). A alternative explanation of queer and trans* youth experiences that is based on a resistant sociality may be as simple as creating "a new story of the self" (Lugones 2000, 180) for LGBTQ+ street youth, whether in the tight spaces of the hidden transcript or the hanging out practices of the streetwalker, which in turn offers the possibilities to create ways of being and acting in the world outside of the constraints of power.

Notes

1. My work with LGBTQ+ street youth had strict protocols for anonymity under Institutional Review Board (IRB) that did not allow for any names, places, or information collected that could be linked back to the identities of the youth I talked with. I never asked for names, and my original field notes are strictly redacted. This may have freed youth to talk openly, yet the politics of the public/hidden transcript seemed a part of every public observation and every interview. The Human Subjects Protection Program (HSPP) is the administrative and regulatory support program for the IRB and works in collaboration with the research community to maintain an ethical and compliant research program. It is a necessary step in research design that oversees any potential problems or unethical treatment of subjects in a research project.

References

Cruz, Cindy. 2011. "LGBTQ Street Youth Talk Back: A Meditation on Resistance and Witnessing." *QSE: International Journal of Qualitative Studies in Education* 24 (5): 547–58.
Fanon, Frantz. (1961) 2004. *The Wretched of the Earth*. Translated by Richard Philcox. New York: Grove Press.
Giroux, Henry A. 1981. *Ideology, Culture and the Process of Schooling*. Philadelphia: Temple University Press.
Kelley, Robin D. G. 1993. "'We Are Not What We Seem': Rethinking Black Working-Class Opposition in the Jim Crow South." *Journal of American History* 80 (1): 75–112.
Lefebvre, Henri. (1974) 1991. *The Production of Space*. Translated by Donald Nicholson-Smith. Cambridge, MA: Blackwell.
Lugones, María. 1987. "Playfulness, 'World'-Travelling, and Loving Perception." *Hypatia* 2 (2): 3–19.
———. 2000. "Multiculturalism and Publicity." *Hypatia* 15 (3): 175–81.
———. 2003. *Pilgrimages/Peregrinajes: Theorizing Coalition against Multiple Oppressions*. Lanham, MD: Rowman and Littlefield.
———. 2010. "Toward a Decolonial Feminism." *Hypatia* 25 (4): 743–59.
Scott, James C. 1990. *Domination and the Arts of Resistance: Hidden Transcripts*. New Haven, CT: Yale University Press.
Zahniser, David, and Benjamin Oreskes. 2021. "L.A.'s New Homeless Encampment Laws: A Humane Approach or Cruel to Unhoused People?" *Los Angeles Times*, August 2, 2021, sec. California. https://www.latimes.com/california/story/2021-08-02/los-angeles-new-homeless-anti-camping-law-humane-cruel.

Cindy Cruz is Associate Professor of Education at the University of Arizona. She received her PhD from UCLA, was a postdoctoral fellow at Cornell University, and faculty at UC Santa Cruz. Her research on the narratives of homeless queer and trans* youth in Los Angeles centers the work of US feminists of color and Latinx and decolonial feminist theory.

10
ON A NONDIALOGIC THEORY OF DECOLONIAL COMMUNICATION

Gabriela Veronelli

Introduction

In this chapter, I examine how decolonial thinking informs a critical theory of communication beyond the confines of modernity/coloniality. I begin by investigating the importance given to the question of communication within the Decolonial Turn, including my interpretation of what some of the authors have claimed on the matter. Then, I make my own intervention regarding decolonial communicative possibilities, going back and forth between a metapragmatic critique and pragmatic questions. Finally, I introduce Édouard Glissant's ([1990] 1997) notions of *Échos-monde* and *Relation*, and María Lugones's (2006) *complex communication* to think through possible answers to these questions to further a decolonial theory of communication; that is, of communication that disrupts the logic of coloniality.

The Decolonial Turn and the Problem
of the Coloniality of Language

Epistemically, the Decolonial Turn stands on the premise that Eurocentrism is basically a question of a long-term imperial project in which the emancipatory potential of modern reason (as practiced by Christianity, Enlightenment, Positivism, Developmentalism, and Neoliberalism) hides and disguises the logic of coloniality, a logic that justifies domination and brutal exploitation of bodies and nature in the name of emancipation (Escobar 2010).

Given this premise, modernity presupposes coloniality and will always accommodate it, and, thus, there is no way out of coloniality from within modern categories of thought. To reveal the logic of coloniality embedded in Eurocentrism is a necessary step toward decoloniality and undoing the modern/colonial matrix of power (Lugones 2007; Mignolo 2010; Quijano 2007)—a necessary step, but not a sufficient one in itself. What is needed to fulfill the incomplete and unfinished project of decolonization is a spatial epistemic break, what Nelson Maldonado-Torres (2005) called a Decolonial Turn, a shift in the geopolitics of reason so as to break away from Western representations and modes of knowing what the world is and should be.[1]

The Decolonial Turn speaks of a deep epistemic shift in critical thought that expresses itself in a commitment to both reject the tendency to reassert the geo- and body-political limits of knowledge production as defined by modernity and move toward ideas, projects, and concerns that emerge from different geopolitical and body-political positions marked by coloniality in order to build alternative projects to modernity. This double commitment stresses that making what the Zapatistas call "a world in which many worlds fit" or realizing the idea of the World Social Forum that "another world is possible" involves not only a list of possibilities but, most fundamentally, the materiality of creating, expressing, and carrying out possibilities that are Other—that is, not only what is possible within modern enunciation but also what can be imagined as possible from the outside.[2]

Something that I find key about the Decolonial Turn is that it does not provide a counterhegemonic alternative, but rather, it appears to point to a horizontal global projection toward which dialogic connections are imperative. Manifestations of decolonial alternatives reappear everywhere across the globe as a consequence of the changes, adaptations, and new modalities of the modern/colonial matrix of power. So, if there is a common condition of living under coloniality and receiving it resistantly or responding to it, then we could ask whether there is a possibility of adumbrating something like a *decolonial totality*.

Although not all the scholars within the Decolonial Turn hold to the idea of totality, for me it is relevant as a point of entry to raise the problem of communication that I am exploring here. In giving some substance to this idea of decolonial totality from a decolonial standpoint, Quijano (1992, 20) tells us that while the modern concept of totality is exclusionary and totalitarian in character, it is also provincial. It is possible, then, to hold to some idea of totality that would be nontotalitarian and would not deny but desire and rest on the unforeseeable heterogeneity of all reality. It would also be necessary to imagine that heterogeneous totality is not a different totality leading to a different global design but a network of local alternatives emerging from the perspective and lived experiences of a politically enriched exteriority (Escobar 2010, 40). Informed by the copresence and articulation of diverse locals that proceed from no absolute, it would close the road to all reductionisms—that of abstract generalizations as well as that of incommensurable localism (Quijano

1992, 16–17). Such decolonial totality would look like a global remade from below—or, better, horizontally, local to local, and dialogically sought. It is this question, the question of dialogues that bring together critiques, responses, or resistances to coloniality from different geo- and body-political positions and how it is related to the project of decoloniality, which I want to examine.

Resistance through dialogue is central to many of the authors who work on resistance to colonization. The contemporary foundations of this idea can be found in the work of Brazilian educator Paulo Freire, whose critical idea is the relationship between dialogue and education for transformation-liberation. Let's examine this idea as illustrated in *Pedagogy of the Oppressed* ([1970] 2005, 88–91).

> As we attempt to analyze dialogue as a human phenomenon, we discover something which is the essence of dialogue itself: the word. But the word is more than just an instrument which makes dialogue possible; accordingly, we must seek its constitutive elements. Within the word we find two dimensions, reflection and action.... When a word is deprived of its dimension of action, reflection automatically suffers as well; and the word is changed into idle chatter, into verbalism.... On the other hand, if action is emphasized exclusively, to the detriment of reflection, the word is converted into activism. The latter—action for action's sake—negates the true praxis and makes dialogue impossible.... If it is in speaking their word that people, by naming the world, transform it, dialogue imposes itself as the way by which they achieve significance as human beings. Dialogue is thus an existential necessity.... Founding itself upon love, humility, and faith, dialogue becomes a horizontal relationship of which mutual trust between the dialogues is the logical consequence.

And furthermore, "Critical and liberating dialogue, which presupposes action, must be carried on with the oppressed at whatever the stage of their struggle for liberation. The content of that dialogue can and should vary in accordance with historical conditions and the level at which the oppressed perceive reality. But to substitute monologue, slogans, and communiqués for dialogue is to attempt to liberate the oppressed with the instruments of domestication" (65). This distinction between dialogue and monologue is key to Freire's understanding of the nature of education. To Freire, educating is always a political act. It can be used to maintain the status quo or to bring about social change. Through what he creatively terms *banking education*, the authoritarian educational system isolates the learner from the content and process of education. Because it assumes that the teacher knows everything and the students nothing, the latter are not encouraged to think critically and consequently do not challenge their social and political position. In other words, in banking education the teacher is the subject of the learning process, while the students are objects-containers that are filled by deposits of information, which they must mechanically receive, memorize, and repeat without reflection. In response to these forces that inhibit the transformation of an oppressive reality, *Pedagogy of the Oppressed* promotes a problem-posing methodology and philosophy of education based on dialogue and a democratic relationship between teacher and student. Dialogue changes the contradictory nature of education because the teacher-of-the-students and the student-of-the-teacher cease to exist and a new term emerges: *teacher-student with student-teachers* who are jointly responsible for the learning process. In short, Freire's dialogical thinking shows the way to a displacement of hegemonic notions of scholarly or disciplinary knowledge, from *thinking about* to *thinking with*. Students not only are taught facts and information but learn along with the teacher to critically acquire knowledge of reality, which is imperative to human action and social, economic, and political transformation.

An important relation between dialogue and the decolonial project of shifting the geopolitics of knowledge appears in Enrique Dussel's (1995, 131–32) idea of transmodernity.

> Authentically liberating projects must strive to lead modernity beyond itself to transmodernity. Such projects require an amplified rationality which makes room for the reason of the Other within a community of communication among equal participants.... Within such projects, all ought to be welcomed in their alterity, in that otherness which needs to be painstakingly guaranteed at every level.... This book serves only as a historico-philosophical introduction to an intercultural dialogue that will encompass diverse political, economic, theological, and epistemological standpoints. Such a dialogue endeavors to construct not an abstract universality, but an analogic and concrete world in which all cultures, philosophies, and theologies will make their contribution toward a future, pluralist humanity.

One can enter this quote from various angles. The one I am trying emphasizes the question of dialogue. Dussel's idea of transmodernity offers both a description of a state of affairs and an ideal of conviviality that goes beyond the liberal style of multiculturalism. Instead of a single modernity centered in Europe and imposed as a global design, transmodernity (in the sense of moving across) calls for a diversity of epistemic positions and productions responding to Euro-centered modernity from the cultures and epistemic locations of *other* people around the world. By radicalizing the Levinasian notions of "other" and "exteriority," Dussel locates a potential in those relatively exterior spaces not fully colonized, subsumed, or instrumentalized by European modernity. The Other—the oppressed, the poor, or the colonized—far from being ontologically constructed (abstraction as an "absence") is, on the contrary, thought out as the location of what will be elaborated as an epistemic irreducible difference (Maldonado-Torres 2005). To listen to the Other qua Other—as difference that cannot be told instead of an object to be colonized and studied—it is necessary to go beyond the epistemic confinements of modernity. Transmodernity (in the sense of transcending modernity) moves along the diversity of the historical process itself. Such dialogic possibility requires, first, to be attentive to listening to the Other in their diversity-plurality and, second, to be attentive to the Other's exteriority.

Walter Mignolo (2005, 112–13) is another important figure within the Decolonial Turn who remarks on the centrality of dialogue for the project of decoloniality, as he sees manifestations of resistant dialogical actions already in practice.

> Afro-Andeans—those who speak Spanish rather than French Creole—are in the process of reactivating their own principles of knowledge and memory. By creating a series of theoretical concepts that allow them to conceptualize themselves ... they enter into critical dialogue with the unavoidable Western categories of thought that were implanted in their souls by the Spanish language they had to learn.... Instead of "alienating" themselves by thinking from conceptual frameworks that do not belong to their experience ... [it] allows them to define ideas and experiences for themselves. It is an energy and a conceptual matrix of "appropriation," enrichment, and empowerment that liberates by decolonizing and works towards a possible future that will no longer be dictated by the church, the capitalist states, or the private sector (and neither, of course, by honest liberal, Marxist, Christian intellectuals with prescriptions for the good of everyone.)

And he continues, "Some Latins in the South confront these struggles and are threatened while others are joining forces with Latinos/as, Afros, and Indigenous people and working in solidarity on common projects. Thus an "intracultural dialogue," to use an expression learned from Afro-Colombian activist Libia Grueso, is taking place *among political projects originating in diverse but parallel experiences* of the colonial wound. Intracultural dialogue among subaltern projects and communities generates intercultural struggles with the state and institutions managing the spheres of the social" (160; emphasis added). Here Mignolo exhibits how, by thinking from the personal and historical experience of coloniality, in critical dialogue with Western historiographical categories that negate them as people with history, Afro-Andean communities engage in a nontotalitarian geopolitics of knowledge in which the West is relocated. I add that the same dialogical move by which the West is displaced from the center of enunciation allows the Afro-Andean intellectual and political project—and other projects coming from the histories of Indigenous and Black communities in South America and the Caribbean and those of Latinas/os in the US—to transcend the confinement of the duality center/periphery and travel to other nonhegemonic locations. In other words, transcending the idea of "Latin America" of Euro-American capitalism and reimagining its logics and temporal-spatial parameters of being and belonging from the colonial wound of Euro-American capitalism seem to encourage a kind of solidarity that modernity/coloniality has denied. This solidarity expresses itself in what Mignolo calls, borrowing from Grueso, *intracultural dialogues*. While the use of the prefix *intra* seems odd as it conveys a dialogue that is situated and carried on within a cultural community (an "in-house dialogue"), my understanding is that the *intra* is itself being reimagined against imperial and national orders and their homogeneous political imaginary. The possibility of intracultural dialogues suggests to me a nonessentialist sense of identity and solidarity conceived in terms of a revaluation of local knowledges without the terms of modernity, knowledges for liberation being produced and enacted inside and outside the academia and "originating in diverse but parallel experiences of the colonial wound." So, one does not have to be Black, Indigenous, or Latina/o to join, support, and participate in their epistemic and political projects, not because "allies are welcome" but because the colonial wound is our common ground.

Fulfilling the unfinished project of decolonization necessitates connections, putting decolonial alternatives in conversation so that they can inform each other as well as the larger conception of a decolonial totality. On this, I believe Freire, Dussel, and Mignolo agree. However, besides emphasizing the central role that dialogue has within a process of liberatory transformation, there is a need to provide theoretical examination of the conditions of possibility of such dialogue across manifestations of decolonial alternatives within educational spaces or in the society at large.

Dussel (1996) gives us an understanding of speech act. In his debate with Karl-Otto Apel, in which he criticizes Apel's approach to discursive ethics for being formalistic and reductionist, Dussel examines interpellation as the speech act, which allows him to expose the excluded Other as "poor" and to underscore the importance of materiality for ethics from the perspective of philosophy of liberation. But, as I argue here, Dussel's theory of interpellation falls short of providing us with an insight into horizontal dialogue. As constructed by Dussel, in attending to the interpellations of excluded people, the listener (the intellectual, the philosopher of liberation) seems to speak for (and not to) them and fails to see them as actually engaging in their own resistant projects.

Mignolo gives us an understanding of connections and connectors among projects of decolonial thinking and action. These connections and connectors are the common ground of coloniality and the colonial wound. It is important that he talks about projects, intellectual and political projects that are fracturing the hegemonic discourse of modernity. A central aim of Mignolo in *The Idea of Latin America* (2005) and more generally in *Local Histories/Global Designs* (2000) is reaching and linking these projects to build the foundation of an epistemology that he describes as the "spatial epistemic break" (2005, 179n40) and further elaborates as "un paradigma otro" (2003, 19). In chapter 6 of *Local Histories/Global Designs*, Mignolo (2000, 277) proposes "bilanguaging" as that foundation, "the movable ground on which educational projects and the decolonization of scholarship can be located." I later examine "bilanguaging." I agree with Mignolo in the usefulness of Humberto Maturana's conceptualization of "languaging" for shifting paradigms of language decolonially. Languaging, like thinking, locates the interaction among people instead of in preexisting ideas (Mignolo 2000, 253). The move from language to languag*ing*, from noun to verb, allows the turn from abstract universal to pluriversal ways of living together. Bilanguaging is a way of life between languages. In my examination, I sketch out some important questions that the concept of bilanguaging opens for rethinking practices and conceptualizations of dialogue and translation. My concern is that bilanguaging is, so far, limited to the politics of knowledge and scholarship and that the emphasis on bilanguaging epistemologies does not allow us to grasp the intersubjectivity among people thinking together.[3]

Whether our communicative frameworks are or are not up to the task of shifting the geopolitics of knowledge is a question that cannot be left undertheorized. Thus, I believe that beyond asking how differently located resistant communities and groups contending with the ways in which capitalism makes sense of them (as not quite human, exploitable bodies, dispensable, damned, etc.) have been remaking sense of and to themselves (in-house dialogues and dialogues with the state), the project of decoloniality requires asking how they and we could make sense to each other (dialogues across communities and projects). More concretely, the question I believe needs to be asked is, granted that dialogic connections are necessary for projecting a decolonial totality or at the very least a decolonial alternative, how do the communicative conditions created by coloniality restrict building such connections? We can admit that a decolonial geopolitics of knowledge is about rethinking the relation between global and local *dialogically* so as to contrast the monologic character of global designs in modern/colonial systems of thought. We can also admit that this alternative does not yet exist, that it has to be built. And finally, we can admit that this enterprise is first and foremost a question of constituting connections. If so, I am arguing, we need to examine the conditions of possibility of such connections regarding the communicative arrangements normed by what I have called the *coloniality of language*.

The Coloniality of Language and Speech

To take up the coloniality of language in terms of language theory and dialogism is to introduce a perspective that proposes a critical understanding of the cognitive and historical process by which communication has been intertwined, articulated, organized, and ranked within the modern/colonial matrix of power. The concept of coloniality of language refers to the process of racialization of colonized populations as communicative agents and its contemporary legacy. It centers on the reduction of colonized peoples of the Americas to nonhuman status and the concomitant dismissal of their languages and ways of knowing as the simple expressions of their "nature" as "inferior beings." The idea is that through the sixteenth-century, Spanish and Portuguese conquest of the peoples of what would become North, Central, and South America and the Caribbean, European colonizers imposed not only their languages but also their conceptual systems on the populations they conquered and colonized. In particular, European philosophies of language imposed a racialized hierarchy of languages based on a prescribed relation between language and humanity: the languages spoken by Europeans were real, human languages; those of colonized populations were not. Among the elements in these philosophies that make a language a *real language,* or a *language in the full sense,* are literacy, grammar, and bonds to Latin. Real languages unify a territory, are written in alphabetic characters, and express truth and knowledge. Given these criteria, the languages of colonized beings were not languages in the full sense but what I call means of *simple communication,* and those who spoke them were not rational speakers but *simple communicators.* Something like a tower of Babel attitude (Maturana 1999, 242) was used against and in relation to the colonized as there was an impossibility of believing that they were people with whom the colonizer could engage in dialogue. *In denying the colonized the communicative ability that colonizers believed themselves to possess, coloniality of language closes communication.* Even when colonized people used colonial languages, the coloniality of language constitutes the structure of their thinking and their mental connections as not those of civilized beings.

In this sense, the coloniality of language is more than the colonization of systems of meaning. It is the coloniality of power in its linguistic form: A process of dehumanization at the level of communication that blocks dialogic creation of meaning (Bakhtin 1981) between colonizers and colonized. This lack of communicative possibility produces a deafness that makes impossible any entrance into the ways of knowing and living of colonized populations and may lead them to internalize the belief that they are linguistically and culturally inferior. I argue that there is a link between reducing colonized populations to nonhuman status through racialization and a language ideology and practice that I analyze as *monolanguaging* and that obscures colonial oppression discursively. More specifically, monolanguaging names the material and discursive praxes of linguistic racialization: a sociality that creates a dehumanizing way of living for the colonized.[4]

Limitations of *Dialogue*

Dialogue is indeed a strong word, which at some point we may need to drop as too enmeshed in colonization and racialization. Some authors use *plurilogue* (Shohat 2001; De Sousa Santos et al. 2008). I do not deny that changing from *dia-* to *pluri-* makes a difference, but are there not problems with the *-logue* part, as well, that is, with the centrality of logos? Using this question as pivot, I move now into a more detailed critique of how the Decolonial Turn has theorized communication across resistant manifestations.

In building up my argument, I look at dialogue in Bakhtin's conception. A condition sine qua non of dialogue in Bakhtin is that the speaker presupposes a response, some understanding of how she will be heard or, at minimum, that she will be heard (Bakhtin 1981, 281–82). That is precisely what is not happening under the coloniality of language, and cannot happen, because there is no communicative disposition but *monolanguaging*.

María Lugones speaks of a tendency in the Decolonial Turn not to enter the subjectivity of, and intersubjectivity among people or groups of people thinking and acting together (personal interview, 2012). I see this tendency showing itself in all the quotes I examined in the first section. I am not saying that Dussel's *transmodernity* and Mignolo's *intracultural dialogue* are proposing the same thing but that in both proposals, dialogue is assumed. They both seem to take for granted that peoples who have diverse but parallel experiences of (linguistic) coloniality would see, hear, and understand each other. I am arguing that linguistic coloniality includes the colonization of dialogue. And I am suggesting the possibility of rethinking dialogue from the colonial difference. First, I briefly state my claim regarding Dussel's and Mignolo's proposals.

I stated earlier that Dussel's idea of transmodernity as dialogic epistemic possibility depends on being attentive to listening to the Other in their diversity-plurality and their exteriority. He unpacks this task in his examination of interpellation as speech act, which now I examine critically, looking, first, at his depiction of the Other as speaker-interpellant: "By interpellation, then, I will understand a preformative, sui generis statement uttered by someone (S) which is, regarding a listener (H), 'out' or 'beyond' (in this sense, transcendental) the horizon or institutional frame, normative for the ruling 'system,' beyond the Husserlian-Habermasian Lebenswelt or the Hegelian Sittlichkeit, which acts as the totality for Levinas" (1996, 23). Following Marx, Dussel further characterizes the interpellant Other as a specter, somebody who does not exist in the capitalist relationship of production (24). We get here the first glimpse of the way in which Dussel's theorization presupposes dialogue, by simplifying the understanding of intersubjectivity to capitalist organization of social relations. There is something abstract and empty about the specter to the extent that one cannot imagine anything about her.[5] Indeed, at the ideal level, the speaker is reduced to a lacking body, a suffering corporality, and at the real level, in the provided examples, the speaker is always placed in terms of hegemonic communities of communication that exclude her "of the genocidally murdered Indian, of the African slave reduced to merchandise, of women as sexual objects, of the child pedagogically dominated" (21). Regarding the speaker, then, Dussel's concept of the interpellation gives us nothing about her diversity-plurality and exteriority as her own understanding of herself, the world, culture, cosmology, sense of freedom, and sense of well-being or being well are left out.

I find a similar lack in Dussel's depiction of the listener. The listener in the interpellation speech act is placed in the position of liberator. She has this capacity to listen beyond, from the outside of her own Lebenswelt. The listener is someone who can articulate what it is that the specter interpellant is trying to communicate, from a meaning that the specter interpellant, as it were, only inhabits because, while she is in the midst of oppression, she has not the means to validly express; the listener does. The suffering body of the Other stimulates the listener-liberator to form of a critique of the prevailing system as it exists: "We [who practice Philosophy of Liberation] pretend to validly express the reason of the Other.... We pretend to be the expression of reason, a reason of one who places him/herself outside eurocentric, machist, pedagogically dominated, culturally manipulated, religiously fetishist reason" (1996, 21). But what allows this is not clear, and to me, Dussel takes this capacity very lightly. How is it possible that people who are just intellectuals, and who have not occupied or attempted to live with the Other in a way that her meanings are learned, can comprehend the Lebenswelt and then make a critique? What is the relationship between that critique of the system and the order of the Lebenswelt and the meaning of the interpellation from somebody who is outside that order? There is nothing in the interpellation that refers to actively learning and understanding the world of the oppressed Other. Understanding that learning is not about empathy but about being able to see the world the way oppressed peoples see it so that one can perceive and visualize how it is that, for example, the colonial capitalist world or the world of racist domination is part of what the oppressed sees. Therefore, I argue that the possibility of understanding is presupposed in Dussel's interpellation. Even with the inclusion of the negative moment in the ideal communicative community, this element does not really allow the listener to have an intimate position in the community of those who have been treated unjustly. To me this is profoundly arrogant in a philosophical sense of arrogating (Frye in Lugones 2003, 78) the very possibility of meaning from the interpellant and imposing, as the meaning is opaque, a world of reason that is a world that has not been crafted with others.

Even when Dussel does consider the question of intelligibility and puts us on guard regarding the possibilities of achieving full communication between interpellant and listener, he continues to presuppose the listener's capacity to interpret the meaning of the interpellation. He tells us that at the beginning the speech act is merely quasi-intelligible: "The speaker (S), being an excluded 'pauper,' in the exteriority, may hardly formulate a sentence correctly, due to a certain linguistic incompetence—from the hearer's (H) point of view—a phonetically defective pronunciation along with the S's lack of knowledge of the H's language and, essentially, the meaning in its full pragmatic sense [full in the sense of both conceptual content and mental intention]" (1996, 24–25). "Incompetence not because of irrationality, but because the institutional world of His unknown, it is not the same as that of S" (1996, 40). Dussel is not telling us that the speech act is quasi-intelligible because the hearer does not understand the speaker's life, way of thinking, or values. No, the problem of intelligibility is due to a linguistic asymmetry between S and H, and it is S who seems to be at fault. Such an understanding of the problem of communication and interpretation of meaning in terms of "incompetence," "mispronunciation," and "lack of fluency" does not make room to reveal the coloniality of language and understand the other as someone linguistically and communicatively dehumanized.

My last point regarding a presupposition of understanding in Dussel's conceptualization of the interpellation as speech act done from the exteriority is about assimilation. When Dussel (1996, 29–31) gives concrete types of interpellations, he tells us that these are interpellations "from those excluded from *their* respective hegemonic communities of communication" (emphasis added). I want to contest that these hegemonic communities are *their* (the Others') communities of communication, when in fact within these communities, they have been constituted in such a way that, for example, akin to African American people or Latinxs in the United States, they have no voice. To speak in terms of the hegemonic community, to speak the hegemonic voice and to think of it as your own is, to me, assimilation. Again, I find that there is no attention in Dussel's concept of interpellation to any creativity or community of the Others as sources of liberation. Their diverse understandings of themselves and the world, their philosophy, poetry, art, and all they have done in becoming who they became in societies that are colonial societies, in spite of the attempt to disintegrate them as a community, all that is left out. In fact, it is not clear in Dussel's examination whether there is a community of the excluded, that is, whether people in the exteriority have a community or not. In this sense, as defined by Dussel, the interpellation is not, and cannot be about a dialogue across communities of resistance, but a means by which those who are excluded appeal to be integrated into hegemonic communities of communication *in terms of those communities*. In other words, to be included is to be granted equal, universal rights (30). But such rights, as critical race theory has made clear, are not real for racialized people and are constitutively racist (e.g., Crenshaw 1991).

I suggest previously that what I see as Mignolo's main aim entails building the foundation for a spatial epistemic break, for a *paradigma otro* on which decolonial intellectual and political projects can be located. In "Bilanguaging Love: Thinking on between Languages" (2000, chap. 6), Mignolo explores this potential by attempting to theorize the possibility of breaking the ties between the three "prestigious" languages (English, French, and German), the territoriality of languages, and the complicity between scholarship, territoriality, nation-states in the erasure of Amerindian and other suppressed and border languages from scholarship. He does that by drawing on Humberto Maturana's concept of "languaging," (1987) which enables him to talk about thinking beyond language and thinking in between languages.

> Reason and knowledge in the modern world, presupposed the purity and the grammar of a language and, without mentioning it, epistemology became entangled with national ideologies ... Subalternization of knowledge was not only possible because a given concept of "reason" became hegemonic and the point of reference to evaluate other logics and ways of thinking at the same time ... hegemonic languages were imposed upon others ... Today ... new forms of knowledge revealing the limits of Western epistemology are emerging in the borderlands of ... modernity/coloniality, borders inhabited by the colonial difference. Border thinking demands a bilanguaging rather than a territorial epistemology, which supported ancient religions and science, its secular Western expansion, as well as economic planning and social organization. (250–51)

In his analysis of the politics of knowledge articulated around language, the philosophy of language Mignolo unearths is one based on early modernity's linking of language and territories (grammars), and late modernity/Enlightenment's one language, one nation, one people construct. He examines the consequences of such imperial and national language ideologies for the cultures of scholarship, including the complicities between language, texts (i.e., ideologically limited to alphabetic literacy and the book, where some books became icons of national culture and all other written forms were relegated to the realm of folklore) (2000, 260), disciplinary structuring of knowledge, and capitalist corporate values. This is the territorial epistemology foundation (the "from where to think") from which Mignolo moves away, and he does so by shifting paradigms of language: from the idea of language as an object of desire linked to territories and nations to the idea of languaging as a way of life, of signs and memories inscribed in the body (the body in history and the body on which history has been inscribed) rather than inscribed on paper (252).

Mignolo thinks his argument from within the languaging (bilanguaging) practice of Gloria Anzaldúa (1987). Anzaldúa refers to Chicano Spanish and code switching as the language of the borderlands, *un language que corresponde a un modo de vivir* (Mignolo 2000, 253, 256). This is the conceptualization of language as bilanguaging that Mignolo picks up: a way of living in the borderlands, a way of living between languages, an interaction among people instead of in preexisting ideas (253). The modern/colonial territorial ideology of living and thinking (monolanguaging), "particularly the idea of national languages in the imaginary of modern states, that is, of speaking, writing, thinking *within* a single language controlled by a grammar in a way similar to a constitution's control over the state" is revealed from the way of living and thinking, the bilanguaging, of the borderlands (252)

Mignolo also draws from Freire's ([1970], 2005) "dialogical thinking" as evidence for bilanguaging. Freire sees dialogical thinking as a means for action and liberation and, Mignolo emphasizes, this is not just liberation from social and economic oppression but also and mainly as intellectual decolonization, liberation from coloniality. Mignolo thinks that dialogical thinking shows the way to displace the hegemonic notions of disciplinary or scholarly knowledge, particularly because he sees a close link between the human sciences (and the thinkers of human science as the thinkers of the state) and the impossibility of thinking with the people (265). Mignolo (2000, 266) also finds support for bilanguaging in Abdelkebir Khatibi's "un pensée autre" and in Cherríe Moraga's notion of the "bicultural mind" and defense of "tribe" as community bond made not by the state but by language, land, spirit, history, and blood (Mignolo 2000, 267). With Moraga, "bilanguaging acquires a new dimension, not just dimension of the linguistic per se, or of dialogical thinking, but languaging in the sphere of sexuality, race, and human interactions" (Mignolo 2000, 269).

To speak with a forked tongue (Anlzaldúa) or to use a bicultural mind (Moraga), bilanguaging (Mignolo), un pensée autre (Khatibi), dialogic thinking (Freire), or double consciousness (W. E. B. Du Bois) are (some of) the dialogical, ethic, aesthetic, and political practices of social transformation as well as conceptualizations of such practices that form the network of spaces and references of bilanguaging epistemology. My concern, as I explained it previously, is that bilanguaging as an educational and epistemological project tends to assume the interactions and intersections that form the network. But how to hear against this territorial way of languaging and thinking about language and knowledge? How to hear against monolanguaging? Mignolo does not engage these questions.[6]

As I have been arguing, the conditions for entering conversations and making sense to each other across the cracks created through several centuries of colonial and national territorialities are not given. And they are not given precisely because of the linguistic arrangements defined and produced by coloniality. Perhaps the assumption could be valid for conversations among intellectuals (in the case of Dussel and Mignolo) or at the structural level of a set of intellectual and political projects (in the case of Mignolo), but I believe it is not valid at the level of *regular people* interacting with each other—people who have been communicatively racialized and reduced to beings incapable of interlocution.[7]

Another way of building my critique on how Decolonial Turn thinkers have taken up the question of communication across resistant manifestations is as follows: As we have seen, linguistic coloniality involves more than destruction, that is, burning of codices and other Amerindian means of expression and representation of knowledge and memory. It constitutes a sophisticated apparatus of legal, religious, civil, and educational *monolanguaging* agents, institutions, and practices that systematized colonial domination and naturalized the linguistic colonial difference. This naturalization makes coloniality and the mechanisms that produce the colonized as inferior invisible. The process of racial hierarchical classification of a great number of different peoples (each with their own history, language, cultural products, and identity) is a prescription that does not have to make rational sense.[8] To unveil the colonial difference, on the other hand, reveals that *colonization creates more than one reality* (Lugones 2003). The colonizers do not have to see the colonial difference; for colonized people, it is their place of existence. And it is not a "pure" place of existence because colonized people have to see reality both in their own way and in the colonizers'. This creates a composite perception, a mixture that is neither homogeneous nor synthetical. Because these two realities are incompatible, a cycle of coercion/negotiation between them becomes the heart of the process and condition of living under the coloniality.[9] Also, this composite perception of the colonized did not exist before colonization. So, it is not the thinking of Indigenous people living before the conquest; but the thinking of people who have gone through coloniality. In other words, to think from the colonial difference is both to think from a position that is given by coloniality and to assume and realize this difference in thinking. I am arguing that the thinking of people putting themselves together against the grain of colonial violence is not easily rendered into articulated anti-structural projects of a decolonial totality.

When decolonial authors claim, as I am understanding they do, that the colonial difference creates the conditions for dialogic situations, I think they take for granted that people who have diverse but parallel experiences of coloniality would be able to see each other at the colonial difference. But that assumes that the colonial difference is easily seen, when in fact it is not and cannot be (Lugones, personal interview, 2012). One can feel all the time how modernity is reproducing coloniality, and one can imagine, as Mignolo (2011, 45–46) does, that "if coloniality is constitutive of modernity since the salvationist rhetoric of modernity presupposes the oppressive and condemnatory logic of coloniality (from there come the *damnés* of Fanon), then this oppressive logic produces an energy of discontent, of distrust, of release within those who react against imperial violence. This energy is translated into *decolonial projects that, as a last resort, are also constitutive of modernity*" (original emphasis).

Although I agree with Mignolo about this "energy of discontent, of distrust, or release," I do not agree that this "energy is *translated* into decolonial projects," because to me finding or hearing a response in this "irreducible energy of humiliated, vilified, forgotten, or marginalized human beings" (Mignolo 2011, 46) is something too difficult to do. In other words, I argue that a translation does not follow because translation is an act that takes place at a cognitive level, in the representational (signifying, conceptualizing, discursive) function of language, and what comes out of this energy are, I am arguing, nonlogocentric responses and nondialogic terms of cognition.[10] I come back to this point regarding the impossibility of translation when introducing Glissant's *Échos-monde*.

One way of summarizing my critique of the way in which decolonial theorists have taken on the question of communication across resistant manifestations is to say that they imagine a communicative exchange à la Bakhtin putting reason, dialogical communication, and speech—in sum, logos—at the center. I am not saying that dialogue is not possible or desirable. Insofar as Bakhtin's conception points to something that should have happened in the colonial situation but did not and is still not happening, *dialogue* may be synonymous with the destruction of the coloniality of power. And this may be what Dussel and Mignolo are in fact claiming. But if connections among resistant manifestations are not an outcome but the engine of this destruction, then we need another way of imagining communicative interaction at, from, and across the colonial difference.

Toward a Nondialogic Theory of Communication

Problems that concern decolonial thinking are problems that have been set up by the modern/colonial matrix of power. The problem I am presenting here is about exploring the colonized's possibilities of communication in the midst of the coloniality of language. Articulated is this way, the problem addresses the fact that coloniality is not completely successful and that people who have been marked by racial and colonial oppression, and who have been denied having *language in-the-full-sense*, do speak, and they do so in a way that rejects the understanding of language and speech as enunciated by modernity. This does not imply, and this is my central claim, that people across diverse but parallel experiences of coloniality—across the colonial difference—can understand each other. A decolonial theory of communication needs to reject this assumption and face the complications of the erasure of dialogue that coloniality has produced.

In order to advance some analysis and propose insights on such decolonial theory, I pose some concrete questions that complicate the relation between communication and *decolonial totality*: Given that potential interlocutors have been defined and indoctrinated into being "beasts," "non-rational," "backwards," "barbarians," "primitive," "underdeveloped," "in need of guidance," "expendable," "incapable of valid knowledge," or "supposed not to answer back," what constitutes an speech act? (Lugones 2007; Mignolo 1995; Quijano 2000). How can they make sense to each other? How can they see each other in a reality where being perceived as less than human does not make sense, while they exist in a system that denies that reality over and over?

How to bring these discrepant voices together from real places to real places, in such a way that the reductions of transnational capitalism and neoliberal globalization are not being reproduced? How to abandon the colonial logic of representation and its mechanisms, attitudes, and beliefs? What is the task of decolonial intellectuals in building these local-to-local connections? How to denaturalize the communicative privileges that Eurocentric tradition has granted us, that is, the role of the intellectual as mediator, interpreter, or translator?

How can one suggest to an oppressed community to join the nontotalitarian totality? How to delegitimize the authority of sources of fragmentation when these monolithic belongings are the only recourse marginalized communities have had to survive? What communicative practices have colonized people employed to circumvent or challenge the mechanisms by which linguistic coloniality is exercised within their communities? Can these practices inform concrete possibilities to bridge decolonial projects? These practices often involve acts of appropriation or transculturation of colonial languages and mechanisms. But they go beyond categories such as "hybridity," "transculturation," "acculturation," "integration," or "mestizaje," in that they critically acknowledge the experience of being under coloniality and the impossibility of avoiding the need to articulate themselves (directly or indirectly) in relation to colonial languages and categories. Given such unavoidability, how not to miss acts of radical appropriation or not to see them as mimicry and, thus, in complicity with the imputation of the triumphant and devouring march of the West by which *everything* in the colonized world was suppressed?

These sets of questions aim to place us in a philosophical position so as to access people and communities crossed by the coloniality of language and to engage critically with their ways of living and communicating that are not modern and are outside European modernity. It is worth stressing that people at and from the colonial difference are not cleanly emptied out and filled up again but are people who are fractured. People who are expressing themselves linguistically, express that fracturing of their locus of enunciation. The *fractured locus*, in Mignolo's (2000, x; 1995, 303–309) phrase, becomes a new form of coloniality, a new form of inferiority, but it also becomes a new form of creativity. These responses that are produced from *fractured loci* may have some decolonial logic (in the sense of disrupting the hegemonic geopolitics of knowledge) *or may not*. I examine this further with Lugones. But in anticipation, we can think, for example, of a situation like the one Ralph Ellison's *Invisible Man* ([1952] 1995) presents, where the modern/colonial requirement not to recognize him, to treat him as invisible, grants the protagonist certain possibilities to contest the oppressor. With Lugones, we see these responses as complex communicative productions building a locus that might be very minimal because it is constituted by a communicative rejection but is still the site of creativity and *languaging* otherwise.

Those whose speech acts are embedded as dominant in the social organization of the racial split do not language from a *fractured locus*; colonized, subaltern, oppressed people do. But the fact that the colonized, the subaltern, the oppressed enunciate something that is *fractured* does not mean that they can see the colonial difference. The colonial difference has become so normalized that is hidden and not easy to see. And part of that naturalization involves the creation of fictional *natural* barriers to intelligibility that turn oppressed people into *simple communicators* incapable of rational expressivity and who speak inferior languages. People have rejected, resisted, and contested domination at many different levels and with diverse logics. But given the logic of linguistic coloniality, communication across resistances fails. This is the substance of what I have claimed so far. In what follows, I argue for the possibility of nondialogic communication—nondialogic because, as I show through Glissant and Lugones, communicating across, from, and to a fractured locus and enacting a resistant response *is more feasible through emotional tonalities than through the exclusively cognitive.*

Relation, Échos-monde, and Complex Communication

In this section I aim to flesh out a theory of communication that does not play out in the terms of linguistic coloniality but, instead, is attuned to movement and moving in the reconstitution of our colonial legacies. In that vein I analyze Glissant's notions of Relation and Échos-monde and Lugones's complex communication as I believe they privilege the communicative understanding of Indigenous, Afrodescendant, and border-dwelling beings and their complex linguistic creations.

Images of movement, of breaking free from confinement, of departure from the petrified conditions of the colonized imaginary, of *marronage*, of fugitive memories, of openness, are central to Glissant's thinking and vocabulary. The paradigmatic example of this nomenclature is his notion of Relation. In *Poetics of Relation* ([1990] 1997), Glissant offers a new mode of conceiving the world as Relation. More than a picture of a totality, Relation is all about attitudes. Being in Relation is to resituate ourselves—not just differently connected in a complex world, but able to express and hear that complexity in terms of echoes. This connecting attitude is interesting to me because in it I see a way of engaging communication that decenters cognition understood as universal, transparent, and split from emotion and thus communicable under the assumption of uni-versality.[11] Its purpose is not to find results but processes, dynamics, and rhythms that show themselves within the marginal, the incoherent, or the unpredictable that coexist with us in our everyday: "Relation informs not simply what is relayed but also the relative and the related. It is always an approximate truth in any given narrative. For, though the world is not a book, it is nonetheless true that the silence of the world would, in turn, make us deaf. Relation, driving humanities chaotically onward, needs words to publish itself, to continue. But because what it relates, in reality, proceeds from no absolute, it proves to be the totality of relatives put in touch and told" (27–28). Relation abolishes delimitations and trajectories, and makes the world up in terms of an intricate interweaving of communities, an infinite movement across cultures, where each particular pattern is activity implicated in the activity of every other particular.[12] It is with the Antillean experience in mind that Glissant analyzes the possibility of reconceiving these connections into a worldview according to which the logic of the One (of the single-central root) is no longer applicable. His imagination of the world as Relation is centered on the displaced communities, on the diasporic experiences of relocation, on people driven across languages, frontiers, and cultures. We see how pointless and fictitious for Glissant are the results of looking for remote origins, to fix reality by establishing hierarchies of great and small civilizations.

Diasporic experiences make evident that the world can no longer be fixed and shaped into a system, and, therefore, that History with a capital *H* is a fantasy peculiar to Western imagination. The world's dynamics demystifies the desperate attempts to impose order, structure, and stability: "Too many Others and too many elsewheres disturb the flattened surface in order for systematic fixations to catch on in the really livable world" (Glissant [1990] 1997, 33). Linear sense gets lost in *Relation*. It makes no sense and is doomed to failure because it is limited to two dimensions, whereas Relation is three-dimensional: it is *Totalité-monde*, it is *Chaos-monde*, and it is *Échos-monde*. These are not guises of the world but the world's identities, which, Glissant tells us over and over, cannot be proven but creatively imagined. Of Glissant's three identities of the world, I take up that of Échos-monde because, to me, it inspires a communicative attitude that stands in opposition to the longing for the virtues of certainty and transparency characteristic of those who wish to suppress the cross-cultural, pluri-versal imagination.[13]

The Échos-monde provides a profound insight into the drama of cross-culturality taking place on a global scale. It opposes at a practical level the *Generalization* imposed by modernity's uni-versal models hierarchically organizing widely disparate realities.[14] The Échos-monde disorders the assumed order of Generalization addressing the weaving of elements and expressions that struggle against Generalization. The Échos-monde, it is worth emphasizing, does not look to pull together, in some sort of qualitative absolute, all the confronting manifestations of marginalized peoples. What matters are not results but intertwining processes imagined in the concurrences of expressions of a number of people who are asymmetrically located and suffer from a common condition: "For though this experience made you, original victim floating toward the sea's abysses, an exception, it became something shared and made us, the descendants, one people among others. Peoples do not live on exception. Relation is not made up of things that are foreign but of shared knowledge. This experience of the abyss can now be said to be the best element of exchange" (Glissant [1990] 1997, 8). Similar to the Decolonial Turn authors' use of *colonial wound*, this "shared knowledge" does not express sameness. Rather, it is about concurrences or synchronic occurrences that express the image of an echo, an echo that is by no means an exact reproduction; no echo ever is, as Ranajit Guha (2001, 40) explains, "For the interval that separates it from the original is also what reduces it to a mere fraction of the latter, constituting a rather different sound." The echo communicates the multiplicity of worlds of meaning by tracking down the secretive and multiple manifestations of diversity confronting the ideal of cognitive transparency imposed by Western models. Thus, what repeats itself in the Échos-monde is not an identical voice created in expressions of suffering, anguish, fear, anger, or impatience but, rather, a movement that emerges gradually in barely perceptible traces. In *Poetics of Relation*, the Échos-monde is what allows the Antilles to come out of seclusion by transporting the other of thought.[15] The repetition of resistant manifestations does not clarify their expression, it shows nothing revealing on the surface. The attempt to approach a reality so often hidden from view cannot be organized in terms of a series of clarifications. *There is no possible translation*. On the contrary, this repetition leads to perpetual concealment; it compels the adoption of a permanent vigilance against the temptation of certainty and transparency (of translating) because disguising is precisely the act of resistance (Glissant [1990] 1997, 173–74).

The image of Échos-monde addressing, sensing, and citing the rhythm of manifestations against Generalization does not provide the means to fight a total war, a strategy that has been central to nationalist homogenizing movements that Glissant keeps away from. On the contrary, it confronts any attempt to reach a counterhegemonic master discourse. This is evident in Glissant's ([1990] 1997, 189) demand for "the right to opacity," which, to me, reaffirms the need to think resistant manifestations less in a reflective, conscious, or, in a word, agential way. It is not the cognitive level of the articulations that matters because resistant manifestations are acts of survival in the midst of extreme oppressions and so discontinuously organized. It expresses a communicative attitude that is not about predicting and that propels one to ask what manifestations emerging in the chaotic roar of everything one can hear, and how one can hear them. A watchword here is *uncertainty*.

In order not to render this Échos-monde in transparency, one has to resist comprehension and *donner-avec* its disorder, its defamiliarizing force, its discontinuity, its confusion of indicators, its multiple levels of articulation, its secretive and multiple manifestations that with or without words, esoterically or coherently, work to say without saying.[16] In fully sensing communication, one is not representing, clarifying, or translating.[17] All these are monologic practices to know about, to grasp diversity, and conclude in a coherent monologue. All of them assume a cognitive level of manifestation, a logos that would make sense to oneself as if these were expressions informed by a conscious subjectivity. None of them can even glimpse resistant communication. They crush resistance and, therefore, the Échos-monde, by imposing monolithic and monolingual order. The communicative attitude capable of fully sensing the Échos-monde has to first and foremost desire the Échos-monde's defamiliarizing force never culminating in some quantitative discourse.

Such a communicative attitude would strive to break free from the confinement of individualism (of individual agency, of a single linguistic and colonial root, of a pure origin, and so forth). At the same time, an urgent abandonment of the notion of individual agency does not imply that the subject is determined by society. Rather, I interpret that within the Échos-monde, individual agency is replaced by what we may call an *errant attitude*.

Propelled by an *errant attitude*, the subject in Relation (who is no longer traveler, tourist, discoverer, or conqueror) plunges into the opacities of that part of the world to which she has access and strives to voice her reality in a drama of cross-culturality and pluri-versality aiming at perfecting a never complete description of the processes of Relation. It is pertinent to highlight that Glissant does not really talk about people or subjects. *Poetics of Relation*, as I emphasized earlier, is all about attitudes and ways of being-together, about cultures and about literary productions meeting each other cross-culturally and pluri-versally. From this understanding, I am unveiling and gathering tactics and subjects in action. The subject in *Relation* fully senses that she is because of all the possible links to the others, and knowing this compels her to have a generous disposition toward them, not to *comprehend* or to possess them.[18]

The possibility of fully sensing the pattern of such a disordered accord composed by every peoples' own *languaging* requires a sense of orientation; it requires one to *tantear* for meanings, as Lugones tells us, a way of sensing whose main attribute is not destined to be clarity or accessibility: "I use the Spanish word 'tantear' both in the sense of both exploring someone's inclinations about a particular issue and in the sense of 'tantear en la oscuridad,' putting one's hands in front of oneself as one is walking in the dark, tactilely feeling one's way" (Lugones 2003, 1). From a women of color coalitional approach to resistance, Lugones offers us a deep sense of relations of oppressions and relations of resistance. In it, multiple oppressions intersect, there is no clear separation between oppressor and oppressed, the logic of domination is exercised by abstraction (categorization leading to fragmentation), the logic of resistance has diversified concretenesses, and agency, although active, is not necessarily of a conscious intentionality (i.e., actions are always voluntary but not always done with political motivation at the front of consciousness) (Lugones 2003, 1–8). She also gives us an understanding of the barriers to the possibility of coalitions-of-understanding-across-resistances, which include the logic of *narrow* resistant identity base on sameness.

In "On Complex Communication" (2006), Lugones takes up the communicative side of this second issue.

> The limen is at the edge of hardened structures, a place where transgression of the reigning order is possible. As such, it both offers communicative openings and presents communicative impasses to liminal beings. For the limen to be a coalitional space, complex communication is required. This requires praxical awareness of one's own multiplicity and a recognition of the other's opacity that does not attempt to assimilate it into one's own familiar meanings. Refusing the assumption of transparency and operating with relational identities, the complex communication that occurs in the limen—often invisible to dominant groups—can enable genuine coalition and effective resistance to domination. (74)

One important thing that I read in this quote is that Lugones thinks of people in oppressed groups as permeable, and so it is possible to address different interactions and interlocutions. Also, to Lugones, the speech act is cognitively charged *as well as* emotively charged. For some people, what they take out of the speech act is not the cognitive content, and there may be more than one way of participating in the speech act without the cognitive content. Another important thing is that being at the limen is, in a way, methodologically similar to thinking from the colonial difference or responding from a fractured locus. It is so in that it simultaneously realizes both the nonexhaustiveness of the oppressive reality with its dehumanizing practices and institutions, and the local and historical materiality of the freeing reality. That is why the limen offers both communicative openings and communicative impasses. In the abstract, at the structural macro level, there is a commonality, something that puts people who are oppressed on the same side. But the ways in which communicative activities and efforts have been transformed as people have been racialized through legal, political, educational, labor, and civil institutions, and how those transformations have been rejected, resisted, and contested at many different levels and with diverse logics, all of it, necessarily leads to different *journeys* to the limen that are not and cannot be that easily accessible to each other. This communicative difficulty, Lugones emphasizes, calls for reading interlocutions, words, and gestures differently. But differently, how? Away from attempting to grasp the conscious, agential content of what is expressed and toward recognizing one another "as occupying liminal sites" (79), which requires a disposition to enter each other's worlds of meaning.

What interests me most about Lugones's way of thinking is the possibility she opens to dismiss *dialogue* in that she refuses not only the presupposition of transparency (which has been widely rejected) but also the goal of transparency, of reaching a common ground. Complex communication is definitively not about Habermasian communication. Being public-sphere communicators is a condition denied to the nondominant speakers in the sense that they do not have the larger structure of power or its institutions backing up their meaning making. This is consistent with my claim that the logic of linguistic coloniality makes dialogue impossible. What Lugones allows me to add is that there does not have to be dialogue for there to be communication. This is key to the possibility of the nondialogic communication that I am arguing for.

To Lugones, nondominant communicative techniques may not have a decolonial logic (in the sense of pointedly addressing relations established by the coloniality of power and structured by the colonial difference) but still be no less than transgressive acts that take in a situation that is oppressive and develop a complex response (Lugones, personal interview, 2012). Despite the racial split that inferiorizes her, the nondominant speaker has the possibility of making those who despise her very uncomfortable, thus making the oppressive situation one that is less successful. These are not dialogic situations, in the sense of the oppressed being recognized as a person with whom the oppressor can communicate rationally. Nonetheless, there is a transgression of the communicative normalcy. Since the emotional reaction requires that the oppressor see the oppressed, we can say, with Lugones (personal interview, 2012), that "the utterance moves the social; it moves the linguistic terrain; it transforms it."

But beyond transgressive speech acts that disrupt oppressive reality, complex communication can become something that the speaker does with a Du Boisian double consciousness in the sense that she understands herself in two realities: as both nothing (dominant meaning) and not-nothing (resistant meaning created within her "rather narrow" circle of resistance) (Lugones 2006, 78). At the same time, the complex response goes further than *double consciousness* and responds to it creatively in a way that crosses expressive communities. It is in this possibility of going further than double consciousness that I read the distinction that Lugones makes between *deep coalition*, or *coalition against multiple oppressions*, and *narrow coalition*, or *coalitions based on coincidence of interest*. Narrow coalitions close themselves in a sameness that is based on being semiotically transparent to one another and on standing together in opposition to oppression as it affects that particular group. There is a shared vocabulary and a shared wisdom that mark the belonging in narrow coalitions. By contrast, deep coalitions thrive on a disposition to understand each other's way of living in resistance in their opaque particularities, a disposition to see one another with the other's eye accepting that it is not fully possible.

Deep coalition requires complex communication because it depends on neither speaking the same resisting code nor sharing a metanarrative of resistance and, thus, is not based on being able to hear one another in a coherent manner (Lugones 2006, 83–84). But, nevertheless, an utterance might be identifiable as responding to a sign that the other is someone who is taking in a situation of dehumanization. So, while there is no full recognition in complex communication, there is a sense of reading both ways and understanding what is read in such a way that keeps the focus on resistance. In this sense, complex communication is both a transgression and a methodology that enables one to read reality as multiple. It exhibits the fractured locus in ways that enable the speaker to communicate very differently from that fractured locus, away and even against the manyness of dehumanizing, monolanguaging senses related through power.

What is resistant, then, in complex communication is not in the content but in the logic of the communicative act because it goes against the grain of fragmenting meaning by moving-arriving at meaning in nonmonosensical ways. Whereas narrow coalitions are either presupposed or reached through finding equivalences, deep coalitions have to be constructed by learning and exercising "multiple visions, multiple sensing, multiple sense making" (Lugones 2003, 7).

In bringing Glissant and Lugones together, I am not looking for commonalities and differences. Rather, I want to focus on what the combination allows for in terms of a theory of communication that would enable those connections that bring together the decolonial totality. We can imagine the decolonial totality in the way Glissant conceives the world as Relation, and in doing so we can think that its identity as Échos-monde allows immersing ourselves in the possibility of complex communications. The echo moves and transforms these complex communications while maintaining their multiplicity, so monolanguaging becomes less audible and the manyness of the marginal can be accessed and activated.

As a way of imagining the world, Glissant's Relation affects everybody.[19] Given that everybody is in Relation, I want to propose that the act of communication in the midst of and within the coloniality, as Lugones thinks of it, can be understood to be going places. And the places the speech act goes signify different relations between colonized, nondominant speakers and oppression and racial domination, on the one hand, and possibilities that are resistant or liberatory, on the other. One can think of that as an echo, a sense of communication that has no (individual) agency. That is, the speech act does not travel without encountering a recipient somewhere along its path. And when it goes through the person and *across* nondominant speakers, it does so in an active way.

Let us go back to the example of Ellison's *Invisible Man*. From the modern/colonial perspective, the Invisible Man does not exist; monolanguaging agents, institutions, and practices have thrown him out of existence. In opposition, from a decolonial perspective, the Invisible Man exists and communicates. He does so in a way that is nonassimilatory and that is often unintelligible to dominant speakers *as well as* to other racialized groups. It is the latter that matters here as I am exploring horizontal communication and the communicative possibilities *across* daily resistant manifestations and transgressions.[20]

With respect to other groups of people or other communities who are in a similar situation at the colonial difference to that of the Invisible Man, in terms of either language or way of life, or both—that is, people who, like him, have experiences of what I call the "coloniality of language"—the Invisible Man's speech act is not clear in meaning. But even though it is cognitively opaque, it might still be identifiable as friendly or inspiring to their own resistance and creation. It is not necessary that the speech act be directed consciously or intentionally, only that it passes through a person in such a way that if read, or heard, it would be recognized (Lugones, personal interview, 2012). This recognition is a response to the Invisible Man's address not in the Bahktinian sense of *reply* but in a less consequential and attenuated sense: merely as something that is improper, that lacks the mark of acceptability of the modern speech act.

So, the utterance at and from the colonial difference has resonances that are different in terms of sense, not emphasizing the cognitive but the emotional direction of the speech act. Echoing is something that can happen in both cases. One never has a complete sense of the speech act's direction, as it is not in the speaker's control. The speech act encounters and passes through different people in a society linguistically racialized and alters the relation among those it passes through with respect to hiding oppression, ignoring it, or recognizing it. The dominant speaker may think of the Invisible Man with contempt but even in his case, the emotional response can be thought of as an echo.[21] The nondominant speaker hears something that she does not understand, but she knows it is against oppression; this recognition can be thought of as an echo.

With Lugones, we learn that there is no need to think here of willfulness or resistant consciousness. The possibility that the Échos-monde opens to engage with complex communications is neither a linear nor a fully agential sense of communication but, rather, an uncertain one. Opacities need to be preserved, and one is never sure of realizing them. One's self-assertions are inevitably linked to a sensuous physical presence, to an active body. It is not the circulation of ideas but how they resonate in the body—the body as a sort of baffle or acoustic box—so that one does not claim possession of a purer piece of truth but neither seeks to erase the factors of time and place that coalesce as they do in the body, informed by the immediacy and urgency of political, linguistic, and social conditions. In other words, within the Échos-monde, what matters is not *comprehending* marginalized people but, rather, being good at *traveling linguistically*. That is, a way of orienting oneself with a sense of permeability and relationality, and a recognition of being on the same side of things that does not have to be political but is always active. But clearly, it is a communicative act that can be done politically, intentionally, or artistically in a manner that has the complexity of understanding both oppression and liberation.

Conclusion

In this chapter, I explored the call for dialogue in the Decolonial Turn. I introduced the idea of coloniality of language to argue that dialogue is not enough to fulfill the project of decoloniality because dialogue itself has been colonized. We need to rethink communication in a decolonial vein. Coloniality as a communicative relation is not something we can make sense of via modern communicative-action theory. To the contrary, modern communicative-action theories hide and disguise the logic of linguistic coloniality.

By articulating the relations between coalitional methodologies (Lugones) and a global sense of connection (Glissant), I proposed a nondialogical theory of communication that takes up the problem of how to imagine communicative connections *across* horizontal realities of oppression and resistance in a decolonial vein given the arrangements and conditions created by coloniality. One of the questions I problematized has been that from a decolonial perspective the *across* needs to be very different from the dialogical intent of speaking with somebody with only cognition involved. This is why to me dialogue has little to do with shifting the geography of reason. Am I saying dialogue would never be possible? We can think about action in a situation where the action is decolonial in its complexity, but this does not mean that a transformation has happened in terms of the structure, be it linguistic, legal, economic, etc. To go for those changes does not require that one wants to change the structure. One lives and communicates as if the structure is something against oneself, so instead of immersing oneself in it to change it, one directs oneself to it in this more complex way attuned to the echo.

Notes

An earlier and shorter version of this chapter was first published as "A Coalitional Approach to Theorizing Decolonial Communication," in *Hypatia* 31, no. 2 (2016). Portions are reprinted by permission of Cambridge University Press. I want to thank and dedicate this chapter to my *compañeras* and *compañeros* at CPIC (2007–19) with whom I learned to think collectively and move away from a solipsistic way of being and knowing that impoverishes my intellectual possibilities. Over the years, CPIC offered me a site for advancing and deepening my research and place it in provocative, moving, and transforming conversations with radical faculty and fellow graduate students who have been working in nontraditional scholarship and contributing to the attempts to decolonize subalternized knowledges at the tense intersection of multiple oppressions. For all of us, CPIC has been a node for decolonial thinking and building a dispersed community with an eye to intellectual activism.

1. Quijano and Mignolo discuss this move as a process of "epistemic de-linking." Quijano (1992, 19) expressed it first expressed in Spanish: "[Hay que] *desprenderse* de las vinculaciones de la racionalidad-modernidad con la colonialidad, en primer término, y en definitiva con todo poder no constituido en la decision libre de gentes libres" (emphasis added). The first translation into English read: "It is necessary to *extricate oneself* from the linkages between rationality/modernity and coloniality, first of all, and definitely from all power which is not constituted by free decision of people" (Quijano 2007, 177). Mignolo (2011, 45) argued that "de-link" was preferable to "extricate" and made the term into a theoretical concept and method that summarizes the political standing of the decolonial collective.

2. Based on comments made by Walter D. Mignolo during the workshop "Re-articulating the Scenarios of Environmental Catastrophe" at the 2009 transmediale festival, Berlin.

3. I must say, so that my critique of Mignolo's proposal is not misconstrued, that this decolonial struggle for another politics of knowledge and scholarship is very much my/our struggle as well. The university and academia are my political arena. I am part of what Jacqui Alexander called "academics on alert," in her letter of support against the decision of Binghamton University administration to close CPIC in 2009: "We have been placed on alert because decisions such as the one taken by Binghamton threatens to undo the very infrastructure from which we make knowledge claims while we ourselves are deeply involved in the work of wider institution building." CPIC wasn't closed that year and remained officially open for another nine years, and during all those years, it was the place and company I called home in academia (see the introduction to this volume). During this time Mignolo has been an instrumental and strong compañero. I owe much to his work and to him for the many spaces he invited me to participate in and for the many invitations he accepted to join our conversations at CPIC.

4. Later, when discussing Mignolo's proposal of a bilanguaging epistemology, I review his understanding of monolanguaging. It is worth noting at this point that our understandings are different. While Mignolo (2000, 252) refers to the ideology of speaking, writing, thinking within a single unified language controlled by a grammar and aligned with the formation of imperial and nation states, my usage refers to a way of communication that dehumanizes. They are indeed related, but I do not examine that relation here.

5. The choice of the pronouns *she* and *her* to refer to the interpellant Other is mine; Dussel uses *he*.

6. Mignolo (2000, 274) ends the chapter recommending "bilanguaging love" as the final utopic horizon for the liberation of human beings involved in structures of domination and subordination beyond their control: "Love for being between languages, love for the disarticulation of the colonial language and for subaltern ones, love for the impurity of national languages, and love as the necessary corrective to the 'generosity' of hegemonic power that institutionalizes violence; this is love for all that is disavowed by cultures of scholarship complicitous with colonial legacies and national hegemonies.... Love is the restitution of the secondary qualities (e.g., passions, emotions, feelings) and of the impurity of language that have been banned from education and epistemology since the very inception of early colonization and modern rationality."

I wonder whether bilanguaging love could serve as the foundation from where to rethinking dialogue decolonially. I don't engage that possibility here. I am thankful to an anonymous reader for suggesting that I consider how Dussel's understanding of interpellation and Mignolo's bilanguaging complicate my critique and open further questions for investigation.

7. By *regular people*, I mean to expand to the present day what until the nineteenth century was conveyed with the terms "common people," "commoners," or "populace" to denote a broad social

division referring to those people who were members of neither the nobility nor the priesthood, people who are not representatives or officials. In the context of the colonies, the distinction applied as we have seen between members of Indigenous communities (*Indios comunes*), and members of the Indigenous elite or the emperors themselves.

8. One could certainly identify plenty of contradictions between and within colonial projects. It was contradictory that the Crown claimed that the colonized were not people while counting them among its vassals and that in churches and missions, colonized people were baptized, while in mines and plantations they were worked to death, and that the state included colonized populations and their descendants within the body of the nation but did not give them legal standing. But all this was done, and it was done legally and backed up by power.

9. I am thankful to María Lugones, who reviewed the draft version of this chapter and pushed me to think so much harder about this idea of a mixture.

10. I wonder whether part of Mignolo's proposal for a bilanguaging epistemology may include rethinking translation as an agency of languaging. I leave this question open for future investigations.

11. I borrow from Fernando Garcés the idea of hyphenating *uni-versal* and *uni-versality* to stress the etymologic evocation they imply: one verse, one discourse—and only one—that displaces all others. In this sense, the term is suitable for referring to the linguistic and epistemic silence to which colonized people in the Americas and other peripheral populations within Euro-centered colonial modernity were and are subjected (Garcés 2005, 141). The terms *pluri-versality* and *pluri-versal* (combinations of the words *pluri* and *uni-versal/ity*) are not my own; they are used by decolonial thinkers to characterize the standpoint from which they situate their critique (see the introduction to this volume). In opposition to global and totalitarian designs, created in the name of universality, pluriversality is an attempt to make visible and viable a multiplicity of knowledges, forms of being, and visions of the world.

12. It is worth emphasizing that, as is the case with the notion of Relation, the verb *to relate* is used throughout *Poetics of Relation* simultaneously in two of its meanings: to connect, to establish a relation between; and to recount, narrate, tell, give an account of actions, events, and facts.

13. See endnote 11.

14. Glissant (2002, 288) capitalizes *Generalization* to indicate a long process of universalization whose current face is globalization or the global market: "Reduction to the bare basics, the rush to the bottom, standardization, and the imposition of multinational corporations with their ethos of profit [at all cost], circles whose circumference is everywhere and whose center is nowhere."

15. *Poetics of Relation*'s project is first and foremost born from the urgent Antillean need to have a full existence; to restore its collective memory against the pervasiveness of colonialist and nationalist divisive loyalties and corrosive fragmentations; to struggle against linguistic and cultural erosion. Glissant's work opens the local Antillean experience and points to a kind of solidarity and intimacy that colonization has denied.

16. The openness and disposition to learn each other's meaning that validate the opacities, difficulties, contradictions, and uncertainties emergent in communication are how I understand that which Glissant names *donner-avec* (translated as *gives-on-and-with* by Betsy Wing). *Donner-avec* constitutes the understanding on which the nontotalitarian universality must be based. It is a form of understanding that Glissant contrasts with the French word *comprendre*, which, like its English and Spanish cognates, is formed on the basis of the Latin word *comprehendere* ("to seize"), which is formed from the roots *com-* ("with") and *prendere* ("to take"). *Comprendre* conveys an appropriative and almost rapacious form of understanding. In contrast, *donner* ("to give") is meant as generosity of perception and also constitutes a notion of yielding. *Avec* both reflects back on the *com-* of *comprendre* and defines the underlying principle of the nontotalitarian universality (Glissant [1990] 1997, xii, 212). It is worth emphasizing how this contrast illuminates an epistemological relation of domination-resistance: The colonial word *comprendre* signals an appropriation, an act of

totalitarian grasping. In order to open space for a nontotalitarian way of understanding, Glissant pushes the limitations of the imposed language of fixed rules and forces the neologism *donner-avec* that uses French from the perspective of the subaltern. Without a doubt, this is a practice of "changing not only the content but the terms of the conversation" (Mignolo 2000), very much in sync with the spirit of the Decolonial Turn on the part of both Glissant and Wing.

17. Glissant's ([1990] 1997, 154) donner-avec allows us to challenge and discard the totalitarianism of a universal sense (in linear terms) and to plunge ourselves into a sense in circularity, a relational sense, or (to use Glissant's favored expression) a *full sense* that combines signification, direction, and concrete sensory/affective perception.

18. See note 16.

19. Everybody is in Relation, but Glissant lets us think that colonized cultures are in an advantage position to sense the echo. This is because from the very beginning (though to Glissant the question of beginning is always a loose question) these are cultures that are made of variety of elements that are heterogeneous and creolized. Thus, they have a tendency toward mixture and impurity. While colonizing, conquering cultures, because of their history and imaginary, have a tendency toward purity, homogeneity, and for them, Relation is difficult to grasp.

20. In the case of vertical communication, the dominant speaker, though he denies all rational content coming out of the Invisible Man's mouth and *comprehends* nothing, he does sense some things about the speech act. And one of the things he senses is that the utterance comes from someone that is part of the despised people. The dominant speaker may be threatened, scared, or full of contempt, all of which signs that the Invisible Man's utterance has troubled him, has moved him.

21. See note 19.

References

Anzaldúa, Gloria. 1987. *Borderlands/La Frontera: The New Mestiza*. San Francisco: Aunt Lute Books.

Bakhtin, Mikhail M. 1981. *The Dialogic Imagination: Four Essays*. Edited by Michael Holquist. Translated by Caryl Emerson and Michael Holquist. Austin: University of Texas Press.

Crenshaw, Kimberlé Williams. 1991. "Mapping the Margins: Intersectionality, Identity Politics, and Violence against Women of Color." *Stanford Law Review* 43 (6): 1241–99.

De Sousa Santos, Boaventura, João Arriscado Nunes, and María Paula Menses. 2008. "Introduction: Opening Up the Canon of Knowledge and Recognition of Difference." In *Another Knowledge Is Possible: Beyond Northern Epistemologies*, edited by Boaventura De Sousa Santos, ixx–ixii. New York: Verso,

Dussel, Enrique. 1995. *The Invention of the Americas: Eclipse of the "Other" and the Myth of Modernity*. Translated by Michael D. Barber. New York: Continuum.

———. 1996: *The Underside of Modernity: Apel, Ricoeur, Rorty, Taylor, and the Philosophy of Liberation*. Edited and translated by Eduardo Mendieta. Amherst, NY: Humanity Books.

Ellison, Ralph. (1952) 1995. *Invisible Man*. New York: Vintage.

Escobar, Arturo. 2010. "Worlds and Knowledges Otherwise: The Latin American Modernity/Coloniality Research Program." In *Globalization and the Decolonial Option*, edited by Walter D. Mignolo and Arturo Escobar, 33–64. London: Routledge.

Freire, Paolo. (1970) 2005. *Pedagogy of the Oppressed*. Translated by Myra Bergman Ramos. New York: Continuum.

Garcés, Fernando. 2005. "Las políticas del conocimiento y la colonialidad lingüística y epistémica." In *Pensamiento crítico y matriz (de)colonial: Reflexiones latinoamericanas*, edited by Catherine E. Walsh, 137–68. Quito: Ediciones Abya-Yala.

Glissant, Édouard. (1990) 1997. *Poetics of Relation*. Translated by Betsy Wing. Ann Arbor: University of Michigan Press.

———. 2002. "The Unforeseeable Diversity of the World." In *Beyond Dichotomies: Histories, Identities, Cultures, and the Challenge of Globalization*, edited by Elizabeth Mudimbe-Boyi, translated by Haun Saussy, 287–95. Albany: State University of New York Press.

Guha, Ranajit. 2001. "Subaltern Studies: Projects for Our Time and Their Convergence." In *The Latin American Subaltern Studies Reader*, edited by Ileana Rodríguez, 35–46. Durham, NC: Duke University Press.

Lugones, María. 2003. *Pilgrimages/Peregrinajes: Theorizing Coalition Against Multiple Oppressions*. Lanham, MD: Rowman & Littlefield.

———. 2006. "On Complex Communication." *Hypatia* 21 (3): 75–85.

———. 2007. "Heterosexualism and the Colonial/Modern Gender System." *Hypatia* 22 (1): 186–209.

Maldonado-Torres, Nelson. 2005. "Post-Continental Philosophy and the Decolonial Turn: Introductory Comments." Presented at the Mapping the Decolonial Turn: Post/Trans- Continental Interventions in Philosophy, Theory, and Critique, University of California, Berkeley, April 21, 2005.

Maturana, Humberto R. 1999. *Transformación en la convivencia*. Caracas: Dolmen.

Maturana, Humberto, and Francisco J. Varela. 1987. *The Tree of Knowledge: The Biological Roots of Human Understanding*. Boston: Shambhala Publications.

Mignolo, Walter D. 1995. *The Darker Side of the Renaissance*. Ann Arbor: University of Michigan Press.

———. 2000. *Local Histories/Global Designs: Coloniality, Subaltern Knowledges, and Border Thinking*. Princeton, NJ: Princeton University Press.

———. 2003. *Historias locales / diseños globales: Colonialidad, conocimientos subalternos y pensamiento fronterizo*. Translated by Juanmarí Madriaga and Cristina Vega Solis. Ediciones AKAL.

———. 2005. *The Idea of Latin America*. Malden, MA: Blackwell.

———. 2010. "Life: Politics, Resistance, & Beyond." Presented at the Twentieth Annual Philosophy, Interpretation and Culture (PIC) Conference, Binghamton University, April 16, 2010.

———. 2011. "Epistemic Disobedience and the Decolonial Option: A Manifesto." *Transmodernity* 1 (2): 44–66.

Quijano, Aníbal. 1992. "Colonialidad y modernidad/racionalidad." *Perú Indígena* 13 (29): 11–20.

———. 2000. "Coloniality of Power, Eurocentrism, and Latin America." Translated by Michael Ennis. *Nepantla: Views from South* 1 (3): 533–80.

———. 2007. "Coloniality and Modernity/Rationality." Translated by Sonia Therborn. *Cultural Studies* 21 (2): 168–78.

Shohat, Ella. 2001. Introduction to *Talking Visions: Multicultural Feminism in a Transnational Age*, edited by Ella Shohat, 1–60. Cambridge, MA: MIT Press.

Gabriela Veronelli, born in Argentina and migrant in the United States, is an independent researcher of Latin American and Latinx social and political theory, translator, and journalist. She is affiliated with the Center for Global Studies and the Humanities at Duke University and the Escuela Interdisciplinaria de Altos Estudios Sociales at Universidad Nacional de San Martín. She is editor, with P. J. Di Pietro, of *The Maria Lugones Reader* (forthcoming 2025). She also edited a special issue of *Revista de Lenguaje y Cultura* entitled *Decoloniality and English Language Teaching: The South Writes Back* (2022). She is the translator of *Peregrinajes: Teorizar una coalición contra múltiples opresiones* (2021) by María Lugones.

11

FROM NATION TO PLURINATION

PLURINATIONALISM, DECOLONIAL FEMINISM, AND THE POLITICS OF COALITIONAL PRAXIS IN ECUADOR

Christine "Cricket" Keating and Amy Lind

Introduction

A KEY COMPONENT of Ecuador's 2008 constitution is a resignification of the state as plurinational and intercultural, two interrelated terms that mark Ecuador as a pluri-sovereign polity that facilitates the equitable interrelation of the multiple peoples within it. In Ecuador, as in other struggles in Abya Yala, the linked notions of plurinationalism and interculturalism are rooted in Indigenous struggles to defend communal systems and diverse modes of collectivity that have been kept alive through centuries of colonization. While both concepts arise from Indigenous political conceptions and organized movements, other social movements in Ecuador have also begun to use the term *plurinationalism* in order to broaden notions of sovereignty and to pluralize conceptions of democratic, legal, cultural, and epistemic practice. Indeed, in addition to Indigenous activists, LGBTIQ, feminist, Afro-Ecuadorian, and migrants' rights activists, among others, have all participated in public dialogues about the meaning and making of a plurinational democracy in Ecuador. In this chapter, we trace this multipronged struggle for plurinationalism, examining some of its key terms and central features. We call attention to the ways in which the adoption of a plurinationalist and interculturalist framework in Ecuador has been stymied, stalled, and oftentimes obstructed by the Ecuadorian government. We analyze ongoing struggles for its implementation, focusing specifically on what the plurinational and intercultural processes in Ecuador might signal so far about the development of coalitional praxis in Ecuador.

Plurinationalism and Interculturalism in Ecuador:
Key Terms and Central Features

The concept of plurinationalism in Abya Yala is grounded in a demand for the recognition of Indigenous groups as distinct nations within the state, with rights to territorial, cultural, economic, and political self-determination. Since the late 1980s, the demand for the recasting of the state as a plurination by Indigenous groups and others has echoed and intensified across Abya Yala. For example, Bolivia, like Ecuador, adopted a new constitution in 2009 that moved the country toward a plurinationalist model, a shift symbolized in its resignification as the "Plurinational State of Bolivia." Other states in Abya Yala are moving toward institutionalizing plurinationalist frameworks as well. In 2022, for example, the Chilean Constituent Assembly approved a resolution to recast Chile as a "Plurinational and Intercultural State." Although the draft constitution was rejected in a referendum, momentum to rethink the model of the state along plurinationalist lines remains. There are calls for plurinationalist refoundings in Peru, Argentina, and Colombia as well (Merino 2021, 8).

Central to the struggles for plurinationalism across Abya Yala is a critique of the racialized structures of authority and governance that were introduced by colonization and have continued into the present day. Decolonial theorist Aníbal Quijano (2000) refers to the perpetuation of racialized social, political, and economic power relations imposed or exacerbated by colonization yet preserved in postcolonial regimes as the "coloniality of power." Drawing on the work of Quijano, Breny Mendoza (2017, 645) characterizes this continuity in the realm of postcolonial political life as the "coloniality of democracy" and explains that not only was "conquest and colonization . . . defined by the loss of sovereignty and self-government of the colonized" but also that "colonization has meant that the colonized remain expelled from the polity and that Western nation-states and liberal democracies have emerged from and continue to rest upon the ruins of colonialism." Underscoring the coloniality of democracy in Ecuador, Spanish literacy requirements for voting effectively disenfranchised Indigenous communities until the late 1970s. In the words of Ecuadorian Indigenous leader Luis Macas (2004), "For us, independence from Spain only represented a change of masters as the structures of domination and exploitation of our peoples remained intact."[1]

In Ecuador, the conception of Indigenous communities as nations began to take hold in the early 1980s. José Antonio Lucero (2008, 113–14) notes that during this time, "nationality became the political term of choice to encompass the diverse Indigenous groups of the country. . . . Though nationalities as such did not exist in an organizational sense—the movement remained one constituted by local, provincial, and regional federations—they still represented important units of representation." The conception of "nationality" was useful, Lucero explains, because it could be used to address the issues of cultural and political domination in addition to economic exploitation. By referring to themselves as nationalities, as Lucero argues, Indigenous activists took "a term from the lexicon of Marxist and European thought and Indianized it" (113). In an early article, Nina Pacari (1984, 138), an Indigenous activist, scholar, and lawyer who would later go on to serve as the first Indigenous woman in the Ecuadorian Parliament and later on the Constitutional Court, wrote that "in the current Ecuadorian state there are countless Indigenous nationalities such as Quichuas, Chachis, Tzatzilas, Shuars. . . . Our problem is not only one of class struggle, but it is also a struggle of the people, as a people . . . They want us to stop being what we are." In the face of such economic, political, and cultural domination, Pacari explained, "we want our existence to be recognized" as well as a state "in which each nationality has the right to self-determination and free choice of social, political, and cultural life" (138). In the influential essay, "Las nacionalidades indias y el estado ecuatoriano" (Indian nationalities and the Ecuadorian state), Indigenous activist Ampam Karakras (1984, 128) wrote that "we have opted for the term Indian nationalities . . . because we understand that the category 'nationality' expresses the economic, political, cultural and linguistic aspects of our peoples. It places us in national and international life."

There are fourteen Indigenous nationalities, with territories across the Highland, Coastal, and Amazon regions of Ecuador and at least thirteen Indigenous languages. Since 1986, the Confederation of Indigenous Nationalities of Ecuador (CONAIE) has linked together various Indigenous regional organizations and has been at the forefront of several important Indigenous struggles and uprisings. While CONAIE draws its representational strength from the nations, it gets its organizational power from the strong network of Indigenous communities across Ecuador.

> Ecuador has about 2,100 Indian communities, functioning as self-regulated entities based on the authority of their *asambleas* (in which everybody participates) and *cabildos* (executive committees of five members). All important issues are discussed in the *asambleas*, where agreement is usually reached by consensus rather than by voting. The decisions are binding for all members. . . . Thus, joining in a mobilization is always the result of a decision of the community, which exerts its influence to make sure that the members join in the roadblocks and rallies. The secret of CONAIE's power, then, lies in its ability to harness the resources for collective action that exist in the Indian communities. (Zamosc 2007, 16)

CONAIE has played a crucial role in developing plurinationalist theory and practice in contemporary Ecuador since its inception. In 1994, CONAIE published a declaration of its political project. This declaration outlines the theoretical underpinnings of the organization's conception of plurinationalism as well as a lexicon of key terms related to it. In it, CONAIE (1994, 5) calls for a plurinationalist restructuring of Ecuadorian democracy and invites "all political and social sectors that coexist in the current Ecuadorian territory to participate actively and creatively" in its formulation and construction. The group defines plurinationalism as the "principle that guarantees the full exercise of the rights of all the nationalities existing in the country" (53), one that upholds "the right of the Nationalities to their territory and internal political-administrative autonomy, and allowing them to determine their own processes of economic, social, cultural, scientific, and technological development to ensure the development of their cultural and political identity" (12–13). The organization explains that plurinationalism as a political project is grounded in the "historical experiences of the permanent struggle" of Indigenous peoples against Spanish colonialism, postindependence republican rule, and international imperialism (1). Defining the state as the instantiation of "organized political unity" (52), it contrasts the plurinationalist state with the uninationalist state. Exclusionary and repressive, the uninationalist state in Ecuador, it explains, has served to "maintain the subjugation of the Indigenous Peoples and Nationalities, and all social sectors; impeding political participation and denying our individual and collective historical rights" (6). In contrast, the group defines the plurinationalist state as a form of "political organization that represents the political, economic and social power of all the peoples and nationalities of a country" (52).

Closely linked to CONAIE's concept of plurinationalism is the notion of interculturality, with plurinationalism recognizing and affirming the fact of the multiplicity of nations, peoples, and cultures within Ecuador, and interculturality marking the process by which they can become unified. According to CONAIE (1994, 12), "the principle of interculturality respects the diversity of Indigenous nationalities and peoples as well as Ecuadorians from other social sectors. But at the same time, it demands the unity of these in the economic, social, cultural, and political fields, with eyes towards transforming the present structures and building a new plurinational state, in the frame of equality, of rights, mutual respect, peace, and harmony among nationalities and peoples." Thus, in contrast to the so-called unity that is enforced or assumed through practices of uninationalist repression and exclusion, the "unity in diversity" of a plurinationalist framework is actively built through ongoing practices of intercultural dialogue, struggle, and transformation.

In its declaration, CONAIE envisions a distinctly plurinationalist democracy. CONAIE (1994, 53) defines a plurinationalist democracy as "the full and permanent participation of all peoples and nationalities in the decision-making process and in the exercise of political power in the Plurinational State." The building blocks of a plurinationalist democracy in Ecuador, CONAIE explains, are the communitarian practices and systems which are "the way of life of Indigenous Nations and Peoples, based on reciprocity, solidarity, and equality." This way of life, the organization explains, is grounded in "a socio-economic and political system of a collective character in which all its members actively participate." CONAIE argues that Indigenous nationalities and peoples have practiced this way of living since "the emergence of our collectivist-agrarian society" and that the maintenance of these communal practices across the centuries of domination has been "the only thing that has allowed and will allow the Indigenous Peoples and Nationalities to subsist within a colonial and republican legal-political system" and has served "to reduce colonial violence and its disastrous consequences." CONAIE (1994, 11) emphasizes that these communitarian systems and practices are not fixed or set in stone, but rather that they have been adapted to external economic and political processes. As such they have "changed but have not disappeared."

The practice of plurinationalist democracy, in CONAIE's conception, is the ongoing exercise of the principles of self-determination, autonomy, and self-management, each of which CONAIE understands in distinctly expansive and intercultural ways. CONAIE's (1994, 53) definition of self-determination, for example, includes not only the rights of nationalities to choose their political, economic, and legal systems but the right to choose "social, scientific, and cultural development model" as well. Similarly expansive, plurinationalist autonomy means "the capacity for decision making and control of the Indigenous Peoples and Nationalities in our territories in the administrative, legal, political, economic, social and cultural order" (55). Such an expansive framework is a bulwark not only against political and economic subordination but also against cultural, social, and epistemic domination. In the words of CONAIE, "We, the Indigenous Peoples and Nationalities must defend ourselves from assimilation and/or physical and cultural extermination, as well as from economic exploitation, with the practice of communal self-management" (53).

Further, CONAIE's theorization of practices of self-determination, autonomy, and self-management foregrounds questions of relation and interconnection, taking up the question of how to coexist with other groups within a polity. For example, CONAIE notes that being autonomous does not mean "separation or rejection of other sectors of the population . . . it is not only inward looking, a strategy by and for the communities alone, but it is also deeply linked to society as a whole." Similarly, the practice of community self-management is situated in intercultural societal relation. In CONAIE's (1994,

53–54) words, "Self-management does not mean isolation or self-sufficiency, but participation in power and a dynamic, dialectical and human interrelation with all sectors of society."

In the declaration, CONAIE (1994, 1) emphasizes that the plurinationalist political project it envisions is meant for the country as a whole, not only for Indigenous nationalities and peoples: "The Political Project that CONAIE has elaborated and defends is an alternative proposal to the neoliberal system that we, the Nationalities and Peoples, present to the whole society, the Afro-Ecuadorian and Hispano-Ecuadorian People and the different social sectors," with the aim of achieving their harmonious and balanced development. Toward the polity-wide development of such an alternative, CONAIE called for a new constitution for Ecuador, a demand that it and others fought for with major uprisings and protests that took place throughout the 1990s and 2000s.

Although Ecuador revised its constitution in 1998, it did not substantively take up Indigenous demands for a fundamental restructuring of the state (Chuji Gualinga 2008). On April 15, 2007, however, Ecuadorians had another opportunity to do so when they passed a referendum to convene a Constituent Assembly to draft a new constitution for Ecuador—its twentieth—by a huge margin, with over 82 percent voting in its favor. In order to prepare for the assembly, CONAIE held dialogues and gathered input from Indigenous, Afro-Ecuadorian, and Montubio communities from across Ecuador. In addition, CONAIE engaged in dialogues with feminist groups, environmentalists, water boards, migrant organizations, LGBTIQ groups, workers, intellectuals, academics, children, and adolescents (CONAIE 2007a, 1). The group synthesized these dialogues into concrete proposals to be taken up the Constituent Assembly, outlining its vision for the organizational restructuring of a plurinationalist Ecuador. In the proposals, CONAIE (2007b, 42) vowed that "unlike other constitutional processes in which Indigenous groups, women, blacks, workers, and peasants were relegated from the official democracy" and "left out of history," the process of refounding Ecuador as a plurinational country would center on these groups' experience of struggle and resistance. The proposals called for several measures that would affirm and structure plurinationalism in the new constitution. As its first objective, CONAIE (2007b, 5) proposed the declaration of Ecuador as a "plurinational and intercultural state," one that is "unitary, communitarian, equitable, solidarious, inclusive, gender equitable, sovereign and secular." Another key objective, it stated, was to "democratize democracy" by "recognizing and valorizing the diverse forms of democracy that exist in the country" (CONAIE 2007b, 14). CONAIE also recommended a series of measures aimed at rearranging territorial administrative and political governance structures to build a pluralized, viable, and transformative system of community governance structures. In CONAIE's words, such a rearrangement would recognize "the right of peoples to their own forms of authority" as well as the importance of territorial self-governance for "practicing a form of life, a way of living in the world, a civilization" (10–11). Emphasizing that its vision is for a unified state (as opposed to a uninationalist state), CONAIE notes that these communities would not be "isolated or enclosed" (11). The unified state would have the responsibility of enabling and supporting community/communal governments as well as responsibility for "several areas of competence" including international relations (11). In CONAIE's constitutional framing, community governments would serve as an important check on the unified state's exercise of these powers (11).

Besides the question of the relationship of the community governments to the unified state, CONAIE's proposals also address the thorny issues of how to establish and define the community governments, especially in a situation where other units of territorial governance (such as the Ecuadorian provinces) might be threatened by such a reorganization. In such a situation, CONAIE emphasized that "it is imperative that the mechanism for defining the Indigenous territory is transparent, democratic and legitimate to other social and political actors." In order to facilitate this outcome, the organization recommends "conducting a local plebiscite expressing the wish to be constituted as territorial community government" instead of this decision being made by decree by the Ecuadorian government (CONAIE 2007b, 11).

In addition to its territorial community governance proposals, CONAIE called for a series of measures to ensure Indigenous and Afro-Ecuadorian representation in the representative institutions of the unifed government as well. For example, the proposals call for the renaming of the National Congress as the Asamblea Plurinacional Legislativa (Plurinational Legislative Assembly) and establishing the "direct representation of Indigenous and Afro-Ecuadorian nationalities" in the legislatures, with each nationality internally selecting one delegate (CONAIE 2007b, 15).

Questions related to legal pluralism also play an important part of CONAIE's proposal. Noting that "the exercise of justice is part of the community government of the nationalities and peoples of Ecuador and a substantial component of the Plurinational State," the proposal called for the consolidation of Indigenous legal systems with their own "authorities, jurisdiction, and powers" (CONAIE 2007b, 7). CONAIE also proposed the inclusion of an Indigenous Justice on Ecuador's Constitutional Court.

In addition to the proposals regarding the legal and political framework of Ecuador, CONAIE's proposal calls on the Constituent Assembly to defend and deepen "collective economic, social, and cultural rights" through measures enabling and supporting interculturality (CONAIE 2007b, 41). In the proposal, CONAIE emphasizes that interculturality should be viewed as a "right and political responsibility for all Ecuadorians" (41). It explains that "it is impossible to have an intercultural country if this is the work of Indigenous peoples and nationalities alone. Interculturality is a matter for all Ecuadorians" (41). Focusing on education as an avenue to foster interculturality, the group argued that the Ecuadorian education system should establish and guarantee an "intercultural bilingual education system for all" (44). Further, it proposed that Spanish and Kichwa be designated as "official languages of intercultural relations" and that Shuar and other Indigenous languages be recognized as "languages of official use for indigenous peoples" (44).

When the Constituent Assembly met in 2007 to begin writing the new constitution, the first article members drafted formally declared Ecuador a plurination: "Article 1. Ecuador is a constitutional State of rights and justice, a social, democratic, sovereign, independent, unitary, intercultural, plurinational and secular State" (Asamblea Constituyente 2008). Although the Constituent Assembly did not include the descriptors "communal," "gender equity," and "solidarity" that CONAIE had advocated, it was nonetheless the first time that the words "plurinational" and "intercultural" were used to describe Ecuador in its constitution. In addition to this resignification, the Constituent Assembly passed several articles that take up Indigenous demands for plurinational self-determination, autonomy, and self-management in structural and institutional ways. Article 57, for example, guarantees twenty-one collective rights for Indigenous communities, peoples, and nations. These include the right to keep "ownership of their community lands and ancestral territories" as well as to participate in the "use, administration and conservation of natural renewable resources located on their lands." It also stipulates that Indigenous groups have the right to "free prior informed consultation on plans and programs for nonrenewable resource projects that could have an environmental or cultural impact on them, and to receive compensation for damages caused." Furthermore, they have the right to develop and practice their own legal system or common law and "create and uphold organizations that represent them and participate in official organizations that affect their collective rights." These rights also encompass the preservation and promotion of their cultural and historical heritage, as well as the "development and improvement of intercultural bilingual education systems that reflect their identities and methodologies." Furthermore, Article 57 stipulates the right to "freely uphold, develop and strengthen their identity, ancestral traditions and forms of social organization," and to not be subjected to "racism or any form of discrimination based on their origin or ethnic or cultural identity." Articles 58 and 59 guarantee the collective rights of Afro-Ecuadorians and Montubios, respectively. Article 60 further holds that "ancestral, indigenous, Afro-Ecuadorian and coastal backcountry (montubios) peoples can establish territorial districts for the preservation of their culture. The law shall regulate their establishment. Communities (comunas) that have collective land ownership are recognized as an ancestral form of territorial organization." On the issues of legal pluralism and Indigenous justice, Article 171 states that "the authorities of the indigenous communities, peoples, and nations shall perform jurisdictional duties, on the basis of their ancestral traditions and their own system of law, within their own territories, with a guarantee for the participation of, and decision-making by, women" (Asamblea Constituyente 2008).

While these were all victories, there were several ways in which the concepts of plurinationalism and interculturalism were compromised or left ambiguous in the constitution. As Carmen Martínez Novo (2014, 113) points out, "plurinationalism was accepted as a term, but emphasis was placed on the unity and predominance of the central state. The sovereignty of the state supersedes territorial autonomy, and special representation of Indigenous nationalities beyond regular democratic representation was not accepted." In particular, she notes that "the question of Indigenous territories and control of nonrenewable natural resources remains a problematic and ambiguous arena in the constitutional text" (114). For example, as Martínez Novo explains, even though the constitution states that Indigenous groups should be consulted prior to any decision that affects them, there is ambiguity in the clause, an ambiguity that the government has leveraged to ignore this directive, particularly in relation to the extraction of nonrenewable resources.

Furthermore, instead of having both Spanish and Kichwa as Ecuador's official languages of intercultural relation, as CONAIE sought, after much debate and tension, the assembly reasserted Spanish as the official language of Ecuador and designated Kichwa an official language of intercultural relation. Thus, in the new constitution, Spanish retained hegemonic dominance, and languages of intercultural relation remained subordinate, both in practice and in concept. Finally, although CONAIE's proposals included institutional designs for new modes of plurinational representation, such as a plurinational legislature and Supreme Court in which Indigenous groups and Afro-Ecuadorians would be ensured seats, these demands were not included in the 2008 constitution.

Challenging the Gendered Coloniality of Democracy

One significant feature of the collective rights enumerated in the 2008 constitution is the central role of gender justice in their framing. Article 57, for example, declares that the state shall "shall guarantee the enforcement of collective rights without any discrimination, in conditions of equality and equity between men and women." Article 171 establishes the right for groups "to create, develop, apply and practice their own legal system or common law, which cannot infringe constitutional rights, especially those of women, children and adolescents." Further, the article guarantees "women's participation and decision-making" in those systems (Asamblea Constituyente 2008).

This linkage of gender equality and community autonomy in a plurinationalist framework is a deep challenge to the colonial practice of pitting the struggles for community, cultural, or religious autonomy and gender justice against each other, a practice that has all too often been a feature of postcolonial politics as well. Feminist scholars have highlighted the role of colonialism in introducing or exacerbating hierarchical gender relations. In some instances, the colonizing state introduced a notion of gender as a binary, biologically based category among communities where such differentials or epistemic framings had not existed before. In others, the colonial state actively dismantled egalitarian gender relations (Lugones 2007, 2010). In postcolonial polities, this colonial legacy has often resulted in contradictory legal frameworks that consolidate antagonism between group rights and gender rights. For example, the 1996 South African constitution, one of the most progressive democratic constitutions in the world, simultaneously asserts gender equality as a fundamental right yet recognizes customary laws, some of which discriminate against women. Similarly, the Indian constitution also asserts gender equality as a right yet countenances discriminatory personal laws. Such contradictions serve to legitimate masculinist domination in the name of group preservation and differentiation (Keating 2011).

However, if the legal pluralism in many postcolonial polities retains the colonialist framing of gender rights and group rights as antagonistic, the plurinationalism of the 2008 constitution is grounded in an articulation of collective and gender justice. Such a shift is a critically important component of a plurinationalist refounding of Ecuador: while the introduction or consolidation of masculinist rule was a way in which both the colonial and postcolonial state has attempted to fragment communities, the 2008 constitution specifically rejects that formulation of rule.

The centrality of gender justice to the articulation and consolidation of plurinationalism in the 2008 Ecuadorian constitution is in large part a result of the efforts of one group in particular, the Red Organizaciones de Mujeres Kichwas y Rurales de Chimborazo ("Network of Kichwa and Rural Women's Organizations of Chimborazo," or REDCH; also known as Red de Chimborazo or Chimborazo Network). Chimborazo is a largely rural province in the central Ecuadorian Andes. The Chimborazo Network was founded in 2005 in order to bring these women's organizations in the Chimborazo communities to work together "on issues of domestic violence in Indigenous and rural areas" (Picq 2019, 14). Cristina Cucurí (2009, 132), who serves as a coordinator for the network, notes that the motto of the organization is the Kichwa saying "warmindi karindi pacta, pactaashi kawsandapo," which translates, according to Cucurí, as the "equality of men and women for a good life."

In 2006, the group embarked on a province-wide investigation of the issues facing Indigenous women in the region (REDCH 2007). Cucurí explains that 80 percent of the rural population of Chimborazo is Indigenous and that there are more than four hundred women's organizations in these communities. In order to understand their experiences and struggles, the group sent out surveys and held workshops, focus groups, and delegate assemblies with women and men from Indigenous communities across Chimborazo. They published their findings, *Agenda de equidad de género de las mujeres kichwas de Chimborazo* (Gender equality agenda for the Kichwa women of Chimborazo), in May 2007, just weeks after the referendum that called for a new constitution for Ecuador.

In the agenda, the Chimborazo Network writes that by passing the referendum the Ecuadorian people made a "decision for a radical change for the country," one that gives Ecuadorians the chance to "reject society's patrimonialism, corruption, racism, exclusions, profound inequity, and subordination to imperial interests." While recognizing that the Constituent Assembly could not "solve in one fell swoop the vicious circle of poverty and the lack of rights," the network argues that in its deliberations, the Constituent Assembly had the chance to "define a national agreement that can support society's founding aspirations for peace, development and equality for the great majority of its peoples." A fundamental component of any such agreement, it writes, "is the inclusion of the voices of Indigenous women" (REDCH 2007, 5).

Drawing on this analysis, Cristina Cucurí explains in her article "El acceso de las mujeres indígenas a la justicia en la Nueva Constitución del Ecuador" (Indigenous women's access to justice in the new constitution of Ecuador), the Chimborazo Network identified five central demands to bring forward to the Constituent Assembly upon its convening. The first was the demand for the plurinational state, a demand that Cucurí (2009, 133) explains, the Chimborazo Network puts forward "together with the indigenous movements, especially CONAIE." Two of their demands focused on questions of legal pluralism, calling for both the recognition of ancestral legal systems and the full participation of women in these systems. The group also argued for linguistic pluralism, calling on the assembly to make "all ancestral languages official languages in

Ecuador, not only Kichwa." Another demand focused on strengthening public banking and savings systems (133).

REDCH mobilized intensely to bring these demands to the attention of the Constituent Assembly. Despite being sidelined by feminist and Indigenous organizations, they organized marches, met individually with Constituent Assembly members, and even orchestrated a protest within the Constituent Assembly proceedings. In a testament to their ingenuity, hard work, and perseverance, as well as to the relative openness and inclusivity of the Constituent Assembly meetings themselves, the group was able to get their draft proposal into the text of the constitution as part of Articles 57 and 171. In the words of Cristina Cucurí (2009, 135), "We made quite a scene in the assembly but it was worth the disruption . . . because we've now got the new Constitution and Article 171, which says that Indigenous justice must ensure participation and decision making by women." As Manuela Picq (2019, 16) observes in *Vernacular Sovereignties*, "the effort of the Chimborazo Network is notable for its policy achievement: a grassroots organization of Indigenous women singlehandedly succeeded in bringing gender parity into the legal recognition of Indigenous justice and collective rights in the Ecuadorian constitution."

Despite this achievement, ongoing struggles pertaining to how to exercise gender-just plurinationalism undoubtedly exist, and there continue to be large gaps between masculinist state-supported police stations and Indigenous communal systems of justice when it comes to the participation of women and the protection of community members who have been subjected to violence. In the face of these challenges, Indigenous women's groups are developing community norms against violence against women and working toward treating each other well. In the Amazon region of Ecuador, for instance, an Indigenous women's group is developing what they call the "Ley de Buen Trato," or the "Law of treating each other well," which has as its goal the prevention and sanctioning of the mistreatment of women (Andi and Grefa 2009, 142). Similarly, in the Andean region, Indigenous women's groups are working together to develop and foster what they call the Reglamento de Buena Convivencia Comunitaria, or the Rule of Good Community Coexistence, which has as its goal family harmony and peaceful community life (Bonilla and Ramos 2009, 136). Having developed these laws, both groups are working to, in the words of Indigenous leader Rosa Andi, "socialize" it—that is, building community support and agreement for its implementation in community councils (Andi and Grefa 2009, 142). Though many obstacles still exist, these are, in the words of the Chimborazo Network, "times of change" in which Indigenous women are "seeking a profound social transformation that eliminates racism, discrimination, inequalities and builds another society, the society of peace and equitable intercultural development for all" (REDCH 2007).

Coalitional Praxis in a Plurinationalist Frame

In her essay, "Diez conceptos básicos sobre plurinacionalidad e interculturalidad" (Ten Basic Concepts of Plurinationalism and Interculturalism), Indigenous leader and former Constituent Assembly member Mónica Chuji Gualinga (2008) focuses on the coalitional possibilities that emerge from the logic of plurinationalism, arguing that "in Ecuador, the concept of plurinationalism has been proposed by the Indigenous movement to challenge the racism, exclusion, and violence that has characterized the relationship of the modern nation-state with Indigenous peoples, but plurinationalism can also generate conditions of possibility for the state recognition of gender diversity, for example.... Plurinationalism is not only a concept having to do with ethnicity, it is a concept that opens the social contract to multiple differences, be they differences of ethnicity, or of gender, or of culture, or of age, etc." Suggesting an expansive conception of plurinationalism, Chuji Gualinga notes that the concept could affirm the struggles of a wide variety of communities that have been excluded or disparaged in Ecuadorian political, social, and economic life. In Chuji Gualinga's framing, plurinationalism has the potential to be a deeply coalitional term.

> Political plurality is not just a concept that was born by the Indigenous for the Indigenous; On the contrary, it challenges the entire system and has to do with the inclusion of all social sectors: women, youth, men, peasants, because in the end, people who are not part of the capitalist elite are exploited and are not treated as subjects of rights. That is what plurinationality is all about, and as with all processes, it must be realized in struggle, little by little. What is in the Constitution helps us to demand it, assume it, and ask for its implementation. (Sánchez Jaramillo 2022)

A coalitional notion of plurinationalism raises provocative questions about collective autonomy, self-management, and self-determination as goals for marginalized and subordinated groups across a diversity of sectors in Ecuador. The recent work of the Quito-based Proyecto Transgénero (sometimes styled as Proyecto TRVNSGEN3RO, or, in English, Transgender Project), a group that has been at the forefront of the transgender and intersex movement in Ecuador, points to the resonance of these plurinationalist goals to issues of sexual and gender justice as well as to the importance of intercultural organizing to this work. In *Cuerpos Distintos: Ocho años de activismo transfeminista en Ecuador* (Distinct Bodies: Eight Years of Transfeminist Activism in Ecuador), Proyecto Transgénero's cofounders, Ana Almeida and Elizabeth

Vásquez, write that the group's understanding of gender as well as its approach to the law was deeply impacted by Indigenous plurinational and intercultural organizing. Almeida and Vásquez (2010, 88–93) explain, for example, how a series of intercultural "trans runakunawanmi rimay" (trans Indigenous trans dialogues) "made us question not only the binary and patriarchal notions present in society, in gender constructions, but also the racist, colonial notions that are present in the construction of masculinity and femininity. . . . That is, masculine and feminine are not only two genders in opposition, they are also aesthetic constructions, colonial constructions." Further, they note that the organization was also deeply inspired by Indigenous approaches to legal pluralism as a "legal-practical application of the recognition of plurinationality." They suggest that the approach might be applied broadly, to be used by populations "historically excluded from [the formal legal system of the dominant culture], or violated or discriminated against by it, either because, belonging to a different cultural matrix, the logic of the system is not applicable to them, or, more generally, because their social location means that certain norm(s) of the dominant system are not applicable to them" (89).

Taking up this legal pluralist approach to issues facing the trans community in Quito, Proyecto Transgénero developed an "alternative citizenship card" that could serve as "a gender-sensitive document of cultural identification" (Almeida and Vásquez 2010, 89). The citizenship card was geared to address the problem of administrative violence against members of the trans community, who at that time were legally barred from listing their names and gender identifications on their government-issued identification cards.[2] Designed for street-based trans sex workers in particular, the front side of the identification card listed the person's cultural name as well as their state-enforced legal name, their gender, their state-enforced legal sex definition, their occupation, and the neighborhood in which they work. The back of the card, designed to serve as an "instrument of enforceability of rights," enumerated the variety of rights affirmed in the 2008 constitution that the cardholder could invoke in case of arrest or maltreatment by police and other authorities (89). These include the right to nondiscrimination based on gender identity, the right to aesthetic freedom, the right to freedom of movement, the right to work, and the right to identity—all of which were fought for by the trans community. The back of the card also lists clauses in the constitution that decriminalize sex work (89). Almeida and Vásquez characterize these alternative citizenship cards as an example of "micro-legal pluralism" because, in their words, the cards are not indicative of "a whole parallel legal system" but instead are focused "on the process of civil identification." (89) Almeida and Vásquez note that the effort was a success, with profound legal, political, and social consequences. They explain that "for the first time a document, instead of imposing legal institutions that have nothing to do with people's lives, operates in the opposite direction, taking up people's real institutions and giving them legal value: their real name (which is certainly the cultural one and not the legal one), their real gender (which is certainly not that of the legal sex), their real aesthetics" (92).

Almeida and Vásquez further explain that the alternative citizenship card advances the practice of interculturality in two ways. First, it underscores ways that the plurinationalist framing of legal pluralism can be used by other marginalized and persecuted groups in ways that challenge their political, economic, social, and cultural subordination. Second, they note, by "treating collectives of transgender street sex workers as collective subjects with their own territoriality," it advances struggles for cultural rights and public space in ways that not only benefit the trans community but could also benefit "other urban and street collectives" including "street vendors . . . rockers, hippies, beggars, [and] street children" (Almeida and Vásquez 2010, 91–92). Indeed, Proyecto Transgénero's creative and innovative use of legal pluralism to support and enable trans self-determination, autonomy, and self-management underscores the expansive possibilities that emerge from a coalitional logic of a plurinationalism, as well as the importance of concrete coalitional linkages between different dimensions of social struggle, in both the enunciation of the struggles and their practice.

Conclusion

After Ecuadorians voted to ratify the constitution in 2008, Alberto Acosta (2009, 20), former president of the Constituent Assembly, wrote that "the constitutional declaration of the plurinational state opened a road, without a doubt, a very long one, towards the eventual achievement of plurinationalism itself. The constitutional declaration of the plurinational state is an important step, but it is not enough. Now we must build it." Indeed, since the passage of the constitution in 2008, Indigenous groups and others have continued the ongoing work of building a plurinationalist Ecuador. In doing so, they have faced a series of hostile and obstructionist Ecuadorian governments that have privileged extractivist economic policies over the 2008 constitution's plurinationalist commitments. These governments have actively worked to undermine many of the changes mandated by the constitution. For example, in blatant disregard of the constitution's plurinationalist directives, the Ecuadorian government (under both leftist and right-wing administrations) has repeatedly intensified resource extraction in Indigenous territories, excluded Indigenous groups from state planning, and worked to undermine Indigenous social movements by criminalizing and fragmenting them. These moves have been met with vigorous protest from Indigenous movements and others. These movements have continued to struggle against government attempts to bypass constitutional law and engage in extraction activities without seeking adequate consultation from local communities.

In June 2022, Indigenous organizations led by CONAIE joined together with labor unions, women's organizations, student groups, and others in a general strike that included blocking highways across the country and obstructing oil wells and mining sites for more than two weeks (Sempertegui 2022). The strike coalition presented a list of ten demands, including "respect for the twenty-one collective rights provided for in Article 57 of the constitution: bilingual intercultural education, indigenous justice, prior consultation, and organization and self-determination of indigenous communities," and a "moratorium on the expansion of extractive mining/oil borders," in addition to several other economic demands.[3] The strike was met with violent repression from the government: six protestors were killed by the police and the military, and scores more were injured. Key to sustaining the strike in the face of this repression, explains Andrea Sempertegui (2022), "was the solidarity and collective action of organizations from the parts of Ecuadorian society hardest hit by the economic crisis. Feminist collectives like Mujeres de Frente, dozens of communes located in the outskirts of Quito like San Miguel del Común, and young students from public universities like Universidad Central turned lecture halls into shelters, houses into community kitchens, and storage facilities into donation centers for Indigenous and peasant families coming from around the country."

In October 2022, the government and Indigenous leaders reached an agreement on 218 points of dispute. By February 2023, however, the agreement had broken down when CONAIE said it would no longer participate due to the government's routine and ongoing disregard of the agreements as well as its continued repression of Indigenous organizing against the expansion of mining in their territories. In the words of Zenaida Yasacama, who was elected CONAIE's first woman vice president in 2021, "There is no will from the Government to solve the problems that we are going through at the national level, not only with the Indigenous sector, but for all the citizens who work and earn a dollar a day to buy bread" (Fors Garzón 2023).

Building a plurinational and intercultural Ecuador along the lines of what CONAIE, REDCH, and Proyecto Transgénero and others envisioned is no doubt an incomplete project. To date, and despite the 2008 constitution, the most generative visions and work rests in the hands and movements of groups that continue to envision, struggle for, and instantiate more just political, economic, and social frameworks. In Ecuador, the ongoing struggles to challenge the gendered coloniality of democracy underscore the ways that plurinationalist praxis is deeply communal and coalitional: it is in community where alternative meanings, modes of decision-making, and ways of being are preserved, developed, and practiced and it is in coalition where transformative processes of intercultural dialogue, analysis, and discernment are enacted toward new possibilities of being, knowing, and relating.

Notes

1. All translations from Spanish to English are by the authors, unless otherwise specified.
2. In 2016, the Ecuadorian parliament passed the "Gender Identity Law," which formally allows people to change their name and gender identity on their identification card. This achievement was in large part a result of a legislative and public relations campaign entitled "My Gender On My ID," spearheaded by the Ecuadorian Confederation of Trans and Intersex Communities, or Pacto Trans, whose membership includes Proyecto Transgénero as well as other groups (Pacto Trans 2014).
3. The complete list of the demands is as follows: "(1) Reduction and no more rise in fuel prices; (2) Economic relief for more than four million families; (3) Fair prices for farm products; (4) Employment and labor rights; (5) Moratorium on the expansion of the extractive mining/oil border; (6) Respect for the 21 collective rights [as defined in the 2008 constitution]; (7) Stop the privatization of strategic sectors, assets of the Ecuadorian people; (8) Price control policies; (9) Health and education; and (10) Security, protection and generation of effective public policies" (Ángel 2022).

References

Acosta, Alberto. 2009. "El estado plurinacional, puerta para una sociedad democrática: A manera de prólogo." In *Plurinacionalidad: Democracia en la diversidad*, edited by Alberto Acosta and Esperanza Martínez, 1–20. Quito: Ediciones Abya-Yala.

Almeida, Ana, and Elizabeth Vásquez. 2010. *Cuerpos distintos: Ocho años de activismo transfeminista en Ecuador*. Quito: Comisión de transición hacia el consejo de mujeres y la igualdad de género.

Andi, Rosa, and Gilberto Grefa. 2009. "La Ley de Buen Trato y los promotores del buen trato en la amazonía ecuatoriana." In *Mujeres indígenas y justicia ancestral*, edited by Miriam Lang and Anna Kucia, 142–46. Quito: Unifem.

Ángel, Ronald. 2022. "Ecuador: An Indefinite Strike by the Indigenous Movement Registers Clash with Police." *El Ciudadano*, November 7, 2022. https://www.elciudadano.com/en/ecuador-an-indefinite-strike-by-the-indigenous-movement-registers-clashes-with-the-police-why-did-they-call-for-this-strike/06/14/.

Asamblea Constituyente. 2008. "Constitución de la República del Ecuador." Political Database of the Americas. http://pdba.georgetown.edu/Constitutions/Ecuador/ecuador08.html#mozTocId215170.

Bonilla, Inés, and Rosa Ramos. 2009. "La construcción e implementación del Reglamento de Buena Convivencia en Cotacach." In *Mujeres indígenas y justicia ancestral*, edited by Miriam Lang and Anna Kucia, 136–38. Quito: Unifem.

Chuji Gualinga, Mónica. 2008. "Diez conceptos básicos sobre plurinacionalidad e interculturalidad." *América Latina en movimiento*, April 8, 2008. https://www.alainet.org/es/active/23366.

CONAIE. 1994. *Proyecto Político de la CONAIE*. Quito: Consejo de Gobierno de la CONAIE. https://www.yachana.org/earchivo/conaie/proyectopolitico.pdf.

———. 2007a. *Constitución del estado plurinacional de la Republica del Ecuador: Propuesta de la Confederación de Nacionalidades Indígenas del Ecuador*. Quito: Consejo de Gobierno de la CONAIE. https://www.yachana.org/earchivo/conaie/propuesta_constitucion_conaie.pdf.

———. 2007b. *Propuesta de la CONAIE frente a la Asamblea Constituyente*. Quito: CONAIE. https://www.yachana.org/earchivo/conaie/ConaiePropuestaAsamblea.pdf.

Cucurí, Cristina. 2009. "El acceso de las mujeres indígenas a la justicia en la Nueva Constitución del Ecuador." In *Mujeres indígenas y justicia ancestral*, edited by Miriam Lang and Anna Kucia, 132–36. Quito: Unifem.

Fors Garzón, Elsy. 2023. "Peasant Organization Withdraws from Government Dialogue." *Prensa Latina*, February 23, 2023. https://www.plenglish.com/news/2023/02/23/ecuador-peasant-organization-withdraws-from-government-dialogue/.

Karakras, Ampam. 1984. "Las nacionalidades indias y el estado ecuatoriano." *Antropología Cuadernos de Investigación* 3:128–37.

Keating, Christine. 2011. *Decolonizing Democracy: Transforming the Social Contract in India*. University Park: Pennsylvania State University Press. https://muse.jhu.edu/book/13126/.

Lucero, José Antonio. 2008. *Struggles of Voice: The Politics of Indigenous Representation in the Andes*. Pittsburgh: University of Pittsburgh Press.

Lugones, María. 2007. "Heterosexualism and the Colonial/Modern Gender System," *Hypatia* 22 (1): 186–219.

———. 2010. "Toward a Decolonial Feminism," *Hypatia* 25 (4): 742–59.

Macas, Luis. 2004. "Diversidad y plurinacionalidad." *Boletín ICCI-ARY Rimay* 6 (64). http://icci.nativeweb.org/boletin/64/macas.html.

Martínez Novo, Carmen. 2014. "Managing Diversity in Postneoliberal Ecuador." *Journal of Latin American and Caribbean Anthropology* 19 (1): 103–25.

Mendoza, Breny. 2017. "Colonial Connections." *Feminist Studies* 43 (3): 637–45.

Merino, Roger. 2021. *Socio-Legal Struggles for Indigenous Self-Determination in Latin America: Reimagining the Nation, Reinventing the State*. New York: Routledge.

Pacari, Nina. 1984. "Las culturas nacionales en el estado multinacional Ecuatoriano." *Antropología Cuadernos de Investigación* 3:138–49.

Pacto Trans. 2014. "My Gender on My ID: A Letter Away from Citizenship!" Pacto Trans Equador. http://pactotransecuador.blogspot.com/p/campana-mi-genero-en-mi-cedula.html.

Picq, Manuela Lavinas. 2019. *Vernacular Sovereignties: Indigenous Women Challenging World Politics*. Tucson: University of Arizona Press.

Quijano, Aníbal. 2000. "Coloniality of Power, Eurocentrism, and Latin America." Translated by Michael Ennis. *Nepantla: Views from South* 1 (3): 533–80.

REDCH (Red Organizaciones de Mujeres Kichwas y Rurales de Chimborazo). 2007. *Agenda de equidad de género de las mujeres kichwas de Chimborazo*. Riobamba: Centro de Desarrollo, Difusión e Investigación Social.

Sánchez Jaramillo, J. Fernanda. 2022. "Entrevista a Mónica Chuji sobre los derechos de la naturaleza." Indymedia, Centro de Medios Independientes de Argentina, August 9, 2022. https://argentina.indymedia.org/2022/08/09/ecuador-entrevista-a-monica-chuji-sobre-derechos-de-la-naturaleza/.

Sempertegui, Andrea. 2022. "Ecuador's Historic Strike." *New York Review of Books*, October 5, 2022. https://www.nybooks.com/online/2022/10/05/ecuador-historic-strike/.

Zamosc, León. 2007. "The Indian Movement and Political Democracy in Ecuador." *Latin American Politics and Society* 43 (3): 1–34.

Christine "Cricket" Keating is Associate Professor in the Gender, Women, & Sexuality Studies Department at the University of Washington and a collective member of la Escuela Popular Norteña. Her research is in the areas of political theory, decolonial feminist praxis, popular education, and transnational feminisms. She is author of *Decolonizing Democracy: Transforming the Social Contract in India* (2011) and coeditor of *LGBTQ Politics: A Critical Reader* (2017).

Amy Lind is Professor of Politics and Women's, Gender, and Sexuality Studies at the University of Cincinnati. Her areas of scholarship include global political economy; critical development and postcolonial studies; transnational feminisms; Indigenous rights; and neoliberalism, memory, and human rights. She is author of *Gendered Paradoxes: Women's Movements, State Restructuring, and Global Development in Ecuador* (2005) and editor of six volumes, including *Development, Sexual Rights and Global Governance* (2010) and *Feminist (Im)mobilities in Fortress North America: Rights, Citizenships and Identities in Transnational Perspective* (2013).

INDEX

Abya Yala, 6, 9, 13, 18, 29–30, 35, 44, 64, 104n8, 239
Aching, Gerard, 3
Adams, Carol J., 154, 155
advocacy research, 127–30; coloniality of knowledge and, 130–37; colonial relationalities and, 137–41; epistemic shift and, 141–45
aesthetic hierarchy, 187–88, 192n2
aesthetics: as metahermeneutics, 178–86; postaesthetics, 180–81; US Black Aesthetic movement, 180. *See also* decolonial aesthetics
Ahmed, Sara, 67
AIDS/HIV, 53, 204, 206
Alcoff, Linda, 36–42
Alexander, M. Jacqui, 3, 102, 234n3
Almeida, Ana, 250–52
alterity, 69, 71, 73, 178, 211
Amadiume, Ifi, 187
anafemales, 139, 146n7
anamales, 139, 146n7
Anderson, Jackie, 143
antisemitism, 111, 120n1
Anzaldúa, Gloria, 6, 22, 49, 57, 115, 145, 220
Apel, Karl-Otto, 213
Appalachian Participatory Education and Grassroots Development Project, 142
Aryanism, 95, 120n1
Asian American studies, 86, 93, 94, 102

assimilation: adaptation without, 85–86, 91; Asian Americans and, 85–87, 91, 96, 101–3; communication and, 218–19, 229, 232; monstrosity and, 68, 69, 71, 76–77
Association of Indians in America (AIA), 98
Austin, John, 145

Baby Boom Generation, 118
Bakhtin, Mikhail, 215, 216, 222
Barad, Karen, 72
Batra, Ravi, 107, 108, 120–21n3
Beauvoir, Simone de, 151, 157–58, 161
Biden, Joseph, 108
Bierria, Alisa, 3
bisexuality and bisexual communities, 49, 58, 62
Black feminisms, 1–2, 189–90
body and bodies: colonized female body, 43; communication and, 209–10, 217, 220, 232; erotic body, 43; LGBTQ+ houseless youth and, 200, 205–6; lived body, 156–59; mechanics of the, 31–32; objective body, 157; phenomenal body, 156–57; racialized bodies, 42–43; sexual body and sexual difference, 31–44
Bolivia, 17–18, 239
border thinking, 14–15, 104n6, 145, 219
Bourdieu, Pierre, 176
Brady, Mary Pat, 3
Brazil, 29, 50, 78

257

breastfeeding, 37, 38, 153, 163
Brison, Susan, 128, 131
Bryce, Geoff, 142
Buddhism, 123n13
Bugallo, Lucila, 3
Burgos-Debray, Elisabeth, 134
Bush, George H. W., 108
Bush, George W., 108
Butler, Judith, 69–70, 187

cachapera, 44
callejera, 159, 197, 198, 199
capitalism, 7–10; decolonial communication and, 212–14, 217, 220, 223; decolonial turn and, 212–14; extreme capitalism, 107–8; gender and, 30–35, 42–44; racial capitalism, 4; sexuality and, 62–63; transnational capitalism, 107, 223
Caribbean Philosophical Association, 3
Cartesianism, 10, 76, 145, 156
caste systems, 95–96, 99–101, 113–14
Caucasian identity, 96–98
Cavanagh, Chris, 3
Center for Interdisciplinary Studies in Philosophy, Interpretation, and Culture (CPIC), 1–4, 15–16, 19–20, 234n3
CGN (Compañía Guatemalteca de Niquel), 43
Chandra, Shefali, 96, 99
Chinatown (San Francisco), 89
Christianity and Christians, 52, 111–12, 115, 161, 208, 212
Chuji Gualinga, Mónica, 250
Chung Sai Yat Po (Chinese American newspaper), 90–91
classism, 59, 107, 109, 112, 151, 205
Clinton, Bill, 108
coalition, 23–24; advocacy research and, 142, 143; barriers to, 29–30, 185; Chicana/o movement as, 114; communication and, 228–31; deep versus narrow coalitions, 230–31; feminist politics and, 160, 164, 165, 166; interculturality and pluriversality as movers of, 17–18; monstrosity and, 66–67, 79–80; postmodernism and, 107; praxis in Ecuador, 250–52; social justice change and, 114, 118, 119; Third World feminism and, 12, 22
Code, Lorraine, 128, 133–34, 136, 142, 143

code switching, 220
Cold War, 97
Cole, Luke, 128
Collins, Patricia Hill, 2, 128
colonial difference, 14, 17, 20, 101, 219, 221–25, 229–30, 232
colonial fraternalist approach, 94–95
coloniality of Being, 15–16
coloniality of language, 214–16, 218, 219, 223, 224, 232, 233
coloniality of power, 8, 9, 11, 85; Bakhtin and, 215, 230; border thinking and, 15; colonial difference and, 14; communication and, 215, 222, 239; gender and, 44; modern colonial gender system and, 34; modern heterosexualisms and, 43; Quijano on, 8, 34, 220, 239; racialization of culture and, 110; Wynter and, 187
colonial mimicry, 96, 99, 101
colonial/modern gender system, 16, 34, 43, 50, 63–64, 75–76, 91, 138, 151, 155–56
colonial semiosis, 13–14
Columbus, Christopher, 140
Combahee River Collective, 109
coming out, 46–47, 50–61, 62, 100
communality, 4–5
communication and language: bilanguaging, 214, 219–21, 234n4, 234n6; coloniality of language, 214–16, 218, 219, 223, 224, 232, 233; complex communication, 225, 228–33; decolonial totality and, 209–10, 213–14, 217–18, 222–23, 225, 231; decolonial turn and, 208–14, 216, 221, 226, 233; dialogue, 210–17, 219, 222, 229–30, 233; Échos-monde and, 222, 225–28, 231–32; fractured locus and, 224–25, 229, 231; Generalization and, 226–27, 235n14; interpellation as speech act, 213, 216–19; intracultural dialogue, 10, 211–13, 216, 241, 254; language in the full sense, 215, 223; monolanguaging, 216, 220, 221, 231; nondialogic theory of communication, 223–25; Relation and, 225–28, 231, 236n19; resistance and, 209–10, 212–14, 221–22, 224–33; simple communication, 215, 224; speech acts, 213, 216–18, 223, 224–25, 229–32; vertical communication, 235n20
compensatory domination, 95–96, 98
Conner, Randy, 110

contact zones, 132, 134, 135, 143, 145
Coronil, Fernando, 12, 42
Cortés, Hernán, 10, 140
Crenshaw, Kimberlé, 1–2
criminalization, 75, 144, 201, 251, 253
"cross-dressing," 75, 81n1
Crowley, Patrick, 23
Cruz, Cindy, 23
Cucurí, Cristina, 248–49
Cvetkovich, Ann, 79

Dalai Lama, 117
Dalit Indians, 99
Darwinism, 113. 120n1, 183
Davis, Angela, 109, 164
Davis, Karen, 154–55
Decena, Carlos, 3, 54–55
"decolonial aesthetics," use of the term, 192n1. *See also* aesthetics
decolonial communication. *See* communication and language
decolonial feminist working group (Berkeley), 3
decolonial imaginary, 12–13
Decolonial Summer School Middelburg, 3
decolonial totality, 209–10, 213–14, 217–18, 222–23, 225, 231
decolonial turn, 6–7, 11, 208–14, 216, 221, 226, 233
dehumanization, 5, 9, 10, 11; of the body, 31, 33, 42; of Chinese American women, 90; coloniality and, 15, 50, 65, 111, 113; communication and, 215–16, 218, 229, 231, 234n4; resistance to, 114–19, 198; sexuality and, 50, 111; of US women of color, 107; Wynter and, 172, 186, 190
DePietro, PJ, 111
Derrida, Jacques, 140
Descartes, René, 133. *See also* Cartesianism
DesiQ (conference), 100, 104n10
deviance, 50, 60–61, 65, 69, 74–76, 78, 98, 178
dialogical thinking, 211, 220
division of labor: racialized, 89–90; sexual and reproductive, 31, 33, 36–37, 40–42
domesticity, 89
domestic violence and abuse, 138, 162, 248
domestic work, 108–9
Dominican immigrant communities, 54

Do the Right Thing (film), 180, 182, 183
double consciousness, 220, 230
Du Bois, W. E. B., 220, 230
Dussel, Enrique, 9–12, 14, 73–74, 137, 144; *encumbrimiento* of, 10, 12; on interpellation as speech act, 213, 216–19; on modernity's "double face," 9; transmodernity of, 10–11, 211–12 216

ecofeminism, 151, 152, 154–56
Ecuador, 17–18, 239, 253–54; challenging gendered coloniality of democracy in, 246–50; Chimborazo Network, 247–49; coalition praxis in, 250–52; conception of Indigenous communities as nations, 239–40; Confederation of Indigenous Nationalities of Ecuador (CONAIE), 240–46, 248, 253; constitution of 2008, 238, 239, 243–54; interculturality in, 238–39, 241–43, 245–46, 250–54; official languages of, 245–46, 248; plurinationalism in, 238–54; Proyecto Transgénero, 249–53; Rule of Good Community Coexistence, 249
Edelman, Lee, 67
Ellison, Ralph, 224, 231–32
embodied proximity, 4, 156, 163, 164
eros ideologies, 110, 122n7
eroticism, 43, 51, 54, 56, 61, 76, 115, 191
Escobar, Arturo, 18, 170, 208, 209
La Escuela Popular Norteña, 142
essentialism, 109, 150, 151, 154, 156, 164, 170
estar, politics of, 54, 58
Exclusion Act, 89
exoticism, 93

Fanon, Frantz, 114, 199; *damnés de la Terre* of, 7, 15–16, 76, 178, 222; goal of, 146n5; sociogeny of, 175
Fausto-Sterling, Anne, 36, 42
Federici, Silvia, 30–32, 35, 139
femininity, 116, 118, 139, 251
Foster, Sheila, 128
Foucault, Michel, 77, 78, 128, 139, 187
fractured locus, 20, 191, 224–25, 229, 231
Frankenstein (Shelley), 67–69
Freire, Paulo, 210–11, 213, 220
Fusco, Coco, 132–33, 137

Gandhi, Mohandas, 113–14, 115, 117, 199
Garcés, Fernando, 235n11
Gaspar de Alba, Alicia, 3
Gates, Henry Louis, 185
Gaventa, John, 146n12
Gay and Lesbian Alliance (GALA), 56–57
gender system, 16, 34, 43, 50, 63–64, 75–76, 91, 138, 151, 155–56
Generation Y, 118
genocide, 12, 107, 111–12, 135, 217
gentrification, 199
Giroux, Henry, 207
GLEFAS (Grupo Latinoamericano de Estudio, Formación y Acción Feminista), 29
Glissant, Édouard, 129, 135, 143, 208, 225–27, 228, 231, 233, 235n14, 236nn16–17
GLQ (journal), 66
Gómez-Peña, Guillermo, 132–33, 137
Gothic, 68
Griffin, Paul R., 111–12
Grueso, Libia, 212, 213
Grupo Cobra, 43
Guha, Ranajit, 226–27
Gupta, Monisha Das, 97–98

Hames-García, Michael, 20
Haney López, Ian, 97
Hannaford, Ivan, 111, 120n1
Harder They Come, The (film), 180, 182, 183
Haritaworn, Jin, 140, 141
Haslanger, Sally, 36, 38
Henry, Paget, 172–73
hermaphroditism, 34, 76, 155
heteronormativity, 48, 65, 109, 110–12
heterosexism, 67, 75, 80
Hinduism and Hindus, 95, 98, 100, 113–14, 115
Hitler, Adolf, 117
Hoagland, Sarah, 22
Hollywood, 179
homelessness: antihomeless laws, 198–99; the body and, 205–6; trope of, 129. *See also* youth, LGBTQ+ houseless
homophobia, 55, 101, 107, 109, 110–11, 115, 116, 117
Hong, Grace, 87, 103
hooks, bell, 138
Horswell, Michael J., 74–75, 78, 81n1, 118
humanism, 73, 171, 176, 177, 179, 184–85, 188–89

Human Rights Campaign Fund, 57
hybridity, 66, 78, 112, 115, 183, 224

imaginaries: colonial imaginaries, 11–13, 25, 156; cultural and popular imaginaries, 179–80, 182, 184–85; of modern states, 220; political imaginaries, 213; spatial imaginaries, 69–70, 72; white imaginaries, 132
Immigration and Nationality Act (1965), 97, 100
imperial difference, 85–87, 101–3; definition of, 85; model-minority myth and, 86–87, 94, 96–101; Orientalization and, 94, 98–99; racial triangulation and, 87–94; secondary empires and, 85–88, 93–94, 96; US context and, 87–94
imperial myth of grandeur, 88, 91
in-betweenness, 86, 91, 95, 96, 102. *See also* liminality
India, 94–101, 102, 113, 247
Indian American women, 94–101, 102
infrapolitics: coming out and, 53–54, 56; definition of, 200; LGBTQ+ houseless youth and, 200–2002
interculturality, 17–18, 235n11, 238–39, 241–43, 245–46, 250–54
intersectionality, 1–2, 75, 150–51. 154–156, 167n2, 188
intersexuality and intersex communities, 36, 38–42, 50, 250
intracultural dialogue, 10, 211–13, 216, 241, 254
Islam and Muslims, 74, 95, 98–99, 115

Jameson, Frederic, 107, 120n2
Janus-faced logic, 85, 87, 101
Jim Crow South, 204
jota/o, 44, 48, 57–59

Kafka, Franz, 132
Kantian aesthetics, 176
Karakras, Ampam, 240
Keating, Christine "Cricket," 24, 94–95, 96–97
Kelley, Robin D. G., 53, 200, 204–5
Kennedy, John F., 142
Khatibi, Abdelkebir, 220
Kim, Claire Jean, 88–89, 91–93, 99, 102, 103n1
King, Martin Luther, Jr., 114

knowledge: coloniality of, 130–37; geopolitics of, 211, 212, 214, 219, 224; subalternization of, 14, 219
Korten, David, 108, 121n4
Kuo, Jen-Feng, 21
Kusch, Rodolfo, 54, 55

Laqueur, Thomas, 35
las Casas, Bartolomé de, 111
Lee, Erika, 89, 90
lesbianism and lesbian communities, 29, 42, 46–50, 56–58, 100–101, 127–28, 143–44
"lesbian," use of the term, 47, 48
Levinas, Emmanuel, 116, 211, 217
Lewis, Helen, 146n12
LGBTQ+ communities: bisexuality and bisexual communities, 49, 58, 62; coming out, 46–47, 50–61, 62, 100; hermaphroditism, 34, 76, 155; heteronormativity, 48, 65, 109, 110–12; heterosexism, 67, 75, 80; homophobia, 55, 101, 107, 109, 110–11, 115, 116, 117; lesbianism and lesbian communities, 29, 42, 46–50, 56–58, 100–101, 127–28, 143–44; Queering Paradigms, 50; Queer Nation, 48, 49; queer politics, 49, 56, 57, 62, 128; queer theory, 46–50, 59, 61, 66; racialized queer, 49–50; same-sex marriage, 100; sodomy, 57, 74–75, 122n9; third gender and third gendering, 74–75, 81n1, 110, 139–40; use of the term "gay," 47–48; use of the term "queer," 47, 48, 49. See also transgender communities and issues; youth, LGBTQ+ houseless
liminality and limen: communication and, 228–29; human-aesthetic transformation and, 172, 176–79, 182, 184–85, 188, 191; monstrosity and, 67; subject formation and, 102. See also in-betweenness
Lind, Amy, 24
Loewen, James, 89
logic of coloniality, 5, 9, 20, 170, 208–9
Lorde, Audre, 22, 109, 115
Los Angeles, California, 197–99, 202, 206–7
Lucero, José Antonio, 239–40
Lugones, María, 16, 20; colonial/modern gender system of, 75–76, 138–40, 151, 155–56; on complex communication, 225, 228–33; on decolonial turn, 216; on hanging out, 197–200; La Escuela Popular Norteña, 142; on Quijano's use of "gender" and "sexuality," 110; on resistance in tight spaces, 200; on witnessing, 205; on "world"-traveling, 116, 197–98, 203

Macaulay, Thomas Babington, 95–96
Malatino, Hil, 21
Maldonado-Torres, Nelson, 3, 6, 15–16, 76, 209
Marcos, Sylvia, 3, 40–41
margin/center binary, 73, 138
Martínez, Elizabeth "Betita," 109, 110, 121–22n6
Martínez, Ernesto Javier, 3
Martínez Novo, Carmen, 246
Marx, Karl, 32, 34, 217
Marxism, 179, 185–86, 240
masculinity, 72, 116, 140, 247, 249, 251
Mather, Cotton, 111
Maturana, Humberto, 214, 215, 219
McBride, Dwight, 132, 135
McWeeny, Jen, 22–23
Mehta, Brinda, 3
Menchú, Rigoberta, 134
Mendoza, Breny, 239
Merleau-Ponty, Maurice, 151, 157–58, 166
Messing, Karen, 133, 144
mestizaje, 6, 111, 224
mestizas/os, 13, 47, 122
Michigan Womyn's Music Festival, 127, 129
microaggressions, 68, 71
Mignolo, Walter, 3, 9, 12; on bilanguaging, 214, 219–21, 234n4, 234n6; on border thinking, 14–15, 219; on colonization of memory, 64–65; on epistemic de-linking, 234n1; on pluritopic hermeneutics, 13–14; on secondary empires and imperial difference, 85–86, 88, 91–93, 96, 102, 104n6; spatial epistemic break of, 209, 214, 219; on subalternization of knowledge, 14, 219
Miller, Alice, 117
Minh-ha, Trinh T., 135
Mittman, Asa Simon, 80
model-minority myth, 86–87, 94, 96–101
modern colonial gender system. *See* colonial/modern gender system
modernity/coloniality/decoloniality, 2, 9, 12, 15, 23, 44, 93, 170, 171, 186, 208, 213

Modernity/Coloniality/Decoloniality (M/C/D) collective, 1, 2, 3
Mohanty, Chandra, 86, 101, 103, 130–31, 138
monstrosity: borderlands and, 69; as coalitional concept, 79–80; decolonialism and, 73–80; Frankenstein's monster, 66–69; gender nonconformance and, 66–69; margin/center binary and, 73; mixity and, 66, 77; outsiderhood and, 69, 71, 73, 78; reclaiming, 68–71, 73, 78–80; subalterity and, 69, 71, 73, 78–80; trauma and, 79–80
Moraga, Cherríe, 56, 220
Morrison, Toni, 152–55, 165, 166–67
multiculturalism, 17–18, 112, 186, 211
Muñoz, José Esteban, 71
Muslims, 74, 95, 98–99, 115

Nagarajan, Mala, 100
Nagler, Michael, 118–19
narcissism, 136, 176
National Association for Chicana and Chicano Studies (NACCS), 57–58
Nazi Holocaust, 116
Negri, Antonio, 71
neocolonialism, 29, 43, 73, 112, 113, 120
neoliberalism, 17–18, 29, 43–44, 72–73, 206, 208, 243
Nhat Hanh, Thich, 117, 123n13
Nieto Gómez, Anna, 109, 110
9/11, 87, 96, 98, 101
nongovernmental organizations (NGOs), 17, 18, 62, 63
nonviolent activism, 107–8, 113–14, 118–19
Nzegwu, Nkiru, 187

Obama, Barack, 108
Occidentalism, 11–12, 14–15, 42
offstage practices and spaces, 199–202, 205
O'Leary, Claudine, 144–45
One-World World (OWW), 18–19
Orientalism, 11–12, 92–98, 101–3, 140–41
Orientalization, 87, 94, 98
Ortega, Mariana, 3
Others and Othering: advocacy research and, 129–38, 141, 143; communication and, 211–13, 216–18; decolonial communication and, 216; decolonial turn and, 209; dehumanization and, 118, 119; monstrosity and, 68–69, 74, 76; Muslims and, 98–99; Orientalization, 87, 94, 98; patriotism and, 101; subalternity and, 76; Wynter on, 175, 177, 185, 186, 187–88
other-sense, 5, 19, 171
outlaws, 69
Oyěwùmí, Oyèrónkẹ́, 187

Pacari, Nina, 240
pachakuti, 30
Pakistan, 98
pata, 48
patriotism, 90, 96, 98, 101
Peetush, Ashwani, 136
Pérez, Emma, 12–13, 21–22
phenomenology, 151, 156–59, 167
Picq, Manuela, 248, 249
Piercy, Marge, 37–38, 39
pity, 202
pleasure, sexual, 16, 31–33, 40
plurinationalism, 238–54
pluriversality, 17, 18–19, 235n11
positivism, 67, 128, 131, 136, 208
postmodernism, 10, 107, 113, 120n2
Potter, Nancy, 130
poverty: in Ecuador, 248; humanness and, 177, 179, 188; identity and, 46, 48, 49; Kennedy's War on Poverty, 142; neoliberalism and, 29; Otherness and, 211, 213; rural poverty, 142; social justice love and, 115; statistics, 120n3; structural poverty, 19; surrogacy and, 42; violence against the poor, 117; youth infrapolitics and, 201
Prashad, Vijay, 94, 97
Pratt, Mary Louise, 132, 134
prostitution, 31–32, 33, 144–45. See also sex work
Puar, Jasbir, 98
public-sphere communicators, 229–30
public-sphere politics, 5, 17
Puritans, 112

queer. See LGBTQ+ communities
Quijano, Aníbal, 12, 62, 112, 239; colonialidad del poder, 8–9, 11, 14, 32, 34, 85, 87, 192n2; on coloniality of knowledge, 133; on definition of decoloniality, 9; on epistemic de-linking, 234n1; on "gender" and "sexuality," 110;

influence of, 2–3, 8–9; on modernity, 137; on procreation and biological body, 35, 36; on totality, 209. *See also* coloniality of power
Quine, Willard Van Orman, 36–37, 38, 42

racial triangulation model, 87–94, 102; civic ostracism, 88, 92, 101; relative valorization, 88, 92, 94
racism, 46, 86, 87, 109–17; American Christianity and, 111–12; patriotism and, 96, 98, 101; racist heteronormativity, 43–43, 110; sexuality and, 57, 59, 60; violence and, 92
Reagan, Ronald, 108
Renaissance, European, 10, 13–14, 110–11, 188–89
reproduction, biological, 16, 31–43, 63–64
reproduction of labor, 32
reproductive technology, 42–43
REPSA (Reforestadora Palma de Petén SA), 43
rhetoric of modernity, 9, 222
Richardson, Troy, 3
Roelofs, Monique, 3
Roscoe, Will, 110
Roshanravan, Shireen, 21
Rubin, Gayle, 69

Said, Edward, 11
same-sex marriage, 100
Sandoval, Chela, 3, 12, 13, 22, 107, 115, 120n2, 122n7
Scott, David, 188
Scott, James C., 199–200, 201, 202, 205
secondary empires, 85–88, 93–94, 96. *See also* imperial difference
self-interest, 112, 116, 117, 146n3
September 11, 2001, 87, 96, 98, 101
sexism, 115, 116, 117, 140, 150, 151, 154–57
sexual difference, 20, 30, 31, 33–38, 40–43
sexuality, specificity of, 61–62
sexual pleasure, 16, 31–33, 40
sex work, 109, 251, 252. *See also* prostitution
Shakespeare, William, 188–89, 191
Sikh Americans, 98
sin, 31, 111, 122n9
Skeggs, Beverley, 130, 132
slavery, 111–12, 171; in *Beloved* (Morrison), 152–56, 165; coloniality of power and, 34–35;

as institutional past, 143; "institution" of, 135; Middle Passage, 64, 192n3; witnessing, 132
Smith, Linda Tuhiwai, 135–36, 144
sodomy, 57, 74–75, 122n9
Sommer, Doris, 132, 134
Sosa Riddell, Ada, 110, 121–22n6
Sparks, David, 110
spatial epistemic break, 209, 214, 219
spatial imaginary, 69–70, 72
spatiality: coloniality and, 13–14; coming out and, 51, 54; of embodied experience, 159; youth resistance and, 199–200
specificity of sexuality, 61–62
speech acts, 213, 216–18, 223, 224–25, 229–32
Spivak, Gayatri, 131
Stryker, Susan, 66–69, 73, 78, 80
subalterity, 69, 71, 73, 120, 166, 224; monstrosity and, 69, 71, 73, 78–80
subalternization of knowledge, 181, 219
subontological difference, 76
Subramaniam, Vega, 100
surrogacy, 37, 42

tacit subjects, 54
Taylor, Clyde, 180–81, 184, 192n7
Tchen, John Kuo Wei, 92–93
terrorism, 98–99, 108, 139
Thind, Bhagat Singh, 97
third gender and third gendering, 74–75, 81n1, 110, 139–40
Third World feminisms, 1, 12, 21, 87. *See also* women of color feminisms
Thomas, Greg, 187
Tlostanova, Madina, 85–88, 91, 92, 93, 96, 102, 104n6
topographic maps, 159–60, 164
topography of flesh, 152, 160–67
torta, 44, 48, 61
tortillera, 48
totality. *See* decolonial totality
transgender communities and issues, 49, 50; identity and, 49, 50, 58; monstrosity and, 66, 67, 70–73, 79; plurinationalism and, 250, 251–52; queer theory/LGBTQ studies and, 66; sexual difference and, 36, 38, 42; violence against, 250, 252. *See also* LGBTQ+ communities; youth, LGBTQ+ houseless

transgender studies, 66
transmodernity, 10–11, 211–12 216
transsexual communities and issues, 36, 38, 39, 40, 42, 68. *See also* transgender communities and issues
transvestism, 81n1, 118
trauma: monstrosity and, 79–80; queer public cultures and, 79
Trexler, Richard C., 110–11, 122nn8–9
"trickle-down" economics, 108
Trump, Donald, 108
TSQ (journal), 66

United States v. Bhagat Singh Thind, 97

Vásquez, Elizabeth, 250–52
Veronelli, Gabriela, 23–24
Victorian gender norms, 89–90
Vidal, Mirta, 121n6
Vilca, Mario, 3
Voltaire, 94

wage labor, 31, 33, 34, 108–9, 121n5
Walker, Alice, 189
Walsh, Catherine, 3, 17, 18
war, non-ethics of, 15
wealth, 32, 35, 108–9, 121, 205
Weheliye, Alexander, 190–91
Wing, Betsy, 143

witch hunts and trials, 32, 117, 139
women of color: coalitional approach to resistance, 228; erasure of category, 2; feminism and, 138, 140, 151, 155, 164–65; liminality and, 188; use of the term, 119–20n1; "world"-traveling and, 203
women of color feminisms, 1, 12, 21, 86–87, 103, 109, 123n12
Wynter, Sylvia, 15–16, 171–72; aesthetics as deciphering practice, 178–86; aesthetics theory of, 172–78; consequences of her naturalization of sexual/gender dichotomy, 186–91; on gender and sexual difference, 35; on sexual difference, 35

X Encuentro Lésbico-Feminista de Abya Yala, 29

Yeğenoğlu, Meyda, 140–41
youth, LGBTQ+ houseless: faithful witnessing and, 205–6; hanging out, 197–200; infrapolitics and, 200–202, 204, 205; resistance and, 202–5; "world"-traveling and, 197–98, 203
youth trafficking, 203–4
Yung, Judy, 89

Zapatistas, 18, 209
Zhouyi, Mai, 90–91

For Indiana University Press

Tony Brewer, *Artist and Book Designer*
Gary Dunham, *Acquisitions Editor and Director*
Anna Francis, *Assistant Acquisitions Editor*
Anna Garnai, *Editorial Assistant*
Brenna Hosman, *Production Coordinator*
Katie Huggins, *Production Manager*
Alyssa Nicole Lucas, *Marketing and Publicity Manager*
David Miller, *Lead Project Manager/Editor*
Dan Pyle, *Online Publishing Manager*
Jennifer Witzke, *Senior Artist and Book Designer*